THE GREEK ORTHODOX
CHURCH IN AMERICA

D1202790

A volume in the NIU Series in Orthodox Christian Studies
Edited by Roy R. Robson

For a list of books in the series visit our website at cornellpress.cornell.edu.

THE GREEK ORTHODOX CHURCH IN AMERICA

A Modern History

ALEXANDER KITROEFF

NORTHERN ILLINOIS UNIVERSITY PRESS
AN IMPRINT OF
CORNELL UNIVERSITY PRESS
Ithaca and London

First published 2020 by Cornell University Press

Library of Congress Cataloging-in-Publication Data

Names: Kitroeff, Alexander, author.
Title: The Greek Orthodox Church in America : a modern history / Alexander Kitroeff.
Description: Ithaca : Northern Illinois University Press, an imprint of Cornell University Press, 2020. | Series: NIU series in orthodox Christian studies | Includes bibliographical references and index.
Identifiers: LCCN 2019037651 (print) | LCCN 2019037652 (ebook) | ISBN 9781501749438 (cloth) | ISBN 9781501749919 (paperback) | ISBN 9781501749445 (epub) | ISBN 9781501749452 (pdf)
Subjects: LCSH: Greek Orthodox Archdiocese of America—History. | Greek Americans—Religion. | Greek Americans—Ethnic identity.
Classification: LCC BX738.G73 K587 2020 (print) | LCC BX738.G73 (ebook) | DDC 281.9/495073—dc23
LC record available at https://lccn.loc.gov/2019037651
LC ebook record available at https://lccn.loc.gov/2019037652

For Speros Vryonis (1928–2019)
Beloved teacher and friend

Contents

Acknowledgments

This book owes its existence to a generous grant from the Jaharis Family Foundation, which deserves the greatest part of my gratitude. His Eminence Archbishop Demetrios granted me access to the Greek Orthodox Archdiocese's archive, where archivist Nikie Calles was an extremely helpful guide while also sharing the extraordinary knowledge she acquired in her long service first at the side of Archbishop Iakovos and later as archivist. Father Robert Stephanopoulos generously shared his knowledge as well as his extensive library with me. Anita Isaacs helped me plan the project and deal with the logistics of doing research in New York City. My thanks also go to Photini Tomai, director of the Historical Archive of the Greek Ministry of Foreign Affairs, and her staff; Andrea Bainbridge, university archivist, DePaul University Special Collections and Archives; Daniel Necas, archivist at the Immigration History Research Center Archives, University of Minnesota; George I. Paganellis, at the Tsakopoulos Hellenic Collection at the California State University, Sacramento; Rob Haley, interlibrary loans librarian at Magill Library, Haverford College; and Art Dimopoulos, who gifted me a part of the material collected by his father, the late Father George Dimopoulos of St. Demetrios Church in Upper Darby, Pennsylvania. The late Peter B. Christie granted me access to material related to the early history of the Annunciation Church in Philadelphia, which later moved to Elkins Park, Pennsylvania.

Numerous persons with direct experience of Greek Orthodoxy in America's recent history were kind enough to share their knowledge in informal conversations, which provided valuable background information. They are Simos Dimas, a New York–based attorney who served on the Archdiocesan Council; Michael Jaharis, a long-standing member of the Archdiocesan Council; Father Alex Karloutsos, who worked closely with Archbishop Iakovos and later with Ecumenical Patriarch Bartholomew; Christine Lee Vicar at All Angels' Church in New York; Maria Makedon, former education director at the Greek Orthodox Archdiocese; the late Panayotis Makrias, who had a long career in the Greek American press; Peter Marudas, an official of the Orthodox Christian Laity Organization; Fevronia Soumakis, whose doctoral dissertation completed at Columbia University is on the archdiocese's schools in New York; and Rev. Robert Stephanopoulos, former dean of the Greek Orthodox Cathedral of New York.

I made four public presentations based on my ongoing research for this book, and I thank the organizers for their invitation and the audiences for their valuable comments and questions. These were the Annual Zamanakos Lecture at the University of Massachusetts in Lowell; an invited lecture at the Hellenic Studies Program at the State University of California in Sacramento; a conference in Athens on the fiftieth anniversary of the establishment of the Greek dictatorship in 1967; and a paper at a conference in Oxford on Greece's relations with its diaspora. I published an article based on my research about the 1970 Clergy-Laity Congress in the online journal Ergon Greek American Arts and Letters, and I thank the editor Yiorgos Anagnostou and two anonymous readers for their comments that in turn helped me sharpen the relevant section in this book.

My understanding of the interface between Greek America and its church has also benefited from listening to or reading the insights of very many friends and colleagues, too many to list here. I should mention that film director Maria Iliou's invitation to serve as historical consultant in the documentary *The Journey: The Greek Dream in America* helped me focus my long-standing awareness of the importance of the church in the history of the Greek American experience. The late and much missed Charles Moskos always offered great encouragement and inspiration, including how to do on-the-spot research when he bounded up the steps of a Greek Orthodox Church in Astoria, New York, crying out "Kalispera" (good evening) to a startled elderly cleric who was peacefully sitting on a stool at the entrance. Finally, the late Speros Vryonis honored me by praising the way I dealt with the Greek Orthodox Patriarchate of Alexandria in my first book and from then on helped me embark on an academic career. Fittingly, he was able to attend the presentation based on this book I made in Sacramento and commented on the significance of the church's ecclesiastical and legal status in America in understanding its history. I have approached this book by using that particular status and the wider structural context of the interactions between Greek America and Greek Orthodoxy to frame the inquiry.

Books on Greek America are not best-sellers, maybe with the exception of Jeffrey Eugenides's *Middlesex*, so I wish to express my profound gratitude to acquisitions editor Amy Farranto and Orthodox Christian series editor Roy Robson at the Northern Illinois University Press for believing in the value and potential of this book. The two outside readers the press selected both wished to remain eponymous, so I am pleased to acknowledge the advice, comments, and encouragement of Yiorgos Anagnostou of Ohio State University and Theofanis Stavrou of the University of Minnesota. My thanks also to everyone else at the Northern Illinois University Press and Cornell University Press for helping to transform the manuscript into book form.

ABBREVIATIONS

AHEPA	American Hellenic Educational Progressive Association
E&D GOARCH	Encyclicals and Documents of the Greek Orthodox Archdiocese of America
GAPA	Greek American Progressive Association
GMFA	Greek Ministry of Foreign Affairs
GOARCH	Greek Orthodox Archdiocese of America
GOYA	Greek Orthodox Youth of America
GWRA	Greek War Relief Association
OCL	Orthodox Christian Laity
SCOBA	Standing Conference of Canonical Orthodox Bishops in the Americas

A Note on Language and Transliteration

I have transliterated Greek language words according to the guidelines of the *Journal of Modern Greek Studies*. I have rendered the titles of Greek and English-language documents in the Archive of the Greek Orthodox Archdiocese in English for reasons of consistency.

THE GREEK ORTHODOX
CHURCH IN AMERICA

Introduction

Signs with the words "Greek Festival," usually in blue against a white background, signifying Greece's national colors, appear on roadsides in towns and suburbs across the United States in the late spring and early fall. They announce a three- or four-day event, part food fair, part bazaar, and part cultural festival, with Greek music and folk dancing, organized by the local Greek Orthodox church. Although the event takes place on the grounds of the church, which will keep its doors open for worshippers and visitors, the catering and the cultural performances will attract the most attention. In many parishes, especially those in the suburbs and exurbs that have ample space, the food offerings as well as the dancing are rich both in flavor and culinary or cultural sophistication. Some of these events have become famous beyond their locale. For example, the annual Greek food festival held by St. John the Baptist Church in Las Vegas gained national recognition when *National Geographic Magazine* deemed it the top food event in Nevada in its survey of food festivals across the United States.[1] The main purpose of these Greek festivals, famous or not, is to raise funds for the local parish through what is a celebration of Greek heritage. Their predominantly secular, most certainly ethnic, but also festive character is in no way at odds with the church's spiritual mission. On the contrary, ever since Greeks began arriving en masse in the United States more than a century ago, the Greek

Orthodox Church has sought to preserve both their religious and their cultural identity with almost equal zeal.

When modern Greece was established in the early nineteenth century following an uprising against the ruling Ottomans, for many Greeks religion was a constituent element of their identity, along with language and a sense that they were descendants of the ancient Greeks. Although the intellectual authors of the vision of Greek liberty that led to the Greek revolution of 1821 had discounted the role of religion in their definitions of Greekness, most of the rebels saw themselves as Orthodox Christians fighting against Muslim overlords. And locally priests blessed the uprising and even took part in the fighting. But in the two decades following the establishment of the modern Greek state in 1830, the status of religion as a defining criterion of Greekness was debated, as was the question of whether Greece should establish its own Greek Orthodox Church autonomous from the Ecumenical Patriarchate of Constantinople, which had held jurisdiction over the Greek Orthodox throughout the Ottoman Empire, including the lands that had now become part of modern Greece. A resolution of sorts came in the 1850s when Greece sided with Russia in the Crimean War in the name of solidarity with a fellow Orthodox nation, and the autonomous Church of Greece reestablished amicable relations with the Ecumenical Patriarchate. Religion was ascendant, and its centrality to Greek identity was never effectively challenged by a succession of anticlerical and secular intellectual trends that developed over the next decades.[2] Rural Greece, from where most of the transatlantic emigration took place, was a bastion of religion. Thus, Greek Orthodoxy was one of the foundations of Greek American ethnicity, making it an "ethnic religion" in the United States.[3] Most Greeks arriving in the early twentieth century regarded their religion as a constituent part of their ethnic identity, even though they might not be regular churchgoers, restricting their attendance to the bare minimum: baptisms, weddings, funerals, and the major services at Christmas and Easter. The type of work that the Greek Americans sought after establishing themselves in the United States tended to be opening their own businesses, in other words preferring to be self-employed, however small their enterprise was, rather than seek employment as workers or employees. This Greek American business culture also entailed a very strong reliance on the family as the primary economic unit and by the same token a suspicion toward outsiders.[4] The cultural and economic significance of the family for Greek Americans found a receptive ear of course in Greek Orthodoxy, and this connection also served to bring the immigrants closer to the church. Many second-generation Greek Americans went on to work in the corporate world or as white-collar professionals, but they had grown up in an environment in which the family was the main economic unit, and thus the church's emphasis on the value of family struck a familiar chord.

There are about 1.3 million persons of Greek descent living in the United States, and the Greek Orthodox Church is a large part of their lives. The Greek Americans are among the wealthiest and most highly educated of the ethnic groups whose ancestors came from Europe. Ever since the Greeks began arriving in the late nineteenth century, they formed organizations with a wide range of aims, and their churches were and continue to be at the center of this organizational world. At first, most ethnic organizations were meant to preserve ties with the homeland and its culture, especially language and religion, as well as to strengthen cooperation among the Greek immigrants. Soon other aims emerged, such as supporting the process of assimilation into American society, passing on Greek culture to the American-born generations, and organizing efforts to influence US foreign policy in Greece's favor. One cannot fully comprehend the richness of the Greek American experience in the United States without considering its networks of institutions, churches, and range of ethnic associations. While all immigrant groups in the United States produce an array of ethnic organizations, it can be argued that the Greeks were especially active in this sense because there is a long tradition of communal self-government among the Greeks. It evolved when they were under Ottoman rule between the fifteenth and nineteenth centuries and extended to the numerous Greek diaspora communities throughout the Mediterranean and the Black Sea that predated the settlement of Greeks in North America.

In the course of the twentieth century it was the Orthodox Church that became the strongest and most influential Greek ethnic institution in the United States. Aside from fulfilling the spiritual needs of the Greeks, beginning in the 1930s it also undertook the responsibility of running the Greek-language schools, it developed a national network of parish-based women's philanthropic organizations, and it was the only Greek organization to create an orphanage and an old people's home. It also spearheaded all Greek American efforts to offer aid to the homeland and to support Greece's foreign policy goals. It was an ethno-religious institution, but beyond that it spread its reach into almost all aspects of Greek American life. All this happened while the church was also adapting to the American environment, especially in the post–World War II era. By then it was easy to recognize the needs of the American-born younger generations and to gradually allow the use of the English language, first in its youth activities, then in the more informal gatherings among adults, then its newsletters and publications, and ultimately in its more formal functions. In doing so, the church was acknowledging the

Americanization of the Greek Americans, especially the American-born, and by addressing their needs it remained relevant and retained its centrality in community life. And because Greek Orthodoxy was a core element of Greek identity, for many Greek Americans religion began to play a bigger role in the way they experienced and expressed their ethnic identity.

The historical trajectory of Greek Orthodoxy in America during the twentieth century clearly speaks to the significance of religion in shaping the ethnic identity of immigrant groups. Yet the considerable corpus of academic literature on the interrelationship between religion and ethnicity and immigration makes very little mention of Greek Orthodoxy—or even the broader category of Eastern Orthodoxy, which includes the Russian, Slavic, and Syrian churches that are also present in the United States, albeit with a relatively smaller number of adherents. This omission, which this study seeks to redress, might seem surprising. Unlike the case in Protestantism and Catholicism, Eastern Orthodoxy is divided into national churches, and the transplantation of these national churches to American soil presumably would offer fertile ground to study the ties between ethnicity and religion. But the Eastern Orthodox population in the United States is roughly three million, or about 1 percent of the total population, and it can get easily overlooked. There are many general accounts or surveys of religion in the United States that do not include any of the Eastern Orthodox churches. Even so, one may have expected a greater role for Eastern Orthodoxy in studies that explore the ties between religion and ethnicity and immigration. The themes those studies have touched on apply to the Eastern Orthodox churches as well.

The first of those themes that also applies to the Greek Orthodox experience but is not thus employed by scholars is the way church and religion functioned as a haven for the newly arrived immigrants in America, or, as Oscar Handlin put it in his classic study, kept them "sound against the strange New World."[5] And several studies that appeared after Handlin's highlighted the role of the church as a haven, especially in the case of Eastern and Southern European Catholic immigrants. A second theme present in the literature is the ways religious affiliation of ethnic groups proved compatible with the process of Americanization, because religious participation was a major step toward assimilation. Yet the best-known sociological studies along those lines, such as Milton Gordon's on assimilation and acculturation, had relatively little to say about the Eastern Orthodox churches, while the title of Will Herberg's study, *Protestant-Catholic-Jew*, speaks for itself.[6] Andrew Greeley's *Denominational Society*, which stressed the sense of "belonging" that ethnic churches provided, was concerned with Catholic and Protestant churches. When the 1970s brought efforts to study the interrelationship of ethnicity and religion more systematically, Eastern Orthodoxy remained in the margins. Among those scholars who underline the relationship of ethnicity and religion, Preston Williams, a professor at Harvard Divinity School, suggested that because ethnicity was "ambiguous" and "like any human action it can result in pride and corruption as well as good," it needed "the illumination of religion which is capable of steering its community building potential and cohesiveness into societal patterns of harmony and fairness."[7] There followed an even more direct assertion of the transformative nature of the relationship between ethnicity and religion. Timothy Smith argued that immigrant churches had not only sustained ethnic identity in the early phase of the immigrant presence in America but also contributed to the Americanization of the immigrants while remaining relevant to their lives, partially because immigration itself was a "theologizing experience," with immigrants responding to the challenges of resettlement by turning to religion, yielding benefits in the form of mutual assistance and support.[8] Eastern Orthodoxy could have been easily invoked to illustrate those assertions, yet it barely appeared in those studies and the debates they generated.

The field of immigration studies, when several studies appearing in the 1980s began to question the widely held assumptions that America was a melting pot, also bypassed Greek Orthodoxy and the Greek Americans. This new trend regarded assimilation not as an all-encompassing entry into an Anglo-American mainstream but instead as a partial or segmented process in which ethnic ties remained much stronger than the earlier melting pot theorists had assumed. Within a few years the sense that the immigrants had been "uprooted" was itself replaced by the more nuanced sense that immigrant identities were in fact "transplanted" to America and preserved or partially altered, notwithstanding the pressures of assimilation.[9] Here again, the Greek Americans could have functioned as a wonderful example, because even as they experienced assimilation in the post–World War II era, they remained closely tied to the homeland—a connection that was manifested by (among other things) the emergence of the powerful "Greek lobby" that sought to influence US foreign policy toward Greece in the mid-1970s. The lobbying efforts were acknowledged in studies on ethnicity and foreign policy, but this did not earn the Greek Americans recognition in studies highlighting the perseverance of ethnicity in the United States.[10] In any case, the new scholarly recognition of the resilience of ethnicity tended mostly to underplay the role of religion and addressed other aspects of ethnic identity, even though, as one more recent study has suggested, in the case of an ethno-religious community such as the Greek Americans, the motivating force of religion should be taken into account when considering ethnic political mobilization.[11] One important reason why religion faded somewhat in the background was that by the 1970s, the Roman Catholic Church's ethnic moorings had dissolved, at least with regard to serving specifically Irish or Italian or Polish constituencies in ethnic neighborhoods, because these neighborhoods largely no longer existed. Thus, studies on immigrant religion and ethnicity continued to appear, but the two were treated separately.[12] And in both those cases, Greek Orthodoxy and the Greek Americans remained on the sidelines.

This situation remained the same when the study of the relationship of ethnicity and religion received a new boost a few decades later. Scholars noticed that the post-1965 immigrants who arrived in the United States mainly from Asia, Africa, and Latin America availed themselves of church and religion to ease their transition into the US. Their experiences generated a cluster of mainly sociological studies that began appearing in the 1990s. Some of the main themes that emerged from the studies of the new immigrants resonate with Eastern Orthodox experience from the 1970s onward. These included the role of the church as a haven as well as a facilitator of assimilation, imitating Protestant practices and adopting congregational models of organization and worship, and the development of transnational ties as well as ties to the ancestral homeland. Orthodoxy, like many other religions historically transnational—that is, capable of cross-border relationships— patterns on exchange and affiliations.[13] Because of the huge numbers of these non-European immigrants, scholars, already acutely aware of the Eurocentric bias in most immigration studies, with a few notable exceptions perhaps understandably overlooked the Eastern Orthodox, even though they too experienced increased immigration to the United States since 1965.[14] In fact, in the Greek case, the influx was considerable in relative terms, and it would impact the life of the Greek Orthodox Church in America.

While mainstream scholarship on ethnicity and religion overlooked the role of the Greek Americans and Greek Orthodoxy, scholars within the Greek American community undertook the task of studying their ethnic group and its religion, though little was done in terms of explicitly examining their interrelationship. In most book-length studies there was a focus either on the ethnic group or the Greek Orthodox Church, one usually at the expense of the other. This is especially true of the most authoritative study on Greek American history, Theodore Saloutos's *The Greeks in the United States*, which was published in 1964 and adopted a pro-assimilationist narrative. Saloutos's excellent study was critical of the church and its embroilment in Greek politics and underplayed the church's role in Greek American life, regarding it as an obstacle to Greek American assimilation.[15] But almost a decade later Saloutos acknowledged the church's strides toward assimilation that had begun in the 1960s and appeared to restore its significance in Greek America, albeit one that was assimilating.[16] Another moment at which Saloutos acknowledged that the Greek Orthodox Church could move with the times was in a subsequent study where he discussed the new church building in Milwaukee, his hometown, that was designed by Frank Lloyd Wright and completed after Wright's death in 1959. The circular design represented a radical departure from traditional Byzantine church architecture, yet it retained the concept of a domed space and incorporated the familiar symbols of the cross as well as blue and white colors. In Saloutos's words, "to many of the parishioners the new church was a mighty symbol of progress, community spirit, faith, and a blending of some of the most original work in architectural beauty of the New World with the culture of the Old."[17] A riposte to Saloutos's downplaying of the church's relevance came a few years later, in 1980, from Charles Moskos, a sociologist who became nationally known for his work on the American military. He produced a historical and sociological account of the Greek trajectory in the United States written in a lively style and incorporating many of his personal experiences, an account in which the church featured prominently. Moskos, however, who was active in the church's affairs and even acted as a consultant to the archdiocese, thought the church's attachment to ethnicity was outdated, and he signaled his preference for a supra-ethnic American Orthodoxy as the natural outcome of the trend toward assimilation that his book emphasized. The book has been updated twice in new editions, the last one reworked by his son Peter and appearing after Moskos's death.[18] A few years later another sociological study, this one by Alice Scourby, addressed the role of the church at somewhat greater length, portraying it as a major Greek American institution. In contrast to Moskos's account, Scourby's work employed more conventional sociological tools, such as surveys highlighting the gradual distancing of the third generation of Greek Americans from the church but also from other communal institutions.[19] Thus, it was left to authors more closely associated with the church to produce monographs on its theology and history in the United States. These included several books that appeared over the past quarter century by Demetrios Constantelos, John H. Erickson, Nicholas Ferencz, Thomas FitzGerald, John McGuckin, and George C. Michalopoulos and Herb Ham.[20] Out of necessity, most of those studies combined theological exegesis and church history and did not systematically examine the Greek Orthodox Church's relationship with the Greek Americans. Church-community relations was left to a handful of scholars including Anna Karpathakis, Andrew Kopan, George Kourvetaris, and Yannis Papadopoulos, who have produced locally based studies about the church's relationship with the Greeks in Chicago and New York and studies on the overall relationship between the church and the Greek Americans examined over a short period of time.[21] Elizabeth Prodromou has written about Eastern Orthodoxy's place in America and its relationship with the democratic impulses in the era of globalization.[22] Studies on globalization—that is, the post–Cold War phenomenon involving the cross-border spread of goods and ideas through improved transportation, technology, and telecommunications—and its effects on the Eastern Orthodox Church have included treatment of the transnational connections of the church in the United States and especially the "mother church," as the Ecumenical Patriarchate of Constantinople is known, focusing primarily on these churches' doctrinal and institutional ties.[23] There are also a number of very useful doctoral dissertations on Greek America among those that shed light on the relations between church and community for the period that concerns us here, namely the twentieth century. They include those by Athena Sophia Condos on Greek-language schools; Panagoula Diamandi-Karanou on the relations between Greece and the Greek Americans; Anastasios Kourlamanis on the St. Demetrios school in Astoria, New York; Gary A. Kunkelman on ethnicity and religion in one Greek American community; Eric V. Morrow on religion and Greek American political activism; Andrea Simon on two Greek Orthodox churches in Astoria; Fevronia Soumakis on the archdiocese's schools in the New York area; Michael Varlamos on Greek Orthodox political activism in America; and Marc Wisnosky on Eastern Orthodox seminaries in the United States.[24] Finally, scholars based in Greece have also produced works on the history of Greek Orthodoxy in America, primarily its political dimensions.[25]

The church community itself, either through archdiocese-sponsored publications, or through the work of clergy or laity, or thanks to the initiative of a local parish, has collectively produced an impressive corpus of books and articles that are essential to the study of Greek Orthodoxy and its relationship with Greek America. Several parishes have produced useful accounts of their history, which they have included on their websites. The same applies to the other Eastern Orthodox churches in the United States. There are too many of those works and sites to list here, but many appear in this book's citations. Finally, another valuable source is the richly extensive electronic files that Archbishop Spyridon, who served from 1996 to 1999, had placed on his website (http://www.archbishopspyridon.gr/).

The purpose of this book is to provide an account of the Greek Orthodox Church's interrelationship with the Greek Americans throughout the twentieth century. This may sound at first like a tautological exercise, because obviously an ethnic church would have close ties with the ethnic community members that form its constituency, with the exception of those who stay away from religion. But in comparison with the other numerous communities of Greeks abroad, it is obvious that the Orthodox Church in the United States plays a determining role in community affairs not seen anywhere else. Its control of Greek-language schools, for example, can be considered as the "archdiocesan model" of education in the diaspora, in contrast with other Greek school systems abroad that are under secular or shared religious and secular supervision. And in the sphere of the community's relations with its homeland, Archbishop Iakovos, who served from 1959 through 1996, was considered as the leader of the Greek Americans, both in Washington, DC, where a power Greek congressional lobby operated, and in Athens and by the ethnic Greeks in Cyprus. And most, if not all, major initiatives launched by the Greek Americans require the blessing and approval of the archbishop. For example, when wealthy Greek Americans decided to form the Greek War Relief Association, a national organization that would send aid to Greece during World War II, the archbishop presided over their inaugural meeting, which was held at the archdiocese's offices in New York City. The Greek Orthodox clergy always feature prominently in Greek parades that celebrate the beginning of the Greek War of Independence and which are held in cities where there is a large enough Greek American community. The first such parades, which were held in New York City, marched past the Greek Orthodox cathedral before they were moved to Fifth Avenue.

This book goes beyond merely establishing the hegemony of the Greek Orthodox Church over the Greek American community. It argues that the church helped shape Greek American identity throughout the twentieth century and did so by adapting to the steady Americanization of the Greek Americans. In the process, it retained its relevance in their lives. This was especially true for the American-born second and third generation of Greek Americans. Greek-born immigrants, especially those who arrived in the United States in the second half of the twentieth century, became very uncomfortable with the church's efforts to address the needs of the Americanized second- and third-generation Greek Americans. As we will see, they reacted with alarm when the church began tailoring its practices to the Americanization of the second and third generations. Nonetheless, the church persisted, and the religious inflection of ethnic identity among American-born children and grandchildren of Greek immigrants increased steadily as a result of the influence of the church. The trend is confirmed in sociological surveys measuring self-identification among Greek Americans conducted over the past twenty years by Christine Alex, Angelyn Balodimas-Bartolomei, and George

Kourvetaris.[26] The hegemony the church exercised could also be observed both on an institutional level, as for example the prioritization of the defense of the rights of the Greek Orthodox Ecumenical Patriarchate by lobbying organizations in Washington, where the Coordinated Effort of Hellenes includes "Orthodox issues" among its interests—a phrase that was not used in the Greek American lobbying vocabulary prior to the 1990s. And it was in an article published in 1999 that Moskos stated that "Orthodox affiliation rather than language has become the defining trait of Greek ethnic identity in America."[27]

To suggest that Greek Orthodoxy increased its power in the sphere of communal and individual identity goes against the grain of the widely accepted view that the emergence of a "spiritual marketplace" in late twentieth-century America, along with an increase in secularization, diminished the influence of established religions.[28] Yet as this study shows, the Greek Orthodox Church incorporated so many secular communal activities that it blurred the dividing line of the religious and the secular in the minds of many Greek Americans. And the very insularity of ethnic Eastern Orthodox churches protected them from the worst effects of secularization. The ethnic ties have certainly mattered and been recognized in those studies that see secularization trends in Greek America. Perhaps it was put best in the revised and updated version of Moskos's study coauthored by his son Peter, who suggests that "the era of the church as the defining element of the Greek American community may have ended" because the Greek Americans "have become more secular." But, he adds, "despite this a feeling of ethnic attachment to the Greek Orthodox Church remains strong."[29] In the pages that follow we will see how the church became a defining element throughout the twentieth century, and, ironically perhaps, because it managed to adapt to the Americanizing environment, it remained so at the end of the century, as no other Greek American institution could evoke Greek ethnicity in such a deep emotional and visceral way.

The reason why the Greek Orthodox Church maintained its ethnic dimension, beyond the obvious fact that its members included a great many Greek speakers (the addition of non-birthright Orthodox converts was a post-1950s phenomenon), was Greek Orthodoxy's transnational character. From 1922 onward, when the Ecumenical Patriarchate of Constantinople assumed jurisdiction over Greek Orthodoxy in America, the church represented an umbilical cord that attached the faithful to the Old World homeland. That it had to face strictures imposed by the Turkish Republic formed in 1923 did not affect, at least in theory, its transatlantic reach. Aware of the difficulties Greek Orthodoxy faced in America, the patriarchate exercised its jurisdiction lightly, intervening only when the issue of appointing a new archbishop arose. This distance that Constantinople maintained allowed the church in the Americas and especially in the United States, where the vast majority of the Greek Orthodox lived, to adapt to the pressures of assimilation. And naturally the patriarchate stood to benefit mightily from the support the Greek Orthodox offered it in material terms but also politically, by that group's potential to influence US foreign policy, especially when the patriarchate was targeted by the government of Turkey. So light was the patriarchate's touch throughout the twentieth century that when it did intervene dynamically to alter the course of Greek Orthodoxy in America in the 1990s, its actions were met by consternation and surprise by many among the clergy and the laity.

Understanding the relationship of Greek Orthodoxy to Greek America helps us understand the dynamics of religion in ethnicity beyond the confines of one particular ethnic group. This study can operate as a means of understanding the ethnic and religious nexus in the case of other ethno-religious groups in America such as the Russian, Ukrainian, Serbian, and Syrian or Arab Orthodox communities. Both the parallels and the more direct interaction between the Greeks and the other Eastern Orthodox form part of the story that is told in the pages that follow, in particular the initiatives for achieving pan-Orthodox unity in America that increased toward the end of the twentieth century. This book also reaches beyond the domain of Eastern Orthodoxy in America because it illustrates the way a relatively small, ethnically rooted religion can survive, indeed thrive, in the wider religious marketplace of America. Those small religious denominations were helped by the religiosity prevalent in the United States throughout the twentieth century; but on the other hand the inevitable assimilation of their constituents over time poses a threat. Those constituents are pulled in opposite directions, and their future seems to be either to retreat into a small and increasingly irrelevant ethnic cocoon, or Americanize to the extent that they lose their identifying characteristics. Staying in place, let alone growing and moving forward, may seem an impossible task. The case of Greek Orthodoxy in America is an example of how that task can be achieved.

I write as a social historian working within the framework of US-based immigration history that is loosely shaped by the paradigms of "transplantation" of identity as well as immigrant identity being shaped by the transnational influences. The term "transplantation" was used to distinguish a new departure in immigration historiography, setting itself apart from the "uprooting" that Handlin used in his pioneering study of European immigrants to the United States. Since the mid-1980s when the "transplantation" paradigm began dominating, immigration history has continued to transform its approaches, most notably by considering the existence of hybrid identities, a concept that grew out of the field of cultural studies. And more recently, immigration history has recognized the significance of immigrant transnational ties, though, dare I say it, those studying Greek immigrants abroad have long assumed the existence of those ties—implicitly, of course, since the term "transnationalism" emerged more recently.[30] Here, I treat Greek Orthodoxy as a transnational manifestation, and the Greek Americans as a diaspora, one necessarily connected with Greece the *topos* but also with Greek culture and its manifestations.[31]

My approach therefore may not be explicitly theoretical, but the empirically based narrative is placed within this broader analytical context that also considers the conditions prevailing in the United States at any one moment in the twentieth century—the Americanization process of the Greek Americans in other words, but also their conscious efforts to retain their Old World identity, whether as an imagined one or merely one that preserves the heritage of Greekness. Moreover, I treat the Greek Orthodox Greek Americans as a group that possesses a degree of agency: in other words, it is able to confront and negotiate with the changing social mores governing attitudes toward immigrants and their descendants and toward religion in the United States during the twentieth century. This negotiation entails a reconciliation between being Greek and Greek Orthodox and becoming American, an outcome that represents a fusion between the agency of individuals and the social structures that govern their lives, what sociologist Anthony Giddens has termed "structuration."[32] I use the concept loosely, not as a rigorous theory but rather as a perspective that helps us understand human action, especially from the vantage point of a historian's inquiry into the role of institutions. In particular, institutions that are not arbitrarily introduced by an academic observer, but instead, institutions such as the church, which historical agents such as individuals accept as domains that define their actions.[33] The structures—for example religiosity or secular trends in America—shape the way the Greek Orthodox Church evolved, especially when the church is making a conscious effort to integrate into American society. By the same token, powerful historical agents—the archbishops, for example—were often able to navigate within those structures and produce outcomes that confirmed their ability to transform the church's evolution. Structures may enable or constrain but do not determine human actions.

I examine this continuous interplay of agency and structure—the status of ethnicity and religion in the United States—in an empirically based chronological account of the relationship of the community with Orthodox religion by relying primarily on the discussions and decisions generated by the biennial clergy-laity congresses of the Greek Orthodox Church, which is the main venue where the church's concerns and policies toward the laity are aired and determined. While for most of the twentieth century the church's governing body was responsible for Orthodoxy in both North and South America, here I am focusing on the church's history within the United States. I am well aware of the prevailing opinion of most observers that the congresses are a top-down affair, a means through which the archdiocese and in particular its head, the archbishop, essentially legitimize their policies. But it is this single archdiocese, based in New York, that is the Greek Orthodox Church's governing body. Unlike the Roman Catholic Church, which has several regionally based archdioceses and no single leader in the United States, the Greek Orthodox Church produced a single archdiocese with the responsibility to oversee the church's life throughout the country. Therefore, the archbishop presides over the activities of the parishes (presently about 440) and their Greek schools and religious education programs spread throughout the country, plus a range of institutional activities including a nationally based network of women's philanthropic organizations, an orphanage, a home for the aged, a summer camp in Greece, as well as the undergraduate Hellenic College and Holy Cross, a graduate college of theology in Brookline, Massachusetts. As such, the archbishop's influence over the decisions of the clergy-laity congresses is significant, and he and the status of the archdiocese are likely to overwhelm any dissident representatives of a particular parish. Nonetheless, the important fact that there are both clerical and lay representatives of the parishes on the floor of the clergy-laity congresses produces an agenda and conversations that are not about religious doctrines but about the church's social policies. And it is these that will ultimately contribute to shaping Greek American identity.

This book is based on original research I conducted primarily in the archdiocese's well-preserved archives in New York City. I was able to consult all the documents that relate to the church's clergy-laity congresses, and this yielded the bulk of the primary material I relied on in this book. In working with this archival collection, I was made aware of the importance the archdiocese placed on American and Greek American newspapers, and this prompted me to gather information from those sources beyond the clippings preserved in the archive. Additional research in the historical archive of the Greek Ministry of Foreign Affairs in Athens enabled me to study the relevant correspondence between the ministry and Greek diplomats in the United States through the year 1967; the material after that year is not yet open to researchers. In addition, I consulted several collections of the Orthodox

Christian Laity, which is an activist group within the church, and the personal papers of Demetrios Callimachos, a founder of the archdiocese, and those of leading lay members Andrew Kopan, Basil Vlavianos, and Katy Vlavianos. I also made use of material I had gathered in the past at the Gerald Ford Presidential Library. I also conducted informal, information-gathering interviews with key members of the clergy and laity, and I have listed all those persons, along with those who allowed me access to their personal papers and book collections, in the acknowledgments section of this book.

This book is organized chronologically. Chapter 1 recounts the arrival and settlement of the Greek immigrants and culminates in the creation of the Greek Orthodox Archdiocese in 1922. The first churches the Greek immigrants established provided them with a sense of community and security and underscored their ties with the Greek homeland. The decision of these immigrants not to become absorbed in the Russian Orthodox Church, which was already established in the United States, signaled the strong national and ethnic character of their religious life. But this pioneering phase was laden with difficulties, which ranged from the uneven quality of the immigrant priests to friction between clergy and laity, and worst of all divisions that reflected the political polarization that had occurred in Greece. In light of those mounting problems, a dynamic metropolitan sent to the United States by the Greek government decided to restore order by creating a centralized governing body with authority over Greek Orthodox affairs all over the United States. Thus, the Greek Orthodox Archdiocese was born in 1922. Chapter 2 recounts the ways the archdiocese tried to overcome the political divide that affected Greek Orthodox life, while attempting to devise a strategy that would confront the pressures to assimilate and "Americanize" that the Greek immigrants faced in the 1920s. Chapter 3 describes the moment of ascendancy of Greek Orthodoxy in the United States, which came with the newly enthroned Archbishop Athenagoras who arrived from Greece and introduced sweeping changes that essentially meant an effective implementation of the idea of a centralized governing body that would hold sway over the parishes. But more importantly, the archbishop decreed that the parishes should assume full responsibility for all local Greek communal activities: education, philanthropy, national commemorations, and cultural events. Thus, rather than the parish being beholden to the local community organization, the parish assumed the primary role in organizing Greek American activities, both religious and secular. Coming at a time when the Depression had weakened the role of the secular Greek American organizations both nationally and locally, this move cemented the archdiocese's dominant role in shaping Greek American identity. Chapter 4 records how that hegemony was extended during the 1940s. It reflects back on the church's close entanglement with the world of secular politics treated at the very end of the first chapter, in order to understand the astute ways that Archbishop Athenagoras courted both the Greek and the US governments in order to strengthen the status and the influence of Orthodoxy in America in the 1940s. Chapter 5 examines the Orthodox Church against the background of the 1950s, an era that saw both a rise in religiosity and the upward social mobility of the Greek American second generation. For a church such as the Greek Orthodox, which was on the margins of conversations about religion in America, this was a moment that invited it to find ways to become more relevant, if not exactly mainstream. An unexpected development, the importance of the Eastern Orthodox Churches to the Cold War policies of the United States, became an enabling factor.

The next six chapters address the interrelationship between Greek Orthodoxy and Greek America during the tenure of Archbishop Iakovos between 1959 and 1996. Chapter 6 examines Iakovos's call for the Greek Orthodox to consider their church no longer an immigrant church but an American church, and to become involved in confronting the challenges presented by the cultural upheavals of the 1960s. He himself gave the example by marching next to the Reverend Martin Luther King Jr. at Selma, Alabama, in 1965. Chapter 7 discusses how the church, now explicitly in Americanization mode, dealt with the era of ethnic revival that legitimized European white ethnic identities, including that of Greek Americans. A key moment came with the controversy the archbishop generated when he decreed that parish priests could perform parts of the Sunday liturgy in Greek, if they believed that was more appropriate for their flock. Iakovos was telling Greek Americans that many if not most of them were now more comfortable with the English rather than the Greek language, and that that development had to be reflected in practice. Chapter 8 looks at how the church, albeit in a process of explicit Americanization, played a central role in Greek American efforts to shape US foreign policy toward Greece, Turkey, and Cyprus between the 1960s and 1980s but did so not as an advocate of Greek interests but an advocate of American and Christian values. Chapters 9 and 10 chart the church's efforts to accelerate and deepen its American character, keeping up with the Americanized second- and third-generation Greek Orthodox Americans it served and in whom it had instilled a strong sense of Greek Orthodox identity. The process culminated in a pan-Orthodox conference held at the Antiochian Church's retreat in Ligonier, Pennsylvania, and which acquired a degree of notoriety because of the Ecumenical Patriarchate of Constantinople's rejection of its outcome. Chapter 11 takes stock of the state of Greek

Orthodoxy in America at the end of the twentieth century, assessing whether the church under Iakovos overreached in its efforts to Americanize and thus alienated the Ecumenical Patriarchate. The patriarchate's intervention illustrated the administrative limits the Greek Orthodox Church in America faces in its efforts to assimilate and also the patriarchate's ability to invoke the transnational character of Orthodoxy in the new era of globalization. Chapter 12 examines how Iakovos's successor, Archbishop Spyridon, erred on the side of tradition—which in turn illustrates the limits and potential drawbacks of Greek Orthodoxy's reliance on invoking its history—and how the patriarchate recovered the lost ground by appointing Demetrios archbishop in 1999. Even at that early point following the patriarchate's involvement in Greek Orthodoxy's affairs in the US, the religious dimension in several articulations of Greek American identity was becoming more pronounced. I then reiterate the book's main argument by summarizing the Greek Orthodox Church's trajectory throughout the twentieth century and the ways its ability to balance between adapting to the American social context and maintaining its ethnic roots enabled it to play a significant part in defining Greek American identity.

In the mid-1990s, the trend toward Americanization stopped short of creating a pan-Orthodox American Orthodox Church through the Ecumenical Patriarchate's intervention. This, if anything, strengthened the drift toward an even greater religious inflection to Greek American identity. On a theoretical plane, the transnational character of Orthodoxy ultimately prevailed over the structural influence of America. In practical terms, the historical experience of Greek Orthodoxy in America throughout the twentieth century demonstrates that an ethno-religious church encounters limits to its Americanization if it is beholden to a "mother church" that remains in the Old World, and in the case of Greek Orthodoxy, any future steps toward Americanization most likely will require negotiation between the church in America and the Patriarchate of Constantinople.

CHAPTER 1

Greek Orthodoxy Arrives in America

Mass emigration from Greece to the United States began in the late nineteenth century. About four hundred thousand Greeks had gone through Ellis Island by the 1920s when the US Congress restricted immigration from southeastern Europe. The passenger lists of the ships they traveled on recorded the very few belongings they brought with them. Their pockets contained a few dollars and scraps of paper with the address of a relative or a fellow villager who had already settled somewhere in the United States, and the directions of how to get there. Other items, of less interest to the authorities, included photographs of loved ones and a few personal effects. The newcomers, it turned out, were also bringing something else to America: the Greek Orthodox religion. Before the Greeks began to arrive in great numbers in the United States, a few wealthy merchants who were engaged in the cotton trade had established the first Greek Orthodox church in New Orleans in 1864; it served business persons and sailors intermittently in the following decades, until the era of mass immigration gave it a new life. There was another early Greek settlement in Florida in the nineteenth century, but no evidence exists of any organized religious practices. The same is true of the small numbers of Greeks who began arriving from the 1860s onward. It was the mass migration of the 1890s that brought a growing number of Greek Orthodox churches throughout the country. By the end of World War I, after two decades of upheavals, Greek Orthodoxy in

America would acquire a centralized administrative structure and governing body: the archdiocese.

At first, where there were only few Greeks, they worshipped in other already established Eastern Orthodox churches, primarily Russian ones. But they saw that only as a temporary measure and looked forward to establishing their own, Greek church. In the Old World the immigrants had left, Eastern Orthodoxy remained resolutely divided into separate national churches, even though Orthodox ecclesiology did not accept the concept of a national church. National churches functioned de facto if not de jure, and their existence was the norm; indeed, "the transition from a non-national to a national pattern of existence [was] a key characteristic of the Orthodox world in Eastern and South Eastern Europe, starting from the 19th century."[1] The immigrants from the Orthodox lands of Europe and the Middle East carried those divisions with them across the Atlantic and reproduced them in America. Russian émigré theologian John Meyendorff noted that those separate Orthodox jurisdictions born of the importation of nationalism from Europe created the appearance that they belonged to different denominations.[2]

The national character of the church was so important to the Greek immigrants that they ignored the Russian church's canonically important claim to represent all the Orthodox in the New World because Russia established the first mission there—albeit in Alaska, before it was acquired by the United States in 1867. The Russian church had spread its influence eastward by the turn of the century in an effort to incorporate all Eastern Orthodox who began arriving in the United States in the late nineteenth century. Toward that purpose, the Russian Orthodox North American Diocese moved its headquarters first to San Francisco and then to New York. But the Russian church was only able to attract Eastern Orthodox who did not yet have their own ethnic church and mostly those from Eastern Europe whose churches also used a Slavonic language liturgy, which was closer to the Russian. Greeks worshipped in Russian, Slavic, or Syrian Orthodox churches only if there was no Greek church. For example, the first Greek immigrants in Chicago worshipped in rented facilities in cooperation with Slavic Orthodox immigrants beginning in 1885, and the first Greek immigrants who arrived in San Francisco worshipped at a Russian church, as did the first Greeks in Galveston, Texas, and Seattle, Washington.[3]

The growing number of Greek immigrants all over the United States created a Greek Orthodox entity big enough to choose to be separate from the Russians. By 1915 the geographical spread of Greek Orthodox across North America was impressive, and churches were appearing throughout the country all the way to the West Coast. The total number of such churches is difficult to establish with any certainty, but one reliable source estimates there were 105 Greek Orthodox churches in existence by 1915. The first two of this new wave were the Annunciation in Chicago in 1892 and Holy Trinity in New York in 1894, the two cities with the greatest number of Greek immigrants. When Holy Trinity was founded in New York, a Russian cleric arrived claiming authority over it, because the Russian church had registered as the "Greek" church with the State of New York. The parishioners, headed by Solon Vlastos, the editor of the daily Greek language newspaper *Atlantis*, quickly took steps to incorporate Holy Trinity in the State of New York as the "Hellenic Eastern Orthodox Church of New York." The article of incorporation was at pains to show the difference between the Greek and Russian Orthodox Churches, stating that one of the purposes of becoming incorporated was "to distinguish the said 'Hellenic Eastern Orthodox Church of New York' from the so-called 'Greek Church of the Eastern Confession' by which title the Church of Russia and the Church of Greece have been known, although the Greek church has been separated from the Russian since the year eleven hundred anno domini."[4] In contrast to the Greek Orthodox attitude toward the Russian Orthodox in the United States, the Arab Orthodox, also known as Syrian Orthodox, sought and received the support of the Russian church. Their close relationship was not only because of their relatively small numbers but also because the Syrian church in the Old World, the Patriarchate of Antioch, maintained close relations with the Orthodox Patriarchate of Moscow.[5]

When Holy Trinity could not satisfy the needs of the growing numbers of Greeks in Manhattan, two more churches appeared on the West Side: Annunciation and St. Eleftherios. Across the Brooklyn Bridge, the Greeks established St. Constantine's, which later became St. Constantine and St. Helen's Church. Those who went upstate to look for jobs in manufacturing established another four churches, bringing the total in New York State to seven. Many Greeks were settling in New England to work mainly in the textile towns, and the first Greek Orthodox churches appeared in Boston, Ipswich, Lowell, Lynn, and Springfield in Massachusetts and in Providence, Rhode Island, and by 1915 there were thirty-eight churches in New England, nineteen of them in Massachusetts. In Pennsylvania, Greeks took up jobs in manufacturing and in the mining towns in the western part of the state; all together, there were sixteen Greek Orthodox churches throughout the state, the first being the Annunciation in Philadelphia. The total in the mid-Atlantic states was nine, including one that was apparently being set up in North Carolina. In the midwestern states there were twenty-six churches; Chicago, with three churches, was the city with the most, while Ohio, with eight, had the most of all states, because the Greeks had spread out to all the small manufacturing towns. The rest of the country—the South, the mountain West, and the West Coast—was the destination of smaller numbers of Greeks, though more would follow in the decades following World War I. But even then, there were Greeks all the way from Jacksonville in Florida and Savannah in Georgia to Galveston and Oklahoma City, and the total number of Greek Orthodox churches in the South numbered fifteen. There were fewer Greeks in Colorado, Nevada, and Utah, where they went to work in the mines, and in Idaho, were they also found jobs in the livestock industry; nevertheless, in the mountain West they had already established five churches. Finally, the first Greeks had reached the West Coast, and Los Angeles, San Francisco, Oakland, Portland, and Seattle each had a Greek Orthodox church. A sign of the growing significance of Greek Orthodoxy was that where there were no Russian churches; the Greek ones attracted all other Eastern Orthodox. In 1901 the *Chicago Tribune* reported that "Greeks from stores and fruit stands, Russians from the sweat shops and factories, swarthy Syrians and even Arabians crowded the Greek Orthodox Church of Holy Trinity, 34 Johnson Street, to observe the Easter services of their church."[6]

Byzantine Architecture and Social Space

The earliest Greek Orthodox churches in most cases were usually housed in what had been a Protestant church, whose own congregants had already moved away to a better part of town. But sooner or later the Greeks built their own churches. The very first Greek Orthodox church in the United States, in New Orleans, was a small wooden structure of a type common in Louisiana at the time. In the era of mass immigration, buildings that formerly served as Protestant churches housed the first Greek Orthodox churches in Chicago and New York and most other places. In what was the first of many concessions to the realities of the American environment, the Greek Orthodox—at least the early immigrants—had to forgo the luxury of building a church that would conform to the all-important dictates of tradition, at least externally. Tradition called for churches in the form of basilicas, buildings with a long central nave with an antechamber (narthex) and a semicircular apse at the other end, high windows to admit light, and a dome (cupola) on the roof. The cruciform nave is separated from the sanctuary by a wooden screen adorned with icons. This was the original architectural model for early Christian churches. In Western Europe, churches eventually adopted more varied architectural designs following the Renaissance and the Protestant Reformation, but Eastern Orthodoxy remained resolutely attached to the basilica archetype throughout history. The internal layout of the church shaped the way the liturgy was conducted, and its continuity helped keep liturgical practice and experience constant through time and consistent whatever the geographical location. The icons decorating the interior adopted a particular pattern: the dome, with its connotations of heaven, was reserved for the holiest figure, Christ, usually called Pantokrator, or Ruler of All; the apse, the second-most-important space, was reserved for the Virgin Mary; while the apostles and angels adorned the drum of the dome just below Christ. The churches the Greeks built in the New World, or those they refurbished, aimed at adhering to this traditional architecture, which functioned as "a codified container of ritual, iconography, and symbolic meaning."[7] It was the single most nationally distinctive structure that signaled the arrival and presence of the Greeks in America.

The Old World Byzantine-style structure was so important that, wherever possible, new church buildings would adopt the Byzantine form. Holy Trinity Church in Lowell, Massachusetts—a city that boasted the largest concentration of Greeks in New England, numbering nine thousand during World War I—was the first Greek Orthodox church in the United States to be built according to the requirements of Byzantine architecture, with a cruciform nave and a domed roof—the dome distinguished all Byzantine-style churches from the Russian churches, which had an onion-shaped dome. Holy Trinity was built in Lowell's Acre neighborhood, where the Greeks were replacing the older Irish immigrants, and the wish to match the grandeur of other churches in the neighborhood motivated the idea of building a Byzantine-style church. Lowell architect Henry L. Rourke designed the church based on Aghia (Hagia) Sophia, the sixth-century church in Istanbul that served as the Ecumenical Patriarchate of Constantinople's cathedral in the Byzantine era. The total construction cost of Holy Trinity came to $80,000. Thomas Burgess, author of one of the early studies on the Greeks in the United States, called it one of the finest churches in America, and he saw it as an Eastern equivalent of the nearby St. Patrick's: "Directly across the canal stands a beautiful Roman Catholic Church. Here truly meet East and West, two excellent examples of the Byzantine and Gothic fronting each other, the gilded domes and splendid spires rising out of the midst of tumble-down tenements."[8] The interior also elicited his praise: "Nothing in Eikons or paintings is gaudy but all is done with exquisite taste and proportion. Truly this house of God, so full of ordered symbolism and pictured teaching cannot but instill in the Greek reverent thoughts of God and his power and love, and devotion to his Holy Church."[9] Another early architectural bow to tradition came in Chicago when the first church there, the Annunciation, which had started out in a rented hall and later moved to a Masonic temple, got its own home in 1909. The parish purchased the lot on North LaSalle Street in the city's downtown at a cost of $18,000, and a church modeled on the Orthodox cathedral in Athens—a combination of Byzantine and Gothic styles—was completed in 1910 at an estimated cost of $100,000.

Byzantine-style churches, or variations thereof, followed in the wake of the westward travels of the Greeks. A visitor to Pocatello, Idaho, in 1915 would probably have been very surprised to see a Greek Orthodox church dedicated to the Assumption of the Virgin Mary built in a Byzantine Revival style with a gable roof and redbrick exterior with stone accents, topped by a cylindrical roof-tower with a conical roof and twelve small round-arched windows that provided additional illumination for the nave. Gradually, all churches built from scratch adopted the Byzantine style; it would be only in the 1950s when modern designs appeared.

The form that the liturgy and all forms of worship took within the churches and during outdoor processions on important feast days, especially Easter, adhered strictly to tradition and evoked the homeland in the minds of the immigrants. The entire service and the chanting were in Greek, while incense and candles burned in the churches. Grace Abbot, an American social worker who was involved in helping the settlement of Greek immigrants in Chicago, marveled at the Old World character of an Orthodox procession and wrote, "If an American were to visit this neighborhood on the night of Good Friday when the stores are draped with purple and black and watch at mid-night the solemn procession of Greek men march down the street carrying their burning candles and chanting hymns, he would probably feel as though he were no longer in America." She added that "those who marched were homesick and mourning because try as they might they could not quite recreate the atmosphere of Easter in the Peloponnesean home town."[10] Yet church life did go a long way toward reminding the immigrants, if only during the important feast days, of the homes they had left behind to cross the Atlantic. Most of these immigrants were men, either single or having left wife and family back in the homeland, so there was no great demand for the holy sacraments associated with weddings or baptisms. It was only after wives and children began coming over after World War I that this demand increased beyond attendance at big feast days of Orthodoxy, because "the immigrants were neither ardent joiners nor attenders of churches. . . . They attended whenever they felt the need, especially during Holy Week, Easter, Christmas, Epiphany and the Feast of the Annunciation. The church parishes in New York and the United States were much larger than the enrolled membership. . . . It was not uncommon for a parish with 50 enrolled members to minister to the needs of a community that may have numbered several thousand."[11]

But the Greek churches did much more than cater to spiritual needs: to their constituents they functioned as social spaces that brought the Greeks together. The ubiquitous Greek coffee shop that spread throughout the country even faster than Greek Orthodox churches also served that function, but it was a male preserve. In contrast, the parish was much more inclusive, as well as being more formal and representative of the entire Greek settlement. We should bear in mind that the immigrants imported to the New World "highly variable folk practices consisting of multilayered secular and religious elements . . . story telling songs and dances, ritual laments, hospitality, traditions and beliefs associated with Orthodoxy, superstitions, folk healing, oral poetic traditions and divination"[12]—in other words, a rich culture in which tradition determined a moral order and in which Orthodoxy and the church as a meeting place arguably played a central role. And the local parish in the United States resembled the one in the homeland where Orthodoxy took on a particular meaning in each rural locality, fusing with local traditions and thus defining the identity of a neighborhood or a village.

The church became the site of the major religious rites such as baptism, weddings, and funerals, which for many Orthodox, especially in rural Greece, went beyond religious belief and were linked with a metaphysical belief in fate.[13] The particular deity or the saint the church was dedicated to also had a particular significance in fostering local, village identity. The Panagía or Virgin Mary in particular is coextensive with Greek identity writ large, because the national independence day is celebrated on the day the Orthodox Church celebrates her Annunciation; churches dedicated to Mary are distinguished through calling them "Panagía of—" and adding the village's name.[14] Parish leaders would make deliberate efforts to foster community-based activities that evoked the social character of Orthodoxy and especially its philanthropic traditions. Parish-based charity was the sphere in which women, who played a secondary role in all the other affairs of the church, were able to take the initiative and make their mark. One of the earliest examples was in 1902 when women organized a charity group that was associated with Holy Trinity in New York. Among their activities was offering aid and advice to the immigrants arriving in the city, as well as offering help to those who got into trouble with the law. Such women's charity groups, named Philoptochos ("friend of the poor"), began appearing in most parishes and became important sources of help not only to the poor but also to those unfortunate Greeks who fell victim to the xenophobia that began increasing in America in the early twentieth century. There was therefore all the more reason for the embrace of the church by newly arrived immigrants in need.

Church and School, Priest and Teacher

Next to catering to the spiritual needs of the immigrants, connecting them to the homeland, bringing them together and initiating philanthropic activities, the Greek Orthodox churches, along with local secular community organizations, took on the responsibility of running Greek-language schools. Even where the community organization was strong enough to shoulder that task, the parish priest was involved in shaping the curriculum and teaching the children. The purpose of teaching Greek to the children of the immigrants was to help them preserve their Greek Orthodox identity and also be able to understand at least some of the language used in the church, an archaic version of the vernacular the Greeks spoke in everyday life. An editorial in Chicago's Greek language newspaper *Hellenikos Astir* captured the purpose of the schools when it noted "the Greek school will train children to be Greeks so they will not be digested in the vastness of America." And it reported a school principal declaring that the school and the church were "the two pillars which support our national aspirations and they must become our two anchors if we are to maintain our ethnicity in America and remain Greek and Christian Orthodox."[15]

Though based primarily on language instruction, the curriculum of the schools included religion and history, stretching back to classical Greece. The immigrants soon discovered the importance of establishing Greek schools where history would be emphasized. When their children began attending American school, their parents were offended by the absence from the public school curriculum of classical Greek civilization and its achievements. Greek immigrants expressed great disappointment about how the American schools "ignored" the glories of the ancient Greeks, and teaching that history through the Greek school was an essential way of ensuring that their children were proud of their origins—and their parents. The priests were happy to teach about ancient Greece because Greek Orthodoxy maintained that Christianity emerged through the cross-fertilization of early Christian and Hellenic thought; and unlike other Christian churches, the Greek church emphasized the significance of that relationship. In the words of Orthodox theologian and church historian Demetrios Constantelos, "The faith, worship and ethos of early Christianity, rooted in the Scriptures, were defined, formulated and disseminated through the efforts of Greek or Hellenized Church Fathers, theologians, missionaries, and ecumenical synods held in

Greek cities. . . . The Church was implanted by St. Paul and other Apostles in Greek cities and provinces and expressed itself in the Greek language for at least four centuries. . . . The richness of the Greek language and mind provided all the presuppositions and dynamics to make Christianity understood." Constantelos concedes that "the relationship between Christianity and Hellenism is still a problem for some Christian denominations that are offshoots of the Protestant Reformation" but adds that this in no way presents a problem for the Greek Orthodox who see Christianity in a historical context.[16]

Thus, if the Sunday liturgy was a time where the adult Greek Orthodox immigrants connected with their identity in a formal setting, the community school served the same function through language classes. The community organizations and the local priest took the initiative to lay the foundations of Greek language education and teach about classical Greek civilization. In most smaller communities, which lacked the means to support a teacher of Greek, the priest took on that responsibility. In his authoritative history of the Greeks in the United States, Theodore Saloutos, who was not an admirer of the church, acknowledged that the Greek Orthodox churches in America, "despite their endless feuds and shortsighted objectives, fostered whatever semblance of Greek education there was. No other agency proved capable of maintaining this sustained effort."[17]

Getting a school up and running usually involved a couple of false starts, and it is difficult to speak about the "first school" with great certainty. In Lowell, the community founded the Greek Parochial School in 1906, and classes were held in the basement of the Holy Trinity Greek Orthodox Church. In 1915 the school changed its name to the Hellenic American School. In Chicago, the "Greek Institution of Chicago-Hellenism" was formed in 1905 but did not last very long. The community associated with the city's Holy Trinity Church founded the Socrates school in 1908, and the community of Sts. Constantine and Helen Church established the Koraes school in 1910. The choice of names, of an ancient Greek philosopher and an eighteenth-century Enlightenment thinker, reflected the prevailing sense that Greek schooling was an ethno-religious project. The establishment of the Helleno-Amerikanikon Ekpaideutirion, a Greek school in the Bronx, New York, in 1911, was a testament to the urgency surrounding the need to cater to the children's education in a foreign environment. The seed money for acquiring a building came from Solon Vlastos, the owner of the *Atlantis* newspaper. Vlastos, a committed royalist, was also involved in the establishment of the second Greek Orthodox church in New York City, the Annunciation. Despite the simmering rivalry between the Annunciation and the Holy Trinity parishes, the board of

Holy Trinity agreed to support the Annunciation church school. Both New York parish priests, Father Kourouklis of the Holy Trinity and Father Lazaris of the Annunciation, spoke publicly in favor of the school. They both joined the school's board, whose other members were prominent Greek Americans and included tobacco merchants, confectionary-patisserie owners, a doctor, a florist, a fur manufacturer, an importer of Greek food products, and a merchant.[18] The school opened in September 1912 in a building in the Bronx that was purchased for $32,500. There were 125 students on opening day; the enrollment soon grew to 135, among them a number of orphans who were housed on the property.

The great hopes that parish leaders harbored about the Greek day schools were dampened when new federal government regulations designed to improve public school education began limiting the scope of ethnic community schools and forcing them to operate only after normal school hours. The regulations were designed to make the public schools work better and address the ways immigrant children were treated or ignored, with a view of achieving Americanization more effectively. The introduction of compulsory education throughout the country by 1918 made the issue of dealing with immigrant children even more pressing. Public education consisted of "instructing the students on everything from American customs, foods, and dress to patriotic songs and heroes," a socialization in which more often than not whatever was considered "American" was also deemed superior.[19] Thus, the desire for ethnic education would become even stronger after World War I, and by the same token the Greek Orthodox Church's responsibilities would increase.

Clergy-Laity Relations

In Eastern Orthodoxy's ecclesiology, the laity are co-celebrants with the clergy; in practice, however, this symbiotic relationship can break down, either because the laity claim responsibility for what they see as the material aspects of church life, or because the clergy ignore the views of the lay members.[20] The lack of a central Greek Orthodox authority in the first two decades of the twentieth century and the isolation of many small pockets of Greek immigrants throughout the country meant that the local laity played a defining role in the early years of Greek Orthodoxy's presence in America. The churches themselves had emerged thanks to the initiative of local lay community organizations. These possessed great authority in the minds of Greek immigrants because there was a long tradition of Greeks abroad forming community organizations—referred to as "the community"—wherever they settled, and these functioned as their main ethnic association.

An earlier generation of Greek emigrants, who had formed merchant communities throughout the Mediterranean, the Black Sea, and along the Balkan trade routes into Central Europe, established influential and wealthy community organizations funded by bankers and export merchants who had pockets deep enough to fund an entire network of institutions: churches, cultural and social clubs, hospitals, schools and orphanages, and retirement homes. The community organizations established in the United States had less impressive budgets, but there were enough relatively well-off Greek merchants or manufacturers based in Boston, Chicago, New York, and Philadelphia who would contribute generously to the creation of the first of these ethnic associations in the United States. These and other relatively prosperous individuals served on executive committees and would also function as the board of trustees of the local church. Again, most of these early ethnic organizations were simply called "the community," though they might go by other names; in Los Angeles, for example, the first was the Benevolent Society. In the smaller Greek settlements, where the sole purpose of the ethnic association was to establish a church, the community was run as a parish, with a committee of lay members hiring a priest with whom they shared the responsibility of administering religious affairs. In many of the smaller settlements, the Greek immigrants saw no reason not to consider the community organization identical with the parish. All of them considered themselves members of the church—"even the indifferent and the nonchurchgoers regard themselves as Greek church people," in the words of one contemporary observer.[21] Whether they viewed themselves as a community organization running a church, or as a parish, the board members relished the control they had over the affairs of the church. As Chicago's Greek language newspaper, the *Hellenikos Astir* (Greek Star), put it in 1904, "the Church is our creation to serve the spiritual needs of the community. The Church is not the community; it is an institution of it."[22]

One of the main reasons the laity predominated was that the early years of the church were plagued by an influx of persons who were priests or monks in Greece (or claimed they were) but proved to be incapable of serving as parish priests. In 1908, a Boston-based Greek interpreter, Miltiades Constantinides, working for the Bureau of Immigration, reported to his superiors that there were a number of Greeks entering the United States who were impersonating priests or were unordained monks, and therefore any sacerdotal acts they performed were, he believed, illegal. The interpreter had made his own investigations and found that "in most cases their papers show they were inmates of a monastery in Greece or Turkey. On a pretense of going to visit their relatives at their home they escape to America. Here they go from community to community offering their services as fully qualified and properly ordained priests of the Greek Orthodox Church amongst their countrymen at half the salary the real priests of that church demand." And he added (without, however, backing up his claims), "By their actions they only bring trouble and discord and scandal to any peaceful church and congregation." He then went on to suggest that priests traveling from Greece to the United States be supplied with several official documents by the Greek authorities. When the Immigration Bureau forwarded Constantides's letter to the Greek embassy in Washington, which was acting as the Church of Greece's informal representative in the United States, ambassador Lambros Koromilas responded that in light of the newly assumed responsibilities of the Church of Greece, he was confident that the problem would be resolved, but reserved the right to provide details sometime in the future.[23]

The ambassador's optimism proved unfounded, as the problem with the priests continued. Eight years later, the head of the Church of Greece, Archbishop Theokletos of Athens, was expressing his sorrow over the phenomenon of clerics traveling to America without the approval of the church's Holy Synod "solely for the purpose of making money." An account of the Greeks in America published in 1918 by Seraphim Canoutas, a Greek American lawyer, noted that "on every ship leaving for America there were several priests traveling without having been appointed to any parish, but thanks to their own initiatives or those of their friends several small communities were created or broke away from others in order to accommodate them by creating new parishes even though there was no need for them."[24] Two years later the Greek ambassador in Washington, Emmanuel Tsamados, expressed his disappointment with the quality of the clergy he had found when he took up his post. Most priests who had come across the Atlantic to offer their services, he reported to the Ministry for Foreign Affairs in Athens, had done so "to get rich," and therefore they maneuvered to curry favor with the dominant faction in their parish so that they could remain. Ability, ethical values, or vision rarely played any part in determining the appointment of a parish priest, nor could they, given the low standards of most of the priesthood. He recommended these individuals' gradual replacement with more qualified clerics sent from Greece, and that the authorities in Greece should prevent any clerics not approved by the church from traveling to the United States.[25]

Yet for all the complaints of unqualified priests that persons in authority mentioned in their reports, many honest and hardworking priests also arrived in the United States, and they labored away, some unnoticed by the officials filing reports yet gratefully recognized by parishioners. Some were urged to come to America by their own former parishioners who had settled in the United States. Others came of their own volition yet also did not fit the profile of the unqualified adventurer that the diplomats warned about. They proved to be the pioneers who prepared the ground for Greek Orthodoxy to plant deep roots in America. They often faced many and unexpected obstacles, but many would manage to adapt to the changes Greek Americans experienced in the first half of the twentieth century and continue to serve the needs of their parishioners. One of them was Constantine Tsapralis, who arrived in San Francisco in 1903 and became the priest of Holy Trinity, which was incorporated in 1904 as the first Greek Orthodox parish in the city and the oldest Greek Orthodox church west of Chicago. There was considerable wrangling with the church's trustees until they agreed to pay him a meager $1,800 over two years for his services as assistant pastor. That sum was not sufficient for the needs of his family—his wife Eleni, their two sons, and a nephew who lived with them—so he also became the proprietor of a saloon and a candy store. His family members ran the businesses because Father Tsapralis was busy traveling to Fresno and other towns in California, Nevada, and even Arizona to perform sacraments. In 1906 Holy Trinity was destroyed in the earthquake that struck the city, so he used the home of one of his leading parishioners to perform services until a new church was built in 1907, along with a Greek school, which was also the first west of Chicago. After a two-year hiatus, during which Father Tsapralis joined a church established by disgruntled parishioners, he returned to Holy Trinity when the local differences were overcome, only for them to resurface because of political polarization among the parishioners after World War I, which led a group to leave and establish their own church. But in the late 1920s Tsapralis officiated in a joint service of the two churches that signaled their reconciliation. As he neared retirement a decade later, he had another dispute with church trustees because he objected to their holding a fund-raising lottery, and he received the salary they were withholding only thanks to a court decision. But he managed to end his service in the church on a high note when he went to Los Angeles to help officiate in the wedding of Jim Londos, the legendary Greek American champion wrestler.[26] Another priest based in San Francisco, Father Koutouzis, also had a very good reputation and was greatly in demand. He was offered a position in Florida, which he accepted, but when his train stopped off in Los Angeles, two local Greeks who were involved in establishing the community there, George and Louis Alexakis, went to meet him and "took the priest off the train, treated him to lunch and persuaded him to stay in L.A. to lead their parish."[27]

The early years of Holy Trinity Church in New York City provide a good example of a troubled relationship between a parish board of trustees and the parish priest. A community organization, Athena, formed in 1891, requested the Church of Greece to send a priest. The community had rented a formerly Protestant church on Eighth Avenue and Fifty-Third Street and named the church Holy Trinity. But the new priest displeased most members of the community organization—he wanted nonmembers to be able to participate in the lay committee that would run the church. The community requested a replacement, and for good measure contacted both the Church of Greece and the patriarchate in Constantinople. This meant that two clerics eventually arrived, something that turned out to benefit the Greeks living in Lower Manhattan, because one of the two, Father Kallinikos Dilveis, went down the island to form a new parish, Evangelismos (Annunciation). Father Dilveis eventually moved the Upper West Side of New York City, but discontent continued to simmer at Holy Trinity, and after a few years both priests left New York. After a succession of priests who were unable to manage the personal differences among the leading Holy Trinity members, the parish had to turn to the Greek consul in New York, Dimitrios Botasis, to administer elections that would be considered fair by both warring sides. Elections were held, but the division persisted, with one side wishing to affirm that they were under the jurisdiction of the Church of Greece and the other seeking to place the parish under the jurisdiction of the Patriarchate of Constantinople. Even Rev. Zisimos Typaldos, a professor at the Rizareios School of Theology in Athens who knew English, was unable to bridge those differences, and he stepped down as parish priest in 1904. His replacement, Methodius Kourouklis, gained support from both sides, and the parish at last overcame the internal strife.[28] The price they paid was to have a dynamic priest who would be accused by some of being too autocratic. After attempts to merge the Annunciation church with Holy Trinity failed, Annunciation was fortunate enough to obtain a gifted priest, Father Nikolaos Lazaris, who possessed both leadership and negotiating skills and managed to unite the parish behind him. The church's website includes a history of the parish, which proudly notes, "But in 1908, Father Nikolaos Lazaris, who was a prominent priest became our spiritual leader for the next quarter century. He had been a graduate and lecturer at the Athens Theological University and during his tenure he was decorated by the Patriarchate and was given the honorary ecclesiastical title of 'Economos.' The cross and bible that he received from the Patriarchate he donated to our church and his chalice was given to the St. Nicholas Church, Flushing, NY."[29]

The experiences elsewhere in the United States showed that local boards of trustees struggled to guide their churches through the early years. There were serious problems in Chicago, where the first Greek Orthodox house of worship had been established in 1892. There, in the words of historian Theodore Saloutos, "the Greek language press continued to attack what they called greedy, stingy, grasping priests who in league with conscience-less members of the board of trustees were trampling on the dignity of the church and the integrity of their communities. Lengthy court trials, criminal waste and the extravagant use of church funds for litigation and lawyers' fees had become a disgrace."[30] An effort to quell parish-based turmoil over the relations between church boards and priests was made in 1915 with the formation of the United Greek Parishes of Chicago, whose goal was to help the city's Greek Orthodox parishes audit their books and achieve better administration through cooperation. Unfortunately, this initiative was stymied by rising political differences within the community over the next few years. In Philadelphia, where the Stephano family, owners of a big tobacco company in the city, helped establish the first church, there were fewer problems. In 1901, when there were about two hundred Greeks in Philadelphia, Nathaniel Sideris, a Greek Orthodox monk, arrived and set about establishing an Orthodox church; he performed the first services, celebrating Christmas, in a Russian Orthodox church. A group of Philadelphia Greeks rallied around the monk, and they established a community organization to administer the Greek Orthodox church, which moved into a rented space in the city center, near where most of the Greeks lived. With the financial support of Constantine Stephano, the community purchased a former Episcopal church nearby and dedicated it as the Greek Orthodox Church of the Annunciation in 1908. There was turnover in the position of parish priest, but changes occurred without friction, owing to the firm influence of the Stephano family, despite some opposition to the family among a group of parishioners.

A Bishop Is Appointed

The eventual establishment in 1922 of a central Greek Orthodox governing authority in the United States was a difficult process because of the impact of Greece's polarized politics on the Greek immigrants. The first step toward establishing the Greek Orthodox Archdiocese came somewhat unexpectedly with the appointment of a bishop charged with overseeing Greek Orthodox life in America. It was a move initiated in Athens. When emigration from Greece had begun in the early twentieth century, the Ecumenical

Patriarchate of Constantinople had asserted its canonically grounded responsibility for the Orthodox "diaspora." In the Orthodox vocabulary, the diaspora were the Orthodox Christians living in the lands beyond the regions that fell under the jurisdiction of the Patriarchates of Alexandria, Antioch, Jerusalem, and Rome, a vast region that included all of the Americas. That Orthodox diaspora was the responsibility of the Ecumenical Patriarchate of Constantinople. Notwithstanding its claims over the Greek Orthodox in the United States, the patriarchate refrained from appointing a Greek Orthodox bishop across the Atlantic, tacitly acknowledging that "canonically" there was supposed to be only one archbishop in a particular region, and that there was already a Russian Orthodox archbishop in place. Instead it merely responded to requests to send priests and adjudicated where there was a dispute. Very soon, however, problems posed by the five-thousand-mile distance to New York, including poor communications, along with Ottoman political upheavals in Constantinople, persuaded the patriarchate in 1908 to cede jurisdiction over America to the Church of Greece. The Church of Greece was "autocephalous"—a term meaning self-governing, in which the head of a church does not report to, but remains in spiritual communion with, a higher-ranking church—but unlike the Russian Orthodox Church, it had remained close to the patriarchate, accepting Constantinople's "spiritual" authority, even though it administered its own affairs. Thus, the transfer did not mean surrendering that authority over the Orthodox diaspora in the United States.

Both clergy and laity in Greece shared a strong conviction that the Ecumenical Patriarchate of Constantinople was the mother church of Greek Orthodoxy. But there was a potential problem with the Church of Greece—which was totally subservient to the Greek government—overseeing Greek Orthodox affairs in America. In the words of a church historian, the original establishment of the Church of Greece in the early nineteenth century meant that "on paper it was divested of practically all its authority and Caesar had taken what was his and what was God's."[31] This also meant that the political party in power in Athens could, if it chose, influence the church's affairs and certainly indirectly choose its leader. Historically, from the Byzantine era onward, Eastern Orthodoxy had evolved a tradition of cohabiting with whatever political authority was in power.

The negative effects of these arrangements were felt across the Atlantic after Greek politics became hopelessly divided in 1915 between the royalists, who were the supporters of King Constantine, who was the head of state, and the Venizelists, who were the supporters of Eleftherios Venizelos, the prime minister and head of government. Unfortunately, what became a deep divide was reproduced among the Greeks in the United States, and it involved the Greek Orthodox Church as well. The immediate cause of the conflict was that Constantine favored Greek neutrality in the World War that had broken out in 1914, while Venizelos believed Greece should join the side of the Anglo-French Entente, because those allies would support Greece's territorial claims against the Ottoman Empire. This divide would become known as the "national schism" because it created a bitter polarization that lasted through the repercussions of World War I in Greece and among the Greeks abroad. When the Venizelists in New York City produced their own daily Greek language newspaper, the *Ethnikos Kyrix* (National Herald), to counter the city's increasing pro-monarchist daily, *Atlantis*, the political divisions escalated, and it was only a matter of time until they enveloped the parishes. Where the majority of the board of trustees and the parish priest saw eye to eye politically, life went on undisturbed. But more often than not community boards were divided, or the trustees and the priest disagreed. The practice of invoking the Lord's blessings on the country's and the homeland's political leaders in the Sunday liturgy was a constant, public reminder of a parish's affiliations. With both sides disputing the other's legitimacy, the pro-monarchists would mention the king but not Venizelos, while the Venizelists would solemnly invoke the prime minister's name. Thus, the liturgy and by extension the whole parish became hopelessly politicized.

Soon, Greece's church affairs would have an even more direct impact across the Atlantic. When Venizelos prevailed over King Constantine and returned to power in 1917 with the help of Britain and France, he dismissed Archbishop Theokletos, who had previously held a public ceremony in Athens anathematizing the prime minister. Venizelos replaced Theokletos with Meletios Metaxakis, a prelate who was so closely identified with the liberal politician that he later earned the description "a Venizelos in robes." It was this trusted figure that Venizelos sent as an emissary to the United States, to court support for Greece's foreign policy goals and—in a surprise move designed to restore order to the church's affairs—to appoint a resident bishop. Meletios traveled to the US in August 1918, accompanied by two leading Greek bishops, Alexandros Demoglou and Chrysostomos Papadopoulos, as well as Amilkas Alivizatos, an eminent lay theologian. Upon their arrival it became known that Meletios was naming Bishop Alexandros as resident bishop in America and that he would be answerable to the Church of Greece's ruling body, the synod. Not much was known about Alexandros, other than he was born Alexandros Demoglou in 1876 in Constantinople, that he graduated from the patriarchate's theological school of Halki in 1902, and that he was ordained a priest the same year and went on to serve in several districts, including Athens. Most importantly, he was close to Meletios, which meant he was a pro-Venizelist. Normally the appointment of a bishop to oversee Greek Orthodox life in America would have been expected to have a positive impact. But Alexandros's tenure as resident bishop immediately ran into serious canonical as well as political obstacles.

Reactions against Alexandros's appointment came from both the Russian Orthodox Church over its canonical (i.e., church law) status, as well as from Greek pro-monarchists who were not prepared to accept that Meletios was the legitimate head of the Church of Greece. Canonical law stipulated that a bishop could be appointed only by the existing Orthodox Church authorities in a particular region—a legal line the Church of Greece had not crossed so as not to cause further tensions with the Russian Orthodox Church. The Russian church claimed to be the sole authority in America, so it made no move to greet Meletios upon his arrival, lest that be taken as some form of official recognition. But the anger with which the Greek opponents of Venizelos greeted the appointment of a Venizelist resident bishop was much more explicit, and they openly disputed his legitimacy. They "abused and vilified him," and the *Atlantis* newspaper "urged the parish priests to ignore his instructions and refuse him the revenue he was seeking."[32]

It was a bad start for the new resident bishop, and things got even more complicated very soon. Elections were held in Greece in 1920, and Venizelos was expected to win easily because he had persuaded Britain, France, and the United States to permit Greece to play a direct part in the partition of the Ottoman Empire and land troops in the Aegean port city of Smyrna, where there was a large Greek population. But back home the war-weary Greek population voted Venizelos out of office in 1920. The new royalist government would continue the Greek campaign to gain Smyrna and the surrounding region, despite vigorous opposition from Turkish nationalists that swept aside the Ottoman old order. But the pro-monarchists dismissed Meletios and reinstated Theokletos, who immediately demanded Bishop Alexandros's return to Greece to explain his actions in America. Alexandros refused to step down, and Greek Orthodoxy in America was now effectively split in two. As the struggle between the two sides continued, Meletios made it worse by returning to the United States in early 1921 and describing himself as the lawful head of the Church of Greece. In April of that year he shared the podium with Columbia University's president at a celebration of Greek independence in New York City organized by the city's Venizelists.[33] Back in Athens, the Church of Greece responded by declaring both Alexandros and Meletios "schismatic," and it appointed its own representative in the United States, Bishop Germanos Troianos of Monemvasia and Lacedemonia (the region around Sparta in the Peloponnese), a trusted collaborator of Arch-bishop Theokletos. Germanos arrived in New York in July 1921 and trav-eled to several parishes, eliciting a mixed response. An obvious destination was Chicago, where he could expect a warm welcome, because the bulk of the Greek population in the city was from the Peloponnesos, a royalist stronghold. But Leon Pigeas, the pastor of the Greek Church of the Holy Trinity, resigned and closed the church rather than receive Germanos, and so the community board had to step in and allow Germanos to attend the ser-vices and make a speech, though not to officiate.[34] Nonetheless, Germanos, a capable and charismatic personality, gradually gained supporters to claim the backing of a quarter to a third of the total number of Greek Orthodox parishes.

The Establishment of the Archdiocese

At this point, clearly, the future of Greek Orthodoxy in America would be decided by moves that were closer to politics than prayer. Meletios, an adroit strategist, estimated that he had the allegiance of about two-thirds of the clergy and, deciding to capitalize on that advantage, moved before Germanos could continue gaining influence. To bolster his claims to be the official rep-resentative of the Greek Orthodox Church in America, he decided to create a central administrative body, the archdiocese. Meletios evidently thought that the worsening situation demanded a drastic solution. It was not just a move calculated to ensure the ecclesiastical hegemony of the Venizelists; it was also a measure to protect the integrity of the church and its standing in the eyes of the American public. The pitched battles between monarchists and Venizelists during parish board meetings and even liturgies had already involved the police and local judges. The church was getting bad press and an even worse image at a time when xenophobia was on the rise. A central organization could provide a sense of order.

On August 11, 1921, Meletios issued an encyclical calling together the clergy and laity of the parishes in America.[35] The "General Convention of Canonical Clerics of the Greek Orthodox Church" met in New York over three days, September 13–15, and would go down in history as the found-ing moment of the Archdiocese of North and South America, and later be considered the archdiocese's first Clergy-Laity Congress. The gather-ing took place at the Church of the Holy Trinity in New York City, at 153 East Seventy-Second Street, in the afternoon of September 13. Meletios was elected as president of the assembly, Alexandros as vice president, and Deacon Germanos Polyzoides as secretary. Polyzoides was a twenty-three-year-old theology student who had been born in the same Constantinople neighborhood as Bishop Alexandros, had also graduated from the Halki seminary, and had come to New York to continue his studies—he signed the founding charter as "archdeacon." Seventy clerics were either present or represented by proxy vote, and also in attendance were a small number of leading lay parishioners from New York City. Following the blueprint outlined in the encyclical sent out in August, Bishop Alexandros proposed that "the Greek Orthodox Church in America be organized into a corporation in accordance with the laws of the State and the Holy Canon." Holy Trinity's Father Methodios Kourkoulis then proposed, "This corporation shall be known as The Greek Orthodox Archdiocese of North and South America."[36] The convention's resolution described the aims of the new organization as being, first, "to edify the religious and moral life of the Greek Orthodox Christians in North and South America on the basis of the Holy Scriptures, the rules and canons of the Holy Apostles and of the Seven Oecumenical Councils of the ancient and divided Church as they are or shall be interpreted by the Great Church of Christ in Constantinople"; second, "to exercise governing authority over and maintain advisory relations with Greek Orthodox Churches throughout North and South America"; and third, "to maintain spiritual and advisory relations with synods and other governing authorities of the Church located elsewhere."[37]

The convention agreed on a twelve-article constitution that included the provision to establish a nine-member board of clergy and lay trustees, as well as the archdiocese's incorporation under US laws. The elections produced a board to serve under Meletios's chairmanship. It was made up of four clerics: Bishop Alexandros and three parish priests, Demetrios Callimachos of St. Constantine in Brooklyn, who had a theology degree and worked previously as the editor-in-chief of the Venizelist *Ethnikos Kyrix* newspaper in New York; Father Kourouklis of the Holy Trinity Cathedral; Stephanos Macaronis; and Polyzoides. The four lay members were Leonidas Calvocoressis, Panagiotes Panteas, Georgios Kontomanolis, and Alexandros Alexion, all of them residents of New York City. There was no disguising the political preferences of those present. The convention coincidentally took place on the same day that Venizelos, out of office, was getting married. The meeting sent a congratulatory telegram to the former prime minister. A resolution to have the Greek Orthodox Archdiocese of North and South America incorporated under the laws of the State of New York was approved on the final day of the congress. In his address to the assembly, Meletios dwelt on the dual nature of the archdiocese's status as an institution that embodied the spirit and laws of Greek Orthodoxy but also operated within the laws of the United States. Maybe in order to draw a contrast with Greece's politics, Meletios emphasized the freedoms that persons enjoyed in the United States thanks to its laws, and went on to say the Greek Orthodox Church had a duty to take advantage of that situation, which enabled it to establish an ecclesiastical authority that would determine its operation without government interference. "And while America provides with full freedoms," he went on to say, "we, as children of the Holy Orthodox Church[,] we have the eternal boundaries that the fathers of the church delineated." All the archdiocese's decisions had to be within the laws of Greek Orthodoxy as well as the US laws governing ecclesiastical institutions. A great deal of work would still need to be done to establish the archdiocese's authority and ensure its role in fostering Greek Orthodox spiritual life and Greek identity in America. The immediate next step came in early 1922 when the State of New York officially recognized the archdiocese.

Within the space of a little over two decades, Greek Orthodoxy in America had gone from the humble beginnings of the first churches, created in makeshift housing to cater to the needs of the first immigrants, to the level of grand strategy. There were often times when Greek Orthodoxy came close to justifying the derogatory epithets of hostile or unsympathetic observers. "Caesaro-papism" has been used to describe the Byzantine system as one in which the head of state was also the head of the church, or, in the older texts, where the head of the church was utterly beholden to the emperor. The concepts the term denotes are historically wrong; it is nothing more than a caricature and at best an inappropriate term with which "to cover an Orthodox Church that rejects episcopal monarchies of all sorts, in favor of collegial consensus and harmony of spirit."[38] "Byzantine politics" was another opprobrious historical term that unsympathetic Western observers employed, referring to the intricate political manipulations in and around the Byzantine court. There were many things about the Byzantines these observers simply did not understand, whether it was their transitive sense of political power in which a pretender to the throne could overthrow the emperor, or their skilled diplomacy, or their ritualistic courtly practices.

The circumstances surrounding the creation of the Greek Orthodox Archdiocese were not about "Byzantine politics" but a reflection of the unfortunate consequences of the closeness of the church to secular politics at a time of deep-seated ideological polarization. It was a polarization that many clerics and a substantial part of the laity got caught up in and which had to be neutralized by the type of decisive initiatives taken by Meletios. It was not an ideal way for Greek Orthodoxy to acquire a governing authority in America, but it was a step forward. This early phase of Greek Orthodoxy in America contained the seeds that would enable it to grow into the most important Greek American institution. The Greek Orthodox Archdiocese derived legitimacy by evoking the life and value system of rural Greece that the immigrants had left behind. As was the case with other immigrant churches, the Greek church's functions as a mutual-aid community increased its appeal. And finally, the church and many of its priests displayed a keen sense of what was allowed and what was not allowed in the host society and began adapting Greek Orthodoxy to the American environment.

CHAPTER 2

Americanization and the Immigrant Church in the 1920s

The year 1922 was a turning point for the Greek world and the Greek Orthodox in America. When the Allies permitted the Greek army to occupy one of the ethnically Greek regions of the Ottoman Empire, it looked like the century-old quest for a Greece that would incorporate all the historically Greek lands in the Ottoman domains into its borders would be finally realized. Instead, defeat at the hands of the resurgent Turkish nationalists brought everything to a dramatic end; Greece abandoned its claims and had to receive over a million destitute refugees, the victims of ethnic cleansing that was part of the transformation of the Ottoman Empire into the new Turkish Republic. Meanwhile, in the United States, Congress drastically restricted immigration from southeastern Europe, including Greece, a move that was followed by an increase of the pressures on the foreign-born to assimilate and "Americanize." All this changed the way the Greeks saw their presence in the United States. Return to a Greece that was dealing with the refugee influx became much less attractive. The prospect of a long-term presence in the United States became a reality and raised the question of how best to become part of American society, as well as maintain ties with the homeland and preserve Greek ethnic and religious identity. Several strategies evolved within the community, ranging from the advocacy of so-called 100 percent Americanism to a more cautious stance that acknowledged the need for the Greeks to demonstrate loyalty to the country they had settled in, and even acquire US citizenship, but to also work toward preserving Greek identity.

Before it could even begin to confront the challenges posed by the post-1922 era, the church had to get used to existing under a new jurisdiction, because the Ecumenical Patriarchate reclaimed the authority over Greek Orthodoxy in America that it had passed on to the Church of Greece in 1908. This happened thanks to Meletios, whom the synod in Constantinople chose as the new ecumenical patriarch, even though he was in some sort of official limbo, having been dismissed as the head of the Greek church. Meletios had left Greece and continued his work as a kind of archbishop in exile. On the eve of 1922, the Ecumenical Patriarchate's synod, concerned about the escalating Greek-Turkish conflict, decided that Meletios was the dynamic leader it needed at a time of crisis and chose him as patriarch, ignoring the protests emanating from Athens.[1] One of the first things Meletios did after he was installed as ecumenical patriarch was to assume jurisdiction over the Greek Orthodox Archdiocese in America. And in May 1922, the patriarchate officially and canonically ratified the establishment of the archdiocese and appointed Alexandros as the first archbishop. Although this was a deliberate move to cut off the Church of Greece from Orthodoxy in America, Meletios was well within his rights, because of the patriarchate's long-established jurisdiction over Orthodox Churches in the diaspora. Fortunately, the leadership of the Church of Greece changed at the time, and there were no objections from Athens. Soon after Greece's defeat in 1922, the pro-monarchist government in Athens fell, and its successors dismissed Theokletos and installed a moderate, Chrysostomos, as head of the Church of Greece. Chrysostomos recognized the patriarchate's authority over the archdiocese in America, although that would not prevent pro-monarchist clerics in Greece and the United States from rejecting the new status quo.

With Greek political divisions and passions casting a heavy shadow over its early years, the church set out to coordinate and organize Greek Orthodox life in America and to develop strategies designed to help the Greeks maintain their faith, their language, and their culture. The agenda of one of the meetings held by the church's New York district in 1924 underscores the intention of establishing a wide range of activities. Items included the establishment of Greek-language schools, Sunday schools, missionary activity, the St. Athanasios Seminary, and the production of a periodical.[2] The issue of education would quickly spawn a vigorous debate as to whether Orthodoxy should focus on the religious education of the children of the immigrants or offer a broader program of Greek language education. Significantly, because Greek schools were parish based, educational policies were left to the church, even by other ethnic associations that devoted great energies to preserving Greek culture and mitigating the effects of the climate of Americanization.

The Archdiocese and Americanization in the 1920s

The early 1920s brought a renewed wave of anti-immigrant measures designed to force southeastern European immigrants to embrace Americanization and assimilation and adopt US citizenship, and for good measure the government put a virtual end to immigration from that part of the world. The pressures to conform to the ways of the American majority were present everywhere, including the media and the schools and through a reiteration of the racially based theories that had appeared earlier. In one of those works, the author wrote that a continuing deluge of Alpine, Mediterranean, and Semitic immigrants would create "a hybrid race of peoples worthless and futile as the good-for-nothing mongrels of Central America and Southern Europe."[3] This type of thinking animated the drastic restrictions on immigration Congress imposed in the early 1920s. As John Higham put it, "Since the brunt of the restrictionist attack was aimed more than ever at the racial qualities of the new immigration it stung the Jews, the Italians, the Slavs and the Greeks deeply."[4] When Congress completed its imposition of quotas, immigration from Greece was reduced to a trickle.

The anti-immigrant nativism of the 1920s was primarily racist, but its rhetoric and practice also turned against members of non-Protestant religions, especially Catholicism and Judaism. In several instances the Ku Klux Klan's proclamations included the Greeks as targets, but while they were victimized as being not quite "white" enough, Greeks were spared explicit attacks on their religion. The Catholics and the Jews presented such an overwhelmingly big target that the Protestant-inspired nativists did not waste too much time focusing on the Eastern Orthodox. The same was true of moderately minded thinkers who accepted the premises of racial difference but thought that immigrants could be Americanized. For example, John Rogers Commons wrote there was a line running from northeast to southwest Europe that separated races and civilizations, popular government and absolute monarchies, lands where education was universal and lands where illiteracy predominated, and it also separated Protestant Europe from Catholic Europe.[5] With that dividing line assumed, there was no need to think about religions that existed farther away, and thus Eastern Orthodoxy was spared an explicit denigration.

The Episcopal Church, among all those who opposed nativism and xenophobia, was the most outspoken supporter of the Greek Orthodox Church.

In its intervention in the immigration debates of the 1920s through its "studies of immigration," it pointed out the big differences between Catholicism and Eastern Orthodoxy and Orthodoxy's similarities with its own creed: "Our own Communion has much in common with the Greek church. The three-fold ministry, Jesus as teacher, preacher, healer as well as the independence of national churches are cherished alike by Anglican and Eastern Churchmen. The liturgies are similar. Our great Easter hymns, 'The Day of Resurrection' and 'Come, ye faithful, raise the strain' and many others, have come to us from Greek sources." And the passage continued, stressing the comparability of the two churches: "The Anglican and Greek Churches represent a common life, a common spirit, a common fidelity to the historic Creeds, and the common possession of an Apostolic Ministry."[6] The study went on to suggest that the Episcopal Church could help the Greek Orthodox Church in America in many ways. The most practical was to offer its church buildings to the Greeks; and where there was no Greek priest, Episcopal clergy ministered to the Greek immigrant needs. The assistance was also designed to assuage the nativist suspicions of the Greeks: "In a spirit of mutual confidence and brotherly approach, we can do much to strengthen the Greek Church, laboring, as it does, under the limitations in our land. The Greeks have come to stay. One-fifth are already naturalized citizens. They enter heartily into American life. By tradition and temper they are predisposed towards the best ideals of this country, and their ancient Church is destined to become a potent factor in American ecclesiastical life," noted the Episcopal study.[7] The Greek Orthodox Church had acquired an important ally in its struggle to become accepted and rooted in American society. And the relationship between the two churches would grow over the next decades.

With only a few allies and the tide turning against the immigrants, the Greek Americans urgently searched for the right type of response. Their professions of loyalty to America during the Great War and the appeals from community leaders to adapt to the American environment were not enough. Change was not easy, because "inherited traditions and customs did not simply fall away like an old skin," and the challenges the Greeks faced were considerable.[8] Ultimately, as was the case with all groups under attack, Greek Americans produced their own "assimilationists" and "traditionalists." As a leading example, eight pro-assimilationist Greek Americans, all residents of Atlanta, met at that city's Greek Orthodox Church in 1922 and created an association designed to promote the Americanization of Greek immigrants. The idea was that the quicker the Greeks embraced assimilation and were seen to be embracing American values and demonstrating their loyalty to the government, the less likely they were to be singled out as individuals or as foreigners by the nativists. The driving force behind the push to Americanize the Greek immigrants was the American Hellenic Progressive Association (AHEPA), which was founded in Atlanta in 1922. The organization quickly grew in the South, where the threat of the Ku Klux Klan was felt the most, although it also spread throughout the rest of the United States quite rapidly. The founders of AHEPA were openly Christian, but for the first few years they downplayed the Greek Orthodox faith and declared themselves nonsectarian in matters of religion. The group modeled itself on Masonic organizational forms. Throughout the 1920s AHEPA consistently repudiated accusations leveled by suspicious Greek Americans that it was anti-Orthodox.[9] Its traditionalist counterpart was the Greek American Progressive Association (GAPA), formed in Pittsburgh in 1923; it called openly for the safeguarding of Greek identity and the conservation of Greek heritage, especially language and religion. GAPA, which had a smaller membership than AHEPA, accepted only professed Greek Orthodox as its members.[10] GAPA cooperated with the church and did not put forward its own educational plan, allowing the church to remain in control of the schools.

The Greek Orthodox Church, along with the other immigrant churches, had demonstrated its loyalty to America during the Great War. Those years had offered an opportunity to all the southeastern Europeans to deflect nativist sentiment by declaring themselves on the side of America in the worldwide conflict. When Meletios arrived in the United States 1918, he joined the chorus of Greek American public statements of loyalty and urged Greek Americans to buy US war bonds in the campaign for the fourth "Liberty Loan" that began in September 1918. In October, Meletios participated along with Greek ambassador George Roussos in the events of "Greek Day" at the "Altar of Liberty," an open-air structure in New York's Madison Square, which was the focal point of the campaign to encourage immigrants to rally to America's war effort. Later on that month the archbishop made a speech at a dinner at the Waldorf Astoria hotel in which he discussed Greece's territorial claims. He included a reference to how impressed he was by how the American people had embraced the ideals of democracy developed by the ancient Greeks, an indirect way of suggesting that Greeks and Americans shared common intellectual origins.[11]

Faced with nativism of the 1920s, the Greek Orthodox Church began urging the faithful to adapt to their American environment and reap the advantages it offered them, but not to abandon their faith. In 1922 the archbishop noted that "ecclesiastical affairs here are not developing in a satisfactory manner, the Greeks are not showing the interest they should." The typical Greek immigrant "had not begun to think of himself as a permanent resident of this country. Their interest is elsewhere, on making some money and leaving. Therefore ecclesiastical and educational matters related to their presence here do not concern Christians. . . . We believe that when Greeks begin to think of themselves as a permanent and committed residents of our adopted country, then their interest in our religious, educational and national life will be greater as [will] our chances for a fuller ecclesiastical development."[12] By 1924, with nativism unrelenting and the doors closed to immigrants, the archdiocese's synod was advising its members to accommodate themselves to American life. It declared it would assist them to "receive from American life" the methodical practices, the organization, the discipline, the order, and charitableness, and everything else worth imitating that existed "in this admirable and great democracy" in which they all now lived.[13]

The Church and Education

The church responded to the assimilationist pressures of the 1920s by exploring the best ways to preserve Greekness through promoting religious and Greek language instruction, and in doing so it emerged as the main ethnic institution responsible for education. Internally, there was a debate among the leaders as to whether the church should emphasize religious education or divide its resources between religious and language education. Underlying those two perspectives were two different views of the future of the Greeks in the United States. Those who favored religious education, which could take place in English as well as in Greek, shared the view that assimilation was inevitable. In contrast, those who believed the Greeks could resist assimilation supported the view that the church should do all it could to help promote Greek language education. The diplomatic representatives of Greece in the United States naturally favored any measure that would preserve Greek identity and also believed that of all existing ethnic institutions, the church was the best equipped to promote Greek language instruction. Michael Tsamados, the Greek ambassador in Washington, who was embarking on a distinguished career that would culminate in a seat on the Supreme Court of Greece, was one of the first to suggest that the Greek Orthodox Church bear the main responsibility for the education of Greek American children. Writing in 1920, Tsamados told the Greek Ministry for Foreign Affairs that the church was the best hope for the preservation of Greek identity. He mentioned regulations introduced during the Great War to the effect that instruction at schools had to be in English and that there was a set of new requirements "foreign" schools had to satisfy. All this meant that Greek schools—which existed only in large urban centers—were severely limited in the ways they could attract the children of Greek immigrants, let alone teach them effectively. The church had to step in and take the initiative in promoting Greek culture and education, according to the ambassador.

The climate of the 1920s prompted the church to say and do something about education. With the archbishop focused primarily on bolstering the archdiocese's authority and parrying political challenges to his leadership by pro-monarchist clerics, it was left to Bishop Joachim of Boston to take the lead and address the problem of how to navigate between Americanization and preserving Greekness. The *Ethnikos Kyrix* newspaper began surveying prominent Greek Americans about their views on the future of the Greeks in the United States in light of the pressures for assimilation, and Joachim took the responsibility to present the church's views in terms of the curricular content of education. The archdiocese was already committed to promoting the Greek language by the establishment of Sunday schools "through which the beliefs of Greek children will be strengthened and in which reading the Bible in its original language would maintain the ancestral values in a healthy state."[14] And the archdiocese spoke at every opportunity about the significance of standing by the beleaguered Patriarchate of Constantinople. But the value of Joachim's intervention went to the core of preserving Greekness by discussing the content of education.

Joachim was emphatic in his belief that Orthodoxy was at the core of Greek identity, and he was committed to publicizing his views widely. He had already sent a memorandum to the Greek government on the issue of education, and in 1926 he wrote a series of newspaper articles on the subject, which he subsequently produced in a book, along with his rebuttals of his critics. The book, which was in Greek, was titled *The Dangers for Hellenism in America and the Means for Its Salvation*.[15] Joachim envisioned a two-pronged plan, with the church playing the main role in keeping alive the Greek identity and doing so by focusing more on religious rather than language-based education and developing catechetical (Sunday) schools rather than Greek language afternoon schools. He believed that in the long run, what would be preserved was a religiously defined Greek identity. It was a bold vision that proved to be well ahead of its time. Secular commentators within the community criticized it openly; the reaction from within the church was to include his recommendations in a report the archdiocese sent to the Greek government two years later, in 1928. Joachim began by lamenting the assimilation of the Greek immigrants and their loss of their language, traditions, and religion, "especially their national traditions and religion, the principal pillars of their racial existence." The bishop divided the four hundred thousand or so Greek immigrants into two groups: 40 percent of the total he described as on their way to being assimilated; for the remaining 60 percent he listed a series of prescriptions designed to enable them to retain their Greek identity. The reasons adult Greeks were losing their identity, according to Joachim, were the limits on immigration from Greece, the strength of the American environment, and the mind-set of those he considered cosmopolitans, students, and communists. A large number, including the younger generation, would experience that loss of identity, he believed, because of mixed marriages, specifically marriages of Greek males to foreign women. He believed that even if their children were baptized Greek Orthodox, the mother's influence would prevail and be reinforced by American schools.

Another important reason why the Greeks were being assimilated, Joachim went on to argue, was the lack of Greek Sunday schools. These he saw as the antidote to the inability of the Greek-language schools, which were run by communities and their local churches, to fulfill their goals. The establishment of competing churches by rival local factions wasted and drained community resources. Community organizations, moreover, were malfunctioning because of a catalog of problems: a misguided sense that everyone would be going back to the homeland very soon; the lack of clerical leadership figures to guide the administration of churches; the "extreme freedom" that existed in the United States, allowing anyone to have an opinion about the way the church should be run; a lack of respect toward church authorities; the age-old curse of the Greek race, namely of everyone wanting to be in charge; and finally a whole set of flaws with the running of each church, ranging from the liturgy to the interior decoration. Given that situation, the Greek church had to turn to its own resources and bolster the Sunday schools.[16]

Joachim evidently possessed a broader vision, which many believed Archbishop Alexandros lacked. Though Joachim was practical and sought to come up with solutions, the underlying principle of his intervention was that the church was the best guarantor of preserving national identity in America. And in order to make his view more persuasive he claimed that the same applied in the cases of Catholicism and the Irish, Episcopalism and the English, Judaism and the Jews, Lutheranism and the Germans, and Presbyterianism and the Scots. And, of course, he also mentioned that the church had preserved the identity of the Greeks during the four centuries they had been under Ottoman rule. Therefore, he concluded, "Our Orthodox Church in America, even though it started off without a head, uncontrolled and without any system[,] emerged as the only force that guided the immigrant in a national and Christian manner. . . . [The church] took the lead in all our national issues. . . . Are not the Greek schools sustained through the Church?"[17]

Religious versus Secular Education

The 1920s witnessed debates over the effectiveness of church-run or parochial schools. Especially in the case of Eastern or Southern European immigrants, this was a formative period for those schools, and the views expressed were strong and urgent. Middle-class lay leaders in the Polish American community expressed considerable misgivings over whether Polish priests and nuns had the necessary skills and commitment to preserve Polish identity. They feared that at most they would instill Catholic identity but not much of the Polish language or history in their students.[18] In the case of the Greek Americans, the close identification of Greekness with Greek Orthodoxy meant that such concerns were much more limited. The publication of Joachim's plan brought a rebuttal by a young Greek lawyer, Stephen P. Ladas, who had arrived two years earlier in the United States and would go on to enjoy a brilliant career built on his pioneering work on intellectual property law. Joachim responded in what became an important exchange in the ongoing public debates in the Greek American community over its future in America.

In responding to Joachim's series of articles, Ladas wrote that it represented a "theocratic" view of the ways Greek identity could be preserved in the United States and offered a secular-based alternative vision. The young lawyer was suggesting the type of communal organization the earlier diaspora communities had employed, in which there was a separation between secular community and the church, and a secular as well as religiously based pursuit of the preservation of Greek identity. His view was that the Greeks needed better secular, and not religiously inflected, coordination and organization. As he had the opportunity to explain in a letter he sent to the Ecumenical Patriarchate (which had inquired about his views with some concern), Ladas believed in a dual form of organization: a strong autonomous community and a strong church that would be separate from the community. These two institutions would each promote the love of Greek cultural traditions and Greek Orthodox religion respectively. Ladas's vision of a dual secular and religious constellation of organizations was a minority view, albeit one held by prominent Greek American academics, such as Raphael Demos, a Greek from Smyrna who taught philosophy at Harvard University, and Nicholas Kaltchas, who taught history at the University of Michigan. The bishop's response to Ladas was a reaffirmation of the rights of the church and an argument for parity between laypersons and clerics in each community organization board but with the church in a dominant role.[19]

The debate got the full attention of Archbishop Alexandros, and the archdiocese adopted Joachim's vision in an official statement on education and language. What prompted the archbishop to act and endorse the core of Joachim's proposals was the rising concern over the impact of Americanization pressures by the late 1920s. Initially, the Greeks had not rushed to acquire US citizenship, but by the mid-1920s this changed dramatically. In 1927, the numbers of Greeks admitted to US citizenship annually peaked at 9,518. Over 35,000 Greeks had acquired citizenship since 1923. But by the same token, the prospect of the American-born retaining their Greek identity suddenly looked threatened. The embattled Archbishop Alexandros found time to make an urgent appeal to the Greek government, which he regarded as the only potential source in helping stem the tide of assimilation. In a detailed account of the situation sent in March 1928, the archdiocese's synod explained that "the younger generation, lacking a suitable church and school[,] faced the very serious danger of being assimilated" because the Greek-born immigrants were settling permanently in the United States and were using the "local language" and adopting the customs and civilization of that country. Their children were attending public schools and then going to Greek language classes in the church schools between 4 and 6 p.m., "because the laws and the spirit of the country did not favor the existence of regular educational institutions designed to prevent assimilation." But the afternoon school system was not working well, the report continued to say; it did not attract all Greek children, nor did it fulfill its purpose, because of the unsuitability of the teaching staff. After the restrictions on immigration from Greece, the smaller communities had reverted to the practice of the turn of the century, hiring the local priest as teacher without caring whether he was qualified to teach. The situation, the report concluded darkly, could lead to the "loss" of Hellenism in America as soon as the Greek-born generation passed on.[20]

Eventually, the archdiocese came up with a plan that did not fully endorse Joachim's preference for privileging Sunday school education over the regular schools, but it envisioned the church taking over an educational curriculum in which Greek language and religious instruction cohabitated. The plan proposed that the Greek government establish a school for missionaries that would train newly ordained priests in Greece with a view to assigning them to parishes in the United States. The school would be based in Greece, but it was necessary, the report added, for it to provide for the learning of English, because in many Greek immigrant communities English was becoming the dominant means of communication. The report even cited instances in which Greek immigrants could not make themselves understood to their local parish priest because their Greek was too poor, and his English too inadequate, for them to communicate.

By the 1920s, the church was scrambling to address the reality that thousands of Greeks had abandoned the idea that they would stay in the United States for a short while and instead were prepared for a much longer, if not permanent, stay. Many Greek immigrants now had children who were born in the United States. The church estimated that 25 percent of churchgoers were English speaking. Soon, there were demands that the church water down some of its Old World practices and make allowances that seemed appropriate in the New World. One such time-honored practice was the custom of standing in Orthodox churches; indeed, many of the early Orthodox churches in America did not have seats or pews.[21] In response to many inquiries, the archdiocese issued an encyclical explaining that the use of seating (pews) was not prohibited, and seats had been in use in Orthodox churches for many centuries. Seating had to be adapted to the requirements of Orthodox worship, and priests had to teach the congregation when to sit and when to stand during the service. For reasons that are unclear, the issue resurfaced in 1927, and the synod affirmed that seating was allowed and issued an encyclical repeating its request that priests instruct their congregants about when they should stand during the service. At the same meeting, the synod considered the use of an organ during services in response to a request sent by a Greek American group in St. Louis. The archbishop was sympathetic to the request, especially because he saw the use of an organ as a means to retain the interest of the younger generation. Fearing that traditionalists might try to exploit the issue, however, he recommended that the archdiocese seek the approval of the patriarchate.[22] The synod reaffirmed its belief that the issue of music had to be taken seriously, "because without doubt without either Byzantine or European music executed well our churches in America would find it impossible to attract the younger generation."[23]

The Civil War in the Church

The installation of a new head of the Church of Greece looked as if it would restore calm to Greek Orthodoxy in America. Indeed, Archbishop Chrysostomos recalled the pro-monarchist Bishop Germanos to Greece in 1924. At a farewell service at the Holy Trinity Church in Lowell, Massachusetts, parishioners declared they would form a separate church, but Germanos did not publicly condone their gesture and adopted the same attitude to calls for an autonomous church made by several parishes, including the Holy Trinity Church in Chicago and churches in Detroit, in Manchester, New Hampshire, and in Passaic, New Jersey. According to Germanos, there were thirty-six parishes in total that wanted him to lead an independent Greek Orthodox

Church, but he declined the dubious mantle. Plagued by bad eyesight and other health problems, Germanos may have also simply not had the stomach to spearhead a breakaway ecclesiastical movement. In a generous gesture, the Church of Greece permitted him on his return to resume his position as metropolitan of Monemvasia and Sparta, which he held until his death in 1935. Bishop Germanos's departure did not mean that trouble emanating from Greece was over, because the divisions between the pro-republican supporters of Venizelos and the supporters of the king who had been forced into exile continued. The ongoing conflict divided the Orthodox in America and prevented the archdiocese from incorporating all the parishes. In 1923, the Greek ambassador in Washington, Michael Tsamados, reported to Athens that "passions among the Greeks here are great, maybe greater than those in Greece itself," and that the difficulties the church faced were due to a combination of Greek cultural traits and the liberties the Greeks enjoyed in the United States, where "the hereditary defects of our race have been amplified because of a faulty understanding of the idea of freedom." The ambassador noted there were many who were "taking advantage" of the freedom to establish independent churches and using the laws as a way to challenge the canonical practices of the Greek Orthodox Church. The implication was that such challenges would have had little success in Greece because of the church's privileged status in the eyes of the constitution and the laws of the land.[24] The two Greek language daily newspapers in New York—whose circulation relied of course on Greek-born immigrants—contributed mightily to perpetuating political and by extension ecclesiastical divisions. The *Atlantis* and the *Ethnikos Kyrix*, the ambassador reported, "never miss an opportunity to divide Hellenism beginning with local small community affairs and ending with the big national issues." He added that the *Ethnikos Kyrix* also contributed to the divisions by criticizing Bishop Alexandros because one of the newspaper's founders, Demetrios Callimachos, a parish priest in Brooklyn, felt slighted by the archbishop.[25]

The continuing political conflict within Greek Orthodoxy in America was fueled by the arrival of a very able prelate who was a committed promonarchist, Vasilios Komvopoulos. Bishop Vasilios made his own way to the United States in the manner of so many other clerics who had sought to find a place in Greek Orthodoxy in America, and he was armed with a pro-monarchist agenda. As archdeacon on Lesvos (Lesbos), Vasilios had witnessed the liberation of the island from the Ottomans and its subsequent incorporation into Greece in 1912. The church in Lesvos remained under the jurisdiction of the Ecumenical Patriarchate, but when the patriarch promoted Vasilios to bishop of that district in 1917, the Venizelist government blocked the move because Vasilios was an avowed monarchist. In 1922 he suffered a further indignity when Meletios, who was then still the ecumenical patriarch, kicked him upstairs by appointing him bishop of Chaldea, a nominal position because it was in the Black Sea (Pontus region) town of Trabzon (Trebizond), from where all the Greek Orthodox had been expelled in the early 1920s. Scorning that appointment, Vasilios made his way to the United States with an ax to grind and a captive audience, namely all those who were looking for a leader to replace Bishop Germanos.

Vasilios's arrival inevitably exacerbated the ongoing divisions. After receiving a warm welcome from pro-monarchists in New York City, Vasilios settled in Lowell, a city that historian Theodore Saloutos described as "the capital of Greek royalism in America."[26] From there Vasilios worked toward consolidating the bloc of pro-monarchist parishes, inevitably sowing dissent, first and foremost in Lowell, where he alienated the Venizelists. When the first Greek Orthodox Church, Holy Trinity, had opened its doors in that city in 1908, worshippers believed its grandeur was purposely designed to prevent divisions and the possibility of a group of parishioners leaving in order to form their own church. Yet only months after Vasilios's arrival, the Venizelists, who were already worshipping away from Holy Trinity because it had allied itself with Bishop Germanos, founded the Church of the Transfiguration of Our Savior (Metamorphosis tou Soteros). Elsewhere in the country, a small but not insignificant number of parishes, mainly in the northeastern United States, recognized Vasilios as their leader, and he announced his intention to form of a separate, autonomous Greek Orthodox Church. Vasilios did not balk when he was censured and recalled by the Ecumenical Patriarchate in February 1924, and he did not slow down even when the patriarchate defrocked him. He was aided by the pro-monarchists in the United States and their press, including the New York daily *Atlantis* and Chicago's *Hellenikos Astir*. Eventually he established the "Autocephalous Greek Church of the United States and Canada" at a conference held in Boston in November 1924. It is difficult to establish precisely how widespread was the support Vasilios received. According to an estimate made by the archdiocese, there were 148 canonical clerics (i.e., ordained by the archbishop) and 68 clerics who had been ordained by Vasilios.

The Archbishop versus the Ambassador

The arrival in Washington, DC, of Charalambos Simopoulos, the new Greek ambassador, in 1925 would shape the Greek Orthodox Church's affairs over the next few years. With the tacit support of the patriarchate and the Church of Greece, the Greek Ministry of Foreign Affairs would allow Simopoulos to do all he could to resolve the issues facing the archdiocese. The archdiocese's charter prevented the patriarchate from dislodging Alexandros, but it hoped that Simopoulos would persuade him to step down. It was always going to be a difficult task. The ambassador could not have been more different from the dour and uncharismatic archbishop. Fifty-one years old and already an experienced diplomat, Simopoulos was an outgoing cosmopolitan. He and his English wife had an active social life in Washington, where she was considered, according to the *Washington Post*, "one of the best dressed women in the diplomatic corps and the best bridge player."[27] The Simopouloses spent the summer in their "cottage" in Newport, Rhode Island. Prior to being posted to Washington, Simopoulos had served as Greek high commissioner in Constantinople in 1922 when Meletios had been elected patriarch, so he was already familiar with the intricacies of Greek Orthodoxy. He quickly decided that the situation the church faced was critical and that the Greek government should intervene. He sent three long messages to the Ministry of Foreign Affairs that outlined the situation bluntly and eloquently. The ambassador did not take sides; he was as disparaging of Archbishop Alexandros as he was of Bishop Vasilios and believed that the rift was beyond repair, that it would continue even if the monarchist-Venizelist division somehow disappeared. Moreover, he also thought that most of the Greek immigrants were uneducated and thus unable to solve the problem on their own. And freedom of religious practice in the United States, Simopoulos noted, echoing the comments of his predecessor, allowed anyone to do what he liked. But there was one important reason Athens should intervene, he decided: "The chauvinism of the Americans is intensifying day by day. The Greeks understand that in the interests of their jobs one needs American citizenship and after a few years all the Greeks will become U.S. citizens. . . . Only the Church will be able to help them retain their language and ethnicity, although its bonds with those born in the United States are not as strong."[28] The ambassador recommended that the government coordinate with the patriarchate in Constantinople and send a cleric of high enough standing to be able to calm the passions dividing the church in America.

Having to face such outside intervention by the combined forces of the Ecumenical Patriarchate, the Church of Greece, and the Greek government would prove too much for Archbishop Alexandros, who tried nonetheless to assert the autonomy of the Greek Orthodox Church in America. After his requests to the US immigration authorities and the Greek embassy in Washington to deport all those clerics whose actions were against "the nation and the Church" failed to bring results, Alexandros decided the church could not rely on support from American and Greek officialdom.[29] In March 1927 the archbishop told the synod that judging by Simopoulos's behavior, "not only is there no willingness to act against and relieve the Church of the defrocked [Bishop Vasilios] but in contrast there was observed an obvious sympathy towards him, expressed by the efforts of H.E. the Ambassador to persuade the canonical Church to reconcile itself with this ecclesiastical renegade."[30] Alexandros decided that the best way forward for the church was a drastic move: to reject all outside intervention. He told the Holy Synod in March 1927 that based on his nine years of experience in the United States, he felt the church could overcome its problems only if it rid itself of party politics, and all outside influence, either from Constantinople or from Athens. Naturally, he added, the archdiocese respected and honored its higher authority, the patriarchate and the Church of Greece, but it had to make them understand that "we thank them for their interest for which we are grateful but we ask we are left in peace so we can work undisturbed according the circumstances and interests of the Church in America."[31] Proof of the archdiocese's wish to defend itself from what it considered outside interference came in October 1928 when the Holy Synod discussed the patriarchate's suggested amendments to the new constitution that the archdiocese had adopted at its third general conference. The synod respectfully rejected the patriarchate's suggestions, reminding it that the church in America was governed according to the laws of an American corporation, and the laws prevented changes to its deliberations made from "outside." It acknowledged the patriarchate's right not to approve the changes the archdiocese introduced, but it could not directly make changes to the regulations, because that went against the US laws concerning religious institutions.

The archbishop was also rejecting the ambassador's suggestion that he, Alexandros, reconcile with his critics: the church emphasizes the principles of collectivity and community, but not at the expense of doing away with its hierarchical structures. Simopoulos, seeing that he was getting nowhere, sent an eleven-page report to Athens that described a complete standstill and a worsening situation. He had met with Bishop Vasilios and then communicated with Archbishop Alexandros, who was unwilling to discuss any accommodation and fell silent for twenty days without responding to the ambassador's missives. Simopoulos had tried to make Alexandros understand that the Greek government could not get the Church of Greece to recall Vasilios because he was within his rights to establish his own church in the United States. But the archbishop continued to insist that Athens should recall Vasilios, and did so in a way that made the ambassador believe this was no longer about politics but a clash of personalities that had created unbridgeable rifts.

"In most towns we have two churches and two communities, two schools," he reported to Athens, adding that "there are acrimonious court cases contested by each side that absorb huge funds and present a deplorable, impassioned spectacle in American courtrooms." And with evident frustration, the ambassador concluded by saying, "Nothing is holy or sacred for these bickering Greeks."[32]

With no prospect of reconciliation between the archbishop and Bishop Vasilios, Simopoulos proposed that the patriarchate and the Church of Greece should send a representative to the United States with a mandate to resolve the ongoing differences. He believed that Bishop Damaskinos of Corinth, who had visited the United States in a fund-raising mission in April 1928, would be an ideal emissary. Simopoulos had met with Damaskinos and was impressed by him, as had been all the Greek Americans who came into contact with him during his fund-raising tour.

When rumors of Damaskinos's impending visit reached the archdiocese, it issued vigorous protests to both the patriarchate and the Church of Greece, and at its March 1930 meeting the Holy Synod reaffirmed its rejection of outside involvement. Without citing actual figures, the archdiocese backed up its position by claiming that the number of "canonical" parishes was increasing year by year, while the number of those that recognized Bishop Vasilios was declining, and, it added, the quality of church life in the "canonical" parishes was steadily improving. Thus, the visit of an "exarch" would only serve to disrupt the parishes at a time when Vasilios's side was in disarray.[33] Initially designating a regional governor in the Byzantine Empire, the title of exarch had come to be used in the Eastern Orthodox Church for a bishop who was a deputy of a patriarch, with authority over other bishops.

The Exarch Arrives

Damaskinos arrived in New York in late May of 1930 as the Patriarchate of Constantinople's exarch, and he spent the next nine months in the United States dealing with the crisis faced by the Greek Orthodox Church in America. It was his second transatlantic trip in the space of just over two years. In 1928, following the devastating earthquake that destroyed the city of Corinth and surrounding villages, Damaskinos, who was metropolitan of Corinth, had traveled to the United States to solicit relief for the sixteen thousand people who had lost their homes. He made a good impression everywhere he went, and Henry Ford had even invited to him to the Ford car plant and made him a gift of an automobile. It is not surprising that Damaskinos's visit was a huge success. He was a dynamic, charismatic, and politically savvy leader. Indeed, Damaskinos would go on to become metropolitan of Athens and head of the Greek church. Upon his return to Greece after his relief mission in 1928 he had submitted a memorandum to the head of the Church in Greece describing the state of Orthodoxy in America. He was clearly the prelate most likely to resolve Orthodoxy's problems in America.

Prior to his departure for the United States, Damaskinos had submitted another memorandum to the Church of Greece with his analysis of the state of the archdiocese and the solutions he proposed, which were to position the church at the center of the effort to preserve Greekness. Damaskinos began by acknowledging the critical situation of the Greeks in America and that any continuation of the "anarchy" would threaten the Greek and Orthodox ecclesiastical conscience of the Greek-speaking faithful. Damaskinos then summarized the situation of the archdiocese as he knew it and made three major sets of recommendations. The first was the dismissal of both Archbishop Alexandros along with the bishops he appointed, and the forcible removal of Bishop Vasilios. He saw no viable future for the church in America if any of them remained in place. The second recommendation was for a radical amendment of the archdiocese's constitution in a way that would deprive the archbishop of his relative autonomy, which had permitted Alexandros to ignore the pressures for him to be more conciliatory toward the dissidents. The Ecumenical Patriarchate agreed with both those recommendations, rejecting only Damaskinos's third proposal, which was that the Patriarchate of Constantinople cede jurisdiction over the archdiocese to the Church of Greece, which Damaskinos—who belonged to the Church of Greece—thought was better placed to supervise Orthodox life in America.[34] With the exception of this last recommendation, his proposals became the agenda he was asked to pursue in the United States.

Upon his arrival, Damaskinos was met by the Greek diplomatic corps and representatives of the *Atlantis* and the *Ethnikos Kyrix*—both newspapers were pledging their support of his mission. Neither the *Atlantis* nor the *Ethnikos Kyrix* had supported Alexandros's appointment, and both had remained hostile to him throughout the 1920s. Adamantios Polyzoides, editor of the *Atlantis*, was a fanatical anti-Venizelist and considered Alexandros a Venizelist. This should have ensured the support of the *Ethnikos Kyrix* for Alexandros, but despite the liberal newspaper's admiration for Meletios Metaxakis, its editor Demetrios Callimachos never warmed to Alexandros. The reason was probably the one Alexandros suggested in a letter to the ecumenical patriarch, namely that Callimachos, trained as a theologian and an ordained priest, thought he knew best what were the interests of the church in America. In any case, both newspapers rallied in support of Damaskinos. The exarch had won a first, crucial battle.[35] The next day Damaskinos visited the White House to pay his respects to President Herbert Hoover. It was Simopoulos's suggestion and designed to confer legitimacy on Damaskinos's visit. After that, Damaskinos got to work. He began with an unproductive meeting with Archbishop Alexandros, but he continued meetings with all major figures in the ecclesiastical dispute until he was successful. In between his meetings with clerics he took time to receive the acclaim of ethnic associations such as AHEPA and also GAPA, whose convention he addressed. Ambassador Simopoulos was often at his side in important meetings. At public gatherings throughout the United States, Greek Americans expressed their support for Damaskinos. The Greek American media covered his travels and contacts closely, and very favorably. Alexandros, however, clung to the archdiocese's founding charter, which granted the archdiocese a degree of autonomy and granted the archbishop of North and South America tenure and immunity from dismissal. But when Damaskinos won over Joachim of Boston, it was the beginning of the end of the old order. The other bishop that Alexandros had appointed, Kallistos (Papageorgopoulos) of San Francisco, who had arrived in the United States back in 1907, had already demonstrated his willingness to go along with the planned transformation. Alexandros refused to voluntarily step down, only to have the patriarchate strip him of all authority and dismiss him. It then moved quickly to name his successor, Metropolitan Athenagoras (Sperou) of Corfu. Damaskinos left New York in February 1931, his mission accomplished; both Alexandros and Vasilios had already left for Greece.[36] Kallistos was the only one of the four church leaders who survived the changes Damaskinos brought, and remained in his position until his death in 1940 in Chicago, where he moved his office because of the effects of the Depression on his church in San Francisco.[37]

For Greek Orthodoxy in America in the 1920s, salvation came from outside, or rather from its strong links to the Old World, in the form of the authority of the Ecumenical Patriarchate and the weight of tradition that legitimized the intervention of an exarch. Thus, Damaskinos's mission brought an end to a troubled period in the archdiocese's history. The arrangements that his actions produced would define the archdiocese's relationship with Constantinople for the rest of the twentieth century, giving the "mother church" considerable powers over Greek Orthodox life in the Americas. From a narrow perspective of ecclesiastical history, it could be argued whether this transformation conformed to the canons of the church. But if we consider the church as an integral part of the Greek presence in America, it was clear that Greek Orthodoxy ran the danger of becoming fragmented or even marginalized. No doubt it would have survived, but the changes implemented at the end of the 1920s produced a stronger church that was ready to assume a central role in the life of Greek America.

CHAPTER 3

Greek Orthodoxy versus Protestant Congregationalism

The arrival of Archbishop Athenagoras in the United States was the first step in the implementation of the patriarchate's vision for the restructuring the Greek Orthodox Church in America, and it represents a huge turning point in the history of Greek Orthodoxy in the United States. Athenagoras looms large in the archdiocese's history in the 1930s and the 1940s, both literally and metaphorically. His imposing appearance, his dynamism and charisma, as well as his unfailing political instincts have all been credited as contributing to his many achievements. The new archbishop needed all his skills and personal charms if he was going to successfully implement the plan Damaskinos had formulated with Constantinople's approval. After so many years of turbulence, the Greek Orthodox in America welcomed Athenagoras and made his task easier. But it was his personality and the forcefulness and skill with which the new archbishop drew a line between the need for the church to adapt to its American environment and the danger of succumbing to Protestant influences that would make the early part of his tenure successful. And Athenagoras's navigation through the hazards of Americanization could stand as an example of how churches representing small Christian denominations can become rooted and thrive in America.

The New Archbishop

When Byzantium fell to the conquering Ottomans in the fifteenth century, the patriarch of Constantinople was granted religious and civil powers, which made him a spokesman for the Orthodox subjects of the Ottoman Empire. The term that was applied to this type of leader was "ethnarch"— literally a leader of an *ethnos*, the Greek word for nation. Athenagoras may not have been explicitly received as such, but implicitly most of the Greek Orthodox community in America hoped he would fill such a role. He certainly looked and acted like a leader. Athenagoras appears in photographs and the early film clips of the history of Greek America in the 1930s tall and broad-shouldered, towering over everyone surrounding him, his headwear giving him even extra height, his gray flowing beard standing out against his black garb. Visually he presented a dramatic figure that inspired awe and respect. His imposing and confident manner and oratorical skills confirmed first impressions. Spyros Skouras, a first-generation immigrant who became president of Twentieth Century Fox in 1942, someone who knew a "personality" when he saw one, was unrestrained in his memoirs: "Immediately, I became greatly affected by Athenagoras' magnetic personality and manner. He was always dynamic and had a contagious effect on me. He always made me feel I was in the presence of an important and significant personality. He mesmerized me with his views and manner of expression. His kind face, wise sayings, his stature—he was very tall, amazingly handsome with his black beard—played a great part. . . . He was very wise and very practical."[1] According to church historian Demetrios Constantelos, the handsome appearance and Olympian personality of Athenagoras magnetized the people. The chances of the new vision being implemented successfully may have been uncertain in 1931, given the radical nature of the plan, but the obvious leadership abilities of the new archbishop inspired optimism.

Athenagoras was less interested in abstract theological arguments than in the practical art of church governance. He was a protégé of Meletios, who had taught him the ins and outs of church and secular politics, a pedigree that no doubt was critical to his selection as archbishop of North and South America. Born Aristocles Sperou in 1886 in the village of Vasiliko in Epirus, he attended the Ecumenical Patriarchate of Constantinople's theological school at Halki and then became a monk, changing his name to Athenagoras after an early Christian thinker who lived in Athens in the first century. Meletios appointed Athenagoras archdeacon of the Metropolis of Athens in 1916 at a politically charged moment in Greece in which the supporters of Venizelos were replacing clergy identified with the king. Yet when the pro-monarchists ousted the Venizelists in the general election of 1920, Athenagoras retained his position, even though Meletios himself was ousted. Those experiences in the centralized world of ecclesiastical affairs in Greece, along with an understanding of the political intricacies of church and state in Greece, would help Athenagoras meet the challenges he would encounter in America. And the respect both political sides in Greece accorded him was unusual. In 1922, Athenagoras was appointed metropolitan of Corfu, an island that was less politically polarized than other parts of the country in the 1920s, which permitted him to consolidate his position as a nonpartisan prelate. It was from there that he traveled to America.

Athenagoras quickly capitalized on the respectful and enthusiastic welcome he received at his enthronement as archbishop, at the Church of St. Eleftherios in New York on February 26, 1931 (the Greek Orthodox cathedral was undergoing refurbishment because of a fire) and also at a special service to commemorate Greek independence, held at the Episcopal Cathedral of St. John the Divine. That special service, sponsored by both the *Atlantis* and the *Ethnikos Kyrix*, featured thirty Greek American organizations marching to the cathedral with their banners. Athenagoras knew that the support of New York Greeks was not enough, and he soon embarked on a tour that took him to wherever there were significant Greek American communities. He traveled not only to Boston and Chicago but also to towns where there were smaller Greek communities—about fifty municipalities in total. A report Athenagoras sent to the patriarchate on his travels provides an insight into his sense of the state of Orthodoxy in America. He was dismayed by the church's meager resources he found everywhere, including in Boston and Chicago, which had relatively large numbers of parishioners, but was heartened by what he described as the existence of a strong Orthodox faith among the Greek immigrants. Athenagoras was concerned about the overall quality of the priests he encountered, but he noted that a number of them were making the best of the few resources they had available. He suggested that the future of Orthodoxy in America depended on replacing the inadequate clerics with able and qualified ones sent from Greece. Athenagoras met with several bishops of the Episcopal Church, who spoke sympathetically of the Greek Orthodox, and they suggested that because of the Americanization of the Greeks, the Greek church should offer services in English. The archbishop's reaction was not dismissive, but he stressed the need to preserve Greek. "Here is the largest problem for us, the preservation of the mother tongue, the language of the Bible and the

Holy Liturgy." The efforts of the communities in terms of schooling were inadequate, he added, and the only solution was the reorganization of the church so it could confront the problem.[2] There was no doubt in Athenagoras's mind that the Greeks in America were part of a larger Greek and Greek Orthodox entity and that it was the church's responsibility to help them preserve their Greekness. But he was also quickly becoming aware of the significance of the American environment with which Greek Orthodoxy had to contend.

As he proceeded along this path, he would pick up unexpected allies. In August 1931 he was a guest at AHEPA's ninth convention, held in San Francisco. The organization had grown exponentially during its first decade and boasted over 220 chapters across the United States. Throughout the 1920s, AHEPA had steered clear of the affairs of the Greek Orthodox archdiocese and its political divisions, limiting affirmation of its Greekness primarily to association with classical Greece and its legacy. Evidently, Athenagoras represented a new and more reliable face of Greek Orthodoxy in America, and his presence at AHEPA's convention in San Francisco symbolized a new, public acceptance of Greek Orthodoxy by the most pro-assimilationist Greek American organization.

Changing to Adapt to America

The Athenagoras-led transformation began formally with a general assembly, the fourth in the church's history. It met in November 1931 at the Evanghelismos Church in Manhattan. The list of official guests confirmed the significance of the occasion: it included the ambassador of Greece, the Greek general consul in New York, representatives of all the major Greek American organizations, and the Greek American press. Those assembled witnessed a speech that was an elegant and emphatic statement, and one that would set the church on a course of change. The archbishop paid tribute to the earlier generation of Greek American immigrants, recalling their struggles, and praised the role of the clergy and of the Greek American newspapers, which Athenagoras generously described as a great teacher that offered invaluable help to the archdiocese. He concluded the introductory part of his speech with mentions of Ecumenical Patriarch Photios, the prime minister and the Greek government (without uttering Venizelos's name), and Damaskinos, all of whom, he said, had worked toward resolving the ecclesiastic question of America. Then he moved on to outline the proposed changes: the abolition of the archdiocese's autonomy from the Patriarchate of Constantinople; the strengthening of the archbishop's powers over the bishops' synod in America; and a plan designed to make the parishes dominant over the local community organizations.[3]

All three major changes, Athenagoras argued, were designed with the purpose of better adapting Greek Orthodoxy to the American reality. This was the object even in establishing closer ties to the Patriarchate of Constantinople. He told the assembly that when Meletios had established the archdiocese as an autonomous church a decade earlier, many experts on church history and canonical right had raised their concerns and suggested instead that a church established so far away should maintain its administrative and spiritual ties with the patriarchate and become independent only when it gained experience and after it resolved the issue of its relations with the other Orthodox Churches in America—the Russian, the Serbian, the Syriac. With their respective relations unresolved, Athenagoras said, any dispute might be settled on the basis of seniority, something that would put Greek Orthodoxy, a relative latecomer to America, at a disadvantage. Instead, with the new arrangement, Athenagoras argued, the Greek Orthodox Archdiocese in America enjoyed a guaranteed status, thanks to the respect accorded to the Ecumenical Patriarchate. And this position would allow the archdiocese to play the principal role in the future unification of all Eastern Orthodox Churches in North America.[4] Similarly, the particular conditions in America, Athenagoras suggested, justified strengthening the archbishop's powers over the bishops, even though that arrangement courted controversy because it flew in the face of "conciliarity," a long-standing Orthodox tradition and practice in which the assembly of bishops, not a single leader, had ultimate authority over church affairs. The only authority over the synod, according to the church, is Jesus Christ—a principle, again, observed in long-standing Orthodox practice. From an ecclesiological point of view it could be debated whether the Orthodox Church's principle of conciliarity represented a systemic characteristic of the church, something inherent to the content of its nature, or something that had emerged out of necessity.[5] And the enhanced powers of the archbishop made Athenagoras susceptible to accusations that he was acting "uncanonically" (going against the church's own rules.)[6] But it was a pragmatic move for a church riven by internal conflicts, and it had the additional virtue of creating a leadership figure within the community, one that no other ethnic association, even AHEPA or GAPA, could rival (both had presidents who served for relatively short terms).

Both of those first two proposed changes could have been challenged, but there was simply too much goodwill toward Athenagoras, accompanied by a sense that the church needed to follow a different path. The invocation of the need to conform with the church's existence in America was surely a tactical move, but no less important as an indication of how the Athenagoras era would unfold. The implication was that being in America allowed the church to make exceptions to canonical practices. But with the third big change he would propose, Athenagoras drew the line between adaptation and co-optation.

Parish and Community versus Congregationalism

The third set of changes Athenagoras introduced affected the community at large because it involved overturning the balance between the local community organizations and their churches. Essentially what the archbishop prescribed was that local community organization executive committees voluntarily transform themselves into boards of trustees of the local parish and cede the leadership role to the parish priest. The priest, in turn, would be beholden to the archdiocese. The originally secular community organization that had established a church would now be co-opted by the church and the archdiocese. Henceforth, all members of the community, which was renamed from "Greek" or "Hellenic" community to "Greek Orthodox" community, had to be "active members" of the local church. The communities would now be responsible for paying dues to the archdiocese. These arrangements were included in the "special regulations," a detailed document that ran over one hundred printed pages and which accompanied the constitution. It outlined the responsibilities of the archdiocese, the archdiocese's central administrative offices, the parish churches, and the communities. This system was along the lines of the practice in Greece, where parishes answered to the regional bishop and the Church of Greece, with lay members playing a secondary role as parish board members.

Athenagoras affirmed the church's commitment to mixed clergy-laity governance but said that too much control exercised by many of the Greek community organizations was an unfortunate effect of Protestantism. He suggested that the crisis Greek Orthodoxy had faced in America was not because of the political divisions in the parishes but because "a spirit foreign to the traditions and practices of the Church and the Nation" had infiltrated Greek Orthodoxy, a spirit due to the influence "of the social environment and especially the Protestant Church." The drafting of many of the parish constitutions, he added, had taken place influenced by foreign churches and consequently did not adhere to the canons of the Orthodox Church and the collaboration of clergy and laity.[7] He then switched to expressing his admiration for the religious sentiments of the Greek immigrants, claiming the clergy was proud to be shepherding such a people as the Greeks who had achieved so much, thanks to their religion. He cited Homer and the apostle Paul's acknowledgment of the religious sentiments of the Greeks. The accusation of "Protestantism" the archbishop had made was a criticism of the "congegrational" practice of church governance in some Protestant traditions in which every local church congregation is self-governing.

Yet what Athenagoras chose not to mention was that from the late eighteenth century onward, in the Greek community organizations that diaspora merchants established in the Black Sea and Mediterranean seaports, the communities controlled the church. Whether or not it was because those merchants simply wished not to cede control to the local Greek Orthodox authorities and wanted to protect their funding of communal institutions, which included schools, philanthropic organizations, fraternal organizations, and even hospitals, the fact remained that the community leaders held sway over the administration of the churches, at least indirectly. Why the reversal envisioned by Athenagoras of this historical pattern could be possible in the United States was only partly due to the relative weakness of the Greek community organizations. In America, these organizations were typically made up of a few white-collar professionals and many small shopkeepers and small businessmen, along with employees and workers; they could only dream of the huge wealth wielded by the Greek import and export merchants who were part of the social elite in cities such as Alexandria, Marseilles, and Odessa. These merchants ran the community organizations and wielded the power to hire and fire priests at will, without any great objections from the local archbishop. It may be that the early Greek community organizations in America modeled themselves on those Old World institutions. Whether the Greeks were in fact influenced by that tradition or merely wanted independence or community control over their church is difficult to establish. It is doubtful the Greek immigrants had been Americanized enough, had been sufficiently exposed to American Protestant cultural and religious norms, to be eager to endorse them and apply them to their own church life. Yet many certainly wished for independence or self-governance and no doubt had noted Protestant church practices. And certainly the more educated and assimilated Greeks would have compared the practices of their church unfavorably to those of Protestant churches. In his history of the Greeks in the United States, Saloutos expressed certainty there was some American influence at work, writing that "unlike the Protestant churches in which the clergy withdrew from administrative functions and the Catholic churches in which the laymen withdrew, the Greek Orthodox Church employed the mixed system of cooperation between clergy and laymen," but adding, "In a democratic country such as the United States, and among such a highly individualistic people as the Greeks, the principle of lay representation had considerable appeal."[8]

Athenagoras claimed that excessive lay involvement had damaged the status of parish priests, and he sought to praise their contributions. Of course, whether it was a priest's own failings or the wish for power by lay members that had diminished the priest's standing varied from place to place; yet the archbishop was emphatic when he described the need for the parish priest to be invested with more authority and power. Of all the topics he raised in his speech, this was the one he spent the most time addressing. He broached the subject by offering a vigorous defense of the clergy and their efforts, stating that "the Greek priest is from the flesh and bones of the nation and deserves national gratitude for loyally performing his task despite the lack of material and educational resources and despite the humiliating accusations and slander about him being uneducated, untrained and incapable of performing his high duties." Athenagoras pressed his defense of the clergy, stressing that they had been marginalized, ignored, and denied public praise. Moreover, he continued, priests had been barred from exercising any administrative responsibility, "limiting him to performing liturgies and ceremonies and reducing him to cowardice and timidity." The archbishop made a brief qualification to his remarks by acknowledging some problems and saying he was not trying "to excuse the inexcusable," nor was he emphasizing the significance of the priests in a manner that would lead to a "clericocracy" in which the church would impose its will on the rest of the community.

Yet the obvious conclusion of Athenagoras's three-part reorganization of the church was that the archdiocese would become the primary force in the affairs of Greek Orthodoxy in America, and the point was driven home by Bishop Kallistos of San Francisco. Speaking right after Athenagoras, Kallistos described the archdiocese as the wellspring of all "religious, spiritual, educational, missionary, philanthropic and administrative initiatives, activities and life of the Orthodox Church in America." It is right, therefore, he added, that in the new constitution the archdiocese was regarded as "the guardian of the faith, the guarantor of discipline and order," and he went on to describe the institution as "the brain," adding, however, that the rest of the body of the church and the archdiocese inspired each other.[9] The primacy of the archdiocese in church affairs that Kallistos described referred not only to its top-down authority but also to all the nonreligious initiatives the parish would be undertaking now that it had replaced the community, especially running the schools and supervising philanthropic activities. For all these functions, the archdiocese established "national" supervisory bodies and committees: a mixed clergy-laity council that advised the archbishop; a committee that set out the church's policy on marriage and divorce; committees for the archdiocese's overall policies on issues of education, philanthropy, missionary work, and clerical tribunals; plus a periodical and the procedures of general assemblies. The archdiocese had hired a prominent Greek American lawyer, George J. Chryssikos, who had represented the Greek consulate in the past, to ensure that the extensive and detailed regulations governing those committees conformed with the "Religious Corporations Law of New York" while providing the archbishop with as much power as possible.[10] Athenagoras had described these numerous spheres of the archdiocese's activities as the "internal freedom" the institution gained in the new era, hoping it would offset objections to Constantinople's closer control and his own enhanced powers.

Opposition to the Reforms

The general assembly and at least part of the wider community apparently received the entire package of changes willingly but with an important exception: the section of the special regulations that addressed the functioning of individual parishes. The overall reception of the new constitution and the special regulations from the floor of the general assembly was positive. And the Greek American press was supportive. The *Atlantis* described Athenagoras's opening speech as a "rhetorical masterpiece," and the *Ethnikos Kyrix* applauded the archbishop's plans. Ambassador Simopoulos sent a glowing report to Athens, noting that the general assembly represented the first time clergy and laity joined together "in complete harmony and love to set the foundations of their house around which all the forces of Hellenism in America can rally." It was the first time, he repeated, he had seen the Greeks in America as united as they were during the assembly. And he concluded by noting, "One can happily recognize how valuable was the help of the Government in restoring ecclesiastical peace in America."[11] But Simopoulos was underestimating the significance of a long-drawn-out debate on the floor over the "regulations of holy churches and communities"—a revealing sequence of words that reflected the intention of making the parish the dominant part of the equation. It was a sign of the difficulties the archdiocese would have persuading the Greek community to accept the entire package of reforms. Objections were to be expected, because for the first time the church was claiming control of all local communal activities. There was in fact great dissent by many parish board committees over the proposed strengthening of the local powers of priests, as well as over the powers concentrated in the archbishop's hands. Critics described the new constitution as "monarchical" and Athenagoras as being a "dictator."

The critics of the plan to co-opt the local community organizations into a parish controlled by the archdiocese decided to make a stand at the next general assembly, held in Chicago at the end of October 1933. They challenged Athenagoras's right to chair the proceedings, insisting that their leader, Rev. Christophoros Kontogeorge, chair the assembly instead. Christophoros had served as the priest in the manufacturing city of Wheeling, West Virginia, whose St. John the Divine was the first Greek Orthodox church in the state, established in 1914. After just over two years in West Virginia, Christophoros had moved on to Lowell in 1928, and from then his stature had grown. In a repeat of the scenes that churches had witnessed at the height of the monarchist-Venizelist conflict, fights broke out on the floor of the assembly. Christophoros was physically ejected and beaten, and as a result he was hospitalized—and he promptly initiated court proceedings against Athenagoras. Freed of Christophoros's presence, the general assembly issued a sharply worded announcement that was translated into English (in which it referred to itself as a clergy-laity congress), condemning the actions of those around Christophoros and suggesting the archbishop "take the severest steps and apply the most austere Canons and Rules of the Greek Orthodox Church, and the Laws and regulations of the Archdiocese against these few independent and insubordinate clerics, who do not submit to the lawful Ecclesiastical Authority, establish unauthorized assemblies, and live a lewd and scandalous life." They were to be given three months to repent. The resolution's language and exaggerated accusations reflect the depth of feelings Christophoros generated, as well as fears that the climate of old divisions could reemerge.

Christophoros Kontogeorge had a relatively small following, which did not encompass all of archbishop's critics at the time, but he managed to remain a thorn in the side of the archdiocese—even though the Patriarchate of Constantinople had defrocked him. In 1934 he established an autonomous Greek Orthodox Church and was consecrated as its archbishop by two clerics who were not under the jurisdiction of Constantinople, Archbishop Beshara of the Syrian mission of the Russian Orthodox Church and Archbishop Theophan Noli of the Albanian Autocephalous Church. Christophoros, if anything, was tenacious and attracted loyal supporters, especially among traditionalists. He continued his legal battles against Athenagoras through the late 1940s, when compromise was reached; he died shortly afterward, in 1950.

Dissent with the new constitution went beyond the group around Christophoros and was a source of growing concern for the church. Ultimately Athenagoras, in consultation with the Ecumenical Patriarchate, agreed to

changes designed to dilute the centralization and the power of the clergy in
regulations concerning the administration of local parishes, the mixed council, the educational council, the archdiocese's philanthropic association, the
Sunday schools, missionary activities, and the general assemblies. Especially
in the case of the local parishes, Athenagoras's rolling back of his initial plan
arguably created what he wanted to avoid, namely a system that echoed the
practices of Protestant Congregationalism. It could be argued that this was
not "congregationalism," because historically the Greeks formed community organizations first and then churches. But it could be seen as a de facto
type of congregationalism. Moreover, when Athenagoras backed down and
reconciled himself with input from the local lay leaders, this indeed constituted a form of congregationalism.[12]

The Challenges of Education

One serious outcome of the church's rejection of congregationalism was
that it had to assume the responsibility for Greek language education in the
United States. In theory, language instruction might be considered something a church so closely identified with nation and ethnicity could manage.
But of all the other projects that the local parish was taking over, none was
more challenging than running the Greek schools. Athenagoras was aware
of the size of the challenge, and "no other department of the Archdiocese received more of Athenagoras' attention than the Greek language school," his
biographer George Papaioannou notes, and in 1931 "the Congress [general
assembly] enthusiastically approved the creation of a Supreme Educational
Board to supervise the Greek language schools throughout the country."
The delegates were evidently in agreement with Athenagoras's view that
the preservation of Greek language was both a national and a religious responsibility.[13] Athenagoras was not dismissing Joachim's suggestion that the
archdiocese should focus on Sunday schools; rather, he outlined an ambitious pedagogical agenda that embraced both religious and language education. All parishes should undertake this dual responsibility, the archbishop
believed. The newly established Department of Religious Education of the
archdiocese made Sunday schools mandatory for all parishes. Their purpose
was "both to preserve Orthodoxy and also to initiate the youth into Hellenic
ideals, traditions and culture," and their mission was not only to instill Greek
Orthodoxy into the children "but to also make good Hellenes of them by
teaching the customs and culture of Greece," as well as the Greek language.[14]
Greek schools came in addition to all this, reinforcing those goals through a
broader range of instruction. As Papaioannou noted, "the opening of Greek

language schools in every parish, even in towns that had no Greek churches, was Athenagoras' most ambitious plan."[15] The archdiocese's choice of symbols and names for schools underlined the assumption that Greek Orthodoxy and classical Greek civilization were closely associated. The Supreme Educational Board chose as its official seal the *glaux*, the owl associated with Athena, the goddess of wisdom. As Fevronia Soumakis observes in her study of Greek schools in the greater New York area, the decision to adopt a pagan rather than a religious symbol "might seem incongruous, but it reflected the intense symbiotic relationship between Orthodoxy and Hellenism" and the ways that relationship inspired early Greek American immigrants. The choice of the *glaux* was in line with the earlier practice of naming Greek schools in which the local priest taught after classical Greek figures such as Athena, Homer, Leonidas, Socrates, and Plato.[16]

It is always difficult to assess the effectiveness and quality of immigrant-run educational initiatives, and this is certainly true of Greek language schooling in the United States. There can be a glass-half-full tendency: being impressed by the mere existence of such schools and the numbers of enrolled students they reported. After all, they were operating in a "foreign" environment and trying to provide instruction in a language that many of the students' parents were themselves in the process of abandoning. Such an optimistic interpretation of the functions of the schools ignores the actual content and effectiveness of the curriculum and the teaching the immigrant schools provided. And even before those schools can be judged in terms of curricular content, a set of challenges at the administrative level has to be considered, including recruitment and payment of teachers, physical facilities, aligning of activities in relation to the demands placed on students by the host-society culture, and public education requirements. By way of comparison, the Greek community in Egypt, just under half the size of that in the United States but more concentrated in the country's urban centers and incomparably better financed, thanks to the presence of a wealthy elite, were themselves facing serious issues in the 1930s. These included adapting the curriculum, generated by the Ministry of Education in Athens, to the evolving conditions in Egypt, even though the Greeks there were relatively privileged compared to the native population, and choosing between the more formal Katharevousa form of the language and a more accessible vernacular (demotic).[17]

A steady stream of encyclicals on educations and the schools issued by the archdiocese in the 1930s attests to the church's efforts to improve the performance of the Greek-language schools, as well as to the difficulties this project entailed. The major initiatives concerned increasing the numbers of schools and teachers and improving the quality of instruction. The reports of the archdiocese's Supreme Educational Board at the biennial clergy-laity congresses (general assemblies) also attest to the church's investment in this project and the obstacles the Supreme Educational Board identified along the way. There was a steady increase in the number of schools and students throughout the 1930s. For example, Vasilios Zoustis, the secretary of the Supreme Educational Board, reported that in the 1932–33 school year there were 284 schools under the aegis of the archdiocese in North and South America, with a total of 12,712 students and 330 teachers, and that in nine years there had been an impressive increase to 500 schools with 21,834 students and 553 teachers. Eight of those schools were day schools; all except one in Montreal and another in Buenos Aires were in the United States.[18] Yet beneath that statistical façade, serious issues remained. An encyclical Athenagoras sent to the teachers of the Greek schools in 1935 revealed the extent of the problems existing four years into the archdiocese's takeover of Greek education. The archbishop acknowledged that pay was insufficient for many teachers, who were often the target of dispiriting, harsh criticism, and who lacked job security. Moreover, teachers had not cooperated with the archdiocese's Supreme Educational Board, had not sent in reports, had not requested help, and had generally ignored the board's existence. Many teachers also ignored the curricula the board had recommended. Some had even expressed themselves publicly against the archdiocese's centralization plan.[19] In August 1938, buoyed by what was apparently a doubling of the number of schools in the space of three years, the archbishop sent an encyclical congratulating the parish priests and boards and called for further increases in enrollment aimed at the further dissemination of the Greek language in order to educate the new generation in a Greek and a Christian manner.[20] An encyclical the archbishop sent in 1939 noted the doubling of the numbers of enrolled students and schools compared to the 1931–32 school year when the Supreme Educational Board assumed its responsibilities, but also acknowledged shortcomings. The 1939 Clergy-Laity Congress had approved a proposal that teachers be paid twelve months a year rather than only for the months they taught, because the pay was so low. The Patriarchate of Constantinople and the Greek government had also signed off on the proposal and expressed their appreciation of the teachers' dedication. The archbishop also expressed the wish that the church would abolish tuition fees in the near future so as to encourage the enrollment of more Greek children, since many families were not sending their children to Greek schools because of the cost of tuition.

In the late 1930s the Greek government began showing an interest in the state of Greek education in the United States. This was triggered by a sharply worded report sent in 1937 to Athens by Petros Daskalopoulos, the Greek consul in Boston. Daskalopoulos reported that the church and the Greek family had performed miracles in preserving and promoting Greek identity, but the schools were failing badly. The schools were housed in dingy, dark basements that contrasted with the bright and clean environment of the American schools that the Greek children came from for their afternoon instruction in Greek. Two hours later they emerged from these cellars mentally and psychologically exhausted, the consul added. The overall malfunctioning of the schools meant the children learned very little Greek, not even enough to communicate with their parents in that language. If it were not for the efforts of families and the church, he continued, Greek identity would erode dangerously. The situation was so bad that there was a need to offer lectures in Greek and for new priests to know a measure of English so they could communicate with the American-born younger generation.[21]

In 1939, Manolis Triantafyllidis, one of Greece's preeminent educationalists and linguists, came to the United States and visited many communities and schools. At the time, Triantafyllidis was chairing a Greek government committee assigned the task of producing a new grammar for use in schools based on a vernacular (demotic) version of Greek that would replace the older, more stilted and formalized Katharevousa version.[22] Upon his return to Athens, Triantafyllidis gave a public lecture on the Greeks of America— attended by the US ambassador Lincoln McVeagh—and he was effusive in his admiration and praise of the achievements of the Greek Americans, though, significantly, he did not mention education.[23] Indeed, he chose to communicate his views directly to the archbishop, in a memorandum he submitted to the archdiocese. Having established a cordial relationship with Athenagoras, Triantafyllidis felt he could be open about his criticisms and his view that Greek education in the United States was in a sad state because of the poor quality of the overall programming and instruction. He wrote that if the situation did not change, he doubted "Hellenism" would survive for another generation, and the loss of the use of Greek would mean the replacement of Hellenism by philhellenism. There was no direction to the educational program, he noted, and the teachers appeared in general to be incapable of implementing the archdiocese's plan. The plan itself, Triantafyllidis added, was inadequate; it made too many demands on both students and teachers and needed to be redirected from its emphasis on reading comprehension toward helping students learn to express themselves in Greek and also to learn about Greece and its culture. The narrow emphasis on reading instruction, he added, included no attempt to introduce children to Greek stories and poems; they were learning trite patriotic verses that would not generate a true love of things Greek. Triantafyllidis was obviously sensitive to the form of language the schools were using, and he noted that even though the archdiocese favored teaching the demotic form, the teachers instead used the more formal and less comprehensible Katharevousa and in some cases were even teaching ancient Greek grammatical forms, something he considered to be an error of criminal proportions, especially in the case of the afternoon schools.[24]

Adapting the Educational Program to America

About the time Triantafyllidis was outlining his critique of Greek education in the United States from a Greek perspective, the enormous challenges education posed to the church were becoming even more obvious from an American perspective. In short, it was becoming clear that there was also an urgent need to adapt classroom material to an American-born generation. As Papaioannou puts it, "Even with all his zeal and enthusiasm for the Greek language, Athenagoras found, as did his fellow Greeks and other immigrant groups, that teaching the language to American born children was an uphill battle. . . . The children often resented attending the Greek school after their regular school day was over and they resisted anything that seemed old fashioned or strange or set them apart from their American friends."[25] The archdiocese recognized that the effectiveness of the schools depended on staffing them with priests who could relate to the American-born young Greeks. There was a broad understanding that the steadily Americanizing Greek immigrants were growing less and less familiar with the Greek language and mentality, and that the same applied, but even more so, to the younger, American-born generation.

Thus there was a need to train priests from within the community but equip them properly. This of course required a systematic and rigorous training in Greek Orthodoxy and Greek culture. An earlier effort to establish a Greek Orthodox seminary had failed. St. Athanasius Seminary had begun operating in rented accommodation in Brooklyn in 1921 and then moved to near the archdiocese's offices in Astoria. But it lasted for only two years because of lack of funding and very low enrollments. Circumstances were different in the 1930s. Establishing a seminary became one of Athenagoras's priorities, because clearly a "native born American clergy would be needed in order for the future generations of Americans of Greek faith to remain faithful to the religion of their fathers."[26]

The answer to this pressing need came six years after Athenagoras's arrival in New York. The new Greek Orthodox seminary, named Holy Cross

Theological School, opened its doors in 1937 on a rural estate in Pomfret, Connecticut, about 150 miles northeast of New York City. A number of Greek Americans had bought the property for $35,000 on behalf of the archdiocese. Its first dean, Bishop Athenagoras Kavadas, described the school's purpose in its 1939–40 yearbook as a process of instilling a Greek and Orthodox consciousness in the minds of American-born Greeks:

> Young adult Greek boys, born in this country, enter this school with little or no religion and an even lesser perhaps concept of the blameless Orthodox Church of their fathers and with very little feeling of respect and love for the native land whose glorious earth covers the bones of their forefathers. At school, a miracle occurs . . . and they become believing children of the Church; they are watered with dedication towards mother Greece and become enthused with justified pride that they are children of that land that was the cradle of civilization. . . . As such they are prepared spiritually and intellectually go enter our Greek Orthodox clergy and to serve as pastors of our communities. Others among them shall be the teachers in our community schools being properly prepared for this.[27]

In 1966, after it had moved to Brookline, Massachusetts, Holy Cross expanded its undergraduate division to a four-year liberal arts college named Hellenic College. Despite the efforts of educators at both institutions, maintaining high academic standards has been a continuous uphill battle.

The establishment of a seminary was an important development for the Greek Orthodox Archdiocese, and it satisfied the need to produce American-bred clergy; but by the same token it raised another set of problems. One was simply having Greek-born and Greek-trained senior clerics teaching young Greek Americans. The cultural differences boiled over in 1941, before even the first class had graduated. Students walked out of the classes taught by Archimandrite Athenagoras Kokkinakis because "mastering the Greek tongue with its ancient Greek philosophy, theology and attendant courses [was] proving too much, even for the brightest, and the strain was in evidence to all but the faculty"; as a result, "a powder keg of resentment was building up in the pressure packed student body." Kokkinakis's entire class walked out, precipitating an extraordinary class boycott that Archbishop Athenagoras and Dean Kavadas tried unsuccessfully to defuse. Such were the depth of feeling, Kokkinakis's obstinacy, and the archbishop and the dean's lack of negotiating skills that eight students left the seminary and turned their backs on their dream of becoming Greek Orthodox priests. The result was that Kavadas produced a fifty-seven-point list of regulations depriving the students of any rights, and life continued as before.[28] But there would be other, deeper conflicts at the heart of this project, most notably the issue of how much should the Greek language feature in the curriculum at a time when Greek Americans were becoming more and more assimilated. This was not a simply a practical question but one that related to the core question of what type of Greekness the seminary was designed to promote.

The Church and the Great Depression

By the time the sixth Clergy-Laity Congress was held in Boston in 1935, in the midst of the Great Depression, the financial burdens faced by the church began overshadowing the implementation of the new changes and the handling of the thorny issue of Greek education. Across the country, many local Greek American organizations and parishes simply found it impossible to continue functioning. Many Greek Americans moved to big cities in search of the jobs, leaving many small churches threatened with closure. Diminished income for all churches meant that those with large mortgages faced foreclosures or bankruptcy. The last thing on their mind was paying higher dues to the archdiocese or implementing the new measures.

Athenagoras appeared to react slowly to the worsening economic climate, at least initially. The clergy-laity congresses of 1931 and 1933 were almost entirely focused on introducing the new constitutions and regulations. But the changes also entailed creating a new department with a responsibility for charitable activities, the Ladies Philoptochos, which essentially would centralize and coordinate the initiatives of charities run by the women's charity organizations, many of which already existed in each parish. Those initiatives were not fully embraced by priests in all parishes. One of Athenagoras's own first initiatives came during a visit to Chicago in May 1931 when he issued an encyclical appealing to the faithful to support the Ladies Philoptochos organization in the city that was working to aid the many Greeks facing hardship. In a postscript, he requested that priests inform their congregations of the fund drive and also allow the group's collection dish to circulate inside the church because "waiting outside for contributions is humiliating and tiring and unlikely to produce great results." Some believed the church could do more. Seraphim Canoutas, an attorney in New York City and author of books and articles on the Greek immigrant experience in the United States, wrote to Athenagoras that year, respectfully but firmly suggesting that the archdiocese become much more active in helping destitute Greeks and that expensive social events, including dances at parishes, should be curtailed in favor of charity work. Yet at least in terms of the archbishop's encyclicals, there is evidence to suggest he was not overlooking the need for charity, but that he regarded the Philoptochos as the appropriate vehicle for such work. And on several occasions, he offered specific guidance. For example, in Athenagoras's first encyclical letter to the members of the Philoptochos organizations, issued in October 1932, he sketched out their administrative responsibilities and role in the parish before entreating them to help those in need as well as to bear in mind that Greeks were imbued with a sense of honor that made asking for help difficult.

The archbishop's choice to maintain his focus on the archdiocese's organizational structure rather than devote his energy principally to charitable activities was a pragmatic one, which was ultimately justified. The magnitude of want created by the Great Depression was such that most Greek American ethnic institutions were as stricken as the population at large. It took Roosevelt's New Deal to offer real help, and it did so in more ways than one. Southeastern Europeans, once the target of discrimination and exclusion, were slowly being accepted into the "white" mainstream. They benefited from programs created and legislation enacted during the Depression—the Home Owners Loan Corporation, Federal Housing Administration loans, the Social Security Act, and the Wagner Act. These "provided them with enormous advantages over non-European groups in the housing and labor markets when it came to state insurance benefits. It was these programs more than anything else that transformed so many racially suspect working class 'new' European immigrants into respectable middle class 'white ethnic' suburbanites."[29]

The New Deal would also benefit Greek Orthodoxy in America. The circumstances of the Great Depression may have tested the church and caused suffering for many parishes, but in a paradoxical way the turn toward American institutions by those in need leveled the playing field among the major Greek American organizations and helped the archdiocese make up for the ground it had lost in the 1920s. The Depression caused all major Greek American organizations—AHEPA, GAPA, fraternities based on place of origin, and the Greek language press—to lose members and subscribers and also some of their status. AHEPA had achieved its goal of encouraging Greek Americans to become US citizens and was able to relax its hyper-American stance. Indeed, it found that in order to justify its relevance, it had to put more stress on the Greek heritage it had tactically spurned in the 1920s.[30] This also brought about a greater acceptance of the church on the part of such organizations. In 1935, Athenagoras accepted invitations to offer benedictions at the opening of both the AHEPA and GAPA conventions. The response of these organizations was a form of retrenchment and cooperation that led to regular public displays of solidarity. For example, both AHEPA and GAPA initiated common celebrations of Greek Independence Day every March. And both organizations made sure to include representatives of the church in all their activities. And in 1937 Athenagoras could confidently assert in an encyclical that the church was at the center of Greek American life. By way of confirmation, AHEPA reiterated its public embrace of Greek Orthodoxy when its boys' youth organization, the Sons of Pericles, produced its first-ever religion-focused publication, an English-language booklet titled *The Holy Liturgy of the Greek Orthodox Church*.[31]

By the end of the 1930s the benefits of the church's reorganization in 1931 were evident: the parishes had absorbed many of the activities usually undertaken by community organizations, giving the parishes a social dimension well beyond the confines of the liturgy and other religious functions. That transition may have been made in the name of countering Protestant congregationalism, but it also could be seen as consonant with Greek Orthodoxy's own practices in the homeland, especially in rural areas, where religion was lived in an indigenized manner, with the veneration of local saints and other local traditions.[32] Athenagoras, arguably, forced through certain changes that placed the church at the center of Greek American life, but for the Orthodox immigrants with experience or memory of life in rural Greece, the result was an altogether familiar one. And that they stood by their church during the Depression era is amply illustrated by the data recorded in a survey of "Religious Bodies" in the United States. It showed that the number of Greek Orthodox churches across the country had increased from 153 in 1926 to 241 in 1936 and that over that same period the church's membership had increased from 119,871 to 189,368. And the number of church buildings had also increased, and by an even higher proportion, from 138 to 222.[33] The archdiocese's seventh Clergy-Laity Congress, held in Detroit in October 1939, was a celebration of its survival and success during a very difficult decade. Two years earlier, Athenagoras had noted that the community was gradually emerging from the effects of the Great Depression. The numbers indicated the archdiocese was also following an upward trajectory. The budget for 1935 showed a total revenue of $39,680, with an after-expenses profit of $4,332; that of 1937 confirmed the gradual improvement, showing a total income of $53,486, with an after-expenses profit of $4,863; while the income for 1938 was $54,882, leaving a profit of just under $5,000.

Slowly but steadily the Greek Orthodox Church emerged from the worst effects of the Great Depression. It had survived the pressures of Americanization and now those of the economic downturn, and it could look to its

future in America with justified confidence. The re-creation of the archdiocese and the network of its organizations showed how Greek Orthodoxy,
that socially shared and structured set of beliefs, functioned as a mobilizing
force that enabled the strengthening of Greek ethnicity and the reinforcement of its cohesion. The structure of Greek Orthodoxy was counterbalanc-
ing the structural influence of American society on the Greek immigrants.

CHAPTER 4

The Greek Orthodox Church in between Greece and America

The wartime conditions in the United States during the 1940s, with men leaving for the front, disruption of the routines of daily life, and war needs attracting resources that may have gone to religious institutions and channeling them instead toward the war effort, are generally considered to have eroded religiosity throughout the country. But in the case of Greek Orthodoxy, the opposite was true. Greece's entry into the war on the side of the Allies meant that the church, which was identified with the Greek nation, could openly support the homeland. Patriotism fed religious sentiment and vice versa, and when the United States entered the war, the Greek Orthodox Church unambiguously embraced America's war effort. With Greeks fighting on the same side with the Americans, life became much easier for the Greek Orthodox in the United States, and Archbishop Athenagoras made sure that those favorable conditions would benefit Orthodoxy in America.

When Greece entered World War II in October 1940, leading Greek Americans, with the aim of forming the Greek War Relief Association to offer help to the homeland, held their meeting at the Greek Orthodox archdiocese's headquarters in New York City. Athenagoras presided over the gathering and approved the plan. It was another affirmation of the status of the church and the archbishop in Greek American community life. Little did the group know that their homeland was already offering them a huge gift.

By defending itself against Italy's invasion, Greece was joining the side of the Allies. Riding a wave of patriotic passion and against all military odds, the Greek army pushed the invading Italians back over the mountains deep into Albanian territory by the time the harsh midwinter conditions brought operations to a standstill. At that moment, Britain and Greece were the only two free European countries that were confronting the Axis. Overall, the general climate of ethnic relations in the United States in terms of the treatment of European-origin immigrants was becoming more positive. In the battle against totalitarianism and Nazism, leading American figures and the press portrayed the United States as a nation whose values were antithetical to its enemies. This meant that if totalitarianism demanded conformity, mocked freedom, and preached racial hatred, then Americans were surely plural and instinctively democratic. Popular films and novels during the war never tired of celebrating American racial diversity. While this theory did not quite apply in practice to all groups, it functioned as an open invitation to southeastern and eastern European immigrants to feel fully American. But Greece's heroic stance against Italy in October 1940 was an additional reason for the American mainstream to begin regarding the Greeks in a more positive light than before. American commentators were quick to express their admiration for Greece, and the media highlighted Greek military feats, giving the country unprecedented positive coverage. An editorial in the *New York Times* on October 29 was effusive, noting that the Greeks, "outnumbered as they are, poor in the instruments of modern war, remember and defend the glory that was Greece. They recognize at once that this is a fight for independence of all small nations. Whatever happens, their instant determination to prove worthy of their ancestors of their freedom vindicates the heroic tradition of Marathon, Thermopylae and Salamis and establishes once more the title to nationhood of a brave and ancient people."[1] This praise continued even after Greece ultimately fell under Axis occupation in 1941, and it had a dramatically positive effect on the standing of the Greek American community.

The new era presented both advantages and disadvantages to Athenagoras and his task of strengthening Greek Orthodoxy in America. The church could capitalize on the pride Greek Americans felt for their homeland and underscore the significance of Greek Orthodox values. But by the same token, the greater the acceptance the Greeks gained, the easier became their path to Americanization. All this required a balancing act: the church had to work toward consolidating the church as an institution and improving its services to the Greek community, especially Greek language education. On the other hand, it had to be seen as an institution that was also American, especially in the eyes of the American-born Greek Orthodox.

Standing by the Homeland

After Greece rejected Mussolini's ultimatum and its homeland came under attack, there was no doubt the church would support the war. Orthodox doctrine is against war but forgives an armed defense against violence and oppression. Neither in Greece nor among the Greeks of the diaspora was there any theological debate about what the church's duties were at the moment of Italy's attack. In the United States, even some mainstream Christian church denominations adopted what has been described as a "cautious patriotism" at the outbreak of the war.[2] But for the Greek Orthodox, this was a moment for them to demonstrate their unqualified patriotism. Athenagoras was present at the first public events organized in the United States to express support for Greece. For example, in February 1941, a gathering of ten thousand people at the historic site of Valley Forge in Pennsylvania, including seven thousand Boy Scouts, linked the suffering and heroism of George Washington's army in the winter of 1777–78 with the struggle of the Greeks, and a service was held in the chapel with Archbishop Athenagoras participating. While such events with the archbishop in attendance continued throughout the war years, Greek American support on the home front for the war effort manifested itself in two major ways: the sale and purchase of US government war bonds, and efforts to send aid to Greece. These were efforts both individuals and Greek American ethnic associations undertook publicly and with remarkable energy, and the church was involved in both initiatives. Spearheading those efforts was the Greek War Relief Association (GWRA), of which Athenagoras was national chairman.

The patriotic mobilization of Greek Americans in support of their homeland brought increasing prominence to the archbishop since, as in the case of the GWRA, he provided the most powerful and appropriate figurehead. The Greek Independence Day Parade in New York City, an annual event that had begun just before the war, took on a special significance for the Greek Americans and for the church. It was an occasion in which they could publicly display their Greek and American patriotism and one in which the archbishop and the church's hierarchy played a significant role. Independence Day marked the beginning of the uprising against the Ottomans in 1821, and at that moment in Greek history, an Orthodox priest had blessed the flag of the Greek insurgents. The ability to link that event with Greece's involvement in World War II and celebrate it publicly—smaller parades took place in many other American cities—brought the community and the Orthodox Church even closer to each other. The Catholic Church in the United States was similarly involved in supporting the war effort, but very much as an

American church, not one associated with a nation or an ethnic group.³ At its 1941 convention, AHEPA invited other Greek American organizations to a meeting designed to consider the establishment of a "Pan-Hellenic Congress" that could coordinate efforts to aid Greece, for example by helping Greek Americans adopt Greek refugee children and even planning ahead for Greece's postwar reconstruction. Athenagoras was elected the honorary chairman. Even though the Pan-Hellenic Congress never got off the ground, the choice of the archbishop as honorary chairman was another sign that he was becoming the titular head of the Greek American community.⁴

The attendance of the exiled King George II of Greece and the Greek prime minister, Emmanouil Tsouderos, at the seventh Clergy-Laity Congress held in Philadelphia in 1942 underscored the church's position as a link between the Greeks in America and their homeland. The king and the prime minister were on a visit to the United States from their base in London, to where they had escaped as Greece fell to the Axis powers. The king opened the conference's proceedings with a speech on June 22 before an audience of invited guests and delegates in the packed confines of St. George's Cathedral in Philadelphia. Appropriately, the church, originally built to serve the needs of the Episcopalians in Philadelphia, was designed by architect John Haviland in his favored Greek revival style. It featured an impressive façade with six large white Ionic-style columns capped by a large triangular pediment. The presence of both the head of state and the prime minister of Greece at the Clergy-Laity Congress offered considerable political benefits to both the guests and the visitors. It helped transform the occasion into a celebration of Greek patriotism and of Greek support for America and the Allies. The king and government's stature grew in the eyes of the Greek Orthodox faithful, while their participation also confirmed Athenagoras's growing importance.

Within occupied Greece, however, the standing of the king and the exiled government were being challenged by the rise of a communist-led resistance movement, and suddenly Greek politics began experiencing another polarizing divide, this time between the political left and right. This new divide influenced the Greek American community's politics, but the divisions were nowhere near those engendered earlier by the monarchist–Venizelist polarization. There was of course no question about where the archdiocese stood in relation to the right-wing, pro-monarchist exiles versus the left-wing, pro-republican partisans. But the archdiocese sought to keep the effects of the rift in perspective. While no friend of the left, Athenagoras did not let the Greek political conflict interfere with church life directly. Rather, he remained focused on proclaiming the archdiocese's loyalty to American democratic values and its support for postwar relief for Greece and for Greece's territorial claims. Always a pragmatist, the archbishop opposed the communist bid for power in Greece but did not let ideology deflect the archdiocese from its primary task, which was to develop and strengthen Orthodoxy and its church in America. The US Office of Strategic Services (OSS), the predecessor of the Central Intelligence Agency (CIA), compiled a report on the Greek situation in April 1944, which included an assessment of the ideological tendencies within the Greek American community. It described Athenagoras as "perhaps the best known spokesman" of the community, but with critics as well as admirers. "The Archbishop," the report continued, "has stated to this Branch and repeatedly in public that as an American citizen he holds himself aloof from participation in Greek political activities. Those who distrust him however call attention to the fact that in conducting services the Archbishop regularly has included a prayer in behalf of 'our King' George and Prince Paul and his wife Princess Frederica [and] Athenagoras has usually taken care to stand in close relations with the Greek government actually in power for the moment." The OSS's Greek American informants thought that all this was reasonable, because "the Hellenic Orthodox Church in America comes under the ecclesiastical jurisdiction of the Ecumenical Patriarchate in Constantinople which receives a heavy annual subsidy from the Greek government."[5] But it would have also been completely out of character for the archdiocese to support a left-wing government. A few years later, when the right-versus-left divide escalated into a civil war that lasted between 1946 and 1949, the archdiocese came out strongly against the communist rebels.

The Role of the Ladies Philoptochos

The activities designed to offer aid to Greece gave prominence to the church's newly established women's philanthropic organization. A great deal of the practical side of gathering and packaging relief supplies for Greece was undertaken by the parish-based Philoptochos branches, and this highlighted the role women played in the life of the church. In a July 1940 encyclical, before the outbreak of war between Italy and Greece, Athenagoras had praised the organization's work in helping the poor and expressed the wish that all Greek and American wives of Greek males would join the organization, and that priests encourage Philoptochos members to bring their entire families to church.[6] After the formation of the Greek War Relief Association, Athenagoras made a special appeal to all women in the community echoing the appeal that Frederica, the queen of Greece, had issued in Athens. Accordingly, Athenagoras named the wife of Cimon Diamantopoulos, the Greek ambassador in Washington, as being in charge of that effort.[7] The Greek

War Relief Association was aware of the crucial role the local Philoptochos branches could play, so after staffing its boards and committees with men, it created a "women's auxiliary" chaired by Mrs. L. J. Calvocoressi. But it was the parish-based Philoptochos branches, directed by the national president Mrs. Tzina Psaki of Brooklyn, that did all the work. The Philoptochos organized a special "tag day" held in many cities across the country. Philoptochos members solicited contributions on street corners, at restaurants, markets, shops, and theaters, and began a campaign named "knit a sweater for a soldier." The Philoptochos established "sewing centers" first in New York and then in other cities, thanks to the help of Joseph Josephs and several other Greek-Jewish businessmen who generously donated hundreds of new clothing items and a large quantity of cloth. After the local Philoptochos branches more than proved their worth, Athenagoras began issuing encyclicals praising them, listing what they should be doing and how.[8] Coming from him, this was high praise. Public recognitions followed.

In early 1941, the New York City Philoptochos became a member of the city's Federation of Women's Clubs, which worked "to acquaint themselves with a better understanding of the language and customs of this country [Greece]." In its report, the *New York Times* noted that "with a membership of more than 300 the [New York City] branch is one of 350 in North America. . . . The club's charitable program is widespread and includes cooperation with local relief and welfare agencies and with the family and children's courts."[9] During the Clergy-Laity Congress of 1942, when the archdiocese decided to implement a decade-long plan to establish a Greek American orphanage, it gave the responsibility for fund-raising to the Philoptochos. This was a choice governed by the assumption that an orphanage was within the sphere of the traditional caregiver role of women, but it was also a recognition of the achievements of the Philoptochos in their charity work for the poor and the relief campaign for Greece. The number of Greek American children requiring care had been steadily increasing throughout the 1930s, and the risks of their being institutionalized or placed into foster care with non-Orthodox families crystallized the idea of an orphanage and school run by the archdiocese. Similar concerns had led to the creation of Catholic and Jewish orphanages in the United States. In 1944 the archdiocese purchased a 450-acre landscaped property along the east bank of the Hudson River in Garrison, New York, about fifty miles north of the city. It had been the estate of Jacob Ruppert, a brewer, businessman, US congressman, and owner of the New York Yankees baseball team, who had died in 1939. Valued at $1 million but with no buyers, the estate went to the archdiocese for $45,000. It was named St. Basil's, and Athenagoras mandated that one of the ways funds should be raised to support the institution would be through the Philopto-chos's annual cutting of the Basil's pie bread (*vasilopita*) in each parish around January 1, Saint Basil's Day according to the Orthodox calendar.

The institution opened its doors in September 1944, its full name St. Basil Academy because the archbishop decided that it should cover another growing community need, the training of young women to become teachers in the Greek schools. The drafting of young men after the US entered the war in late 1941 had rapidly reduced the ranks of Greek American teachers, and teachers from Greece were manifestly unsuited to teach American-born Greek children. Athenagoras realized "that only a teachers training school with students recruited from among the young American women of Greek Orthodox descent that offered a training program comparable to that of the American teachers training colleges would solve the problem."[10] The school offered a three-year course in liberal arts, with an emphasis on education. In June 1948, eight young women became the first class to graduate from St. Basil Academy.

However, while the orphanage at St. Basil's operated smoothly, the teach-ers' college division limped along without being to attract great interest from young women, either Greek Americans or from Greece, where the church made recruitment efforts. It did not help that instruction was intensive and living conditions somewhat spartan. The top-down nature of the administra-tion, with all final decisions up to the archbishop, a preponderance of fac-ulty members who were either priests or theologians, and very few of those faculty with any pedagogical training, imposed a continuous burden on the teachers' college division, which never gained accreditation from the State of New York. To address its ongoing difficulties, the academy was incorporated into Hellenic College Holy Cross and moved to Brookline, Massachusetts, in the early 1970s.[11]

The Church Ascendant

The mobilization of Orthodox women in the Philoptochos was just one of the signs of an ascendant Greek Orthodox Church in America. At the Clergy-Laity Congress of 1942 in Philadelphia, Athenagoras was able to point to several other achievements in the decade that had elapsed since he had as-sumed his position. The archdiocese, he was able to report, had increased its income to a record $47,233 revenues in 1941, with an outlay of $39,940; it had acquired its own administration building, which was valued at $300,000; and it had collected $30,814 toward rebuilding the wing of the patriarchate. The number of community-parishes under its aegis had grown to 286, of which 270 were in the United States, 6 were in Canada, and the rest in Latin America. Among these parishes, 280 had their own churches, 168 or which were their own property; and other properties owned by the communities included 42 community offices and 21 graveyards. There were 8 day schools and 491 afternoon schools, with a total of 23,000 students; and almost as many students, 20,206, attended one of the church's 309 Sunday schools. The impressive statistics were capped with the information that the archdiocese's publication, the *Greek Orthodox Observer*, had a monthly circulation of four thousand. And with the church poised to grow further, Athenagoras announced the introduction of the so-called "monodollarion," a single-dollar annual contribution to the archdiocese of every member of the church. It represented a radically new form of revenue raising, inaugurating a more direct relationship of each parishioner to the central authority. Until now, the archdiocese had relied on dues paid by each parish and its priests and teachers on a per capita basis and also according to the number of marriages and baptisms performed by each local church. This was a notoriously unreliable system, and its weaknesses were exposed by the unwillingness or inability of several parishes to pay their dues, either because of disgruntlement with Athenagoras's centralization or because of the effects of the Depression, or possibly both. The archbishop told the congress that the communities owed the archdiocese $16,528 and individual priests a total of $14,070. Those dues were to be abolished beginning in 1943 and replaced by the single-dollar contribution by each parish member that would go directly to the archdiocese— irrespective of the dues owed by members to their local parish. But there was a catch. Parish priests were assigned the task of producing lists with the names of the members of their parishes over the age of twenty-one, and the archdiocese would send back "identity cards," which would entitle holders to obtain services from the archdiocese without any additional charge. Parishes that failed to produce these lists would continue to be charged the old dues, and priests would face disciplinary action.[12]

The delegates in Philadelphia accepted the introduction of the "monodollarion" unanimously. The measure took some time to gain acceptance throughout the country, but the first years of its implementation gave cause for optimism. In 1943 the collection yielded $60,253; two years later, the total collected had gone up to $90,206. That year, 1945, a total of 285 parishes contributed an average of $316 each. The largest donors were the parishes of the Assumption in Chicago, with $1,980; the Annunciation in Boston, $1,891; St. Spyridon in Washington Heights in New York City, $1,565; the Annunciation in Baltimore, $1,122; St. Nicholas in St. Louis, $1,114; Sts. Constantine and Helen in Gary, Indiana, $1,059; St. Demetrios in Jamaica, Queens, $1,000;

the Annunciation–St. Demetrios in Chicago, $987; the Holy Trinity Cathedral in Manhattan, $934.50; St. Andrew in Chicago, $926; St. Demetrios in Astoria, $907, Three Hierarchs in Brooklyn, $900; St. Sophia in Washington, DC, $898; St. Nicholas in Newark, New Jersey, $857; the Annunciation in San Francisco, $823.50; St. Constantine in Chicago and Holy Trinity in Lowell, each $810; St. George in Lynn, Massachusetts, $725; St. Constantine in Brooklyn and Transfiguration in Corona, Queens, each $710; and St. Sophia in Los Angeles, $709. The list and the respective sums are a good indication of the geographic distribution of the Greek Americans at the time and the relative wealth in each community, since membership of the church was a common Greek American denominator in the 1940s.

Overall, there were very few signs of any lingering opposition to Athenagoras's policies. On the eve of the gathering in Philadelphia, Detroit's Greek language newspaper *Athenai* was one of the very few that had raised its voice in opposition to Athenagoras's policies. An editorial expressed the hope that the presence of the king and prime minister at the conference would create the opportunity for introducing a separation between the self-governing rights of the community organizations and the church's rights over the community's spiritual life. The editorial described the archdiocese's policies as "arbitrary and autocratic."[13] But otherwise, the Greek language press was falling in line behind Athenagoras. Chicago's *Hellenikos Astir* reported that even though the Philadelphia meeting was described as a "clergy-laity" gathering, in fact "the clergy will have the floor, the clergy is the alpha and omega because it was the clergy that first received the Lord's blessing, the clergy is able to restore our people's failed dedication to our sacred traditions."[14] Another Greek American newspaper, New York's *Atlantis*, was also very supportive of the archdiocese. The possibility of any critical reflections on the proceedings had not occurred to its editors. The reporter covering the conference for the *Atlantis*, Nestor Veniopoulos, was a delegate representing a parish in Springfield, Massachusetts, who was entrusted with presenting one of the committee reports. The newspaper's coverage of the opening day included a photograph of Veniopoulos greeting the king. In one of his columns, he noted that the increase of lay representatives at future conferences meant that the democratic spirit of the times was permeating the structures of the church and the church was taking on greater laical characteristics.[15] Regardless of the accuracy of that assessment, Athenagoras's achievements were evidently considerable. One of the speakers at the banquet on the fifth and final day of the congress may have evoked the spirit of the proceedings when he remarked, "All these days at the conference it was like being in a dream. We thought we were attending a liturgy at Agia Sophia or the Cathedral in Athens. In the welcoming atmosphere in Philadelphia, we did not feel as strangers. We imagined Philadelphia as another Olympia from which we will take the sacred flame and make the Orthodox Christian Church the vanguard in all of America."[16]

Confronting Americanization

The Orthodox Church and AHEPA held national meetings in 1946, at which both institutions addressed the issues of aid to Greece and that country's postwar future. Yet what distinguished the church's clergy-laity conference was the time it devoted to discussions about the effects of assimilation on the church and the ways the church could maintain its members' faith and sense of identity. AHEPA was an organization whose primary purpose was to promote an Americanized Greekness, so assimilation would not have been regarded as a problem—quite the opposite. Thus, the clergy conference's discussions about ways of keeping members of the church engaged in parish life contrasted with AHEPA's relative calm over similar issues. And it was a reminder that however well the affairs of the Greek Orthodox Church in America may have been going, the influences of the American environment on its members were always a source of concern, given the prominence of religion in everyday life in the United States.

Athenagoras addressed the issue of assimilation in his keynote speech to the seventh Clergy-Laity Congress that met in Boston in November of that year. He began by saluting Greece's liberation two years earlier, in 1944, from the Axis occupation. He praised the contributions of the Greek Americans to the war effort and offered thanks to the Lord for making it possible for all to assemble there "in order to solve the vital problems the Church and more generally Hellenism in the United States were confronting."[17] He then raised the issue of assimilation, noting that the theory that America is a "melting pot" was no longer applicable, because instead it had gone from being a "federation of states" to a "federation of nations," a philosophy of liberty, he added, that enabled persons to retain the characteristics of their homeland. This was a fairly appropriate description of the end of the interwar era, with its emphasis on immigrant Americanization and assimilation. The Greek Orthodox Church, he said, could play a special role in helping the Greeks defend their identity and defend Greek Orthodoxy from accusations that it was backward and ossified in the new era.[18]

The issue of identity came up again in the general discussion that followed the committee reports, submitted after the archbishop's speech and specifically in connection with the archdiocese's marriage statistics. The discussion raised crucial questions about to what extent the church could use its functions to preserve Greek identity, and it revealed that Athenagoras held relatively moderate views on this issue. The comparison of the numbers of intra-Orthodox marriages and mixed marriages (Greek Orthodox with a person of a different Christian denomination) and their trend over a period of time has always been considered an important indicator of the strength of Orthodox sentiment. During the discussion on the report on marriages, the pastor of the Annunciation Cathedral in Boston, Iakovos Coucouzes (the future Archbishop Iakovos), spoke about the mixed marriages, which he said were occurring more frequently and were dividing and undermining the Greek American community and Orthodoxy. He recommended that the church insist that children born of mixed marriages be baptized as Greek Orthodox and that parishes obtained signed agreements from the parents to that effect. Bishop Gerasimos, who had presented the report, responded that this idea had been considered but the committee wished to avoid a public debate "out of respect to our country America." The dean of the Annunciation Cathedral in San Francisco, Polyefktos Finfinis, supported Iakovos's recommendation during an exchange of views that followed. One delegate expressed a more moderate view, namely that the church should try to understand the needs of individuals and cater to them rather than alienate them with rules. He added that "we have more girls than boys, and rather than a girl remain unmarried because there are no Greek boys, it would be better to marry someone of a different race." At that point Athenagoras intervened, agreeing with both sides by way of indicating that the debate should not continue.[19]

The discussion on mixed marriages that had begun at the Clergy-Laity Congress in Boston resumed in two years, an indication that clearly it was causing growing concerns. This in fact was a problem that other Christian churches were facing in the United States in the 1940s. One of the more detailed investigations of this phenomenon studied intermarriage patterns among Lutherans and came up with a list of causes for the increase in intermarriage, which included the increased mixing of religious groups in cities and towns and an increased mobility of the population, a decline in loyalty to the church, the decline in number of possible Lutheran mates, changed attitudes toward marriage, and the relative prestige of other denominations.[20] There are cases in which relatively small denominations in the United States are insulated from general trends, but the fact that both the Lutherans and the Greek Orthodox were affected by increasing numbers of persons marrying outside the church shows how general the phenomenon was in the 1940s. Athenagoras issued two long encyclicals that year, in April and September, on the ways the church should treat non intra-Orthodox marriages, and as was his custom, he listed several directives. Couples who were active parish members and baptized their children in the church but had been joined by civil marriage had to be encouraged to have a religious wedding service. Priests could perform the service at home, if the couple did not want to go to church, and it could be free of charge; nor was it mandatory that the husband and wife were fully paid-up members of the parish. Athenagoras suggested it should be easy to persuade those couples, noting, "We are human. We live today and tomorrow we depart this vain world. Why not depart blessed, peaceful and happy?" Athenagoras directed parish priests to make similar concessions to those who married outside the Greek Orthodox Church and performed their weddings in their spouse's church. The archbishop's language reflected the priority accorded to men but also the value the church recognized in women and their traditional roles. He said that the early immigrants were excused for marrying non-Orthodox women, but "for today's young men there is no excuse, because we have many, and in every respect, excellent young women, eager and willing to create happy Orthodox families." But unfortunately, he continued, "many young men and especially those with a university education and from the best families overlook Orthodox women and marry non-Orthodox, and thus do not create a harmonious family life." Nonetheless, they as well had to be persuaded to have an Orthodox marriage. A third category of marriages Athenagoras discussed were those in which Greeks brought over an Orthodox bride from Greece. The archbishop said he could not criticize such a practice, but he could not praise it either, because if that continued, "what would happen to the daughters of the Greek American community?" The way the archbishop decided to address all those issues was by proclaiming a competition among parishes, with a prize going to the one that over the next year would have no mixed marriages and would marry the largest number of those who had civil marriages.[21]

It is not clear whether the archdiocese held an actual competition, but several months later Athenagoras informed the parish priests that his April encyclical had been very well received and that many Greek Americans had asked for an Orthodox religious wedding service. Mixed marriages continued, however, between young Greek American men and non-Orthodox women. Athenagoras repeated his exhortation that something be done about the problem: "We have thousands of young women ready to marry. What will become of them? We will have a major community-wide social problem soon." Another problem with the mixed marriages was that the couples tended to baptize their children in the mother's faith only. And priests shied away from visiting mixed-marriage couples to encourage their involvement in parish life, either because of a lack of time in a busy schedule or because their English was not good enough to communicate with the non-Orthodox spouse. As for the Orthodox unmarried women, whose relative numbers were growing, Athenagoras made a concession, saying they should be encouraged to marry a non-Orthodox, as long as he was Christian. And finally, priests should try to put an end to the existence of bridal agencies that were bringing unmarried women over from Greece.[22]

The Archbishop and the President

For a consummate tactician such as Archbishop Athenagoras, America posed not only the threat of assimilation of the Greek Orthodox but also the opportunity of bringing the Greek Orthodox close to the country's mainstream. And, typically enough, he worked toward that end in a personal way, by forging relationships with religious and secular leaders in North America. He was especially successful in establishing a close bond with President Harry Truman, a relationship he offered as a symbol of America's growing acknowledgment of Greek Orthodoxy.

Speaking publicly a decade after Athenagoras's tenure had ended, Peter Kourides, who had served as his legal counsel since 1935, was effusive about the archbishop's service. He mentioned several major innovations but singled out the promotion of Orthodoxy as the most significant: "The most important contribution of Archbishop Athenagoras undoubtedly was the effect of his personality on the American populace. . . . He became Orthodoxy's super salesman in a back-breaking one-man assignment to sell our church to the Americans and to establish it as an integral part of the spiritual life of this great nation. He became the respected friend of Presidents, Governors and Senators."[23] Kourides's statement, although delivered in the spirit of a eulogy, was an accurate assessment of Athenagoras's championing of Orthodoxy in America.

The archbishop's outreach toward political leaders would have come naturally to him because of Orthodoxy's long tradition of accommodation with political authority. Athenagoras's efforts to achieve public acceptance of the Greek Orthodox Church in America had begun in the 1930s as soon as he assumed the post of archbishop. He set the tone of the whole of his tenure early on when he visited President Herbert Hoover in the White House and, in Martin Marty's words, "worked to become known in Washington."[24] After Franklin D. Roosevelt became president in 1933, the archbishop was quick to declare his admiration. Speaking during a visit to parishes in Georgia in 1934, he described Roosevelt as "a man sent by God to help His people as near divinity as a temporal ruler can be."[25] It was of course very appropriate for the leader of an Orthodox Church to establish a good relationship with the head of state, but at that particular time the symbolism had positive connotations for the church's and the Greek American community's standing in the public eye. AHEPA had made a habit of making annual visits to the White House beginning in the mid-1920s, reflecting the organization's deliberate policy to affirm its loyalty to America and support for assimilation. Athenagoras was doing the same in the 1930s, but his position as a leader of an ethnic church gave those moves even greater significance. And in the 1940s, no doubt Athenagoras took note of the initiatives of the new Catholic archbishop in New York, Francis Spellman, who frequently hosted prominent political figures and became a confidant of President Roosevelt.

Athenagoras did not limit himself to establishing ties with the US government; he sought out Protestant and other religious leaders. Athenagoras became close to the Episcopal Church's Bishop William Manning, the pastor of the Cathedral of St. John the Divine in New York City. The archbishop acted as the bearer of gifts from the Greek church and the Ecumenical Patriarchate to Manning, gestures designed to acknowledge the drawing closer together of the two churches. Both gifts, a rock from the Aeropagus in Athens where Saint Paul had preached, and an icon of Saint John, were presented in 1933 and 1936 respectively at special services held at the cathedral. The icon was a gift from Ecumenical Patriarch Benjamin I and was made by monks at Mount Athos at his personal request. At the service, Athenagoras called the bishop "one of the strongest heralds of the future union between the Episcopal and the Greek Orthodox Church," and Manning responded by describing the gift as a symbol of the brotherhood of the two churches.[26] The archbishop also led the church toward a greater adaptation to American ways. He had presided over the first-ever Greek Orthodox services for the dead held on an American Memorial Day, in May 1931.[27] And in February 1938, seven years after arriving in the United States, Athenagoras became one of the thousands of Greek-born immigrants who became citizens of the United States. In the 1940s this religious outreach extended to contacts with the other Eastern Orthodox churches in America. In March 1943, the Holy Trinity Cathedral in Manhattan hosted a joint evening service with the participation of the city's Russian, Syrian, Serbian, Romanian, Ukrainian, and Carpatho-Russian churches and their choirs.[28]

Athenagoras's outspoken support for the war effort in the 1940s was part of the wider process of Greek American identification with the United States, and it also brought the Greek Orthodox Church closer to the country's political leaders. When the United States entered the war, Athenagoras called a meeting of all Eastern Orthodox prelates to demonstrate support for the president and the government. "Realizing that throughout the world's history," said the statement issued by the prelates, "since the dawn of Christianity, the Eastern Orthodox Church has steadfastly upheld the government in those lands where she has existed since the Holy Apostles, following Christ's command, the Hierarchs make it known to the world, that their entire sympathy and cooperation are with the President, and completely at his command."[29] Athenagoras put those words in practice, instructing parishes to include a talk on the war after the Sunday sermon and to invite senators, congressmen, and local politicians to the Greek Orthodox churches. After the US Army's victories in battles in North Africa in 1943, Athenagoras proclaimed Roosevelt as a new Constantine the Great, who would prevail over the powers of darkness as bearer of the Holy Cross of the Sepulchre.

Athenagoras's greatest success in forging important relationships came when he gained the trust of Harry Truman, who became president in 1945 following Roosevelt's death. The two men appeared to admire each other, and Athenagoras was just as generous in praising Truman as he had been with Roosevelt. In his sermon in Boston during the Clergy-Laity Congress in 1946, Athenagoras called America "a true democracy of peoples living in brotherly love, harmony and cooperation" and "the heart of great humanitarian ideals and the begetter of the greatest and most admirable humanists in the world, who form the pyramid of true glory at the top of which stands today our great and beloved President, Harry Truman."[30] The president would very soon demonstrate his own high esteem for the archbishop. In 1948, Ecumenical Patriarch Maximos was abruptly forced to step down, triggering a search for a worthy successor. The official reason for Maximos's resignation was that he was suffering from clinical depression, and treatment he received in Switzerland did not alleviate the symptoms. One of Maximos's biographers suggests he was forced to step down amid considerable Byzantine intrigue and controversy created by the political polarization between the West and the Soviet Union at the beginning of the Cold War era. Maximos had close relations with Russian Orthodoxy, and consequently he was suspected of being "soft" toward the Soviet Union. In a three-way process of negotiations that still remains shrouded, the US, Greek, and Turkish governments began quietly planning for Maximos's successor. With several prelates serving in Greece vetoed by the Turks, Ankara and Athens "favored the patriarch's replacement by a prestigious leader with international repute."[31]

Truman's strong religious convictions shaped the ways he pursued the policy of preventing the worldwide spread of communism, America's cornerstone foreign policy during the Cold War. Truman understood his so-called policy of containment in religious terms—the nations that believed in God had to contain those that did not—and the president also saw religion as a tool that could undermine the faith in the Soviet system of communism. Truman saw the Christian faith as revolving primarily around ethnical values rather than doctrines of salvation or of the church, which allowed him to conceive of a broad anticommunist Christian alliance that included Eastern Orthodoxy. Truman's point man with responsibility to forge a Christian alliance in Europe that would act as a bulwark against communism was Myron Taylor. In early 1948 Taylor had discovered that doctrinal difficulties were a huge obstacle to forming a united Christian front, and in particular the Catholic Church wanted nothing to do with the Russian Orthodox Church because it considered it a mouthpiece for the Soviet government. Taylor therefore turned his attention to the Church of Greece and especially the Patriarchate of Constantinople.

It was under those circumstances that Athenagoras emerged as a viable candidate to succeed Maximos and received support from Greece as well as Turkey and the Truman administration. The American ambassador in Ankara worried about Athenagoras's selection becoming grist for the mill of Soviet propaganda because he was an American citizen and an anticommunist, but the Turks publicly declared him a friend of Turkey. Maximos's resignation left open the path for Athenagoras's election by the patriarchate's synod. The bonds between President Truman and the archbishop and newly elected ecumenical patriarch were spectacularly displayed when Athenagoras traveled on Truman's presidential aircraft, the "Sacred Cow," a DC-4 military transport, to Istanbul for his enthronement. The *New York Times* reported that "arrangements for the use of the plane were made by President Truman, it is said."[32] Evidently the White House was unconcerned about Soviet propaganda, or perhaps it wanted to make a political point. There was a ceremony at Idlewild Airport, attended by 1,500 communicants, just before Athenagoras boarded the plane. In his speech to them, Athenagoras said that President Truman's inauguration speech, given a few days earlier, would pave the way for a new offensive against tyranny. The plane's departure was an hour late because earlier that day Athenagoras had given personal communion to twenty-five hundred attendants at the Holy Trinity Cathedral in New York City.[33]

In the 1940s, the Greek Orthodox Church continued the upward trajectory it had embarked upon the previous decade. The prevailing circumstances, especially Greece's entry into the war on the Allied side, helped bring the

Greek Orthodox closer to the American mainstream. That shift was abetted a great deal by moves made by the archbishop. His biographer, George Papaioannou, writing in 1976, produced a balance sheet listing Athenagoras's strengths and weaknesses during his nearly two decades at the helm of the archdiocese. The strengths were many and included personal traits such as charisma, an ability to relate to persons, flexibility in decision making, and diplomatic skills. As an administrator, he was forceful in implementing the reorganization of the archdiocese but did so by displaying pastoral love for the wealthy and the poor, the big and the small parishes. He displayed financial acumen—and an ability to raise funds—that led to the archdiocese's addition of much-needed educational institutions to ensure Orthodoxy's viability in America: the theological school, the orphanage, and the teachers' training college. The two criticisms that Papaioannou expressed and which relate to Athenagoras's role as archbishop are his disinclination to permit the use of English and his inability to forge an adequate response to the alienation of many young Greek Americans from the archdiocese. But overall, he notes that Athenagoras inherited a church that was disorganized and divided and transformed it "into the most progressive Orthodox jurisdiction in the New World."[34] It is easy to agree with the biographer's assessment. The achievements were many. Certainly, the kind of centralization and top-down government imposed by Athenagoras did not suit everyone's vision of church life; yet there were many who favored the certainties of a strong leader over the unpredictability of wider participation in decision making.

Athenagoras is an example of how even the leader of a relatively small, ethnically oriented church could, with the right moves, achieve a great deal of respect and prominence in the United States in midcentury. Although the conventional wisdom is that the war had a negative effect on American religiosity, national identities thrive during war, and a church with a strong national connection with its homeland easily embraced the sympathetic national goals of its host society. War and Cold War created circumstances in which Greek Orthodoxy, thanks to the political skills of its leader, made significant gains in midcentury America.

CHAPTER 5

Assimilation and Respectability in the 1950s

A powerful combination of causes, including the Cold War, social dislocation in suburbia, and anxieties of the atomic age, as well as deliberate religious marketing, led to a remarkable spread of religious identification in postwar America. In a 1952 survey, some 75 percent of Americans polled responded by saying religion was very important in their lives, and five years later over 80 percent answered that religion could solve the big problems in their lives. Politicians embraced and promoted the significance of religion, and Congress added "under God" to the Pledge of Allegiance, the widely used statement of loyalty to the United States.[1] In the words of one authoritative study, "the 'return to religion' of the 1950s was formless and unstructured, manifesting itself in many different ways and reinforcing all religious faiths quite indiscriminately."[2] For Greek Orthodoxy, the across-the-board rise in religiosity in America was a relief at that particular moment. If being American meant being religious, this allayed some of the fears that increased assimilation might bring secularist tendencies.

Yet, in the mind of much of the general public, the religious faiths that were publicly celebrated in the 1950s were Protestantism, Catholicism, and Judaism—Eastern Orthodoxy was neither mentioned, nor was it excluded. The signature study that sought to conceptualize the strengthening and drawing together of those faiths in the 1950s was Will Herberg's *Protestant-Catholic-Jew*. Herberg argued that the third-generation immigrants were being assimilated into American life, and the only part of the old ethnic identity they were preserving was their religion. Herberg omitted Orthodoxy from his triple-religion melting pot most probably because he was taking his queues from his mentor theologian Reinhold Niebuhr's 1930s conceptualization of the "Judeo-Christian" idea that stressed the Hebraic and discounted the "pagan" Hellenic roots. Yet Eastern Orthodoxy's omission from the popular idea of a tri-faith America in the 1950s was not necessarily a disadvantage for the archdiocese. The rise of religiosity was enough of an advantage. Greek Orthodoxy certainly wished to enter the mainstream, but it wanted to do so on its own terms, and not sacrifice the all-important ties with the homeland. Thus, yet again, Greek Orthodoxy found itself in an in-between place, having to negotiate between keeping up with the steady Americanization of the faithful while doing all it could to maintain its and their connections with Greekness. But by the same token, Greek Orthodoxy could not step into the same river: the 1950s presented new challenges that made the balancing act different this time around.

The new archbishop, Michael, whom Athenagoras handpicked as his successor, was prepared to confront those challenges. Michael had served the church outside Greece but had never been to the United States prior to his appointment. But he was seasoned in church administration and politics, serving as chancellor in the Archdiocese of Athens and then as the dean of the Greek Orthodox Cathedral in London, a city with a small but wealthy Greek community, where he had acquired a fluency in English. His last post was metropolitan of Corinth, where he had succeeded Damaskinos. The policies he initiated lacked the dramatic tenor and occasional controversy both his predecessor Athenagoras and Iakovos, his successor, could generate. He also eschewed their larger-than-life center-stage public presence. "While others lay the foundations and yet others erected the building, Michael provided the goods with which the structure was filled," according to Demetrios Constantelos; and Michael was a genuinely religious man with deep biblical interests.[3] When the archdiocese decided to commemorate Michael's service to the church a half century after his enthronement, it was able to produce a booklet packed with information about the archbishop's many contributions.

Choosing an Archbishop

Athenagoras had chosen his successor with care. Going against the expectations of many clergy and laity in America, Athenagoras decided not to appoint either of his two most senior collaborators, the bishop of Boston

Athenagoras Kavadas, or the titular bishop of Nyssa, Germanos Polyzoides, who had been one of the signatories of the original charter of incorporation of the archdiocese in 1921. Athenagoras "promoted" Kavadas by appointing him "bishop of Philadelphia," a defunct metropolitan district in Anatolia, which ceased to exist in 1922 when the region was ethnically cleansed of Greeks during the Greek army's retreat westward in the final phase of the Greco-Turkish War. The titular position had vaguely defined responsibilities within the central administrative structure of the Patriarchate of Constantinople. Kavadas was upset and refused the appointment, and he made his displeasure known to the Greek American press, fueling a simmering sense of outrage among New England Greek Americans who believed that Kavadas deserved to be the head of the archdiocese or, if not, at least allowed to continue as bishop of Boston.[4] The impasse involving Kavadas lasted several years, and it took considerable effort from the Greek Ministry of Foreign Affairs to find a more acceptable solution, with Kavadas being appointed bishop in London, where he served until his death in 1962. Germanos Polyzoides, the other likely successor, was a gentle, cerebral cleric. He loyally accepted to stay on and served in several senior positions in the archdiocese.

The tension surrounding Michael's appointment reflected the perennial issues of "sovereignty" that all churches linked to the Old World experience from time to time in the United States. The vigorous debate over who should succeed Athenagoras was about much more than the popularity of or the respect due to someone like Kavadas. The exchange of views was about principle, namely whether the church in America should be led by one of its own or by someone from the senior ranks of the "mother church"—the Patriarchate of Constantinople—or at least the Church of Greece, which had a say in the matter as the homeland church, even though it deferred to Constantinople on this issue. The Greek Americans valued Kavadas's experience and familiarity with the conditions in the United States. But it was evident that Athenagoras and the Patriarchate of Constantinople, as well as the Church of Greece, wanted one of their own, or at least someone they could control, in New York. It was a vital position that overlooked the ongoing need for the church to adapt to American circumstances and deal with delicate issues such as the use of the English language and catering to the spiritual needs of the younger, American-born generations. From this "Greek" perspective, church leaders may have considered Kavadas as perhaps too "American," as he had served in the United States since 1922, even though he had been born in Greece and trained there. Officially, both Constantinople and Athens said very little. But Apostolos Daskalakis, a professor at the University of Athens who had close ties to both church and government and whose columns appeared regularly in the Greek press, came out explicitly for the appointment of someone from within the Greek fold. The Greeks in the United States, Daskalakis claimed with considerable exaggeration, were 99 percent American citizens, and this made it very difficult for the Greek state to influence them. Those born in the United States may have had emotional ties to Greece, but they had no wish to become involved in their homeland's politics, a drawback for Greece, in his mind. Thus, Daskalakis concluded, "the Orthodox Church is effectively the only dominant power of the Greek element in America and functions as the link with the Greek homeland." This meant that Athenagoras's replacement should be chosen among candidates belonging to the Church of Greece, because they had the closest contacts with the mother country and could best serve the national interests.[5]

Athenagoras had clearly decided he wanted someone he could influence (if not control) and who would satisfy all those who wanted close ties between the church in the United States and Greece. In fact, his first choice was somewhat surprising: he had appointed Metropolitan Timotheos of Rhodes, who had no experience of leadership outside the Greek world; but the frail Timotheos had died soon after arriving in Istanbul to confer with Athenagoras. So, the patriarch appointed Michael, evidently believing that he could trust him to be his own, and the patriarchate's, man in New York.[6]

The Cold War, the Archbishop, and the President

Michael arrived in December 1949 in a country where the Cold War climate had begun to define politics and public affairs, and he seized the opportunity to insert Greek Orthodoxy in the mix. Dealing with the problems of Americanization and the younger generation would have to be postponed for now. Weeks after Michael's enthronement, US Senator Joseph McCarthy was unleashing his notorious anticommunist crusade. A few months later, the Korean War broke out. Michael was not taken by surprise. Greece itself had just come out of a similar right-versus-left civil conflict, with the Greek Orthodox Church firmly on the anticommunist side. US intervention had ensured that the right wing's victory meant Greece would remain a close ally of the United States. Michael was no Athenagoras and temperamentally was the antithesis of his predecessor, a quiet and pietistic cleric who would issue long, reflective encyclicals on religious matters. But it quickly became apparent that Michael also had a strong political sense and was not shy about applying it in matters of public affairs that concerned the archdiocese. He wasted no time in picking up where Athenagoras left off regarding the archdiocese's stance toward the Cold War and the American presidency.

On arriving by ship in New York to an official welcome by the Greek ambassador and heads of two hundred Greek American organizations in late 1949, Michael paid tribute to President Truman and how the US had helped the government defeat the communists in the Greek civil war. Michael was following Athenagoras's lead in courting American public opinion and the US government while adding also his own strong commitment to the struggle against communism. He spoke of his firsthand knowledge of the evils of communism, which he had experienced when he was a student in seminaries in Kiev and St. Petersburg between 1915 and 1919. Michael also echoed the Greek government's claim that the communist side's evacuation of twenty-eight thousand children from regions under its control and their resettlement across Greece's northern border in countries with communist governments was a mass kidnapping.[7] The Cold War and the US-Greek alliance became a major theme of the new archbishop's public statements. In his keynote speech at eleventh Clergy-Laity Congress in 1952, he mentioned the need to pray to God to guide all Americans in the upcoming presidential elections in the United States, "a country that was at the forefront protecting the freedoms of the civilized world and was fighting in Korea against godless, materialist and totalitarian communism that was trying to spread its suffocating tentacles throughout the globe."[8]

Public support of the government and anticommunist statements were an obvious way of any immigrant church to assert its patriotism in the early 1950s, yet the Cold War brought a mixed blessing to the Eastern Orthodox Churches in the United States. It was not as straightforward a boost to their efforts to enter the country's mainstream religious life as it might appear at first glance. The Greek Orthodox Church had benefited greatly from the attention lavished on it by Truman and his administration. And naturally the statements Michael made demonstrated his intention to continue and deepen that close relationship. But the other Orthodox Churches—those whose home countries were under communist governments—were not trusted and, in the public's eye, did not reflect positively on Orthodoxy in general.

Had Russian Orthodoxy in the United States not been splintered into several churches and instead housed in a single church autonomous from Moscow, then the story might have been different. Instead, in the words of Orthodox scholar Elizabeth Prodromou, "Washington's ideological and geostrategic map of Cold War Europe meant, at the very least, the implicit political and cultural identification of Orthodoxy with an eastern, communist-totalitarian Other."[9] Indeed, one of Michael's early successes was to drive home the idea that Greece was part of the Western world and the anticommunist alliance. His task was made easier by recent events—Greece's bloody civil war in which the communist side had been defeated with US help, and Greece's subsequent pro-Western moves, including sending troops to fight in the Korean War in 1950 and joining the NATO alliance in 1952, while its conservative governments espoused fervent pro-American and anticommunist positions.

Reward for Michael's staunch anticommunist stance came when President Eisenhower attended the Clergy-Laity Congress held in Washington in 1956 and invited Archbishop Michael to offer a prayer at his second inauguration in 1957. During the Clergy-Laity Congress, Eisenhower and his wife, Mamie, participated in the laying of the cornerstone of the city's Saint Sophia Cathedral. They took part in a service at which the archbishop officiated, and at the conclusion both the president and the First Lady received the Golden Cross of St. Andrew, the highest award that the Greek Orthodox Church awards to laypersons. And on January 21, 1957, Michael became the first Orthodox hierarch to take part in the inaugural ceremony of a president by delivering a prayer. He was one of three religious leaders who participated; the other two were from the National Presbyterian Church in Washington and the Jewish Theological Seminary of America. It was a rare case of Protestant-Orthodox-Jew.

Eisenhower's gestures of recognition of the Greek Orthodox Church continued Truman's use of Greek Orthodoxy as a weapon in the Cold War. Early in Eisenhower's administration the National Security Council warned that the Soviet government completely dominated the Russian Orthodox Church and was making inroads with Orthodoxy throughout the Eastern Mediterranean. The memo addressing this situation noted that both Athenagoras and the "Orthodox community" in the United States could be relied on to offset that influence. The government's "Psychological Strategy Board" produced a program for supporting the Orthodox Church. The program's contents remain classified, but according to William Inboden's study of religion and foreign policy, it encompassed several countries and, coordinated by the CIA, the Pentagon, and the State Department, was designed "to bolster anti-communist leaders within the Church, likely including significant financial support."[10] Whatever the case may be, Eisenhower's acceptance of the invitation to attend the Clergy-Laity Congress and then his inclusion of the archbishop in his second inauguration were invaluable gifts to the Orthodox Church in America.

The Archdiocese and the Community

The increase in wealth and social status of the Greek Americans was encouraging for the archdiocese and Greek Orthodoxy, but the parallel process of Americanization threatened to diminish any advantages, and this posed challenges to the new archbishop. But even before the church confronted the perennial problems of language and education and ties with the homeland, it addressed two more mundane but crucial issues: strengthening its control over the parishes, and raising more funds through increasing their contributions. The agendas outlined in the three clergy-laity congresses held between 1950 and 1954 reflected the archdiocese's plan to continue the transformation of local community organizations into parishes and thus place them under the church's central control. It was in a sense a reinforcement of the measures Athenagoras had introduced in the 1930s.

There was always that feeling that greater assimilation might bring "congregationalist" democratic tendencies, and that had to be avoided at all costs. Concerns about what assimilation would mean for the cohesion of Greek Orthodoxy were pronounced in the early 1950s and would also influence other issues the church had to deal with, particularly the language problem. Next to tightening up the administrative structure, Archbishop Michael introduced a dramatic increase in the dues each member of the church had to pay annually, from one to ten dollars. The need to substantially improve the church's educational infrastructure, including provisions for the training of priests, was the primary reason given for the steep rise in dues.

The original centralization plan introduced in 1931 was represented in the articles of the constitution and a separate set of regulations. At the Clergy-Laity Congress of 1950, the archdiocese presented a new, expanded version of the constitution, which incorporated several of the clauses of the regulations governing the parishes, in an attempt to give the centralization project more legitimacy and sharper teeth. The amended constitution spoke exclusively of a religiously based association of Greeks in America in which "community" would now mean ipso facto religious, or rather parish, community. Now one could refer, for example, to the Greek "community" in Chicago meaning all the Greek Orthodox who belonged to its various parishes, and the term "parish" would indicate those belonging to one of the city's local churches. There was even more specificity: "Believers or Members, in a wide sense, shall be all Christians without restriction of age, sex or race, duly baptized according to the Eastern Orthodox Church's Rite and in good standing with the said Church."[11] The other major administrative step Michael took, raising individual annual dues to ten dollars per family (the "dekadollarion"), a tenfold increase, caused great consternation, and it took almost a decade to be implemented properly in all parishes, but it ultimately bolstered the archdiocese's finances.

The need to increase the monetary contribution of the church's membership brought a public recognition of the role that women members played in raising funds. More often than not, women were the unsung heroes of parish life, excluded from holding office on the boards but making a significant contribution through organizing fund-raising bazaars and social gatherings, as well as cultural events that were also fund-raisers. In this instance, the executive committee of the Philoptochos immediately appealed to all the local organizations to begin working in order to raise the additional funds the ten-dollar contribution required. Michael recognized their role and encouraged them to become even more involved in the church's affairs. And it was his decision that the Ladies Philoptochos hold its first national biennial congress in conjunction with the church's thirteenth Clergy-Laity Congress held in 1956 in Washington, DC. Previously, the Ladies Philoptochos had sent representatives to the clergy-laity congresses and had convened national assemblies separately. In recognition of its importance to church life, the Ladies Philoptochos had earned the right to hold its own congress. As the archdiocese's press release announcing both congresses mentioned, "The Church can only progress with the active participation of the entire Greek congregations in America. The Greek Orthodox Church is in a critical period of development and needs the united support of all its communicants."[12]

There were other signs that the role of women in church affairs was gaining public recognition in the 1950s. In 1954, Bishop Athenagoras Kokkinakis, whom Michael had entrusted with overseeing Orthodox affairs in the western United States, visited Las Vegas to discuss the establishment of what would be the first Orthodox church in the region. The bishop requested that women participate in his meeting with the Orthodox faithful and convinced them that the most effective first step in the process of establishing a church would be to organize a local Ladies Philoptochos chapter.[13]

In addition to raising funds internally, the Greek Orthodox Church benefited from donations from other Greek American organizations, yet another sign of its growing stature with the ethnic community. In the early 1950s the United States began admitting victims of the world war—"displaced persons"—from Europe, including Greece. Among the arrivals from Greece were a number of orphaned children, and the obvious place to settle at least some of them was the church's St. Basil Academy in Garrison, New York. AHEPA was instrumental in getting the US government to agree to the admission of the displaced Greeks, and it also assumed the responsibility of contributing funds to St. Basil's orphanage and school. This was the beginning of a long association of St. Basil's with AHEPA, which resulted in the building of a dormitory, the AHEPA Hall for Boys that opened in 1959, followed by the opening of the AHEPA School for Boys and Girls in 1962. The attendance of church and AHEPA leaders at the opening in June underlined the growing confluence of the two institutions. Taking into account the funds for both the hall and the school, AHEPA's total contribution to St. Basil Academy had reached $335,000.[14]

Religiosity and the Official Recognition of Orthodoxy

The Greek Orthodox Archdiocese was not in a great hurry to become part of an expanded Protestant-Catholic-Jewish constellation. It did not want to risk having Greek Orthodoxy absorbed into a bigger, inchoate whole. There was always the danger that members of this relatively small church could be enticed away by bigger and more influential churches. At least one encyclical issued by the Greek Orthodox Archdiocese in the 1950s warned that Episcopalian ministers had taken advantage of the close relations between the two churches and persuaded several young Orthodox to become Episcopalian.[15]

There were efforts on the part of the church and its members to connect Orthodoxy to the burgeoning religiosity in America. Archbishop Michael frequently referred to America as a Christian nation. Leading laymen also played their role. One of the earliest, fullest statements connecting Americanism with Orthodoxy came from Spyros Skouras. The president of Twentieth Century Fox, who had played a leading role in the Greek War Relief Association in the 1940s, had remained involved in the archdiocese's affairs, and he addressed the Clergy-Laity Congress in 1950 in St. Louis, the city where he had begun his successful career in the film business. As a private individual involved with domestic and international affairs, Skouras sat on the boards of Catholic and Jewish organizations and thus had seen the tri-faith alliance work in practice. Speaking in English, Skouras opened by saying, "We are meeting here to cope with problems which are peculiar to the Greek Orthodox Church. But we are meeting primarily as American citizens, who cannot be unmindful of the crisis that confronts western civilization. . . . All the world is in a state of fear and insecurity because of the heathen philosophy that has risen up in Moscow to plague humanity and threaten freedom." And then he referred to the significance of religion: "The Church has always had a restraining influence upon those who break the rules of human conduct. But for Christianity and Judaism, and the other great religions, which accept man as a kindly, considerate creature, this would be a chaotic world indeed. The Greek Orthodox Church has played a classic role in fulfilling its moral responsibility." And in underscoring the connections between Hellenism and Christianity, he added, "The Greek language and the Greek philosophy and Greek culture expounded by men like Socrates, Plato and Aristotle, prepared the Greek mind and the Greek conscience for Christianity. When our Lord,

Jesus Christ, came into the world, all of this background of Greek morality was a great benefit to Christianity and an impetus to its development
throughout the world."[16]

The rise of religiosity in the postwar era also brought unsolicited recognition to Greek Orthodoxy in America. The archbishop was invited to speak
on CBS Radio's *Church of the Air* program, a weekly religious broadcast that
had begun in 1931. By the 1950s it was featuring broadcasts from representatives of many different denominations. Speaking from Pittsburgh on December 31, 1950, Michael delivered a sermon titled "The Efficacy of Christian
Virtue and Prayer in the World Today," which was followed by songs from
the choir of the city's St. Nicholas parish. It was the first time that a representative of the Greek Orthodox made a national "coast-to-coast" radio broadcast to American listeners. Michael's sermon was focused on the significance
of Christian faith and love in the context of current world affairs, and it
included two lines from the scriptures in Greek; but overall it was a sermon
delivered from the vantage point of an American Christian. He concluded
by saying, "We Americans take pride and comfort in the knowledge that our
nation is the bulwark of democracy and the arsenal of freedom throughout
the world. But we take greater pride and greater comfort in the realization
that ours is a nation of God and that its fortunes are entrusted to the steady
hands of men of God."[17]

The archdiocese also sought to use the climate of increased religiosity to
gain Orthodoxy official standing in the armed forces, as well as on a state-by-
state basis. Following a 1947 US Supreme Court decision putting an end to
the practice of states granting only certain religions legislative privileges, the
way was open for Orthodoxy to also gain public recognition. The initiative
to gain recognition of Orthodoxy by the US military began as the campaign
by a lay member of the Greek Orthodox Church, Nicholas Royce (who had
changed his name from Nicholas Vlangas), who had grown up in Pennsylvania, the son of Greek immigrants from Sparta. When he enlisted in the Army
in World War II, he saw that the "dog tag" identification that soldiers were issued designated only three religious identities: Protestant, Catholic, and Jew.
He began a one-person campaign to have his own and other major religions
also officially recognized by the armed forces and continued his effort after
the war, when the cause was picked up by the church and politicians. In the
mid-1950s the military eventually agreed to add "EO" for Eastern Orthodox
to the dog tag identifications.[18] Royce was honored by the archdiocese at a
later date. At the time, Archbishop Michael offered thanks and described
the issue as "so important in the life and the progress of our Church in the
freedom-loving land of ours."[19]

Orthodoxy's Youth Outreach

The beginning of Archbishop Michael's tenure coincided with the rise of the American-born Greek generation. This brought the first instances of intra-generational differences within the church. In one parish in Baltimore, for example, the arrival of a young American-born priest, Soterios Gouvellis, at the Evangelismos (Annunciation) Church galvanized the younger Greek Orthodox. Many parishioners liked his informal ways and liberal views, which contrasted with the conservatism of the senior priest, who was Greek born and much older. A bitter two-year intra-parish generational war broke out, until both priests were reassigned to other positions.[20] Gouvellis—"Father Sam," as he was known—would eventually be posted to a church in Birmingham, Alabama, where he became one of the few Greek Orthodox priests in the South who took a stand against segregation and for the civil rights movement (he would join Archbishop Iakovos at the march in Selma in 1965).[21] Father Gouvellis was an example of how the occasional young priest could have an impact, but more important, his experience in Baltimore demonstrated how the church had to take into account the needs of the young Orthodox.

Two major steps the church would take to adapt to the Americanization of the younger generation were the official introduction of English in the Sunday schools and the establishment of the Greek Orthodox Youth of America (GOYA), which used English as its official language. There were and would continue to be objections to the use of English in other spheres of church life, but in these cases nobody seemed to mind. The establishment of GOYA, originally proposed by the future Archbishop Iakovos when he was a priest in Boston, was the culmination of a process that had begun in the 1940s with the formation of locally based youth organizations. Michael Sotirhos, a leading GOYA member in the 1950s and its first treasurer, recalled that those local organizations formed citywide federations. He was president of the federation of New York that encompassed fourteen youth groups, while other such federations existed in Chicago and other midwestern cities and towns.[22] The formation of a nationwide organization under the aegis of the archdiocese was discussed at the 1950 Clergy-Laity Congress in St. Louis, and the next year sixty-one parishes sent representatives to Chicago for the founding conference. Most of those parishes were in fact from the Midwest—ten from Chicago and six from the rest of Illinois, five from Michigan, four from Indiana, and three from Iowa and Wisconsin. After another year of deliberations, GOYA held its first national conference in Washington, DC, in August 1952. President Truman sent them a message, as did Archbishop Michael, calling on them "to prove once again that we are worthy of the Greek Orthodox Church and the lofty and noble traditions of mighty and glorious America."[23] The archbishop took a special interest in the organization, and it flourished under his guidance, acquiring junior and senior sections based on age. Not all parish priests shared his enthusiasm, so in 1955 he issued a very strongly worded appeal expressing his deep sorrow at the apathy of some and exclaimed, "In the name of our Lord, my dear brethren let us review our stand and attitude toward the organization of our Junior and Senior G.O.Y.A. Indifference to this organization is indifference to our Church itself. . . . Those who have not displayed any interest or were not moved, so far, for the success of this organization should reconsider their attitude and approach to the youth."[24] The message had its intended effect. By the end of the 1950s, GOYA had reached a membership of thirty thousand, with 240 parish-based chapters, and had become "the most vital segment of the Archdiocese," with chapters in practically every parish community in the country. Appropriately, GOYA would honor Archbishop Michael by raising the $150,000 to build a chapel on the grounds of the theology school in Brookline, which was dedicated to him and to the Greek immigrants, the parents of the GOYA members who had built the foundations of Greek Orthodoxy in America.[25]

There were several young Orthodox who threw themselves into GOYA work with great enthusiasm. Ernest [Anastasios] Villas, born in Minneapolis in 1924 and a graduate of the University of Minnesota, was the first GOYA national chairman and became the organization's driving force. He had been the founder of one of GOYA's predecessors, the Upper Midwest Orthodox Federation, created in 1940. Like many other GOYA members, he met his future wife at a GOYA convention. Vickie (Vasiliki) Shuris, whom he met in 1954, would join him in the task of building the organization. And like many other GOYA members, Villas continued to serve the church, in his case by becoming director of the archdiocese's newly created Department of Laity in 1961. Other GOYA members would either become priests or prominent lay members in their parish. The organization's first decade, the 1950s, was its heyday precisely because those were the years when it was able to attract the American-born children of immigrants who otherwise might not have remained close to the church. It was a case of the archdiocese creating the right institution at the right time that employed the right approach to attract the young Americanizing Greek Orthodox generation. In a message to a regional GOYA conference held in Seattle in 1957, Michael said the organization, nationally and locally, had made great progress in the very few years of its existence and added, "Your period of trial is over. You are now established as a great organization, which is the hope and pride of our Greek Orthodox

Church, and an integral part of our beloved United States. You should be double proud that you represent both your noble Greek heritage and the aspiring idealism of America."[26] The 1960s would prove more challenging than the 1950s, as that decade brought much more serious issues for the younger generation. The concerns of the 1950s over such problems as "juvenile delinquency" (which Michael addressed in a message to GOYA in 1956) would pale in comparison with the challenges of the next decade and make GOYA's task of keeping the young close to the church much more difficult.

How Far to Go in Allowing English?

"The most difficult and perhaps the most dire problem that the Greek Orthodox Church in America will have to face in the coming years, by all evidence, will be the language problem," wrote Georgios Theotokas in 1954, reflecting on a recent visit to the United States. A distinguished Greek author, Theotokas was one of several leading Greek intellectuals who traveled to the United States with the help of politically motivated programs designed to familiarize influential minds in Europe with the United States during the early years of the Cold War. Most of them came into close contact with Greek Americans, and some of them expressed views about whether or not the church should allow English beyond its youth organization and its Sunday schools. Theotokas compared the state of the Greek language in America with that in Greece and found it lacking. "The Greek language is fading in the United States day by day, there is no point in denying it," he wrote, adding, "It is fading in all forms, it is losing its color, the richness of its words, its syntactical potential, but the church, continuing its centuries-long sacred and heroic traditions, is trying to save it and keep it somewhat alive." The ten or so day schools did a good job, according to Theotokas, but the rest of the Greek American community had to rely on afternoon schools, which focused exclusively on language, without, however, any great effectiveness; their staff was below standard, the instructional materials poor, and the children considered the experience of attending a burden that deprived them of their free time. Overall, Theotokas noted, a third of Greek American children received Greek language education, but most retained few of its elements. This assessment, based on a several months' stay in the United States, came from a relatively open-minded visitor from Greece and a friend of the church. Theotokas wrote admiringly about the architecture of some churches and the choirs of some parishes. Concerning the role of the Greek language, he encountered two opposing views: one that held that services should be performed exclusively in Greek, the other that some English needed to be introduced because a large number of the faithful did not understand Greek.[27]

Theotokas believed it was not for him as an outsider to take sides in the debate, but other visitors from Greece thought they should—and, oddly enough, some of them came out in favor of allowing the use of English. Vasilios Laourdas, a Greek academic who was a visiting professor at Georgetown University in the early 1950s, wrote a column in the *Ethnikos Kyrix* suggesting that the archdiocese should allow the use of English in churches or otherwise lose its influence. He feared that the growing assimilation of the Greek Americans and the serious weaknesses of the community's educational system meant that the insistence on preserving language as a way of preserving Orthodoxy was a losing battle. A decade earlier, another visiting Greek intellectual, Manolis Triantafyllidis, had been disappointed by the poor level of Greek language education but had not seen it as a threat to Orthodoxy. But it was one of Laourdas's main concerns, and he believed the introduction of more English would prevent the weakening of the church's influence. His views were challenged by another Greek-based intellectual sojourning in the United States, the writer Kostis Bastias, who had worked as the New York correspondent of several Athenian newspapers since 1946. Bastias also wrote a regular column in the *Ethnikos Kyrix*, and it was there he had a public exchange with Laourdas and vigorously defended the principle that the Greek language and Orthodoxy were intertwined. Members of the archdiocese senior staff, including Nicholas Vavoudis, the director of education, rushed to his support, contributing their own articles.

Archbishop Michael decided to enter the conversation. The archbishop agreed with Laourdas's point that Orthodoxy did not depend on the Greek language and that not only Greek speakers could be Orthodox. But then he embarked on a long explanation of how the Greek language had functioned as the tool through which Orthodox Christianity was promoted, especially in the hands of Saint Paul. He went on to discuss the significance of the translation of the Old Testament into Greek as a way of illustrating "the historic mission and unique position of the Greek language in God's plan for the salvation of humankind." The archbishop concluded that Orthodoxy survived and spread thanks to the Greek language and the Christian Greek spirit that transmitted the faith and Christ's teaching to the present-day Orthodox nations. And he posed the question: "If the Roman Catholics preserve the dead Latin language without that causing any decrease in the number of their followers, what should we do and how should we think about the Greek language in which the most beautiful, loftiest and most spiritual thoughts have been articulated"? Michael ended his article on a conciliatory note by acknowledging that the church was pragmatic enough to permit the sermon and Sunday school religious instruction in English, but it would never allow the divine liturgy to be performed in English.

The archbishop's intervention calmed the waters for the time at least. Laourdas wrote a letter, which Bastias hosted in his newspaper column, agreeing with Michael's pragmatism and calling for an end to the debate, acknowledging the archbishop should have the last word. But the debate was not over, and the archbishop soon found himself refuting the views of two respected figures, the Athens-based professor of theology Amilkas Alivizatos, and Archimandrite Ieronymos Kotsonis, the pastor of the royal palace in Athens and a future head of the Church of Greece. Alivizatos had visited the United States back in 1919 as a member of the Meletios delegation that helped establish the archdiocese. He had maintained an interest in Greek American affairs and especially the church and education. He had published two series of newspaper articles, in 1945 and again in 1949, in which he expressed pessimism about the potential of both the archdiocese's theological school and the St. Basil Academy, doubting that they would be able to produce a high level of priests and teachers respectively. In the articles published in 1949 he expressed the view that because Americanization of the Greeks was inevitable, the church should begin to use English extensively. After visiting the United States again in 1953 and in 1954, when he lectured on Greek Orthodoxy in Chicago, Alivizatos, in a small book published in Athens in 1955, repeated his views about the need for the church to use English much more extensively. "The language of the American-born Greeks is disappearing," he wrote confidently, "and the desperate efforts of the Church leadership to save it and Greek sentiments, are certainly quite laudable but are destined to fail. Its motives are sentimentally noble because it aims to educate by strengthening national traditions through the preservation of language. But," he added, "the language of the Americans of Greek descent is English," and therefore the Greek Orthodox Church had to use it in the liturgies and the sermons.[28] Alivizatos saw a future in which the alternative to complete assimilation and deracination of the Greek Americans was for them to retain their Orthodox identity through English and retain ties to the homeland as philhellene Americans. The theologian also noted that Orthodoxy, when it was transmitted to other countries beyond he Greek lands, had adopted the local language. He acknowledged that in the case of Orthodoxy in America, the church could not allow the wholesale introduction of English from one day to the next but that it had to be phased in. A more unyielding call for the introduction of English came from Archimandrite Kotsonis, who agreed with Alivizatos's views.

Archbishop Michael rebutted the arguments put forward by Alivizatos and Ieronymos in a thirty-one-page booklet, making a vigorous defense of the archdiocese's use of Greek. He dealt mostly with Alivizatos's essay, dismissing Ieronymos's claims because the archimandrite did not have direct knowledge of the situation in the United States. He also believed Ieronymos had seized on Michael's public admission that the numbers enrolled in the Sunday schools were not increasing in order to disparage the value and the potential of Greek language education. In dealing with Alivizatos, Michael accorded him the respect of citing each of his arguments and then carefully deconstructing them. He based his counterarguments on the contemporary demographic and cultural characteristics of the Greek Americans and on the religious significance of the Greek language. The Greek Americans, he noted, both clergy and laity, were in large part still Greek speakers, as were, naturally, those who were part of a recent stream of new arrivals. They all would find a switch to English disorienting, if not worse. Michael reminded Alivizatos that the Greek Americans were not foreigners, but of Greek origin. And as far as transmission of Orthodoxy in a different language was concerned, the Greek language, he went on to say, was the language of the scriptures and integral to the resonance of the Lord's words. And even though English could be used in sermons and in Sunday schools, it could never be used in the liturgy, where Greek was part of its very meaning. Michael pointed out that the Catholic service was performed in Latin, which none of the American Catholics used at home or anywhere else, and yet Catholicism was flourishing in the United States. That would all the more support the case for the Greek liturgy, since Greek was a living language. Finally, Michael cited surveys in a parish in Ohio and at a GOYA conference in which young respondents overwhelmingly favored the use of Greek in the liturgy.[29]

The debate on the value of the Greek language among learned clergy and laypersons tended to mostly overlook the views of parents and their children. Memoirs of Greek Americans offer insights on the ground-level conversations that went on in the community. The issue was not as black and white as might be assumed, given the popular scenario of parents insisting that the children should go to Greek school and the children finding it an unbearable burden. Aphrodite Matsakis, who went on to become an accomplished counseling psychologist, presents a mixed assessment of the Greek afternoon school she attended in St. Louis in the 1950s. She notes there was an egalitarian atmosphere in the school because it brought together the children of dishwashers and hotel owners, while the teachers did not care about who was from a wealthy or poor family and were concerned only with their pupils' handwriting skills, their knowledge of Greek grammar and history, and the respect they showed their ancestors and the teachers themselves. The most telling of all her memories is that the schools could be a haven for the children who had grown up in Greek immigrant households and had yet to become Americanized. "Despite all my complaints about Greek school," she writes, "it was fun being with children that looked like me and had long names like mine. In contrast, in American school, I often felt like an outsider."[30]

The Archdiocese and Greek National Issues

While some concessions were to be made over the use of English in church life, there was no relaxation of the archdiocese's efforts to keep Greek Orthodoxy closely connected with the homeland. In the early part of the decade, when Archbishop Michael underscored the common stance of the Orthodox Church and the Western allies in the Cold War, he also pointed out that Greece itself stood on the same side and used the opportunity to praise the homeland. Michael reminded the delegates to the Clergy-Laity Congress in 1952 that the children of heroic and glorious Greece, the sacred country in which democracy was born and "where hideous communism was crushed and buried," were also fighting against communism in Korea, side by side with the Americans.[31] Supporting the West in the Cold War was not only taking a stand with America but also a way of connecting with Greece. The archbishop had made the same connection in his first message to the clergy and laity. In offering thanks to President Truman for his interest and support of Greece during the civil war, he noted that at the same time "we have the saintly and sacred duty not to forget our Greek descent and nationality, or our Orthodox faith and Church," adding, "We have Greek nationality. We were born of Greeks. Through the blood that flows in our veins we belong to Greece, the cradle of civilization, the mother of freedom, the country that has always fought for the highest and most sacred ideals of the human spirit." Going on to praise Orthodox Christianity, Michael spoke about how the Orthodox do not criticize other churches or religions, nor do they proselytize, because that would go against Christianity's message of love, but that they practice their own faith through their lives, their study, and their prayer. Turning to the clergy, he exhorted them to instill in their parishioners the justified pride in their Greek descent and their Greek Orthodox faith.

The archbishop made sure that ties with the Greek homeland would remain strong during his tenure. Beginning in the early 1950s, he sent several messages urging members of the church to support charities engaged in postwar reconstruction in Greece; and in 1953 and 1954 he requested aid for the victims of earthquakes in several areas of the home country. Michael did not shy away from endorsing nationalist and political causes. In 1950 he took the unusual step of appealing to the members of the Greek Orthodox Church as well as to the American public in general to support the struggle of the ethnic Greeks on British-controlled Cyprus for the island's union with Greece. The appeal included sample telegrams to be sent to the president and the secretary of state. And the archbishop unfailingly produced patriotic proclamations every March 25, Greece's Independence Day, underlining the association with the Annunciation of the Virgin Mary celebrated the same day. And in an appeal for the return of Greek children removed from the country during the recent civil war, he sounded more like the leader of a Greek, rather than an American, church: "Greece appeals to the nations of the world to aid her in the repatriation of these children." The archbishop reiterated his political beliefs during his enthronement ceremony a few days later and added that religion was strengthening in Greece as part of the struggle against totalitarianism.

When Archbishop Michael arrived in Salt Lake City for the fourteenth Clergy-Laity Congress, he was in poor health, and he appointed his counsel, Peter Kourides, to be in charge of the procedures. Michael alternated attendance at the congress with rest in his room, though he addressed the grand banquet on the closing night, when there were almost a thousand people in attendance. He conveyed an ecumenical Christian message, saying "Our Church never felt it has a monopoly of salvation over other religions," and declared, "We must cooperate with other Christian denominations all over the world to settle social and moral questions." As he stepped down from the podium he paused as he passed the GOYA representatives and told them, "Look after GOYA." He left directly for the airport, where an army plane sent by President Eisenhower flew him to a hospital New York, where he was operated on for an intestinal disorder. He died there on July 13, 1958.[32]

The archbishop's decision to speak on the topic of ecumenism on what he may have suspected would be his last clergy-laity congress reflected a confidence in the state of Greek Orthodoxy in America. Michael had been an active contributor to debates over ecumenism earlier in his career—the urgent tasks he faced as archbishop in the 1950s had necessarily curbed his output on that issue, even though he continued to produce theological studies. His tenure in office had been taken up mostly by other issues, such as gaining greater acceptance and recognition for Greek Orthodoxy by the American mainstream, dealing with the challenges that assimilation presented (especially the language issue), forging close relations with the homeland, maintaining and enhancing the archdiocese's control over the parishes, and augmenting its educational institutions. By 1958 he could justifiably look back and see that a great deal had been achieved in all those spheres, and this freed him to talk about ecumenism, which among all the challenges the church faced was evidently a long-term one that would unfold very slowly into the future. Michael's successor, Archbishop Iakovos, wrote that Michael took over at the moment when Athenagoras had led the archdiocese "from childhood to adolescence and from adolescence to manhood," and he praised Michael for paving the way for the younger generation to take over.[33] To stay with Iakovos's metaphor for a moment, we can say that Michael's intangible achievement was to instill a sense of confidence and empowerment to the adult he led through the 1950s. Michael displayed a great deal of respect toward other Greek American institutions, and he lavished praised on AHEPA, GAPA, and the Greek American press. It was a sign of how confident he was that he could count on their support, and indeed all three responded by backing all of the archdiocese's projects, both with words and with deeds. The debate over the value of the Greek language also demonstrated the predominance of the church and Greek Orthodoxy in the life of Greek America. As Theotokas noticed during his visit in the early 1950s, the "defense" of the Greek language was being argued purely on religious grounds. All those arguing for the preservation of Greek—not only Michael, who was focused on the liturgy, but also all others who entered the debate—were focused on the language's significance in maintaining Greek Orthodox identity. There were virtually no voices within or without the community suggesting that the preservation of Greek could be of value as a secular tool, say of literature or as a means of maintaining political ties with the homeland. Greek language retention had become important primarily because it would help shore up Greek Orthodox identity. Greek Orthodoxy's transition out of adolescence also tells us interesting things about religion in the United States in the 1950s. The first is that the "Protestant-Catholic-Jew" model of understanding the relationship between Americanness and religion was not all-inclusive, that in fact it excluded several smaller religions, including all denominations of Eastern Orthodoxy. Notwithstanding the rise in religiosity, those smaller churches, such as the Greek Orthodox, had to actively seek acceptance into the mainstream. The Cold War, in the case of Greek Orthodoxy, provided crucial leverage through which the church strengthened its standing, certainly in the eyes of policy makers in Washington, DC. The second is that the postwar era of greater US involvement in world affairs also brought closer contacts with countries that were its allies; this brought mixed results for nationally oriented churches because it brought increased intervention from the homeland. In the case of the Greek Orthodox Church, this meant closer interaction with Greece—there was much less contact with the Ecumenical Patriarchate because the serious difficulties it faced in Istanbul—and Greek intervention was not always welcome. At a time of increasing integration of the Greek Orthodox into American society, the church had to find the right balance between Americanization and retention of ethnic characteristics that benefited religion—and outsiders, however well-meaning, could not appreciate the complexities of America's religious landscape in the 1950s.

CHAPTER 6

The Challenges of the 1960s

The cultural and social upheavals of the 1960s that affected all major religions in the United States also presented challenges for Greek Orthodoxy. There were declining levels of religious involvement, including church attendance, and fewer people believed that the influence of religion in America was increasing.[1] These trends were somewhat muted in the Greek church in comparison with other major Christian churches because of Eastern Orthodoxy's long-standing position that the ideal form of relationship between church and state is synergistic, which discouraged social activism from within the church's ranks. There was and still is a debate within Orthodoxy over whether the synergistic relationship was merely convenient in the past and has wrongly been assumed to be part of traditional practices, and arguments can be made that a more active stance on reforming society is closer to the true teachings of the church.[2] Nonetheless, a conventional wisdom favoring limited social activism certainly prevailed in the 1960s. But if doctrine, or rather a particular understanding of it, insulated the Greek Orthodox Church from the challenges to the status quo in American society rampant in the 1960s, the church was directly exposed to the continued assimilation of the Greek Americans, along with the proportional increase of the American-born second and third generations.

In an article published in a major Orthodox theological journal in 1961, a Greek Orthodox priest noted, "The threat of assimilation for the Orthodox communities in the United States is, indeed, a very real one."[3] And assimilation, in turn, brought the culture wars more sharply in focus for the church's hierarchy, because "Americanization" at that particular juncture could also mean exposure to the fissures that Protestantism and Catholicism experienced in the wake of the social and cultural upheavals of the 1960s, as well as the emergence of the so-called new religions that were shaped by Asian philosophical concepts or a syncretism between religion and popular psychology, science, or mysticism.[4] The Greek Orthodox Church faced the need to make its presence felt at a time when its faithful were confronted with the dilemmas posed by the swirl of new ideas and values.

Fortunately for the church, Iakovos, who took the helm of the archdiocese in 1959 following the death of Archbishop Michael, was a gifted and visionary leader familiar with American society and also willing to take bold and even controversial initiatives. Born Demetrios Coucouzes in 1911 on the northern Aegean island of Imvros (Imbros; now Gökçeada and part of Turkey), he enrolled at age fifteen in the Ecumenical Patriarchate's Theological School at Halki; he took the name Iakovos when he was ordained a deacon in 1934. Iakovos had observed the community's steady assimilation firsthand, as he had already served in several posts in the United States. He had arrived in the United States at the invitation of Athenagoras and was ordained priest in 1940 in Lowell, Massachusetts. He subsequently served in several parishes, as assistant dean of the theological school, and as preacher at the cathedral in New York City, and from 1942 to 1954 he was dean of the Annunciation Greek Orthodox Cathedral in Boston. Along the way, he had earned a master of theology degree from Harvard Divinity School. Iakovos rose to prominence early in his career thanks to his strategic sense of how best to navigate the growing demands made on him by the church hierarchy. In 1950, newly enthroned Ecumenical Patriarch Athenagoras had identified him as the most suitable person to replace the director and reorganize the Ecumenical Patriarchate's seminary on the island of Halki (present-day Heybeliada). The Greek ambassador in Ankara reported to Athens that Athenagoras held Iakovos in the highest esteem, and everything had to be done to persuade him to take up the Halki position.[5] Greece's general consul in Istanbul, Michael Melas, also confirmed that he heard "good things about the Rev. Coucouzes." But Iakovos probably rightly thought that being tucked away in the patriarchate's theological school did not offer many prospects for the future. When his possible reassignment to Halki became public, an uproar of protest erupted among his numerous loyal parishioners, most probably orchestrated by Iakovos himself. Alexis Kyrou, Greece's Permanent Representative to the United Nations who was involved in the exchanges, explained in a message to Athens that the Greek Americans were displeased about losing Iakovos because "the rarity of educated clerics here in the United States is well known as is the need for able Bishops."[6] In the end, Iakovos remained at the cathedral in Boston. In 1954 Athenagoras named him as his personal representative at the World Council of Churches in Geneva. It was a much more senior and influential position than being dean at Halki, and Iakovos was happy to accept. He spent five years at that post, and in 1959 he became the first Greek Orthodox archbishop to meet with a head of the Roman Catholic Church in 350 years, visiting Pope John XXIII as a special emissary of Patriarch Athenagoras. By then, he was well prepared to take center stage as archbishop of North and South America.

In the wake of Michael's death, Iakovos was one of the favorites to succeed him as archbishop not only because of his abilities but also because he had already served in the United States. But another favorite was Metropolitan Meliton (Hadjis), who was senior to Iakovos and crucially a member of the Holy Synod of the patriarchate, the body that would elect the new archbishop, albeit under Athenagoras's guidance. Sending their "own man" over to America was an attractive proposition to many other synod members. Iakovos did have the edge in that he was much more aware and supportive of Greece's foreign policy issues. The Greek prime minister, Constantinos Karamanlis, wrote to Athenagoras and asked him to consider Iakovos's candidacy in light of the many issues of national importance that Greece would be facing in the near future. Iakovos's "abilities, moral standing and attunement to the nation," Karamanlis wrote, enjoyed the highest regard and the complete confidence of the government of Greece.[7] He could not have stated his position more strongly without overstepping the mark. Four decades earlier, the patriarchate's synod had elected Meletios Metaxakis as patriarch despite protests from Athens. But now, only four years after the anti-Greek pogrom in Istanbul, an already weakened patriarchate could not afford to alienate the Greek government. And yet, several hierarchs dug their heels in, and there followed a seven-month impasse, with Athenagoras unable to persuade them to abandon their support of Meliton. Having failed to achieve his goal through negotiation, Athenagoras exercised his right of dismissing members of the synod. He forced seven out of the twelve members to step down, tipping the balance in favor of Iakovos, who was duly elected on February 14, 1959. Years later Athenagoras would say that he believed at the time that Iakovos was the best person to lead Orthodoxy in America and that Meliton was the best person to uphold Orthodoxy's interests in Istanbul.[8]

Speaking less than two months after Iakovos's inauguration as archbishop (which took place six weeks after his election), the man who would serve next to him as his close confidant and legal adviser, Peter Kourides, echoed the general confidence Iakovos's past record inspired: "Though it is always difficult to foresee the future, it can be safely noted that no Archbishop in the Americas has ever come better prepared by training, education and temperament than Archbishop Iakovos. He has the great advantage that he has served amongst us, he knows our people, he knows our problems, and he is equipped to deal with them."[9]

In many ways, Iakovos's first decade represented both a new beginning for the Greek Orthodox Church in America and continuity with the past. Through the 1950s the church had worked diligently to consolidate its internal structures and its position as the most influential Greek American institution and to gain legitimacy in they eyes of the US government. In the 1960s, as Iakovos liked to say as often as possible, it was no longer an immigrant church; it had "arrived" and had every right to claim its place in the mainstream of American society. Iakovos liked to promote the idea of an Orthodox arrival in America. In an English-language volume of essays that Iakovos commissioned in 1964 to mark the centenary of the establishment of the first church in New Orleans, Walter Wiest, a professor at the Pittsburgh Theological Seminary, wrote in the opening essay that his purpose was to voice "the greetings of fellow Christians to the Greek Orthodox people" and went on to explain that Greek Orthodoxy had gone unnoticed until then by most Americans.[10] Yet the Orthodox Church under Iakovos was going to show it had arrived and was going to return that greeting without abandoning its ethnic characteristics, especially the use of the Greek language in its liturgy and the promotion of Greek education. Navigating between an opening up to America while preserving the uniqueness of the church was not an easy undertaking, but Archbishop Iakovos was not one to doubt his own abilities or shy away from challenges.

Iakovos's inauguration ceremony took place on April 1, 1959, and it was fittingly impressive for a prelate who would soon display great leadership and initiate an opening up of the church. On that day, he entered Holy Trinity Cathedral on Seventy-Fourth Street in New York City in the presence of three thousand worshippers. He was surrounded by a procession of 250 persons that included 25 black-robed bishops of the Greek, Albanian, Armenian, Carpatho-Russian, Romanian, Russian, Serbian, and Syrian Orthodox Churches, as well as the Coptic and American Protestant Churches.[11] Among them were the elite of the Greek American community. It was a glorious occasion, and it reflected the growing status of the Greek Orthodox Church and the new archbishop's popularity. A wide-held conviction that Iakovos was the personal choice of Ecumenical Patriarch Athenagoras, whom he had served under as archdeacon, strengthened the sense in the community that the archdiocese was destined to play an important role not only in the Americas but also globally.[12] George Cornell, who served for decades as the Associated Press's religion editor, described the new archbishop as "a tall handsome man of 48" and wrote admiringly that Iakovos "personifies some of the distinctive qualities of his Church—qualities that are giving it increasing impact and esteem. Like the church, he is urbane, cheerful, learned, cosmopolitan, warm-hearted, tolerant and immensely confident. . . . Archbishop Iakovos' conversation sparkles with scholarly references and homey anecdotes. He is genial, informal with an easy smile."[13] Soon Iakovos was also recognized for much more: his forceful leadership that made him architect and engineer of the church's exponential growth over the next three and a half decades, which he oversaw with a combination of authoritarianism and charisma.

Americanization in the 1960s

The Greek Americans constantly agonized about their survival as a community and the preservation of the Greek language, viewed as always as the litmus test of a continued Greek existence. Veteran journalist Demetrios Callimachos, who as parish priest in Brooklyn had been present at the founding meeting of the archdiocese in 1921 and was in his eighties when Iakovos became archbishop, led the charge by launching a public campaign lamenting the state of Greek education in America.[14] Others defended the efforts of Greek-language schools, but both critics and defenders of the schools were well aware that the use of Greek was declining and that the move of many to the suburbs was diluting the compactness and cohesion of the community. The 1960s was an era in which the second and third generations, the children and the grandchildren of the Greek-born immigrants, were reaching their prime in terms of age and place in society. The Greek-born generation was slowly disappearing. The remaining prominent foreign-born Greek Americans had arrived as children, and gradually the American-born were supplanting them, and several were being elected to public office. In 1958, John Brademas became the first Greek American to be elected to the US Congress since the era of mass migration had begun. There had been an increase in emigrants from Greece, such as "displaced persons" and relatives of those already settled, but overall the community leadership was made up of the American born. According to the US Census, the number of native-born (in the United States) persons of Greek parentage stood at nearly 220,000 in

1960, an increase of 25,000 compared to 1950, and almost 60,000 compared to 1940.

Mixed marriages continued to be one of the clearest indications of increased assimilation. In 1959, the church began recording the number of these mixed marriages, comparing them to the number of intra-Orthodox marriages. That first year of recordkeeping indicated the number of mixed marriages was about 10 percent that of the total intra-Orthodox marriages, but the numbers of mixed marriages would increase steadily over the next years. For example, the archdiocese reported to the Clergy-Laity Congress of 1964 that of a total of 7,165 marriages performed by the Greek Orthodox Church the previous year, 28 percent were interfaith marriages (1,079 with Catholics and 905 with Protestants). By 1968, the numbers of intra-Orthodox and mixed marriages were roughly the same.[15]

The 1960s also transformed the Greek American community's geography, and this in turn created a new type of parish that no longer benefited from being located in an urban ethnic enclave. Upward social mobility meant that the Greek Americans, like many other white ethnics, chose to move away from the inner cities, and this generated a different type of suburban Greek Orthodox parish, one conscious of its privilege and social class and in many cases less beholden to the church's central authority. Many new and prosperous congregations came into being in the suburbs of cities such as Baltimore, Boston, Chicago, New York, and Philadelphia; their new environment made them very different from the older parishes that had benefited from the cocoon of their ethnic urban enclave. The new, suburban parishes, "especially those whose membership was composed overwhelmingly of third- and fourth-generation Greek Orthodox and many proselytes, became more cosmopolitan and socially involved."[16] The new parishes required the archdiocese's special attention to their suburban needs, from bigger parking lots to more concerted efforts to draw in parishioners who were much more geographically dispersed. These new suburban or even exurban parishes began appearing across the country. The chronology of appearance of new parishes in suburban Long Island through the mid-1960s typifies the trend. Before 1959 there were three parishes in existence: St. John in Blue Point, founded in 1942; St. Paul in Hempstead, 1950; and St. Paraskevi in Huntington Station, 1956. Their number doubled in the space of five years, from 1959 to 1964, with the establishment of the Assumption Church in Port Jefferson Station, in 1959, and St. Nicholas in Babylon and St. Demetrios in Merrick, both in 1961.[17]

In some cases, the church building relocated to the suburbs even though many parishioners were still left in the original location—needless to say, an unpopular decision. The decision to move the Annunciation Church from downtown Philadelphia ten miles north to the suburb of Elkins Park caused great consternation among the church's female parishioners. Two hundred women held a sit-in, which they described as a vigil, in the original building, and threatened to remain there until the archbishop reversed the decision to close it down. The church nonetheless moved to Elkins Park, but the incident remains a rare example of women's mobilization over issues of faith and community in opposition to the hierarchy.[18] Locally based issues had that effect on the women of the parish, while Orthodox women in general were not as active over the issues of discrimination and inequality that were a cause for mobilization in the major denominations in the 1980s.[19]

The spread to the suburbs in the late 1950s and early 1960s meant that opening more and more churches to reach the faithful became a permanent concern. According to the archdiocese's best estimates, there were 335 churches, with one hundred thousand members in good standing; and since only the head of the family counted as the paid-up member, the total active membership was closer to half a million, or about half of the estimated total persons of Greek ethnicity in the United States. The archdiocese believed that of the rest, two hundred thousand attended church sporadically and did not join, and the remaining three hundred thousand were "totally lost," either because they did not live near a church or because "they have through choice or intermarriage voluntary withdrawn from our church."[20]

A Greek Orthodoxy Open to America

Iakovos confronted the Americanization of the Greek Orthodox in a variety of ways. His keynote speeches at the Clergy-Laity Congresses held in Buffalo in 1960, Boston in 1962, Denver in 1964, and Montreal in 1966 provide the clearest picture of the breadth and boldness of the policies he initiated. At the first two of those congresses, Iakovos affirmed of the value of Greek language education and called for an expansion of the church's educational mission. He also introduced a new set of regulations governing the archdiocese's relations with the parishes, which placed them under even closer administrative and financial control. Then, in Denver in 1964, he used the occasion of the centenary of the establishment of the first Greek Orthodox church in America to expand on a theme he had already touched on in the earlier congresses, namely that the Greek Orthodox Church was not an immigrant church. He said the church had to become open to American society, grapple with the cultural and moral issues swirling around it by underlining Greek Orthodoxy's attachment to traditional values. But he also decided to

allow the use of English in some parts of the Sunday liturgy as a way of ensuring that the Greek Americans who were growing less familiar with Greek
would not be alienated from the church's Greekness. But in 1966, the archbishop openly addressed the culture wars, staking out a conservative position, and he also criticized the more "irresponsible" protests against the war
in Vietnam. He was being liberal in terms of language use but conservative
in other ways that the Greek Orthodox related to American society. The reason was that Iakovos was well aware of the developments within American
Catholicism at the time. John Kennedy's election as president in 1960 and the
liberalization of Catholic life brought about by the decisions of the Second
Vatican Council that concluded its work in 1965 have been described as the
"de-ethnicization" of Catholicism or its emergence from a cultural ghetto.[21]
Different opinions over issues from birth control to the Vietnam War may
have divided Catholics as they did Protestants, but this did not necessarily
mean an overall weakening of a denomination or a diminution of its stature. But a relatively small church such as the Greek Orthodox may have suffered irreparably from too much internal dissent, so falling back on its ethnic
moorings was an obvious way to maintain its membership and its cohesion—
even if the church was going to make concessions toward "Americanization."

The choice of Denver as the venue of the formal call for Greek Orthodoxy's opening to America was appropriate in many ways, because the Greek
Americans in Colorado were representative of the distance the Greek immigrants and their children had traveled since the early twentieth century.
Hundreds of Greeks had gone to Colorado to work in the mines and the
railroads, and many of them subsequently filtered to the West Coast or the
American Southwest. Those who remained—there were over one thousand Greeks in the state in 1940—and especially their children, gradually
made their way into less strenuous jobs as shop owners and white-collar
professionals. In 1960 there were over fifteen hundred Greeks in Denver,
most of them members of their parish, the Assumption of the Virgin Mary,
which had been established in 1906. The church ran two afternoon language
schools, two Sunday schools, a youth organization, and a women's Philoptochos charity organization. It was typical of the many parishes dotted across
America where the early settlers had survived and flourished.

Evoking that trajectory, Iakovos spoke of the church being on the threshold of a new era that made it imperative to look ahead to new challenges.
The recent past, he told delegates, had been consumed by the need to bolster
the organizational structure of the church to ensure its survival. The numbers indicated that the existence of the church was assured and that it was
growing. Over the previous two years the number of heads of household

registered as members of the parish communities had risen to 91,100, the establishment of 14 new parishes brought the total number to 424, the number of priests had grown to 525, and the archdiocese's income had reached $1,847,248. But the church was not only an organization, he stated; it was also the body of Christ, and most forgot this and considered themselves as members of a community and talked about rights, not about the responsibilities they had as members of a church. And the new era that lay ahead of the church, Iakovos said, entailed an engagement with American society: "Our Church has to move out of the margins and on to the arena of American life. To work, to struggle, to develop its spiritual life, to take its place among the other Churches as a living entity, active, bold, ready to shoulder its responsibilities and eager to make sacrifices."[22] The archbishop then became specific, explaining that a church of the future should not spend its time on mundane matters such as payment of dues, parish boundaries, uniform regulations, irregularities in elections, and local interests. "A Church of the future should engage in different issues of central importance, the marriages that take place outside the Church, fluid Orthodox conscience, pantheistic or pan-religious syncretism, the superficial sense of Orthodoxy, the secular spirit, the dissolution of morals, fraud, crimes against children." And he concluded this list of social ills by adding the need to raise the spiritual level of the faithful. The church spent too much time instead on less substantial things, he said, and quoted Matthew 23:23: "Woe unto you, scribes and Pharisees, hypocrites! For ye tithe mint and anise and cumin, and have left undone the weightier matters of the law, justice, and mercy, and faith: but these ye ought to have done, and not to have left the other undone." Iakovos went on to speak about it being time that the church heeded God's messages and the needs of the times. He was referring to the means through which the church would address those big social issues. The church, he said, needed major educational and philanthropic institutions, its own radio and television programs, a publication read by all Greek American families—the church had not properly weighed the significance of the Greek press and books in the preservation of its spiritual heritage. He concluded by proclaiming that the church's roots went back deep into history, but it now had to make history by confronting the future.[23]

Iakovos's 1964 speech was a call to arms, an exhortation aimed at guiding the Greek Orthodox Church into the mainstream of American society. His view was that the church should engage with the issues of the day as a way of retaining the involvement of the Greek Americans who were inevitably being drawn into those debates. He reiterated his exhortations at the following Clergy-Laity Congress, held in Montreal in 1966, telling delegates that "since we are living in an extremely revolutionary era which is toppling everything ranging from knowledge and methodology to popular faith and morals, we should not delay in reassessing our Christian values and beliefs . . . that is the revolution that Christ himself proclaimed." The functioning of local Greek Orthodox communities in the United States, Iakovos averred, reflected the spiritual crisis of the times and was characterized by a low morale and lack of intellectual vigor. The community was not considered a community of faith, of intellectual pursuit, of religious vision and moral obligations. It had turned toward secular, inward concerns, he implied. Iakovos spoke about the need to enact a revolution internally as quickly as the external revolution was taking place, the goal being a resurrection, a world of a new life, a world of a new faith, a world of light, and this was the only guarantee that the Greek Orthodox could avert degradation and the dangers of dissolution as a church and as a race and a people of God.[24] Iakovos was reassuring his audience that Greek Orthodoxy could respond to the crisis and social upheavals of the times through a reawakening and renewal. His words echoed those he uttered at the previous clergy-laity congress, when he urged the Greek Orthodox to look to the future and to engage with the wider social issues outside the confines of the church and the ethnic community. At the core of his message was the need to cultivate and strengthen a Greek Orthodox conscience, to thrust the church among other churches in America, as one possessing its own identity, tradition, and life.

The Archbishop Goes to Selma

Iakovos was photographed next to numerous world political and church leaders during his long tenure as archbishop, but the most iconic of those images shows him standing next to Martin Luther King Jr. on the steps of the courthouse in Selma, Alabama—it appeared on the cover of *Life* magazine on March 25, 1965, to the surprise and even horror of most Greek Americans. From the time the popular weekly magazine had appeared in 1936, its iconic single-photograph covers had featured very few religious leaders. Aside from the popes, who had appeared three times, evangelist Billy Graham had appeared twice and Cardinal Spellman, the Catholic archbishop of New York, once.

The image conveyed in a most dramatic way Iakovos's determination that the Greek Orthodox Church engage with the burning issues of the day in the United States. Against the wishes of his closest advisers and indeed the sentiments of most Greek Americans, including the community leaders, the archbishop had taken the brave decision to respond to King's invitation and take part in the civil rights demonstration in Selma. In the process, Iakovos demonstrated how committed he was to take the Greek Orthodox Church in a direction that would ensure it became a living part of American society. A year earlier, the Archdiocesan Council, the archdiocese's governing body, had produced a statement supporting racial equality, and then, at Denver, Iakovos publicly praised President Lyndon Johnson's signing of the Civil Rights Act, which outlawed discrimination on the basis of race, color, religion, or national origin. The archbishop said it marked "a most significant milestone in our history and in the history of mankind" and brightened "the horizon of the world with the refreshing hope that justice and equality for all men regardless of race, color and creed, shall fill the hearts of all men."[25] No one within the church or the community objected to the archbishop's words, but they took a different view of his actions when he traveled to Selma to join King in March 1965. Iakovos regarded the civil rights movement as not only a social and political one but also a religious one, and he was cochairman of the National Council of Churches, which supported the civil rights movement. In 1963 the council had called on all Christian churches to acknowledge their sins of omission and move forward to witness their essential belief that every child of God is brother to every other.[26]

The Greek Orthodox Church had joined the Council of Churches—which brought together Christian denominations in the United States—when the council was established in 1950. Iakovos flew to Alabama on an airplane the council had chartered, and he participated in the second march from Selma on March 9 that dispersed peacefully at the Edmund Pettus Bridge where two days earlier, on "Bloody Sunday," the marchers had been violently attacked by the police. On the night of the second march, Rev. James Reeb, who had traveled from Boston and participated in the marches, was attacked by pro-segregation thugs and died two days later. Along with King, Iakovos spoke at a memorial service for Reeb. It was that day he was photographed with King on the steps of the courthouse in Selma. Iakovos spoke about the reasons he was participating in Reeb's memorial:

> I came to this Memorial Service because I believe this is an appropriate occasion not only to dedicate myself as well as our Greek Orthodox Communicants to the noble cause for which our friend, the Reverend James Reeb, gave his life; but also in order to show our willingness to continue this fight against prejudice, bias and persecution. . . . In this God-given cause, I feel sure that I have the full and understanding support of our Greek Orthodox faithful of America. For our Greek Orthodox Church and our people fully understand from our heritage

and our tradition such sacrificial involvements. Our Church has never hesitated to fight, when it felt it must, for the rights of mankind; and many of our Churchmen have been in the forefront of these battles time and time again.[27]

Those were fine words but not the whole truth. Iakovos had received threatening phone calls from Greek Americans at his hotel room during his stay in Alabama, and criticism within the community would continue long after his return to New York. It would continue after President's Johnson's speech to Congress a few days later in support of the Voting Rights Bill, in which Johnson quoted the famous civil rights movement cry, "We shall overcome," affirming his endorsement of its demands.

Where Iakovos could easily see the religious dimension of the civil rights movements, most Greek Americans saw a racial blacks-versus-whites divide and viewed the civil rights movement and their archbishop's presence in Selma with distrust if not downright hostility. Their response reflected the pattern of reactions of white ethnic Americans, who were enjoying their relatively recent acceptance by the WASP establishment coupled with their post-1945 upward social mobility. They regarded the civil rights movement with guarded suspicion, and the youth-driven rebelliousness and questioning of the status quo, including the sexual revolution, with more open resentment. Certainly many, if not most, Greek Americans held negative views of black Americans and saw the civil rights movement as threatening their newfound middle-class security. There was roiling discontent among parishioners with Iakovos's bold move. Many Greek Americans, especially southerners, flooded the archdiocese with messages of denunciation.[28] Secure in the comforts of recently acquired prosperity and "respectability," many Greek Americans echoed White American aversion to the civil rights movement. Iakovos's embrace of Martin Luther King Jr. made them angry and embarrassed. The prewar depictions of Greeks as nonwhite and the attacks of the Ku Klux Klan on the Greeks had been conveniently forgotten.

Faced with this outburst, the archdiocese drafted a special set of instructions to the clergy to help them portray the archbishop's actions in a positive light. The text stated that the archbishop traveled to Selma because he felt that was what his people wanted to do, and went on to state that Greek Orthodoxy stood for "justice, freedom and equality for all." To drive home the character of the civil rights struggle, the statement added that the situation in Selma reminded the archbishop of the Greek struggle for freedom from the Ottomans. And it brought to mind the noble words of the philhellenic poet Lord Byron, who fought on the side of the Greeks and who died as a champion of Greek freedom. Iakovos recalled the words in one of Byron's last poems: "The land of honorable death is here—up to the field and give away thy breath."[29] If some Greek Americans would not see the civil rights movement through a religious lens, maybe they would warm to it if they saw it as a struggle of the oppressed, like the Greek fight for liberation from Ottoman rule.

Moral and Social Issues

The Greek Americans who considered themselves as belonging to the established mainstream of American society were relieved to see the archdiocese come out in support of the war in Vietnam and had harsh words for the antiwar movement. In the discussion about "World Peace," the Committee on Moral and Social Issues at the Clergy-Laity Congress of 1966 affirmed that

> the eternal commitment of the Greek Orthodox Church to the cause of world peace will not permit it to ignore the suffering and oppression of our fellow-men and therefore wholly supports America's commitment to the pursuit of peace in Vietnam. We deplore however, such hypocritical acts of pacifism as draft-card burning and the evasion of military service, for we affirm that freedom is not and has never been totally free. The preservation of our cherished rights and liberties requires the solemn obligation and duties of citizenship among which the Church recognizes as most important, the service to and defense of the country in time of need.[30]

There was also a resolution that expressed the church's wholehearted support of the United States' stand against "all aggression, particularly in Vietnam." The minutes report it was passed—apparently unanimously—though no floor debate was allowed.[31] Following the statement on the Vietnam War, the committee issued statements on several contemporary social ills, yet another demonstration of the archdiocese's wish to engage with the world beyond the parish's boundaries. They began by addressing "moral disintegration," defined as the rise of materialism, the breakdown of family life and the failure of parents to provide proper leadership for their children, and crime and juvenile delinquency. This all meant, the committee suggested, that church members should strengthen the inherent Greek Orthodox family structure that emphasized "self-respect, discipline, pride, obedience, and respect for authority." The archdiocese also called on parishes to observe Law Day on May 1, and, paraphrasing Abraham Lincoln, stated "let reverence for the law become the political religion of the nation." The pairing of Greek Orthodox

family values and the words of a president who had been in office decades before mass migration from Greece reflected the archdiocese's determination
to enter the American mainstream. The archdiocese also decided to establish
a Department of Social Action and recommended each parish form a social
action committee to address those areas of social concern.[32] The call for such
committees suggests that these social ills affected the Greek Orthodox community in North America, although the way these were discussed was very
general, and reading through the clergy-laity materials begs the question of
whether all those problems affected society in general or the Greek American
community in particular. There was reference to disintegration of the family
among the community, "the denial of Greek Orthodox family traditions and
a lack of loyalty and concern for the home by members of the family." And
there were specific recommendations to parish priests to help them prevent
divorces, which extended to appealing to Greek lawyers in major cities and
generally adopting a more "austere" approach to requests for divorce.

The Clergy-Laity Congress formally constituted the "United Greek Orthodox Charities" modeled on the Church World Service (a charity representing several Protestant and Orthodox churches in the United States), the
Catholic Relief Services, and the United Jewish Appeal. Iakovos named Spyros Skouras as the chair and Nicholas B. Macris of New York as president,
and they planned to raise $3 million to $5 million for hospitals, homes for
the aged, shelters for the poor, child education, and literature and the arts.
It was an ambitious agenda, and a symbolic one. The archbishop told the
New York Times, "This is a major step in the transition of Orthodoxy into the
mainstream of American life. . . . We recognize that as Greeks we have made
little contribution to the culture of America, but only taken advantage of the
opportunities this nation has offered."[33]

The Church and Greek Language Education

In his first Clergy-Laity Congress, held in Buffalo in 1960, Iakovos spent the
most time in his keynote speech addressing a topic always closely tied to the
opening (or not) to America: Greek language education. He invited the delegates to consider what would have happened to the Greeks during the time
they were ruled by the Ottomans if they had decided to become assimilated
linguistically, socially, and in terms of religion with the Turks, and then drew
the parallel with their own present situation.

> Would you ever wish that because of us there would be no Greek
> community or Orthodoxy in America? Of course you do not. And this

because we are Americans, by that I mean citizens of this country that has enormous admiration and respect towards Greece and Orthodoxy. We are also children of Greeks, the Greeks that brought over to America and honored the Greek name and Orthodoxy. So why should we disrespect our Greek descent and our Orthodoxy? We pose this question because we want this Congress to provide a dutiful answer: the answer that as long as it up to us, we will not become the gravediggers of Greek Orthodoxy; that we will not become the gravediggers of our fathers; that in contrast to all this we will foster as much and wherever possible, the resurrection of the meaning of Greek Orthodoxy. . . . If you want to know what the Archdiocese believes, listen to this: we proclaim Orthodoxy and Greece: the Mother of Churches and the Mother of letters, of arts and civilizations, and we proclaim Christ in the first language he was proclaimed: the Greek language.[34]

Language and religion were interconnected, according to the archbishop, because Orthodoxy was Greek. The ethnic character of the church enabled this reiteration of the significance of the language of the Old World because it was also the language of the religion. "It is Greek in spirit, in its intellect, its thought, its sensibility," he said, adding, "Orthodoxy and generally religion is one, but in practice it varies. Because religion is not dry dogma, it speaks to the spirit." Iakovos went on to acknowledge that the Catholic Church in America was reconsidering allowing English instead of Latin, but he suggested that would not have happened if the worshippers were only of Latin descent. And in any case, with thirty-five million faithful, the Catholic Church had nothing to fear. Instead, interfering with the original language would break up the Greek Orthodox Church, according to Iakovos. The reason was that the Greek Orthodox were a small minority in America. The community possessed "solidity" because there was a common sense of its Greek origins. But over time, he noted, this solidity would weaken, because the numbers of the Greek-born would decrease. And when the Greek language was not used anymore, and when the Greek Orthodox person did not feel the need to belong to an ethnic group, Iakovos asked, what would keep that person close to the church, if in addition the church became just any other church, without its own distinct features?[35] It was a rhetorical question, and Iakovos said he would not ask any additional ones so as not to fill his audience with pessimistic thoughts, and instead he returned to the need to improve education, the only means through which the church could be preserved in America. Observing the proceedings was G. D. Vranopoulos, the consul general of Greece in New York. In his report to the Ministry of Foreign Affairs in Athens, he remarked approvingly, "It is fortunate that His Eminence the Archbishop is fully aware of the national significance served by the intense cultivation of the Greek language and familiarization of the American-born Greeks with the classical tradition. . . . Despite certain objections, thanks to his undoubted prestige he will ultimately achieve the structural reform of all educational programs."[36] Also in attendance was the Greek consul in Boston, who had a less optimistic view. In his own report to Athens on the Clergy-Laity Congress of 1962, he observed that even though the congress's official languages were English and Greek, almost all the formal debate took place in English. And he worried that the overwhelming presence of second-generation Greek American delegates might mean there would be little interest and lukewarm support for promoting Greek-language programs.

But the practice of educating young Greek Americans in their ancestral language, everyone agreed, was becoming increasingly difficult. The Greek General Consulate in New York produced a report on Greek education in the United States in 1963 that typified the pessimism the Greek observers had about the community's educational program. The number of schools listed by the archdiocese, the report noted, was impressive, but the output could certainly be richer. Two reasons for this were the lack of funding compared to the needs, and the resultant lack of teachers. The lack of direct funding on the part of the community, despite the archdiocese's appeals, made the schools dependent on the local church and reliant on its surplus income, if any. There were other problems as well, as far as the consulate was concerned: teaching revolved around religion, and language instruction was based primarily on religious texts. Greek history and geography were inadequately represented in the curriculum. The school was the "Greek school," and it taught Greek, but "the Greek spirit" was absent. Many of the priests who acted as teachers were American born, as were many on the local parish school boards, and therefore the education offered was geared more toward "Greek Orthodoxy and less toward Orthodox Greekness." The report's conclusion was that the Greek state ought to stir itself and become more involved in Greek education abroad and provide the necessary funding.[37]

Church-sponsored education may indeed have been too religious according to the standards or the expectations of the Greek diplomats, who no doubt had the school curriculum in Greece in mind. But the church had nothing to fear; it was very unlikely that the government in Athens would devote any serious effort and resources to bolstering Greek education abroad. Historically, Greek governments expect the diaspora communities to contribute to the homeland, while the homeland's response has usually been limited to words, not deeds. The curriculum would therefore remain weighted toward religion, as was school life more generally, with the class starting with prayers, for example, and important dates on the Orthodox calendar being observed inside and outside the classroom.

Promoting Greek Orthodoxy through Language

Unencumbered by interference from Athens or by any serious objections from within the community, the archbishop decided to make allowances for the use of English in the life of the church, while doing all he could to bolster education as a means of preserving Greek Orthodoxy. In 1964 he announced that English could be used by priests for certain sacraments, namely certain prayers at baptism, the marriage ceremony, the service of betrothal, the funeral service, and also at the readings of the Epistle and Gospel. The reason was the great number of requests for some English by those entering the Greek Orthodox faith from other religions, especially through the growing number of interfaith marriages in the church. Out of a total of 7,165 marriages performed by the Greek Orthodox Church the previous year, 28 percent were interfaith marriages (1,079 with Catholics and 905 with Protestants).[38] The permission to use English in parts of the church services was a major step in acknowledging that the archdiocese had to adapt to the changing times when the understanding of Greek, not to mention its use, was declining. The move was potentially controversial, but the archbishop anticipated any complaints by the traditionalists and especially the Greek language media by reiterating the archdiocese's commitment to Greek language education. At the Clergy-Laity Congress in 1966, the Church and Education Committee made the core commitment to Greek as explicit as possible by issuing a statement that read, "The Greek language is rightly considered to be the principal means by which the Greek Orthodox culture and tradition can be transmitted. . . . The Greek School should be basically in all aspects dealing with the Greek education of a child. The Greek language introduces the child into the world of the Greek spirit, Greek ideals, Greeks Arts and Greek civilization."[39]

Iakovos outlined his views in a confidential report he sent to the Greek Ministry of Foreign Affairs with his thoughts on the state of the Greek American community. He made the connection between language and religion quite clear and suggested that among the younger generation, Orthodoxy (rather than a secularly defined Greekness) was becoming a form of identity. Thus, he continued, the erosion of Greek language use endangered not only "Greekness" but "Orthodoxy" as well. And the archbishop doubted that Orthodoxy "could be expressed authentically in English." To promote

Orthodoxy through Greek language education in an era of Americanization presented more and more challenges and absorbed more and more of the church's energies and resources. Iakovos outlined a five-point plan: the resurrection of Greek Orthodox consciousness even among those in whom it had withered; a reorganization of the day and afternoon schools on a Greek Orthodox basis and according to the directions of the archdiocese; the establishment of kindergartens and schools even when these would be attended by only five or six children; the prioritization of education expenditure in a community's budget (communities would model themselves on the archdiocese, which devoted three-fifths of its budget to education); and full moral and material support of the archdiocese from the communities. The program that grew out of this plan would unfold through successive stages that corresponded to the growth of each Greek American child. The first was the kindergarten; the second was the afternoon school that was easy to run and that every community should create; the third was the day school, which ought to exist in communities with over four hundred members; the fourth was the middle school (two were coming into being that year, at the Greek Orthodox Cathedral in New York City and at the St. Basil Academy); the fifth was high school (the aim was to create one in Chicago and another in New York); and the sixth and capstone of the process would be a Greek university associated with the theological school, a vision that was growing in popularity.[40] The entire program was a grandiose vision, typical of Iakovos's wish to take bold steps to expand the church's role and to make ethno-religious education the key to the future of Greek Orthodox and Greek American identity. Echoing the archbishop's optimism, the archdiocese's Education Office expressed the hope that improved Greek language education would help children go back to their families and make everyone speak Greek.

The decade that followed the Clergy-Laity Congress of 1960 witnessed the church's concerted efforts to implement the ambitious plan to expand Greek language education throughout the United States. It was not easy, despite the progress being made. Resource allocation and questions about how useful Greek would be in the long term were on the minds of many parishioners. In 1960 three newly established day schools, the Socrates school in Chicago and two in Manhattan parishes, St. Spyridon in Washington Heights and Sts. George and Demetrios in East Harlem, brought the total number of Greek schools in North America to twelve. All of them were in areas of high concentration of Greek immigrants: the greater New York area, Chicago, Lowell (Massachusetts), and Montreal. The total number of students was 2,138. There were 397 afternoon schools, with 7,306 boys and 7,482 girls. Two years later, at the Clergy-Laity Congress held in Boston, the archbishop noted that some parishes faced the dilemma of whether to devote funds to create a community center where social gatherings could be held, or use the available funds to establish a day school. Iakovos recommended that these be combined, and proudly announced that three more day schools had been established, in Brooklyn, Detroit, and Washington, DC. It would be commendable if others also took the "heroic initiative to break the bonds of small-minded accounting and fears and dig deeper in their hearts. . . . The thought that one day the Greek language would be replaced by the language of this country does not justify a defeatist attitude toward Helleno-Christian education and Greek American day-schools." Indeed, the day schools guaranteed the future of the Greek American community. He reminded his audience that the archdiocese assisted day schools annually with the symbolic sum of $3,000 and wished to help in any other way it could for those schools to maintain a high standard, follow the same curriculum, and share the same goals.[41]

The more the school program expanded, the greater the needs and the problems. In November 1962 the archdiocese's Education Office took stock of what had been achieved since the 1960 Clergy-Laity Congress where the archbishop had set out his ambitious plan. The numbers may have been up, but so were the obstacles in the way of making Greek language instruction effective. The gradual relocation of Greek American families to the suburbs created logistical difficulties; the unfamiliarity of teachers from Greece with Greek American life was another issue. The report identified four areas of concern with regard to parents: parents did not speak Greek to their children at home; parents did not let their children attend Greek school every day; children lived far away from churches and schools; the mothers in the parent-teacher organizations did not help because in many cases they wanted to run the school themselves. The solution to those problems, according to the Education Office, lay with greater engagement by the mothers, and it specified what had to be done in considerable detail. The mothers should be talking to each other, carpooling, organizing parties on every last Friday of the month so that the teachers, mothers, and children joined in song, games, and Greek-language conversation. Another recommendation was that the parish mothers could help out more with the kindergartens, not only by taking their children there but also by staying and playing and singing and speaking Greek. Several kindergartens, the report noted, had closed because mothers were concerned a Greek environment would slow their children's ability to learn English.[42]

The uphill struggle continued over the next few years, and the archdiocese kept on issuing recommendations about how to increase the numbers of schools and enrollments. The archbishop thought it important to produce a statement affirming the value of Greek-language-based Greek Orthodox education. At the Clergy-Laity Congress of 1966 in Montreal, the education committee's report endorsed Iakovos's ideas as a way of offsetting what it acknowledged were "the many and serious obstacles" in promoting Greek language education. The solutions were a more sophisticated administrative structure within the archdiocese, better organization, more suitable textbooks, closer monitoring, greater involvement on the part of families, and a more active role for the parish priests.[43] This new long list of remedies suggests the archdiocese may have underestimated the challenges of running day schools and had focused more on increasing the numbers rather than helping schools consolidate and gain acceptance in the community. In January 1967, on the occasion of the "Day of Letters" celebration—an annual event celebrating the Orthodox Church's three great hierarchs and ecumenical teachers, Basil the Great, Gregory the Theologian, and John Chrysostom—Iakovos acknowledged that the perpetuation of Greek in the United States required a concerted effort. He recalled that his predecessor, Archbishop Michael, had introduced the annual celebration of Greek letters in 1951, a time when there was great concern about whether the Greeks in America would be able to retain their Greek Orthodox identity. It may have been, he added, a measure designed to offset wrong impressions caused by the permission given to use English in Sunday schools the previous year. Then as now, his encyclical pointed out, the Greek Orthodox Church in America faced a huge problem of determining its spiritual identity. As the church became more "indigenous," he said, the greater the effort had to be to preserve the knowledge of the community's spiritual and national origins. This effort had borne fruit over the time that had elapsed since the Day of Letters was introduced: more and more Greek schools had appeared, even though Greek was spoken less than ever since the beginning of the big wave of Greek immigration at the turn of the century. Greek families faced growing pressures of assimilation, and the trend toward moving to the suburbs weakened the bonds of the once tightly knit Greek unit. Priests and teachers were doing their best to preserve Greek identity, but "the education of our children in the language of our fathers is a struggle, often uneven if not unrealistic. . . . We ask of our children to be educated in both Greek and English, fully and at the same time." So great were the problems, the archbishop said, that the archdiocese, which retained the major responsibility for the education of Greek American children, would accept the input of all those who wanted to study the issues facing Greek education—he mentioned the Greek language press and radio stations, as well as Greek American organizations such as AHEPA and GAPA. He offered no easy solutions but concluded by suggesting that the Greek language educational program would benefit if the community supported the Greek press and radio programs and programs promoting Greek and Byzantine arts. It was the first step toward envisioning the educational project in broader terms than merely language instruction, and a way of insulating it from the effects of Americanization.[44]

Archdiocese versus Parish

A consequence of archbishop Iakovos's ambitious programming was, in his mind at least, the need to strengthen the archdiocese's control over the parishes and their finances. The archbishop told the 1960 Clergy-Laity Congress he estimated that 393 community-parishes (95 percent of the total) had endorsed the successive measures introduced by his predecessors to effect greater control and yield more funding, leaving about 20 that had still not accepted the measures. Iakovos told the delegates that they should not dwell on the refusal of those parishes as much as notice "the distrust and negativity of the soul towards the Archdiocese. Maybe this phenomenon is because that some community leaders have not read the Constitution or because some parish communities have never been represented at Clergy-Laity Congresses." Many parishes had in fact accepted the tighter control but were not necessarily abiding by the rules, especially when it came to paying their dues to the archdiocese. Iakovos emphasized that the acceptance of the uniform regulations and constitution and their faithful implementation "would give the Archdiocese the prestige and the power you all wish it could possess. It would present itself as disciplined whole, which freed from small distractions would focus on more serious matters such as our place as a Church with recognized prestige, high educational level and influence in America."[45] Over the next few years the archdiocese would make every effort to incorporate the twenty or so outlier parishes, but with mixed results.

Iakovos exhorted the convocation at Buffalo to address more directly the serious financial issues the church faced due to the lack of incoming funds from the parishes. He began by gently criticizing the parishes for not paying their ten-dollar-per person dues to the archdiocese, a shortcoming that was widespread. This, he said, left the archdiocese unable to cover its monthly expenses, which Iakovos proceeded to list in some detail: $10,000 for the theological school, $7,000 for the St. Basil Academy, $40,000 for the Ecumenical Patriarchate, $10,000 for the Patriarchate of Jerusalem, another $10,000 for the teachers' pension fund, $40,000 for the clerics' pension fund, $5,000 to the Greek Orthodox Youth Association, $33,000 for the eleven day schools. The total was $155,000, and this did not include the salaries of the archdiocese's staff, the staff of the nine bishops, and the costs of publications and philanthropic donations. He concluded by saying that the archdiocese was considering a number of remedies, including the creation of a trust fund, but that in his view the solution was a transformation of the attitudes of parishioners toward donations to their churches and toward the archdiocese.

A survey conducted by one of the dissident parishes in 1961 indicated a much bigger proportion of parishes resisting the archdiocese's pressure. The idea of the survey was born of the polarization that divided the community-parish in Memphis, Tennessee, when it came to decide whether or not to accept the archdiocese's constitution and uniform parish regulations. The group that wished to retain local autonomy sent a questionnaire out to all Greek Orthodox community-parishes and received responses from 157. Of them, 83 stated they had adopted the new constitution and regulations, 22 replied they had adopted an earlier version, and, significantly, 52, or about a third of the total number of responding communities, reported they had not adopted the centralization plan.[46]

The case of the parish-community in Memphis illustrates the deep divisions that opened up in some community-parishes over the archdiocese's constitution and uniform parish laws and also provides us with a sense of why certain parishes resisted centralization. It is a story that historian Speros Vryonis Jr., who had grown up in the Memphis community and whose father was one of the leaders of those who rejected conformity with the archdiocese, has recounted in book-length form. Vryonis, with the help of records kept by the opponents of the archdiocese, documents the clash and polarization in the community over the constitution and the uniform parish laws. In the end the opponents were defeated and left the Church of the Annunciation, establishing their own independent community and church, St. George's, in 1962. The crisis in Memphis had broken out in the wake of Iakovos's call at the 1960 Clergy-Laity Congress for the outlier parishes to accept the regulations and uniform parish laws and reflected the wish of parishioners to instead run their own affairs. The community president at the time, Nick Capadalis, appointed a committee headed by Speros Zepatos, the owner of the Arcade restaurant in town, and tried to ensure a quick approval of the archdiocese's demands. But a group that included Speros Vryonis Sr. and Mike Zambelis (who would draft the questionnaire sent out to all community-parishes) opposed this move, and there followed a yearlong struggle between the two sides. The local priest, Nicholas Vieron, inevitably sided with those who supported the archdiocese. In his account, Vryonis explains how difficult it was for a local parish priest to go against Iakovos: "It would have taken a priest of consummate diplomatic skills to navigate between Archbishop Iakovos and the Memphis community in 1961, and it would have taken a priest of steel character to withstand the withering rage of a displeased Archbishop Iakovos. The Reverend Vieron was a good man, generally well disposed to all the members of his community, but he was placed in a situation beyond all the abilities and strengths of most ordinary mortals."[47] The conflict the Greek community of Memphis experienced no doubt was intensified, as are most local disputes, by personality clashes, but it primarily entailed a clash of principles over community and church relations, and it was played out elsewhere in the United States. In Vryonis's words, it was a conflict between "the older congregational spirit of the Greek-American communities, as they had historically evolved, and the centralization of ecclesiastical authority now being fervently pushed by Archbishop Iakovos, a prelate dominated . . . by a spirit of pure authoritarianism."[48]

Iakovos refrained from describing the dissident parishes as animated by a spirit of congregationalism, because he was also calling for the church to become more open to American society while retaining its ethnic character. Tellingly, Archbishop Athenagoras, who in the 1930s initiated the process of centralization at the expense of parish autonomy, had justified his moves as preventing the disruptive influence of Protestant congregationalism. But that was the era of what Iakovos would describe as the immigrant church. Now, in the 1960s, the church was opening up to America, but obviously not reconciling with "congregationalism." In Iakovos's view the transition from secular organizations running a church to parishes belonging to the archdiocese had happened organically, thanks to the inherent piety of the Greek Americans. "Our parishes," he said in 1968, "are the center of our total life—our family and social life, as well. . . . Our parishes began as organizations, and developed into religious communities. Today, they are Churches. Around them our whole life is entwined and is developed. . . . Quietly and subconsciously we have accepted that basic factor of life, that which the Apostle Paul stated with natural simplicity with the words: 'whether we live or die, we are the Lord's' (Romans 14:8). We are born and die in the bosom of the Church." And if the parish was at the center of Greek American life, it was of course also at the center of the preservation of Greek identity in America: "The Church is everything for us. Through the Church we endeavor to retain and develop and pass on to the future generations whatever we have received: religion, language, tradition, manners and customs, and whatever else is connected with or contributes to the fulfillment of the feeling of our common religious and cultural heritages."[49]

By the mid-1960s Iakovos was well aware that the church's central administrative body could not take for granted cooperation and support from the parishes. Of course, one damaging effect of troubled relations with any parish was delay or even withholding of their financial dues. In a move that demonstrated the archbishop's keen understanding of his fellow Greek Americans and the ways that the wealthy among them could be persuaded to make donations, he established an organization that offered membership to prominent lay members of the church. Officially named the "Order of St. Andrew of the Ecumenical Patriarchate" but known as "the Archons," it inducted members through Iakovos's awarding them one of many titles that the Byzantine church had awarded to worthy laypersons. It was a very clever way to reward contributors and in some cases at least also stroke egos, and it further strengthened the stature as well as the budget of the church. And it was historically well timed. This was the moment in which many Greek Americans had achieved upward social mobility and wealth. With that came the sense that they should be making philanthropic contributions, and in turn receiving some form of social recognition. The church was there to address those needs in a much better way than could any other Greek American organization.

The life of an ethnic church is isolated from the mainstream because of its inward focus, and that insulates it from wider social trends. Greek Orthodoxy stood to the side as the "sixties" swept through America, challenging the status quo. And the Greek Orthodox who had gained acceptance into the American mainstream relatively recently were not prepared to suddenly start criticizing what they had worked so hard to achieve. This enabled Archbishop Iakovos to advocate more steps toward the Americanization of Greek Orthodoxy while maintaining a conservative stance toward the various social movements in the name of preserving the church's ethnic character. The more the hierarchical and undemocratic structures of church life could be cloaked in the mantle of ethnic mores and age-old traditions, the less likely it would be that anyone from the within the church would come up with a version of Orthodox liberation theology.

The church was the only Greek American institution that was explicitly confronting this transition phase in Greek American life. The membership of GAPA, the organization that had favored retention of ethnic identity, had declined precipitously as its agenda was less and less appealing to the younger generation. AHEPA continued to be active and develop, but its members already considered that they had moved from being Greek Americans to being Americans whose heritage was Greek. This left the church to articulate the dilemma facing most Greek American Orthodox, which was how much of the homeland's culture they should retain, and how to balance it with the drift toward Americanization. Iakovos's vision entailed an ambitious agenda, and not all its projects went forward. An example is the outreach directed toward the other Eastern Orthodox Churches that was initiated through the establishment of the Standing Conference of Canonical Orthodox Bishops of the Americas (known by its acronym SCOBA) in 1960. It would not really gather momentum until much later. Issues such as the role of women also remained sidelined. The transition from an immigrant to an ethnic church was difficult to enact across the board, and Iakovos tried to steer the church in that direction and Americanize, but on his, and the church's, own terms.

CHAPTER 7

Greek Orthodoxy and the Ethnic Revival

When the phrase "it is chic to be Greek" appeared in the *New York Times* in 1975, the revival of white ethnic identity in America and especially Greek American identity had reached its apogee. This revival was a roughly decade-long phenomenon, a somewhat unexpected consequence of the success of the civil rights movement that legitimized the celebration of black identity. Southeastern European immigrants could now similarly claim pride in their own origins and ethnicity. In a polemical book published in 1971, author Michael Novak wrote provocatively, "Let us suppose that in the 1960s the blacks and the young had their day in the sun . . . and now it is the ethnics' turn. Perhaps the ethnics can carry society further, more constructively, more inventively."[1] The "ethnics" he had in mind were the Poles, the Italians, the Greeks, and the "Slavs." The new public respect for identity that the civil rights movement had generated allowed these white ethnics to reassert their identity. The revival of white ethnicity was a cultural force that had its effect on government policies, implemented in response to demand by all those caught up in this new assertion of identity. The passage of the Ethnic Heritage Act through Congress in 1974 was a high-water mark in an effort to restore the purportedly lost heritage of white Americans, and it brought an institutionalization (albeit underfunded) of ethnic studies in elementary and secondary schools.

The Greek Americans experienced perhaps the most sustained revival of their identity of all the European "ethnics" because of a big influx of immigrants from Greece in the wake of the immigration reform of 1965. Prior to that, about 75,000 Greeks had entered the United States after the end of World War II; now another 75,000 would arrive from the late 1960s through the mid-1970s, when the numbers dropped significantly. The 150,000 or so Greeks who arrived in the postwar era became a separate subgroup within the Greek American community, one that used the Greek language and maintained ties to Greece. The most tangible result was the exponential growth of the Greek presence in the New York borough of Queens, especially in the Astoria section that became a "Greektown," brimming with Greek restaurants, coffee shops, groceries, and entire neighborhoods populated by Greeks. The new influx, made up of many students and young professionals as well manual laborers, reinvigorated the ethnic character of community life not only in New York City but also in Chicago and other big cities. Philadelphia, for example, acquired its own scaled-down version of a Greektown in the neighborhood of Upper Darby. The overall climate generated by the revival of ethnicity would also embolden those among the Greek-born who considered the community and the church as extensions of the Greek homeland and did not see an urgent need to adapt to American society, let alone assimilate.

All this came at a somewhat inconvenient time for the church. It threatened the archbishop's balancing act between, on the one hand, pushing the church away from its immigrant past and toward an Americanized future, and on the other positioning the church as the repository of Greek culture in the United States. The influx of the Greek born, especially after 1965, and their concentration in New York City, created a Greek-oriented Greek American constituency that had certain distinct features. The new Greek immigrants shunned the well-established ethnic associations such as AHEPA and gravitated mostly to the geographical-origin fraternities (e.g., the Pan-Macedonian Federation or the Cretan Association), which were by definition more oriented toward the homeland. Sociologist Charles Moskos described the differences between the old and new Greeks, noting that "the newcomers did not always meld easily into the Greek American community. . . . Some tended to view the Greeks already established in America as boorish and uncultivated," while the older Greeks saw the newcomers as averse to the hardships and dutiful playing by the rules that characterized the pioneer immigrants.[2]

The new Greeks also had an ambivalent relationship with the church. Church theologian Nicon Patrinacos believed the newcomers lacked a religiously formed character and that their piety was superficial. Although they would turn to the church for the sacraments and other religious services "that answer to their religious fear and the need for a form of pseudo-piety which they have retained from childhood, their conscious attitude towards the Church is anticlerical and anti-ecclesiastical." He ascribed this both to the failure of the Church of Greece to win over the educated class, "whose members by personal philosophy consider themselves superior to clergymen and who still bear an intellectual allegiance to the credos of the French revolution," and to "the low level of education of the clergy in Greece and the scandalous lives of some of the leading clergymen."[3] Patrinacos may have been overestimating the philosophical moorings of the secularism of the incoming Greeks, but he was right to point out their relationship to Greek Orthodoxy that was shaped by increasing cynicism toward the church in Greece. For the new Greeks, language rather than religion functioned as a marker of their ethnic identity, and it also distinguished them from the older Greek immigrants. Moskos also observed that "the recent arrivals were perhaps too quick to contrast their good Greek with the deteriorated Greek, which in any event was less polished to begin with, spoken by most of the old-timers."[4]

Language thus became a badge of honor that distinguished the new Greeks. They took pride in using Greek in their ethnic organizations and their social gatherings. Their high concentration in certain neighborhoods reinforced the ethnic and linguistic bubble they lived in, at least during their first years in the United States. There was nothing profoundly philosophical about their association of language with their Greekness; it was something no one questioned.

The Liturgical Language Issue Erupts in 1970

In what seemed an innocuous next step in the church's Americanization process, at the Clergy-Laity Congress of 1970 in New York, Iakovos stated that priests would be allowed to deliver the Sunday liturgy in English if they considered this would be more appropriate for their parish. Though he never acknowledged as much, it is very likely that this move had been partially shaped by the Second Vatican Council's decision to allow the use of the vernacular in church liturgies. Vatican II, as it is better known, was a series of meetings of the Catholic hierarchy held in Rome between 1962 and 1965 at which representatives of the Eastern Orthodox Church were present as observers. Phasing out Latin in favor of the vernacular language was a huge turning point in the history of Catholicism in the United States and signaled its embrace of modernity and adaptation to the realities of post–World War II America. Iakovos, who had served on the World Council of Churches in the 1950s, would have surely followed the proceedings very carefully. Moreover, Iakovos was becoming increasingly sensitive to the need for Greek Orthodoxy to follow suit, as the Greek Americans were becoming assimilated as fast as the Irish, Italian, and Polish Americans. The archbishop had already revealed his concerns at the 1964 Clergy-Laity Congress at Denver, where he recommended that certain readings and prayers for the liturgy be repeated in English for the benefit of the non-Greek-speaking congregation. In fact, many priests, responding to parishioners' requests, had begun to use the English version of the services, and the archdiocese did not openly challenge that practice. And there had been only limited dissent after the Congress in Denver endorsed Iakovos's proposal.

But now the archbishop and like-minded lay members would be pushing for more. In 1968 two Greek American academics, James Counelis and Andrew Kopan, coauthored an article published in *Logos*, a journal focused on Eastern Christianity, in which they expressed their attachment to the Greek language but called for a greater use of English because Orthodoxy's teachings could be expressed "in all tongues of man" and because, they held, the Orthodox Church could never exert social, moral, and religious influence in the New World without becoming a part of its culture.[5] Six months before the opening of the 1970 congress, Iakovos told the archdiocese's council that the church would have to tackle the language question, in particular the use of English in the liturgy, in the coming decade because the emergence of two American-born generations, the increase in mixed marriages, and what he called the "indigenization" of the church, as well as the limited Greek academic education of the priests, all demanded a reevaluation of the insistence on the use of Greek.[6] Just before the congress opened, the *Orthodox Observer* carried an article proclaiming that the church needed to change and align itself with contemporary American society and that Greek Orthodoxy in America had emerged from its adolescence and was facing a hopeful and painful adulthood.[7]

The article in the *Orthodox Observer* was by the publication's editor, Nicon Patrinacos, who was the intellectual author of the shift toward English in the liturgy. Patrinacos had been born in Greece, in the province of Laconia in the Peloponnese. In 1936, when he was twenty-five, he was ordained a priest and received his diploma from the School of Theology of the University of Athens. He then moved to Australia, and after earning a degree from the University of Queensland he moved on to Oxford, where he received a doctorate in psychology in 1950. Next he moved to the United States, serving as pastor of St. Nicholas Orthodox Church in St. Louis and also teaching at Washington University in that city. In 1953 Patrinacos was appointed dean of Hellenic College Holy Cross. It was from that vantage point, training the young American born who would serve as priests in parishes across the United States, that Patrinacos gained an appreciation of the growing use of English in church life. It was three decades since the arrival of new immigrants from Greece had been limited to a trickle, and both the students at the school and the parishes they would be serving were mostly American born. Nevertheless, Patrinacos's policies were considered too liberal, and he stepped down the next year; but during his short tenure in Brookline, he founded the *Greek Orthodox Theological Review*, an English-language academic journal of which he was editor. Patrinacos viewed the liturgical language question as part of a much broader set of requirements the Greek Orthodox Church had to satisfy in order to remain relevant in the America of the 1970s. That same year, Patrinacos published a book titled *The Individual and His Orthodox Church*. It was addressed, he wrote pointedly in the introduction, to the American born "who now comprise the bulk and make up the strength of the Orthodox parish in the New World," men and women "who are Orthodox by baptism and outward conformity but scarcely so by inward choice."[8] It consisted of four chapters that dealt with the sacraments, the content and meaning of Orthodox worship, the teachings and practices characteristic of Orthodoxy, and with facing the present and future of Orthodoxy in America. Patrinacos carefully avoided the term "Greek Orthodoxy" throughout the book. His purpose was to explain the religious content of Orthodoxy and how it could be practiced in present-day America. He argued that in its current state, the practice of Orthodoxy did not entail the conscious participation of individuals, who he wished would embrace the essence of Orthodoxy rather than its culturally determined rituals to which they were attached because they wrongly considered them as timeless and fundamental to the faith. The division of the Orthodox Church along ethnic lines, and by extension the use of different cultural practices and languages, were becoming outdated, in his opinion. "For the American born Orthodox" he wrote, "the existing liturgical and cultural diversity is something they cannot comprehend and a definite impediment toward having a unified Orthodox congregation that could be at home in any Orthodox church."[9] Patrinacos called for more fundamental changes: "Few can perhaps realize that our real problem at this stage of development is not which tongue we should use in our worship, English or any other, but what do we mean by that which we express. . . . Worship is man's way of communicating with God and as such reflects the individual's and the group's development through the ages in their understanding of

God and of themselves. . . . This means that a liturgical reform should not be limited to form and language but it should be primarily concerned with and reflect the thought and personality attitudes of contemporary Orthodox as regards the problem of human placement within the world of matter as well as within the world of spirit."[10]

As the 1970 congress approached, Patrinacos and others on the archdiocese's staff prepared a "Delegates' Workbook" designed to inform delegates about the issues to be discussed in New York. It included advance notice of the proposed permission to use English in the sacraments of baptism, marriage, penance, Holy Unction, and Holy Communion, and it explained that "the Archdiocese does not rule out this eventual changing from one language to the other" but qualified this by mentioning the need for an appropriate translation, aimed "at rendering our ritual not only understandable but forceful and effective enough so as to elicit, and even inwardly compel, a true participation on the part of our people during common worship."[11] There were distinct echoes of Patrinacos's ideas but also an evident unwillingness to make the use of English a rushed, overnight affair. Reinforcing the attempt of the archdiocese to maintain a position of moderation, its chief secretary and adviser to Iakovos, Basil G. Vasiliades, issued a statement to be included in the materials distributed to all delegates. It reiterated that the archdiocese was proceeding with prudence, allowing both English and Greek, and that the use of English should be adopted for the purpose of maintaining "the retention of the Greek Orthodox nature and character of our Church."[12] Iakovos had done all he could to smooth the way for the optional use of English in Greek Orthodox life. Now he had to persuade the Clergy-Laity Congress to approve the measure. But all the preparation and publicity had caused rumblings of discontent among the Greek-born Greek Americans.

The Twentieth Clergy-Laity Congress

Iakovos was a big believer in pomp and circumstance, so the 1970 congress took place at the Waldorf Astoria Hotel in midtown Manhattan. Addressing a record number of one thousand delegates, Iakovos spoke about the adoption of English in the liturgy in parishes where the priest deemed it more suitable than Greek, explaining the proposal as a way of ensuring greater and more meaningful participation of the congregation. Iakovos elaborated on the former need—greater participation—by making two points: that the minimal participation of the Greek Orthodox due to their decreasing comprehension of Greek would soon lead to their alienation and the spiritual death of Orthodoxy in America, and that language reform would make Orthodoxy more widely accessible in America. "The greatest mystery which God has revealed to the Orthodox Christian in America, is the fact that Orthodoxy is not exclusively the religion of the Hellenes, but the religion of all those who, as a result of mixed marriages or contact and study of Orthodoxy, have come to know and relate to it and therefore that Orthodoxy has already found its place and mission in the Western Hemisphere."[13]

The archbishop qualified his proposal by reassuring the delegates that this was not a "repudiation or denial of the Greek language in the ecclesiastical services" and reminding them that there had been a limited authorization of languages other than Greek at the 1964 Clergy-Laity Congress held in Denver. He went on to explain he was responding to an existing situation in allowing a wider use of other languages, because a committee of the archdiocese had ascertained that "languages other than Greek are in fact being used in various parishes throughout the Archdiocesan districts to meet a specific local situation." The last phrase meant of course parishes where most could not understand or use the Greek language.[14] The recommendation that the church permit the use of the "vernacular" (i.e., English) language as needed in its services, according to the judgment of the priest in consultation with the bishop, "was enthusiastically adopted by an overwhelming majority of the 1,000 delegates"[15] Clergy-laity conferences rarely even questioned proposals by the archdiocese, so the vote on the floor and the wide margin of approval were not surprising—which is perhaps why the report also mentioned the delegates' enthusiasm.

The opponents of any changes in the status of the liturgical language also took issue with a relatively minor point the archbishop made in his speech. As part of his long-standing position that the church adapt to the American environment, Iakovos spoke about the need of the archdiocese to determine issues relating to mixed marriages autonomously—that is, on its own, and not be bound by the church's established doctrines. For example, if the wedding ceremony of a Greek Orthodox with a person of a different denomination did not take place in an Orthodox church, according to doctrine the Orthodox Church did not recognize that marriage and denied the Orthodox person any rights, including burial. With the number of mixed marriages between Orthodox and non-Orthodox increasing steadily, and with many of the wedding ceremonies taking place in Catholic or Protestant churches, the archbishop believed that the archdiocese should be allowed some leeway and the right to recognize such marriages. Although his use of the term "autonomy" in this respect was correct, it conjured up notions of independence from the Ecumenical Patriarchate, at least in the eyes of those who were assuming that permitting the use of English in the liturgy in some parishes amounted to a repudiation of the Greek language.

It was the Greek language press that spearheaded the protests, often employing hyperbolic rhetoric and claiming that the archbishop was attacking the Greek language and was bent on "de-hellenizing" the Orthodox Church in America. Several ad hoc commiittees also emerged, purportedly in defense of the Greek language and Orthodox traditions. An organization calling itself the "Panhellenic Fellowship," dedicated to the protection and preservation of the Greek language, organized a demonstration outside the archdiocese's offices on Seventy-Ninth street in Manhattan. About one hundred people participated, and their president, Michael Halkias, said they were opposed to the use of English and what that implied, namely that Archbishop Iakovos was establishing an independent church.[16] The Greek language press seized on the idea that Iakovos was "breaking away," because that accusation, coupled with the assertion that the congress had voted to replace the Greek language, made their attacks more sensational. On July 20, a "Pan-American Conference for the Preservation of the Greek Language and the Greek Orthodox Church" was hastily convened in New York, and it issued a manifesto against Iakovos and his policies. It appealed to Ecumenical Patriarch Athenagoras to dismiss Iakovos and appoint a new archbishop, and it initiated a stream of letters and pamphlets to parishes and Greek American organizations urging them to turn against the archbishop. The Greek language press continued its own assault on the archdiocese: Gazouleas, the editor of the *Atlantis* newspaper, resorted to biblical imagery, claiming "the glorious Greek language is driven to Golgotha."[17]

Iakovos had traveled to Greece as soon as the Clergy-Laity Congress ended, and from there he issued his own stream of encyclicals and statements explaining that the congress had only voted to permit the use of English, not to abolish the use of Greek, and that it was vitally concerned in the ways it could attract the younger, English-speaking Greek Americans.[18] He got no help from the government in Greece, which called for the end of the feuding within the community but came out in support of the "preservation" of the Greek language. And in Constantinople, Athenagoras—who had to approve of the congress's decisions—adopted a wait-and-see attitude, not wanting to alienate the traditionalists and strangely insensitive to the need to attract the English-speaking Greek Americans to the church. He may have been unaware of the extent that assimilation that had taken place within the community since the time he left New York, twenty-two years earlier.

The conflict elevated the Greek language as a contested symbol of Greek identity and took on a much bigger meaning than anyone had anticipated.

Ironically, the language employed in the liturgy was an archaic form of the Greek that the immigrants actually spoke among themselves. It was closer to the formal Katharevousa Greek that was familiar only to those who would have completed higher education in Greece. In contrast, the sermon was usually in a mixture of the formal Katharevousa and the vernacular *demotiki* and much easier to understand. The majority of Iakovos's opponents spoke *demotiki* but would have had difficulty with the Katharevousa and even greater trouble understanding the liturgical language. Moreover, Katharevousa was taught in only a few of the existing Greek parochial high schools in the United States, while the many more afternoon schools taught *demotiki*. The Greek American press adopted a mixture of the two versions of Greek. So relatively few Greek Americans would have been able to follow the liturgy word for word. But there were important reasons for retaining the old version of Greek used in the liturgy. The liturgy itself was a reenactment of the sacrifice of Jesus Christ, a cornerstone of Orthodox belief, and therefore possessed a powerful symbolic character. This symbolism was conveyed through a set of ritualistic practices that served, along with the chanting that was part of the service, as a venue of continuity between the world of Greece the immigrants had left behind and their lives in America. Thus church attendance on Sunday mornings was a form of spiritual but also mental return to the homeland. And this gave the language of the liturgy a powerful emotional weight in the minds of parishioners. Germanos Polyzoides, a senior and well-respected bishop of the church in America, sought to explain the significance of the liturgical language in a short book about Orthodoxy addressed to the younger and American-born members of the church. The book, published in 1961, was written in a question-and-answer format, and in response to the question why the church retained the old language in the liturgy, Polyzoides's explanation was threefold: "1) This language became respectable for its antiquity since it was used even during the Apostolic times, 2) it is sacred as long as it is not the common language of the street and 3) it always remains the same."[19]

Athenagoras eventually sided with the traditionalists, upholding the function of the Greek Orthodox Church in America that he himself had created, namely the dual preservation of religion and ethnic identity. His official letter to Iakovos conveying the Ecumenical Patriarchate's view praised Iakovos and expressed full confidence in him, but it made clear that it did not favor the liturgical and linguistic reforms. The letter referred to the archdiocese's constitution where it was stated that Greek was the language of the archdiocese and that the archdiocese's purpose included preserving the ethnic identity of its people and teaching the original language of the Gospel, meaning Greek.

The patriarch also addressed a letter to the Greek Orthodox in America in which he expressed his sorrow at the divisions and strife and called on them to remain united, because he believed the language controversy had simply been a misunderstanding. He also praised the archbishop and even suggested that some good had come of the affair because the community had the opportunity to affirm its attachment to its ethnic identity.

Iakovos Strikes Back

The fallout from the 1970 decision on language continued unabated on the eve of the next Clergy-Laity Congress, which opened in Houston in July 1972. The views expressed publicly for and against the archdiocese's new policy fell along predictable lines, with the English language newspapers backing the decision and the Greek language media keeping up their relentless criticism. Harris P. Jameson, a columnist for Boston's *Hellenic Chronicle*, noted there was a petition being circulated that demanded the ouster of the archbishop and added that "the men behind the petition are fanatical ethnocentrics who are barking up the wrong tree: this is America we are living in, not a Greek colony within America."[20] He blamed the Greek-language press for distorting the archbishop's message by claiming he wanted to replace Greek with English immediately. For its part, the *Ethnikos Kyrix* carefully distinguished between its opposition to replacing Greek and its attitude toward the archbishop, whom it still considered the leader of the Greek Orthodox Church and deserving respect.[21] The *Atlantis* expressed the hope that the congress convening at Houston would reverse the consequences of the "coup d'état" against the Greek language that had taken place in 1970.[22] Greek Americans were waiting for Iakovos's keynote speech at Houston to get a sense of the status of the language issue, although Iakovos had already shown his hand earlier that year in a text that commemorated the archdiocese's fiftieth anniversary. It encapsulated Iakovos's overall strategy, which was to reassure all of the significance of the Greek language but to place it in a broader context in which it was necessary for both Greek Orthodoxy and the Greek Americans to adapt to American society. Unlike the traditionalists who insisted, somewhat shortsightedly, solely on the preservation of the Greek language, Iakovos unfolded a much broader and sophisticated vision of the current state of Greek America in which the church was trying to balance between its past and future. The archbishop reiterated the church's commitment to Greek language education but also presented the church's fifty-year trajectory as one in which it had transcended its narrow national origins and become an American church; and the evolution of the community (he used the Greek term *omogeneia*, which is used in Greece to invoke the same racial origins of the Greeks in Greece and the Greeks abroad) meant it had become integrated and successful in American society. This in turn made the maintenance of ethnicity and religion much more challenging and complex. The church, Iakovos wrote, was going from being "national" to becoming "above and beyond national, in the nature of our Ecumenical Patriarchate." The *omogeneia* "was neither wholly Greek nor wholly American but Greek-American, a synthesis strongly bound together." The community's values that had to be addressed in light of an uncertain future were "our religion, our Greek education, Greek culture and civilization, our love for our country, our ambition to survive," and the way these could be preserved was for them to "be embodied in our Church and in our traditions, the guardian of which is the very Church." After placing the church at the center of the community's life and future, Iakovos added that there was a collective responsibility not to keep that heritage "for ourselves" but instead "to share it with others and multiply it," a process he regarded as going from mere physical to spiritual growth. He acknowledged that this had meant the community had to "pain and sigh together on account of the difficult questions of this time, such as the Greek language which is ignored, through no fault of the Omogeneia, but because of the need to become familiar [with]," if not equal to, "the environment in which they live."[23]

The 1972 Twenty-First Clergy-Laity Congress at Houston

The calm and order of 1972 Clergy-Laity Congress belied the fact it was convening two years after probably the most controversial congress in the archdiocese's history. It had originally been scheduled to meet in New Orleans, but it met in Houston instead. The delegates did not miss out on festivities they might have expected with the earlier venue, and in fact much of the congress, at least in the opening days, was nothing less than a Texas-size party. There was a visit to the NASA Manned Spacecraft Center led by the archbishop, a "Welcome Reception" with "delightful background music provided by a string ensemble comprised of talented young musicians from Houston's Annunciation Cathedral," a special youth forum that included guitar and vocal performances, a luncheon address by astronaut James Irwin, an evening "Freedom Ball," and on July 4, a service at the Annunciation Cathedral followed by a "Texas style barbeque" on the church grounds. The clergy-laity congresses always combined prayer meetings, serious deliberations (or at any rate discussions) on prepared committee reports, and visits to local sights and evening entertainment, so the one in Houston was no exception. And beginning in the 1950s, the biennial congresses were always scheduled over the Fourth of July holiday and therefore included an American patriotic component. An extra bonus in the 1972 Congress was a brief address by Spiro Agnew, the Greek American who was President Nixon's vice president. Agnew's father was Greek Orthodox, but Agnew himself had become an Episcopalian.

It was in this atmosphere that Iakovos addressed the serious business of language controversy by responding firmly to the traditionalists. The official agenda of the congress did not include a specific item on the language question, but Iakovos mentioned it in the preface to his keynote report:

> I want to reaffirm for the record, without the slightest reservation whatsoever, that Articles I and II of the Charter of the Archdiocese which provide that the Greek Orthodox Archdiocese of North and South America, is part of the Holy Apostolic and Patriarchal Throne, and that the liturgical language of the Holy Archdiocese shall be principally Greek, are valid and in full force and effect, and will continue to be so, for as long as I serve as your Archbishop. . . . In connection with this, let me say unequivocally the position of the Archdiocese. With respect to the language issue: the Greek language continues to be the official language of the Divine Liturgy.

The archbishop also reminded his audience of the decision at the 1964 Clergy-Laity Congress at Denver, ratified by the Ecumenical Patriarchate, according to which certain essential parts of the divine liturgy, the sacraments, and other religious services could also be offered in English, "when and where it is deemed appropriate and necessary in the judgment of the Church."[24] It was a way of reminding all that English had already been in use before 1970. In his report to the congress, Iakovos linked its theme, "Speak the Truth in Love," with what had happened at the 1970 congress, during which "certain persons did violence to truth and love as expressions of Greek Orthodoxy, at the very time when its influence was on the rise" and that "it was not the language of the Greeks that was threatened in that Congress, but the language of God: the language of truth and love in our Church life and our personal lives."[25] And a little further on, after he spoke of the need for the church to confront the pressures of assimilation and dangerous social trends, including a loosening of morals, Iakovos proclaimed a church deeply rooted in the past and the present whose mission was to bring the message of Christ to the world, and that toward that purpose it would "utilize the Greek as well as well as all other languages in fulfilling its mission."[26] Iakovos's words were met with widespread approval from the floor of the congress. The Committee on Laity Relations took the unusual step of referencing the language controversy in its recommendation that the archdiocese establish a Commission for Spiritual Renewal. It expressed its frustration that there existed a language barrier in the church's spiritual outreach and declared, "Let it be made abundantly clear that we love and respect the Greek language, and recognize it as the historic and original vehicle for transmitting the beauty of our worship services," but, it added, it placed its confidence "in the leadership of His Eminence, praying that it will lead us very soon to a proper solution in meeting this crucial need of greater linguistic flexibility."[27]

By way of reassuring those concerned with the weakening of Greek in the church's life, the reports of the Committee on Education confirmed the church's commitment to promoting the Greek language. In 1972 this was the case with the committee responsible for the schools but also the committee that oversaw the theological school, where there had been long-standing problems and complaints that the Greek language instruction was subpar. Indeed, the archdiocesan staff was working hard to provide support of Greek language education at all levels. In what turned out to be among his successful choices, Iakovos had appointed Emmanuel Hatziemmanuel as director of education of the archdiocese in 1968. Hatziemmanuel served for the next twenty years and oversaw the spread of Greek language education that took place in the 1970s.[28] Born in Greece and equipped with a degree in theology from the University of Athens, from where he went on to study theology in the United Kingdom with a scholarship from the World Council of Churches, Hatziemmanuel arrived in the United States in 1950 and began working as a teacher in an afternoon school in Brooklyn. From there he went on to hold teaching and senior administration positions at St. Basil Academy, the archdiocese's residential school for children in need and the women's junior college for teachers. Hatziemmanuel presided over what was an exponential growth of the archdiocese's education program that represented the growing sophistication it had begun to acquire in the 1960s. He developed a course for the teaching of Greek as a second language for the day and afternoon schools and a curriculum for teaching modern Greek in high schools in the United States. The US Department of Education subsequently granted the archdiocese the right to develop Greek language examinations used in high schools. Hatziemmanuel introduced seminars—in the US and Canada—for the professional development of teachers of Greek, as well as summer seminars in Greece with the collaboration of the Greek government; and he succeeded in getting full status recognition of St. Basil Academy as equal to the pedagogical academies of Greece.

Athenagoras's Death

Iakovos linked the commemoration of the jubilee of the archdiocese's foundation with the jubilee of Athenagoras's elevation to bishop, which had happened the same year. The archdiocese even published a booklet in early 1972 titled *The Double Jubilee*. The archbishop and other speakers at the Houston congress mentioned the jubilee frequently, and the archbishop also kept the congress abreast of the patriarch's condition, as Athenagoras had suffered a broken hip as the result of a fall. On Wednesday, July 5, the archbishop informed delegates that the patriarch would have to be flown to Vienna for surgery; that same day, several events had been scheduled honoring Athenagoras, including a luncheon, tributes, a showing of a film by the Knights of St. Andrew about Athenagoras's life, and an "ecumenical tea" hosted by the Ladies' Philoptochos. The next day, July 6, Vice President Agnew gave his speech and hailed Athenagoras "as a great international figure in world peace." That evening, at an official banquet attended by one thousand guests and dignitaries, Iakovos rose to speak about Athenagoras's life and achievements. Suddenly, he paused. Ernest Villas, the congress coordinator, described what happened next: "Then he dramatically and tearfully added 'but Patriarch Athenagoras is no longer with us, he is home, he is back with God.' The statement electrified everyone. Open sobbing punctuated the otherwise silent hall. His Eminence then bravely continued on to the conclusion of his address, but for all practical purposes his message ended both the Congress, and a never-to-be-repeated era in the history of our Church in the Americas."[29] Athenagoras had died of kidney failure in Istanbul at age eighty-six. His death was reported on the front pages of major newspapers in the United States and across the world, and the obituaries noted his contributions to bringing the Orthodox and other Christian churches closer, and his historic meeting with Pope Paul VI in 1964.

Upon hearing of Athenagoras's death, more than a few Greek Orthodox would have recalled his conciliatory efforts to resolve the language crisis in 1970 and the way he gently curbed Iakovos's push to allow English in the liturgy. That had been an unexpected move, because Iakovos had been and still was in some ways Athenagoras's protégé. For his part, Iakovos had responded wisely so as not to allow the traditionalists to drive a wedge between him and the patriarch. And in linking the archdiocese's jubilee with Athenagoras's elevation to bishop, Iakovos had underscored his own identification with the patriarch. And indeed, Iakovos had long been considered Athenagoras's possible successor. And even in death, Athenagoras served to bolster Iakovos's standing, if not his prospects for succession. The Turkish government banned Iakovos from attending the funeral in Istanbul, describing him as undesirable and a persona non grata. Four American religious leaders who were to have formed an ecumenical delegation with Iakovos— the Catholic archbishop of New York Terence Cardinal Cooke, the Episcopal bishop of Long Island Jonathan Sherman, rabbi Marc Tanenbaum of the American Jewish Committee, and Edwin Espy of the National Council of Churches—canceled their plans to attend the funeral, in solidarity with Iakovos.[30] The ban was very distressing for Iakovos personally, and it also signaled the unlikelihood that he could succeed Athenagoras, since the Turkish government exercised a veto on the patriarchate's choice for its leader. In the election, Metropolitan Meliton of Chalcedon, the powerful dean of the Holy Synod whom some considered Iakovos's rival, was struck off the ballot by the Turkish government, and this led to the election of a less experienced cleric, the recently appointed metropolitan of Imvros and Tenedos Dimitrios, whose candidacy Meliton ultimately supported.[31] Iakovos would have to wait, assuming he was interested in becoming patriarch, something he had always denied.

The Archdiocese, the Ethnic Revival, and Greek Language Education

The revival of ethnicity in the US in the late 1960s and early 1970s disrupted Iakovos's push to make Greek Orthodoxy more accessible to the American born, but it ultimately worked in the archbishop's favor. The Greek-born Greek Americans and their media had regarded the revival of ethnicity as a license to regard the community and the church as extensions of the homeland, and this had given a militant edge to their protestations about the need to preserve the Greek language. Their achievement in the momentary shaking of Iakovos's authority in the immediate aftermath of the 1970 Clergy-Laity Congress gave that particular conference a special notoriety. But it cannot be regarded as a turning point in the church's history. At most, it was the high-water mark of the traditionalist demands for the preservation of the Greek language, which would continue as a permanent low rumble in the background in the decades that followed. Rather, it was the 1972 Clergy-Laity Congress that was a turning point, because the vision Iakovos articulated of a church adapting and continuing to become part of the America mainstream while retaining its spirituality and its ethnic roots—and using the Greek language wherever possible and promoting it in its schools—shaped the future of the archdiocese. The revival of ethnicity could not and did not bring a revival of the Greek language in a steady assimilating Greek America.

The plan to hold the 1976 Clergy-Laity Congress in Philadelphia so as to coincide with the celebrations of the nation's bicentennial in that city said a lot about Iakovos's understanding of the place of the Greek Orthodox Church in America in the 1970s. And he was backed up by the parishes, which overwhelmingly dismissed a proposal that the congress be moved instead to Athens as a gesture of solidarity with the homeland following Turkey's invasion and occupation of the northern third of the island of Cyprus. Logistical and practical reasons were cited, but the choice of Philadelphia over Athens spoke volumes in terms of its symbolism. The program of the 1976 Clergy-Laity Congress that awaited delegates at the city's Sheraton Hotel prepared them for a serious reflection on America's ethnic revival and what it meant. The archdiocese had commissioned eminent Byzantine studies professor Deno J. Geanakoplos to contribute an article on ethnicity. American-born himself but with cosmopolitan scholarly experience, Geanakoplos could be relied on to evoke Greek ethnicity in American rather than Greek terms. And the Yale professor delivered. Geanakoplos explained that scholars had discounted the theory that America was a "melting pot" and recognized that immigrants such as the Greeks "insisted also on maintaining their own particular cultural identity" but did so "while offering sincere allegiance to America and to the process of Americanization." Indeed, he added, "We can now see that through maintaining the roots of their own traditions, the immigrants were able, in the long run, to become even better Americans" because "our free, democratic American society has discovered that it operates most effectively when it actively encourages cultural and religious diversity."[32]

And in his keynote speech, Iakovos spoke of the church "acting and living in America" and repeated his vision of a church adapting and continuing to become part of America while retaining its spirituality and its ethnic roots—and using the Greek language wherever possible while promoting it in its schools. The congress also heard how the revival of ethnicity was benefiting the archdiocese's programs. Hatziemmanuel noted in his report to the congress, "Today, more than ever before, conditions are very favorable for the development of Greek education. . . . The multi-national synthesis of the American society, far from destroying national unity . . . gives to the nation a kind of unique uniformity and strength. . . . This new thesis . . . has considerably strengthened the endeavors of various ethnic groups to maintain and cultivate their native language together with their cultural traditions. Religion, language and cultural tradition," he added, "make up, as is known, one's identity and prescribe his style of life." And "as a result of this climate, the faith of the Greek Orthodox in the value and worth of Greek education has been encouraged and considerably strengthened."[33]

The efforts the church made in the 1970s to strengthen education were in fact helped by Iakovos's close contacts with Athens. Back in 1961, Iakovos had met with the Greek prime minister Constantinos Karamanlis to discuss the ways in which Greece could assist. A decade later, with two government bills in 1972 and 1973, Greece's Ministry of Education offered accreditation to all ninety-five US Greek Orthodox parochial schools and the afternoon schools that operated five days a week. Between 1974 and 1977, the prestigious Anavryta School in Athens had a special curriculum for Greek American high school students who spent the academic year studying there. And the Greek Ministry of Education accredited teachers working for the archdiocese and began awarding pensions to a number of retired long-serving teachers. The pension arrangement lasted, but that was not the case with the plan for a permanent Greek American school. It never materialized because of what Hatziemmanuel described delicately as "the frequent changes in Greece's political life and as a result the change of personnel in the Ministry."[34] There was a general election in Greece in 1977, and even though the incumbent Karamanlis administration won, the changes of personnel at the ministry—a regular practice after an election in Greece—contributed to the discontinuation of Anavryta's Greek American connection. Yet Athens continued its modest efforts at offering help to the archdiocese. In 1977 the Greek government appointed "educational advisers" who took up positions in the Greek consulates in New York, Montreal, Ottawa, and Toronto. Iakovos presided over a conference held at the archdiocese in January 1978 and attended by the Greek ambassadors to the United States and Canada and the four newly appointed advisers at which he suggested the parameters of their work and the ways Greece could continue its help. Overall, a very close relationship developed between the archdiocese and Athens until new elections in 1981, when the coming of the socialist party to power would bring another temporary disruption.

The church's efforts and the Greek government's support meant no one could question the archdiocese's commitment to promoting Greek language education in the 1970s, even though a fine-grained study of the educational program in this period by Fevronia Soumakis suggests that the program continued to display weaknesses as well as strengths. The archdiocese's representatives liked citing statistics, especially when the numbers showed an increase. For example, in a presentation that Rev. Nomikos Vaporis, the dean of Hellenic College, made in Athens in 1980, he cited data collected by the archdiocese's Education Department that showed the church ran 27 nursery and kindergarten schools, 22 elementary schools, 409 afternoon language schools, and 23 junior and high schools. Some 29,600 students were enrolled in the afternoon schools, a figure that represented a 23 percent increase over the past ten years, and 6,890 students were enrolled in the other schools. There had also been an increase in the number of teachers during the previous decade, from 500 to 853.[35] But the progress made throughout the 1970s in terms of establishing new schools and introducing the archdiocese's curriculum was mostly in the Greek American enclaves in the states of Connecticut, New Jersey, New York, and Massachusetts. For example, of the four new parochial schools in the 1970s, half of them were in New York City (Brooklyn and Queens), while the two others were in Houston and in Northridge, California. And overall, there was a drop in the numbers of enrolled students in most of the existing parochial schools. The figures Soumakis gathered show a small drop in the numbers enrolled in the parochial schools in the Bronx and Manhattan, both the school at the Cathedral and the one in Washington Heights, and also in three schools in the rest of the greater New York area. And controversies continued around the underfunding of the schools and the low salaries of teachers. There were claims that some teachers were unqualified, and—especially galling to the Greek-language press—revelations that several principals of parochial schools in the greater New York area were not Greek or even Greek American.[36]

Yet there remains a sense that the archdiocese's educational program was a success—if not in strictly pedagogical terms, then in the wider sense of the church's being the main force shaping Greek American identity. Simply put, the church was running the schools, and there was very little scrutiny of the premise of that project, let alone any secular-based alternatives. For instance, debates in the Greek American press no longer raised the possibility of alternatives to the religious administrative and curricular paradigm. No wonder Hatziemmanuel could assert in 1975, "Our work in cooperation with the Greek Ministry of Education is based on the premise that our system of education is bound by its nature to pursue ideals of the Greek culture and Christian tradition."[37] Even when logistical difficulties meant there were times that certain parochial schools did not include classes on religion, religion was always present. As Soumakis found in her research on Greek schools in New York City in the 1970s, "While religion may not have been taught regularly or systematically it was practiced throughout the school year. . . . From the start . . . of the school year, when the priest would offer a blessing to students and faculty in every classroom, to the celebration of important feast days that punctuated the parochial school calendar, all students and faculty alike practiced religious observance. Icons were placed in every classroom. Prayers were often recited at the beginning and at the end of the school day. Additionally, students were taught hymns and attended church on a regular basis."[38]

There was one instance of a critique of the concept of the church running Greek education in the United States, but its impact was limited because it came from a maverick parliamentary deputy of an opposition party rather than the Greek government. Virginia Tsouderos, daughter of the wartime prime minister Emmanouil Tsouderos who had visited the United States and attended the 1942 Clergy-Laity Congress along with the king, was a Center Party deputy and a member of a Greek parliamentary delegation that visited New York in the spring of 1980. In an interview with the *Ethnikos Kyrix*, she upheld her reputation of espousing liberal principles as well as not mincing her words. Greek American education was in a poor state, she said; it was suffocating under too much control and had to be freed from the church in order to gain a new lease on life. Greece, she continued, should produce a special curriculum and books for young Greeks abroad, and the schools should be run by teachers and parents. This was a rare occasion in which a prominent Greek personality—albeit a deputy of a small party with no real clout in parliament—called for an alternative system of Greek language education in the United States. There was no real cause for concern for the archdiocese, but Hatziemmanuel was sufficiently upset to pen a long rebuttal that appeared in a weekly Greek American magazine. If anything, it would serve to respond to the complainers in the United States who had seized on Tsouderos's comments. Any other system than the present one was inconceivable, the archdiocese's director of education argued back, because autonomous, secular communities did not exist: "Greek American education," he noted, "developed with the initiatives and sacrifices of the Greek American ecclesiastic community," and a separation of education from community would mean alienating the children from the community home and housing them instead in a "commercially" driven type of school. And for good measure, Hatziemmanuel estimated that the total monetary investment of the "ecclesiastic communities" throughout the United States amounted to $100 million, and he wondered where Tsouderos would find that money to finance the changes she advocated.[39]

In his December 1980 presentation in Athens, Vaporis came to Hatziemmanuel's support. He quoted Iakovos's words about the difficulties the archdiocese faced: "The education of our children in the language of our fathers is a struggle and often an uneven if not unrealistic one. We ask our children to be educated in Greek and English and indeed in both simultaneously and completely." Iakovos had also pointed out that the Greeks were the only ethnic group whose church was fully responsible for its schools.[40] Vaporis went on to tell his audience that Archbishop Iakovos would "gratefully accept the cooperation of those who would truly wish to study this problem of education seriously and extensively and to contribute—their experience, counsel, and other resources, so that our [the church's] stance and policy with regard to the subject of Greek education in America can be placed responsibly in the light of today's realities." He could have added that the archbishop was not holding his breath. Greek language education in the United States was firmly under the control of the archdiocese. No one in the Greek American community was contemplating the launch of an alternative, secular-based education initiative, given where Greek America was headed. And the Greek government, even it had the political will and financial ability, was facing the prospect of a difficult election in 1981 and was therefore very unlikely to become seriously involved.

In contrast to the church's hard-earned successes in the field of Greek language education, however, Hellenic College, the liberal arts institution that was added to Holy Cross Theological School in 1966 and with which it shared resources on their Brookline, Massachusetts, campus, seemed to face perennial difficulties. Costas Maliotis, a leading Greek American businessman and philanthropist in the Boston area, had contacted the archdiocese back in 1970 expressing grave concerns about the financial viability of the college and the harm its problems may cause to the entire archdiocesan financial structure.[41] The archdiocese agreed with Maliotis's recommendation to commission a report on the future possibilities of both the college and the theological school from Arthur D. Little Inc., a management-consulting firm headquartered in Boston. The firm's report, which was completed in May 1970, confirmed that the cohabitation of the two institutions on their campus was mutually detrimental; the faculty of the theological school felt that the presence of the college threatened to secularize the seminarians, while the faculty of the college, inevitably perhaps, prioritized secular cultural education over religious instruction. The report offered a total of ten alternative scenarios for the future, which ranged from closing down both institutions and moving theological instruction to Harvard's Divinity School, to continuing their cohabitation. It ended by noting that if the decision was to continue both schools and have them share the same resources, "commitment to the religious and secular aspects of life need not be conflicting, but it is necessary to work hard at making them mutually supporting commitments. Without that effort, fragmentation of resources and development will continue."[42]

Iakovos's decision was that the two institutions remain together, with their administrators and faculty taking heed of the consulting firm's recommendations. Within a few years, a generous contribution to Holy Cross by Maliotis and his wife, Mary, created the Maliotis Center, a facility with an auditorium and areas for exhibitions and lectures whose purpose was to showcase Greek religious and secular culture and nurture the growth of both institutions at Brookline. Yet both Holy Cross and Hellenic College would demonstrate a mixed record in the decades to come, achievements tempered by difficulties that served as a reminder that the wide scope of the Greek Orthodox Church's educational agenda in America stretched the church's capabilities to the utmost. Significantly, perhaps, Peter Kourides, Iakovos's legal adviser whom Maliotis had contacted initially and who had conveyed the philanthropist's concern to the archbishop, also noted his personal view, writing, "Though I do not have any expertise in the educational area, I am convinced that our people's interests is limited to the education of our priests and teachers and to the care of our orphaned and abandoned children. I think they are willing to pay the bill for these services but they are unwilling to contribute almost $1,000,000.00 per year for the maintenance of a non-sectarian college for the general public."[43]

During the ethnic revival of the 1970s that swept over Americans, including those of southeastern and southern European origins, community leaders soon realized that ethnic groups were experiencing this phenomenon in different ways, in some cases more profoundly and in other cases more superficially as the mass culture co-opted it, as the proliferation of ethnic-pride bumper stickers demonstrated. In the case of the Polish Americans, for example, several Catholic parishes with a preponderance of members of Polish origin asserted their Polish-ness and broke with Rome; for other parishes, the revival remained at the level of expressing pride in their heritage.[44] In the case of the Greek Americans and the Greek Orthodox Church there was a similar range of responses, though the embrace of the Greek language remained central. Ironically, the ethnic revival threatened the Orthodox ethnic churches much more than the Catholic ones, at least those ethnic churches that were attempting a careful integration into the American mainstream. In the case of the Greek Orthodox, the postwar immigrants who came to the United States (and in much bigger numbers than Poles or other Eastern Europeans whose communist rulers imposed strict travel restrictions) embraced the ethnic revival in visceral ways. Also, although ritual is part of all religious services, the vehement insistence by many on preserving the Greek-language liturgy may have been a reflection of the significance of ritualized practices in Greek Orthodoxy. In any case, yet again, a strong leader, this time Archbishop Iakovos, was able to determine the direction the church would take. Greek Orthodoxy's reliance on a single leader in America has resolved the issues that the ethnic church periodically encountered.

CHAPTER 8

Church and Homeland

"Ethnarchy," according to the archdiocese's theologian Stanley Harakas, "occurs when the highest ecclesiastical leader of the church in a given area assumes political leadership. . . . This rarely practiced institution occurs only in periods of crisis, when lay civil leaders cannot, because of extraordinary reasons, exercise normal political powers." Thus, "When only a Church leader seems to be able to embody the identity of the people of the nation, the hierarch may assume political and government leadership by general consensus."[1] Not all prelates of the Greek Orthodox Church play an overtly political role, much less that of ethnarch. In his reflection on the ethnarchy principle, Harakas provides two examples of ethnarchs in the twentieth century: Archbishops Damaskinos and Makarios. Damaskinos, the metropolitan who arrived in the United States to resolve the difficulties the church was experiencing in the 1920s, was archbishop of Athens and of Greece during World War II and served as regent (head of state) from the time Greece was liberated from Axis occupation in 1944 until the return of King George in 1946. Makarios, the leader of the autocephalous Greek Orthodox Church of Cyprus, served as the first president of the Cyprus Republic between 1960 and 1977. Scholars who have studied Makarios's role in the 1950s, when the Greek Cypriots launched a struggle to put an end to British colonial rule and to unite their island with Greece, agree that he played an ethnarchic role. Makarios led the Greek Orthodox Church's effort to position itself as the leading vehicle of the national aspirations of the Greek Cypriots.[2] And Makarios's political language throughout the 1950s and the 1960s was inflected by a markedly religious imagery.[3]

While the Greek Orthodox Church has not acknowledged Archbishop Iakovos's role in shaping diplomatic relations between the church and the United States as a form of ethnarchy, the archbishop earned that title in the eyes of many of the faithful on both sides of the Atlantic. And there are certainly parallels to be drawn between Iakovos and the best example of a Greek Orthodox ethnarch in the twentieth century, Archbishop Makarios of Cyprus. When Iakovos was twelve years old and living on the mostly Greek-populated island of Imvros (present-day Gökçeada) in the northern Aegean, he witnessed the raising of the Turkish flag that signaled that the Lausanne Treaty of 1923 had awarded the island to Turkey. For the young Iakovos, seeing the Turkish flag flying over his island was a traumatic event, and it remained etched in his memory and stayed there because of the mistreatment of the ethnic Greeks by the authorities. Years later, that memory would animate Iakovos's keen sense of injustice and his solidarity with the ethnic Greeks on Cyprus and Istanbul when they would be targeted by Turkey in the decades from the 1950s onward.

Next to that personal investment, what also shaped Iakovos's leadership in forging close ties with the homeland was the worsening of Greek-Turkish relations in the 1960s and the 1970s. In Istanbul itself and in the wake of a pogrom against the ethnic Greeks in 1955, the status of the Ecumenical Patriarchate was under threat, and the well-being of the remaining Greeks in the city remained precarious. The tension between Greeks and Turks on Cyprus was escalating. Iakovos confronted the Greco-Turkish crises in the 1960s and the 1970s by becoming an unofficial ethnarch, availing himself of the Greek Orthodox tradition that recognized the right of certain church leaders to represent a national or ethnic group in political affairs.

The Archdiocese and the Homeland in the 1960s

Iakovos, following the steps of his predecessors, cultivated close relations with the Greek homeland soon after his appointment as archbishop. He went beyond issuing encyclicals commemorating the two Greek national holidays that marked the Greek revolution against the Ottomans in 1821 and Greece's entry into World War II. Iakovos was very vocal over the deteriorating state of Greek-Turkish relations that had already been strained since the mid-1950s because of the interethnic conflict in Cyprus. Cyprus had gained independence in 1960, but the delicate balance between the Greek majority and Turkish minority on the island was shattered when intercommunal clashes raged in the following years. As the conflict on Cyprus unfolded, the Turkish authorities began applying pressure on the Ecumenical Patriarchate and the Greek community in Istanbul. This included shutting down several of its schools, its orphanage, and its printing press, seizing two Greek Orthodox churches, and expelling thousands of Greek Orthodox. By early 1965 the authorities were talking openly about the possibility of entirely eliminating the Greek presence in Istanbul, prompting the *New York Times* to declare in an editorial that "the Turkish threat to expel all Greek nationals from Turkey and to 'control' or even deport the Greek Orthodox Patriarchate is clearly a political move. It is part of the game of trying to force Greece to accede to talks between Greeks and Turks on Cyprus. . . . For all Orthodox Christians, the menace to their Patriarchate will be most disturbing. . . . It would shake up the whole of the Orthodox world if the Patriarchate were now expelled; and it is hardly an exaggeration to say that the Patriarch is being held to ransom."[4]

Iakovos tried to balance between a humanitarian and a nationalist tone in his public statements. He urged the parishes to respond by informing elected officials and the American public of those events overseas and to take steps to offer relief to the Greek victims. In his encyclicals he spoke of the victims of "Turkish barbarism," mixing nationalist with religious vocabulary: "As free and prospering people, we have a sacred obligation to face the dictates of our conscience and our souls," he wrote in August 1964. "Thousands of souls are at this very moment in deadly peril in Cyprus and Turkey. . . . The ideals of freedom and justice are so flagrantly being violated by the Turks, tolerated unfortunately by us, as Greeks and Americans."[5] There were occasions when Iakovos's fervor over Greece's "national issues" made him adopt positions more radical than those of Greece, whose official policies sometimes veered to circumspection rather than explicit condemnation of Turkey's actions. For example, at a meeting of the World Council of Churches held in January 1965, Iakovos put forward a resolution that deplored Turkish depredations against its Greek subjects and its actions on Cyprus. But two bishops who were representing the Church of Greece did not support the resolution because they knew that the Greek Ministry of Foreign Affairs would view it as too radical a move. Informed of this, the Greek general consul in New York, Georgios Gavas, echoed the view that Iakovos's resolution could have had "negative consequences for our national issues."[6]

The Archbishop and the Colonels

Iakovos wished to establish close relations with the homeland, so he scheduled a meeting of the Archdiocesan Council in Athens in August 1967, the first ever outside North America. He went ahead with the meeting even though four months earlier, in April, a group of Greek colonels engineered a military coup and established a dictatorship. They seized power, abolished democracy, and arrested or interned many elected political leaders, labor unionists, and other public figures and placed the media under their control. While loudly proclaiming their Orthodox piety and the Christian character of their regime, the colonels forced the resignation of the archbishop of Athens and of Greece, Chrysostomos, and appointed their own favorite prelate, Ieronymos Kotsonis, whose extreme right-wing and anticommunist views were well known. The colonels' regime took its name from the date of the coup, the twenty-first of April. The purpose of the archdiocesan meeting in Athens in August 1967 was to plan the next clergy-laity congress to be held in that city. The decision to go ahead with the planning for Athens is surprising, given that the dictatorial nature of the regime had become obvious within a few months. All this was in complete contradiction to the American principles of democracy that Iakovos praised so frequently and to the civil rights movement's principles that the archbishop had so publicly endorsed by going to Selma in 1965. It should be acknowledged, however, that what solidarity there was on civil rights had increasingly given way to polarization between religious liberals and religious conservatives. The conservatives were concerned that too much liberalism might erode the foundations of tradition and, by extension, of Christianity, and it is likely that Iakovos shared those concerns.[7] Many years later, Iakovos claimed that by maintaining good relations with the colonels' regime he could use his influence to pressure them to restore democracy, and he attempted to do so in his correspondence with its leaders. But if in his private communications Iakovos tried to exert gentle pressure on the colonels, in public their relations were close and even cordial, with the archbishop always stressing the Greek American community's national and religious ties with its homeland and his own role as an ideal intermediary. The archbishop always referred to the "Greek" or "national" government, never to the colonels' "regime" or "junta," used by most who were opposed to the colonels. The stated reason for taking the clergy-laity congress to Athens was always the need for the Greek Americans to remain in touch with their cultural origins, including Orthodoxy, and the preparations confirmed this but also showed that the archbishop saw himself as well as the archdiocese as the primary link between Greek America and Greece.

The Clergy Laity Convenes in Athens

The opening of the Clergy-Laity Congress in Athens was heavy on pomp and Greek symbolism and conveyed the archdiocese's close embrace of both the homeland and its government. The *New York Times* reported on the two-hour opening ceremony that took place at the foot of the Acropolis in the restored second-century CE Roman theater of Herod Atticus close to Mars Hill, where the Apostle Paul had preached: "High above the ancient amphitheater the evening sunlight dimmed on the smooth white sides of the temple of the Wingless Victory. . . . As a choir of Greek-American clergymen sang the national anthems of both countries and a program of Greek and religious songs, the sky darkened into a deep blue, and yellow spotlights played on the walls of the ancient backdrop." Outside, and on all the city's major avenues, Greek and American flags decorated the lampposts. Greece's prime minister (and dictator) George Papadopoulos greeted the three thousand persons in attendance and formally opened the congress. Archbishop Ieronymos, who had been appointed head of the Church of Greece by the regime and had clashed with the World Council of Churches over its concern about the regime's surveillance of Greek emigrants in Europe, received a standing ovation. Following various greetings by officials, Iakovos took the podium and set out the goals of the congress, including the strengthening of the cultural and religious ties of the Greek Americans with their homeland. He told his audience, "We want the Greeks in Greece to see the children and grandchildren of the immigrants are not just preoccupied with material gain. . . . We also want to discover the principles and ideals that we can share and work for a renewal of Orthodox theology throughout the world."[8]

The return-to-the-homeland theme featured prominently the next day, in Iakovos's formal speech at the first business day of the congress. The entire speech was geared to explaining the evolution of the archdiocese in America, describing its functions and outlining the problems Greek Orthodoxy faced in the New World. Unlike all other keynote speeches at these congresses, it was not a framed by a pronounced spiritual message, although the archbishop spoke of how the Greek Americans and the Greeks of Greece were coming together to become "of one accord, of one mind," a phrase from the Apostle Paul's Epistle to the Philippians. The speech could be read as a report that the archbishop was making to the Greek homeland, with him in the role of an independent narrator and interpreter. He opened with one of his favorite topics, how the communities had become parishes, a necessary introduction for the Greeks of Greece who were more familiar with the older diaspora model in which the community organization was separate from and sometimes more powerful than the church. He described the mission of each parish as above all religious: "the instilling and perpetuation of the faith, ecclesiastical order, the Holy Canons, the Worship and Holy Tradition, and above all the educating of the new generations in the history of our people and our church." The archbishop was quoting from the Uniform Parish Regulations, which were of course weighted toward religion.[9] From there Iakovos went on to describe the challenges the church was facing in America, noting that two-thirds of its members had been born in the United States and speaking at length about how social changes there threatened the church's values.

The archbishop painted a dark picture of American society, which would have certainly accorded with a conservative assessment of the 1960s. The Greek Orthodox were "exposed to every imaginable danger" because, Iakovos continued ominously, "today's political, economic, social and spiritual climate in America is not at all conducive to favoring the normal development and shaping of the mind and the ethos of the average man. . . . Everything: religion, language, family tradition, ethnic heritage, are under judgment . . . all these are being overturned."[10] Faced with this imminent catastrophe, the Greek Orthodox Church in America was drawing from its homeland and becoming of one mind with it, strengthening and broadening its front and making it impenetrable: "And Orthodoxy as a way of life and ethos shall persist."[11] Referring to the homeland, Iakovos was careful not to mention the Twenty-First April regime by name, though he presented Greece as possessing regenerative qualities, and reassured his hosts that the connection he sought was in the name of the Orthodox religion that united the Greek Americans with the Greeks of Greece, noting nonetheless that the Greek Orthodox in America were not interested in becoming involved in the politics of Greece. He told his Greek audience that the Greek Americans had come "to seek together with you the sound from the blue heaven of Christian Greece, and to be moved with you by the thrill of new life when it comes with a rushing mighty wind to sweep away all that is decayed and old around us and within us." This all sounded very similar to the claims made by the regime about cleaning up Greek society and politics and its vision of a "Greece of Christian Greeks." Iakovos made sure to cast the intended rebirth in spiritual terms, but there were certain echoes of the regime's political rhetoric. He described the Church of Greece as "the only truly free Orthodox Church," the implication being it enjoyed freedom under an anticommunist dictatorship while the other Orthodox churches under communist dictatorships in Eastern Europe were not free.[12] And the connection with the homeland, Iakovos explained, was based on a shared Greek Orthodox identity and patriotism, and the pursuit of national interest: "Of course we have our political views too, but these refer to the politics of our new country. . . . We recognize the value of patriotism, but we are careful not to confuse real patriotism with the voicing of political expressions that are not truly national." It was nation above everything else, Iakovos said: "Greece as a nation is more sacred to us than any political set-up. The politics of Greece are most important, but they are a matter that concern you." He added that Greek citizens could have "the determining vote about them"—a strange thing to say, since the regime had abolished democratic elections.[13]

The Archbishop Plays Wait-and-See

For a prelate who could show considerable dynamism when dealing with the church's affairs, Iakovos was remarkably reticent in dealing with the Greek dictatorship in the aftermath of the Clergy-Laity Congress of 1968. He continued to offer it cautious support, and he did not back the efforts of Democratic Party congressmen in the United States to persuade the White House to disassociate the US from the colonels. And he most certainly did not condone any of the anti-junta activities pursued by a few, or in any case a small part, of the Greek American community. The archbishop preferred to play the role of power broker between Athens, Washington, and the exiled Greek politicians, including King Constantine, who after initially aligning himself with the regime had turned against the colonels and engineered a counter-coup in December 1967, which failed and forced him into exile. But Iakovos's role as power broker was extremely cautious; it was a mixture of praising the colonels publicly and gently admonishing them privately, putting himself forward as a mediator but tactically retreating when he thought the stakes were too high. The published diary of Orestis Vitalis, a former officer who was a supporter of the king and who was permitted to leave Greece and settle in the United States in 1968, attests to Iakovos's constant maneuvering and the ease with which, after communicating with the State Department, exiled politicians, the king, and the colonels, he could simply refuse to do something that might anger the colonels, because, after all, he was not a political figure, and the Greek Americans he was asked to influence were not "political."[14]

It took Iakovos five years to express public criticism of the regime and Washington's policy of support, and he did so in the summer of 1973 when Secretary of State William P. Rogers stated that the abolition of the Greek monarchy by the regime was an internal Greek matter. In June of that year, the regime declared Greece a republic and held a plebiscite, widely considered

to be rigged, in which the electorate supposedly approved of the establishment of the republic. The State Department's reaction was too much even
for Iakovos, who may have thought he had been quietly chipping away at
Nixon's policy of supporting the colonels. The archbishop wrote a letter
to the secretary of state protesting the administration's position, and most
probably he leaked it to *New York Times* journalist Nicholas Gage, a Greek
American, whose byline appeared in the article that made the letter public.
In response, the State Department expressed its surprise, because until then
it had "no hint of the Archbishop's feelings."[15]

The archbishop had chosen the right time to distance himself from the
regime, albeit in a restrained way: a year later Greece's seven-year military
rule would come to an end. While he maintained cordial relations with the
regime and its diplomatic representatives in the United States, in the summer
of 1973 Iakovos began contacts with the White House and Congress with a
view of finding the best way to effect a restoration of parliamentary democracy in Greece. In a private letter to Secretary of State Rogers, he described
the colonels' government as "a tyranny."[16] The replacement of Rogers with
Henry Kissinger in September 1973 ensured that the United States would
continue its support of the regime, and that support continued even after a
student uprising at the Athens Polytechnic in November led to a change of
leadership of the regime. On July 15, 1974, in a misguided attempt to revive
the nationalist dream of uniting Cyprus with Greece, the regime engineered
a coup d'état on the island with the help of Greek forces stationed there, in
an effort to overthrow President Makarios and install a right-wing nationalist government. The coup was successful, but Makarios managed to avoid
arrest and left the island. Days later he appeared in London, where he spoke
out against the coup and prepared to go to New York to address the United
Nations. Greece's obvious connection with the coup provided Turkey with
the pretext to intervene, which it did, invoking its diplomatic status as one of
the international "guarantors" of the island's security. On July 20, Turkey's
military launched a successful attack on the island, while Washington stood
by, with Secretary of State Kissinger unwilling to intervene. The regime in
Athens, unable to defend Cyprus from the Turkish invasion it had provoked,
hastily handed over power to former conservative prime minister Constantinos Karamanlis, while on Cyprus itself the Greek-Cypriot military officers
who had seized power also stepped down and handed over power to the politicians. Ultimately, with Greece unable to respond militarily and the United
States standing by, the Turkish forces overwhelmed the Greek Cypriot army
within a few weeks, occupied the northern part the island, and forced the

Greek Cypriot population to flee to the south, which remained under the control of the legitimate government.

The Archdiocese and the Greek American Lobby

The church's reaction to the events on Cyprus was twofold: mobilization to offer relief to the uprooted Greek Cypriots, and, on a political level, involvement by Archbishop Iakovos in the Greek American lobbying efforts to put pressure on the US Congress to censure Turkey for the invasion and pressure it to end its occupation of the northern part of the island. The effort to help the suffering Greek Cypriots was relatively straightforward; it entailed encouraging all Greek Orthodox parishes across the country to raise funds for that purpose. On July 30, Iakovos convened a meeting of the Archdiocesan Council, which included representatives of the Federation of Hellenic Societies of New York, to coordinate the campaign to support Cyprus and announced the establishment of the Archdiocesan Cyprus Relief Fund. Throughout the United States, Sunday services at Greek Orthodox churches offered Greek Americans the opportunity to gather and organize relief initiatives and also coordinate political activities. Many parish priests encouraged those efforts. The archbishop himself issued appeals to the faithful to rally to the side of the Greek Cypriots who were fleeing from the advancing Turkish forces and creating a growing refugee crisis on the island.

The archbishop's involvement in the lobbying campaign was more challenging, as it entailed adopting a confrontational stance toward the White House. If Archbishop Iakovos was to retain his unofficial position as the head of the Greek American community, it behooved him to go along with the pro-Greek lobby's demands, indeed lead them. But in doing so, he ran the risk of failing to appear as a reliable mediator between the US administration and the Greek and Greek American sides, especially in the eyes of the White House. He would ultimately address the need to balance between endorsing the Greek American demands and retaining the trust of all sides by separating himself from the actual lobbying activities through the creation of a lobbying organization not officially connected to the archdiocese. In the meantime, Iakovos publicly identified himself with the cause of helping Greek-Cypriots but in ways that underscored his status as a religious leader. He called for more relief for the refugees and welcomed Cypriot leader Makarios at a special service held at Holy Trinity Cathedral in New York. He also sent telegrams to President Nixon, Henry Kissinger (who was serving as both secretary of state and national security adviser), and the

UN secretary-general, Kurt Waldheim, urging them to bring about a cease-fire.[17] Iakovos would continue to play his intermediary role in the months that followed, as the Greek lobby's gigantic effort would bear fruit.

In August of 1974, it appeared that the entire Greek American community, including the church, was mobilizing over the crisis on Cyprus, gathering relief funds and demanding that Congress persuade the White House to put pressure on Turkey to relinquish its control of the northern part of the island. The pro-Greek lobbying campaign only became stronger as the Watergate affair culminated in Nixon's resignation and Gerald Ford assumed the presidency. The lobbying effort was spearheaded by the newly established American Hellenic Institute, which was led by Eugene Rossides, a Greek American lawyer of Cypriot descent and a Washington insider, having served as assistant secretary of the treasury during the first Nixon administration. AHEPA joined the lobbying and relief efforts and rallied its membership to the cause during its annual convention held in Boston in August 1974. Other, smaller Greek American organizations also joined the campaign. Seeing this groundswell of activities persuaded Iakovos to go ahead and create a lobbying organization that he could influence unofficially. The inaugural meeting of the new organization took place in Chicago in September and was well attended, not only by those whom Iakovos had appointed as state chairmen to coordinate activities, but also by representatives of all major Greek American organizations, including AHEPA, GAPA, and the regional fraternities. The meeting reiterated the three major goals of the archdiocese's pro-Cyprus campaign: influencing public opinion in the US and Canada in order to bring about a just solution to the crisis; urging support for the resolutions introduced in the US House of Representatives and the Senate designed to stop military aid to Turkey; and the expansion of the relief activities that were being undertaken by the Cyprus Relief Fund the archdiocese had established. The meeting also decided to establish a coordinating organization that would take on those goals. Initially named the United Hellenic Council, in January 1975 it joined up with another organization, the Congress of American Hellenic Organizations, to form the United Hellenic American Congress (UHAC), chaired by Chicago-based Greek-American steel magnate Andrew Athens.[18]

The archdiocese stepped up its activities in connection with Cyprus over the next months, continuing to support the lobbying effort, which was succeeding, and focusing on the need to address the humanitarian crisis on Cyprus. Congress had voted in favor of the arms embargo in December 1974, and the president was able to veto only parts of the plan. The embargo went into effect in February 1975, but pressure by the administration led to a new round of votes in Congress the following July. UHAC's representative in the capital, a Greek American doctor, Andrew Tegeris, appeared before a House of Representatives committee that July and echoed the position that Turkey's actions had violated the rule of law.[19] The failed effort to lift the embargo coincided with the first anniversary of Turkey's invasion, and the archdiocese moved a memorial service it had scheduled in the cathedral in New York City to St. Sophia, the Greek Orthodox Cathedral in Washington, DC. Iakovos also sent a message of support to a Greek American rally held outside the White House.[20] The administration's pressure continued, and it succeeded in getting Congress to agree to an easing of its sanctions against Turkey in late 1975; but what remained of the embargo survived the end of the Ford presidency, which came after he was voted out of office in 1976. In the meantime the refugee crisis on Cyprus had become acute.

The Archbishop as Intermediary

Throughout this period, from August 1974 through the end of the Ford presidency, Iakovos played the role of go-between, meeting with American and Greek and Cypriot government officials and Greek American leaders and passing messages from one to the other, as well as making his own policy recommendations. Early on he had been invited to the White House to meet President Ford and Henry Kissinger (whom Ford had retained as secretary of state) in the hope that he could convey to the Greek Americans that the administration was working carefully behind the scenes to bring about an end to the hostilities and reverse the effects of Turkey's intervention. In December 1974 Iakovos had testified before a Senate subcommittee, urging America to do better in sending humanitarian aid to Cyprus. The archdiocese continued its fund-raising campaign and by mid-1975 had collected about $1.3 million. The lobbying campaign had gained momentum throughout the rest of the summer, while on Cyprus itself the situation worsened.

Iakovos's contacts with policy makers had in fact begun almost immediately after the Turkish invasion. He had requested a meeting with the president in mid-August; at the time, though, the National Security Council had recommended against the meeting because "the archbishop is intensely disliked by the Turks, and in the current, highly charged climate if he were to meet with the President we could expect that this would be interpreted by the Turks as a very provocative and unfriendly gesture." The memorandum (which misspelled Iakovos's name) went on to warn, "It is also possible that the Turks might be moved by the visit to do away with the Greek Orthodox Church in Turkey, an action they have refrained from taking."[21]

The memorandum confirmed the high political profile Iakovos had already achieved because of his espousal of Greek national concerns and the respect with which the National Security Council treated Turkey. But Kissinger decided that it would be best to meet with Iakovos, and he briefed the archbishop at the State Department on August 24. With the embargo legislation continuing to make headway in Congress in September, the administration decided to raise the stakes and invite the archbishop to the White House in the hope that "he could be helpful."[22]

At the White House meeting, Iakovos parried the president and Kissinger's request that he dampen down Greek American pressure on the administration. Iakovos had brought with him the two pastors of the Greek Orthodox churches in the District of Columbia, Demetrios Kalaris of Sts. Constantine and Helen, and John Tavlarides of St. Sophia. Also present, aside from Ford and Kissinger, were two deputy assistants to the president, Brent Scowcroft and Greek American Tom Korologos. Ford and Kissinger spoke of how their efforts to bring about an understanding between the Greek and Turkish sides was being undermined by the push for the arms embargo on Turkey, and the president added he would veto such a plan. They implied that the Greek government understood the need to show restraint at that moment, but they wanted Turkey to make concessions without the United States' role in obtaining these to become public. The minutes of the meeting indicate that Iakovos demurred from making any statement himself about the embargo, or intervening with Athens, saying "I can't reason with my people . . . they are demonstrating against me"—an acknowledgment that there was an antiestablishment element present in the pro-embargo mobilization and that many Greek Americans were critical of the archbishop's stance during the 1967–1974 dictatorship. Iakovos suggested that the White House improve its image in the eyes of the Greeks and the Greek Americans by focusing on the issue of the Greek Cypriot refugees, whose number had reached two hundred thousand, and then asked Kissinger if he could also make a statement that would "calm" the Greek Americans. Father Kalaris added that the Greek Americans believed the US had done nothing to alleviate the suffering of the refugees. Kissinger responded that the US could not say it would help with the return of the refugees because that would alienate the Turks. Iakovos insisted on some kind of statement, to which Ford replied that the White House could maximize the humanitarian aid it was offering. The outcome of the meeting was inconclusive, though it did provide Iakovos with a great deal of political capital, and he was wise enough not to squander it by doing Ford and Kissinger's bidding and come out against the campaign for the embargo.[23] The White House press secretary's answers during the press briefing later that day tried to evoke an anodyne version of what happened. He emphasized the president's concern with relief aid, and he responded negatively to a question as to whether the archbishop had been critical of US policy. He confirmed that the topic of US aid to Turkey had come up but said he had no "specifics" for the press.[24]

Iakovos's visit to the White House acquired an unexpected and quite public footnote when it became the topic of an article by syndicated columnists Rowland Evans and Robert Novak that appeared in the *Washington Post* and other newspapers. Writing a week before Greece held its first national elections following the collapse of the colonels' junta, Evans and Novak described the meeting based on a memorandum drawn up by the archdiocese, which they say had made its way to the Greek government in Athens. The article provided an accurate description of the essence of the meeting as portrayed in the memorandum—Iakovos confirmed its contents—and made the point that Karamanlis did not want his dealings with the Americans known because the socialist party of Andreas Papandreou would portray the United States as Greece's patron and in doing so could increase the support the socialists would receive at the polls. Evans and Novak spiced up their piece by including a critique of the president by Iakovos in his memorandum: "I think he is a good man of good intentions but too weak to take a position by himself." In a possible tit for tat, administration officials told Evans and Novak that they were "expecting a firebrand in Iakovos," but instead they found him "unimpressive and insecure."[25] Despite that sting in the article's tail, most Greek Orthodox may have regarded the column as contributing to the archbishop's aura because two well-known columnists were talking about their church's leader.

The archbishop had maintained contact with the Greek government during the Cyprus crisis in the summer of 1974, and he used the access he enjoyed in Washington as a way of offering advice to the Greek government on how to deal with the Americans. He hastened to Athens in August, days after the Turks completed the second phase of their occupation of Cyprus. Initially he was met with suspicion by part of Greek public opinion; his support of the colonels' regime had earned him the name "CIAkovos" in the left-wing press, but his mobilization over the Cyprus issue gradually reinstated his standing in the eyes of most of his critics. His visit elicited a long, detailed telegram from American ambassador Henry Tasca, who reported that the stated purpose of the archbishop's visit was to examine "possibilities for assisting efforts of Hellenism at present time" and to convey the greetings of "two and a half million Greek Americans to the new government." In fact, at a sermon delivered at the Greek Orthodox Cathedral in Athens,

Iakovos told the congregation he was bringing "the unanimous support of two and half million Greek Americans and that support would be accompanied by material assistance and by strong protests in the U.S." The archbishop also "denounced the Turks for fighting an unjust and bandit war" and asserted "they had violated all international principles." Over the next few days, in meetings with Prime Minister Karamanlis and other Greek government officials, Iakovos discussed "the moral and political support as well as material assistance" Greek Americans could provide to Greece. The Athens-based *Vradyni* newspaper claimed that Iakovos would collect $100 million for Greece. Meanwhile, Iakovos spoke on the Greek state radio station about the strong interest of the Greek Americans in the Cyprus problem, declaring that they were aware they had a voice, which would be effective because their cause was just. He concluded by expressing the hope that Kissinger would understand what was going on in Cyprus and would "adjust his original positions."[26]

Iakovos was back in Athens again in January 1975, where he met twice with Prime Minister Karamanlis and twice with the US ambassador, Jack Kubisch. In a cable to the State Department, the ambassador reported on the visit, mentioning that during Iakovos's stay in Athens, all his interviews to the Greek media "contained consistent and supportive themes," and that he described US policy toward Cyprus as "equitable" and said good relations between Greece and the United States were "essential." Speaking at a nationally televised interview, the archbishop said "the Greeks in America are trying to contribute as much as possible on all issues that help the mother country." But Greek reactions to Iakovos's pro-American assessment of the diplomatic goings-on were mixed. The extreme right and left newspapers "bitterly condemned Iakovos' analysis of the issues," and "the more moderate press simply expressed varying degrees of surprise regarding the basis of his optimism." Iakovos went as far as recommending that the United States invite Prime Minister Karamanlis on an official visit to Washington, to which Kubisch added, "Any such proposal should be most carefully evaluated."[27]

Tensions with the Patriarchate

Iakovos's diplomatic initiatives in the 1970s left their mark not only in Athens and Washington but also in Istanbul, the seat of the Ecumenical Patriarchate. It was there, ironically, where his dynamism was least appreciated—not for ecclesiastical reasons, but because of differing policy concerns. Metropolitan Meliton and members of the Holy Synod had tolerated if not welcomed Iakovos's strong advocacy of the rights of the patriarchate during

Athenagoras's tenure. Iakovos was, after all, the patriarch's protégé. But following Athenagoras's death and Dimitrios's enthronement in 1972, Meliton and his fellow hierarchs felt the time had come for the patriarchate to speak out for itself whenever it considered that prudent, and not have others do their bidding, lest that created difficulties with the Turkish authorities. If Iakovos was informed of this, it apparently did not stop him from speaking out whenever he saw fit. In late 1977, Iakovos had written to the secretary of state listing a series of incidents of harassment of the patriarchate and the minority and Greek schools in Istanbul. This brought a detailed explanation of the situation, provided by Turkey, to the State Department.[28] This did not satisfy Iakovos, and he made his concerns public in an interview to the *New York Times* that appeared on Christmas Day, 1977. The patriarchate quickly showed its displeasure, and significantly it was through Meliton of Chalcedon. Iakovos's old rival, traveling through Athens, was asked about the archbishop's statements on the situation in Istanbul. He acknowledged there were serious problems between the patriarchate and the Turkish government but stressed there was no real danger because it would not be in Turkey's interests to take any restrictive measures. Meliton added that problems existed between the government and the Greek minority in Istanbul, but all issues would be dealt with through dialogue and without any foreign interference. The US embassy in Athens considered that Meliton "clearly aimed at disassociating the Patriarchate from the critical remarks" that Iakovos made publicly "about Turkish mistreatment of the Patriarchate and the Greek minority in Turkey." The message added that according to the Greek Ministry of Foreign Affairs, "the Patriarchate had warned Iakovos recently to avoid making public statements critical of the Turks in order not to exacerbate its relations with the GOT [Government of Turkey,] however, for his own reasons Iakovos chose to ignore this advice." The embassy's cable went on to explain that the Greek government agreed with the patriarchate's tactics, and then it listed the serious problems faced by both the patriarchate and the Greeks of Istanbul.[29]

In August 1978 another incident confirmed Iakovos's difficult relations with the mother church. The White House invited Iakovos to join the US delegation that was traveling to Rome in August to attend the funeral of Pope Paul VI. Iakovos had met the pope in 1959 in the first meeting of an Orthodox leader and the pope in 350 years, and that meeting had paved the way for the meeting between the pope and Ecumenical Patriarch Athenagoras in 1964. But Athenagoras's successor Dimitrios was less eager to allow Iakovos to thrust himself in the limelight, and—no doubt at Meliton's urging—refused the archbishop permission to go to the funeral. The patriarchal delegation may not have wished to be overshadowed by Iakovos's participation with the Americans, who were sure to attract more media attention. It sent the archbishop a laconic message forbidding him to go in the name of the highest interests of the patriarchate. Iakovos tendered his resignation, but he submitted it to the Ministry of Foreign Affairs in Greece, not the patriarchate, a ploy to publicize his anger and also get the Greeks involved. Prime Minister Karamanlis acted quickly to defuse the situation and did not forward the resignation on from Athens to Constantinople. It was a temporary resignation. When the pope's successor, John Paul I, died only a month later, Constantinople sent Iakovos a message asking him to go to the funeral. Iakovos did not miss the opportunity and responded curtly that the highest interests of the archdiocese prevented him from traveling to Rome.

Jimmy Carter and Iakovos

In his campaign leading up to the presidential election in 1976, Jimmy Carter had made statements criticizing Ford's Cyprus policy and favoring a solution that would remove the Turkish occupying forces and allow Greek Cypriot refugees to return to their homes. A month prior to the 1976 elections he sent Iakovos a message on the occasion of the prelate's sixty-fifth birthday in which he repeated his views, saying "These have been trying years for the Greek Americans. . . . They have seen the U.S. government tilting away from Greek democracy and away from a principled policy concerning the tragic events in Cyprus. They have seen our government ignore the rule of law and pursue a course on Cyprus that has failed . . . to bring about the end of the division of the island . . . to remove foreign troops . . . and to make possible the return of the refugees to their homes."[30] Next to his attractiveness because of his position on Cyprus, Carter's publicly professed religiosity matched him well with the archbishop. And yet their relationship proved to be the most turbulent of all those between a US president and a Greek Orthodox archbishop.

The archbishop, along with the rest of the Greek American community, had assumed that Carter would keep his promises, but his policy advisers persuaded him to change his mind and push for lifting of the embargo. Soon after moving into the White House, Carter publicly spoke of separating the issue of a solution for Cyprus and the Turkish arms embargo. In November 1977, the archbishop led a group of Greek American leaders at a meeting with Vice President Walter Mondale. According to Iakovos, Mondale was cordial and said he understood the frustration of the Greek Americans, adding that the administration was not going to renege on its promises. The archbishop had raised concerns about Turkey's violations of human rights and conversions of Christian churches into mosques in the Turkish-occupied territories. Toward the end of the meeting, Carter walked in and greeted the archbishop and the others warmly. The event had been very positive in the archbishop's view, because Carter and Mondale had acknowledged Greek American frustrations and given assurances they had not forgotten their pre-election promises, and because there had been a pervasive atmosphere of "trust." As Greek Cypriot scholar Chris Ioannides noted, however, the arch-bishop was being somewhat naïve in believing the president and the vice president, and moreover had not questioned Carter on his statements about separating the issues of Cyprus and the embargo. Following that meeting, Iakovos appeared confident that the United States would move toward end-ing the Turkish occupation. It is possible that the usually politically savvy Iakovos was taken in by Carter's religiosity, and this may have blunted his political acumen. In Ioannides's words, "the Archbishop's optimism was not rooted in fact but, rather, reflected his own expectations based on the trust he and most of the Greek Americans had in Carter."[31]

In April 1978 the archbishop was demonstrating against the White House rather than visiting it: a period of strained relations between the archbishop and the president had begun. Carter had made public his intention to lift the embargo for reasons of national security and not alienating Turkey. Greek American organizations joined in a huge protest rally at Lafayette Park across from the White House on April 16; estimates of the number of dem-onstrators ranged from fifteen thousand to forty thousand. Among them was Archbishop Iakovos, who had written to Carter that day expressing his opposition to lifting the embargo. Two weeks later he was able to meet with Mondale to discuss the meaning of the Greek American demonstration, and he sent along a gift for the president.[32] Carter responded two weeks later to thank him and added, "I appreciate the forthrightness with which you have expressed your views. All of us must be patient and determined if we are ever to solve the problems in the Eastern Mediterranean. The United States does not intend to prescribe specific steps to the parties involved."[33] In the months that followed, his administration launched an all-out effort to get Congress to the lift the embargo. It was a long, drawn-out battle, but in the end the president prevailed after two cliffhanger votes, in the Senate on July 25 and the House of Representatives on August 1. Iakovos, despite his bitterness, was careful not to alienate Carter and communicated with him in September, congratulating him on his peace initiative that led to the Camp David accords between Egypt and Israel. In June 1979, Vice President Mondale was the principal speaker at an event in Chicago held in honor of

Iakovos's twentieth anniversary at the helm of the Greek Orthodox Church in America. In his remarks, Mondale avoided any talk of politics and focused on the value of the Orthodox Church's moral principles.[34]

The attempt to patch up any bad feelings between the archbishop and the president was made obvious when Carter announced in September 1979 that he would be awarding Iakovos the Presidential Medal of Freedom. Iakovos became the first Greek American and Greek Orthodox to receive this highest civilian honor bestowed by US presidents on extraordinary individuals. At that event Carter avoided any mention of the recent campaign to maintain the Turkish arms embargo, which had caused so much bitterness. Instead he focused on Iakovos's contributions to humanitarianism, his religious community, and American society, saying, "We could not have a better exemplification of the finest aspects of human life than His Eminence Archbishop Iakovos. His life is one which has been dedicated to the pursuit of the broadest possible realm of basic civil rights, basic human rights, not just in this country but throughout the world. . . . Although he only has 3 million communicants who look to him with direct religious conviction, and a common, narrowly defined religious conviction, he has many millions of other Americans who look to him for spiritual inspiration and who admire his great contributions to our country and to the kingdom of Christ."[35]

The Ethnarch as Intermediary

Iakovos's rapprochement with Carter sums up the way the archbishop saw his dual role as both an ethnarch and an intermediary. He inserted himself in the policy process and navigated according to the circumstances, benefiting from his position as leader of an ethnic church and one associated with a homeland that was affected by US foreign policy. But he could not act against the prevailing climate, and in this case he could not afford to alienate a president, even one who lifted the arms embargo on Turkey, and over the next years he would demonstrate that he would be able to approach if not win over politicians in Greece and Turkey with whom he did not see eye to eye. In the meantime, Iakovos easily slipped into a comfortable relationship with Ronald Reagan, who would defeat Carter in the 1980 elections. Prior to the election both Carter and Reagan invited Iakovos to their party conventions that took place over the summer, and not wanting to offend anyone, Iakovos attended both, beginning a tradition of sorts in which he would be the only religious leader who went to both party conventions in election years.[36] Iakovos was astute enough to adopt a bipartisan approach, proclaiming that the archdiocese "was not political."

Iakovos continued to play the role of intermediary between Washington and Athens in the Reagan era, after a difficult couple of years because the socialist government in Greece led by Andreas Papandreou was openly critical of the United States and chose to ignore the archbishop. But after two years, the frosty relationship melted away. In November 1983 Turkey announced the establishment of the "Turkish Republic of Northern Cyprus" in the territories its army had held illegally since 1974. It was an audacious act that flew in the face of all the United Nations decisions that had gone against the Turkish actions on Cyprus, and it was serious enough to bring Iakovos and Papandreou together. As soon as the Turkish announcement became known, the Greek lobbying organizations and Iakovos launched a flurry of messages to the White House and Congress demanding that the United States not recognize the so-called republic and oppose Turkey's action. Iakovos met with the UN secretary-general Javier Pérez de Cuéllar and then traveled to Washington and met with Secretary of State George Shultz. Within a few days, deputy secretary of state Richard Burt wrote to Iakovos to confirm that the United States condemned the Turkish announcement and called for its reversal. Meanwhile, Iakovos and Papandreou were in direct contact, and at the end of November the archbishop arrived in Athens along with representatives of Greek American lobbying organizations for consultations. The pomp surrounding the official welcome signaled the thaw in the Iakovos-Papandreou relationship. The archbishop had regained his place as ethnarch and intermediary.

Iakovos, having established a close relationship with Papandreou, went on to demonstrate his ability to woo almost anyone when he was also able to sit down with Turkish prime minister Turgut Özal. A political moderate who emphasized economic modernization and tried to downplay the nationalist issues that always predominated, Özal visited New York in 1985 and requested a meeting with both Iakovos and representatives of AHEPA to discuss the normalization of Greco-Turkish relations. When Iakovos pointed out he was still persona non grata in Turkey and therefore it was strange that the Turkish prime minister should be asking him to intercede with Papandreou, Özal told him he would resolve the problem so that Iakovos could visit Turkey. He also pledged to allow the refurbishment of the patriarchate, which Turkish authorities had refused to allow for over four decades. Following the meeting, the archbishop and the Turkish prime minister continued their conversation through an exchange of correspondence, with Iakovos conveying Özal's views and proposals to Papandreou and, in return, Papandreou's views to Özal. The Greek Orthodox Church began to experience the pre-1955 atmosphere of cordiality toward Turkey. In December 1987,

Iakovos hosted a luncheon in New York City in honor of the visiting mayor of Istanbul, Bedrettin Dalan. The archbishop and the mayor avoided sensitive issues such as the situation in Cyprus, and Iakovos told the *New York Times* "it was not a business meeting but a meeting of hearts" and that he was determined to develop "warm and friendly" relations.[37] Despite a sudden and serious crisis in the relations of the countries earlier in 1987 over their respective rights in the Aegean Sea, Özal and Papandreou met in January 1988, on neutral ground at an international gathering at Davos, Switzerland, and even issued a common statement about the prospect of normalizing relations between the two countries. A Turkish newspaper described Iakovos as the "architect of Davos." On his part, Iakovos, delighted, congratulated both leaders and offered to take on the role of intermediary in their future negotiations, this time in an official capacity.

The year 1988 represented the culmination of Iakovos's dual role as ethnarch and intermediary in the diplomatic triangle between Greece, Turkey, and the United States.[38] The following year Papandreou lost the elections in Greece, and the Greco-Turkish rapprochement lost momentum. Although it is always difficult to weigh the contribution of an intermediary in diplomacy, there is no question that Iakovos played a crucial role in the coming together of Özal and Papandreou. It is also difficult to know what the clergy and laity thought of his initiatives, though it is certain that the coverage the media provided to Iakovos's initiatives, when those became public, helped raise the profile of Greek Orthodoxy in America, even though his critics suspected his only motivation was his wish to become the next ecumenical patriarch.[39] The particular circumstances governing US–Greek relations from the 1960s and 1970s enabled the leader of Greek Orthodoxy to play a political role, and Iakovos adroitly exploited the conditions he encountered to maximize his political influence, albeit as an intermediary. The Orthodox Church may not have been the most influential of all Greek American actors over that period, but the archbishop most certainly played an important role, which helped the status of the church as a force in shaping Greek American identity.

Next to Greek Orthodoxy's conception of an ethnarch, what helped Iakovos assume the role of diplomatic intermediary was the role that US politics reserves for leaders of American religions. There is of course the ceremonial part they play in the inauguration of presidents, but also, more informally, political leaders frequently solicit the advice and input of religious leaders. And some of those leaders offer their own input, such as Martin Luther King Jr.'s leadership in the civil rights movement or when, in the mid-1980s, New York's Catholic archbishop John O'Connor and many other bishops all but decreed that Catholics should not vote for political candidates who did not agree with the Catholic stance against abortion rights. And if we add, in this case, the significance of ethnic lobbying, which is another feature of American politics and also of Greek Orthodoxy's identification with Greek national issues, we can appreciate the combination of factors that enabled Iakovos to become an important element in the diplomatic sphere. While members of Congress and professional lobbyists did most of the work, the presence of the archbishop gave the Greek American cause an important and influential figurehead. And by the same token, the archbishop's presence in the White House, and the way presidents treated him as the unofficial head of the Greek Americans, served to confirm and consolidate Greek Orthodoxy's position at the center of Greek American life.

The structural framework that guaranteed Iakovos a privileged position in American political culture enabled him to play the role of ethnarch and cement his own authority as the undisputed leader of the Greek American community. The archbishop, knowledgeable and politically savvy, also showed himself to be a master tactician. Significantly, Iakovos maneuvered carefully and chose the role of intermediary rather than advocate of the community's, Greece's, or the US government's position.

CHAPTER 9

Toward an American Greek Orthodoxy

Greek Americans were becoming more American than Greek, suggested sociologist Charles Moskos in his book *Greek Americans: Struggle and Success*, published in 1980. Moskos, the American-born son of Greek immigrants who became an authority on the sociology of the US military, was involved in the church's life, and he supported Iakovos's efforts to adapt Orthodoxy to the American environment. Moskos believed that Greek immigrants had to reorder their lives on arrival and conform to the socioeconomic realities of the New World and to its cultural norms. His conclusion was that "among those born in this country it seems clear that one's identity is not that of a transplanted Greek, but rather the sensibility of an American ethnic."[1] Moskos anticipated a clear trend in American culture. His was a post-melting-pot view that acknowledged the persistence of an ethnic identity in an Americanizing community.

As the 1980s unfolded, trends in the church and community life confirmed Moskos's view. For the archdiocese, the number of intra-Orthodox and mixed marriages, as well as the number of baptisms per year, had always been closely watched figures and functioned as a barometer of the cohesion of the Greek American community and its attachment to its identity. By 1980 the numbers of baptisms and intra–Greek Orthodox marriages, both indicators of the community's growth and cohesion, were dipping significantly. The number of Greek Orthodox baptisms recorded by its Registry

Department in 1975 had reached 10,435, one of its all-time highs, but over the next four years it steadily decreased, and the number of intra-Orthodox marriages was also declining. And they continued to do so. In 1984 the number of baptisms, 8,109, was the lowest since 1961, and the intra–Greek Orthodox marriages, 1,821, were the lowest in the post–World War II era.[2] Meanwhile, the post-1965 surge in immigration from Greece ended in 1974 when democracy was restored there and the country prepared to join the European Common Market. Throughout the 1980s the numbers of persons born in Greece recorded in the US Census would drop steadily, from 210,998 in 1980 down to 177,398 in 1990.

These trends toward Americanization did not mean that ethnic identity was disappearing, but it was changing in ways that would benefit Greek Orthodoxy. As Yiorgos Anagnostou has argued, what in fact was happened in the Reagan era of the 1980s was that ethnicity was being transformed, with the various European ethnicities becoming part of mainstream views of America. Their public acceptance, indeed their incorporation into the narrative of a multiethnic America, enabled first-, second-, and third-generation immigrants to continue to celebrate their ethnic roots as a way of expressing both their Americanism and their individualism. What eroded was the umbrella term of white ethnicity used to describe the immigrants from Eastern and Southern Europe. In its place grew a culturally defined "multitude of unique ethnic identities, and the language of distinct ethnic hyphenations— Irish Americans, Polish Americans, Jewish Americans," and of course Greek Americans. Ethnicity, according to Anagnostou, became "a powerful source of identification because it anchored cultural uniqueness and belonging, interests and affective ties, all central ingredients in the search for combating modern anomie."[3] Moreover, it also became a matter of personal preference, as Mary Waters has suggested, allowing persons to construct and express their ethnicity if and how they pleased and in whatever ways that fulfilled them most.[4] In the case of the Greek Americans, the hegemonic presence of the church in community life meant that it became increasingly likely that an à la carte ethnicity would include some form of ties with Greek Orthodoxy.

Decentralization

The Greek Orthodox Church entered the 1980s in an especially strong position to move toward Americanization and to augment its role in community life because it was granted somewhat greater autonomy by the Ecumenical Patriarchate. The crisis of the language issue in 1970 had also entailed accusations by the traditionalists that Iakovos desired too much autonomy from Constantinople. But developments in the Russian Orthodox Church in America prompted a reconsideration of the autonomy issue in a more favorable light. In 1970, the Orthodox Patriarchate in Moscow had granted autocephaly (i.e., autonomy) to the main body of the Russian Orthodox Church in America, known as Metropolia. It had been a long process that took place primarily within Russian Orthodox Churches and without the approval of the Patriarchate of Constantinople. This step upset the balance among the Eastern Orthodox Churches in North America. The Metropolia had not only become self-governing, but it was also taking on the responsibility or at least making the claim of being the instrument of uniting all the Eastern Orthodox and changed its name to the Orthodox Church in America. The Patriarchate of Constantinople had shown its displeasure at Moscow's granting autonomy to the Metropolia, and Athenagoras had appointed Iakovos as its "exarch" or representative in the United States, giving him the authority to preside over the standing conference of Orthodox bishops, in an attempt to bolster its authority over all the Orthodox Churches in America.[5] But the Metropolia's claim to represent potentially all Orthodox in America required a stronger response from the archdiocese, so Iakovos had proposed that the Patriarchate of Constantinople consider and approve a new charter for the Archdiocese, one that would make the Greek Orthodox Church more attractive to the faithful by providing more local decision making and allowing the church to seek to attract all those of Eastern Orthodox faith in the Americas. It was an obvious countermeasure to the Metropolia's new status and would be granting the archdiocese greater autonomy.[6]

Four years later, in 1977, the patriarchate finally approved a new charter that would make the archdiocese more attractive to all the Orthodox in America by decentralizing its structure, but for good measure it rhetorically affirmed the archdiocese's close dependency on Constantinople. The new charter stated that the church in America was "by canonical and historical right under the supreme spiritual, ecclesiastical and canonical jurisdiction of the Ecumenical Patriarchate." It also affirmed that the archdiocese served "all of the Orthodox living in the Western Hemisphere." And in a significant acknowledgment of local conditions, while the new charter was set out in both Greek and English, "in the event of a need of interpretation, the English text shall be deemed the official and legal text."[7] Ecumenical Patriarch Dimitrios asserted that the patriarchate was mindful of the needs "of the whole of Orthodoxy in the Americas," and it offered itself "in service for the increasing growth and development of the Holy Archdiocese in a fashion so that the Archdiocese may give—together with all of the Orthodox in America—a united, eloquent and powerful witness of Orthodoxy in the

New World." And Metropolitan of Chalcedon Meliton, an influential member of the patriarchate's synod, wrote that Constantinople was initiating the conversations with the archdiocese in a climate that combined "the ancient Orthodox tradition of the Mother Church, her canonical order, ecclesiastical ethos, and American reality, and with the service of the faithful people of God in America and the common Orthodox witness in America."[8] The new charter established regionally based dioceses headed by a bishop, restoring the synod of bishops and the authority of each bishop in his diocese that the patriarchate had abolished when it installed Athenagoras as archbishop in 1930. The new dioceses were Boston, Charlotte, Chicago, Denver, Detroit, Pittsburgh, San Francisco, Toronto, and Buenos Aires, and each would elect its own bishop who would handle religious matters on a local level. Significantly, the bishops would be answerable to the archbishop.

In his keynote speech at the Clergy-Laity Congress in Detroit in 1978, Iakovos made it obvious that the reforms reflected a step toward Americanizing the church. He said it was a "Congress which initiates a new period of Church Life, the Congress that signals the end of the transition; from an immigrant status to a state of permanency; from a state of parochialism to the status of a national church," a trajectory that he had always spoken about. He did not use the words "an American church" but sought to explain the arrival of the Orthodox to the United States in providential terms and entailing a responsibility to spread their religion: "Orthodox Christians were led to these shores by the same God Who led the Pilgrims, and with the same purpose; i.e. to share their faith and tradition with other people who migrated earlier with all American believers." And he continued driving home the point that the ethnic boundaries had to be superseded: "It becomes incumbent upon all the Orthodox in this country, therefore, to rise above phyletism and self-righteousness, and discern the signs of our times and the writing on the wall," and added that "we certainly can preserve our particular language and liturgical traditions, even our dependency on Mother Churches, without losing sight of the mission of Orthodoxy." Addressing his "fellow Greek Orthodox believers to whom Orthodoxy was either a birthright or a faith by choice," he reminded them that "Orthodoxy, by its very nature, excludes no one from approaching and examining it" and that the principal task of the church was "to unite, not to divide, to embrace, not to reject . . . to heal, not to wound."[9]

Speaking to the *New York Times* a few days after the congress, Iakovos suggested that the greater autonomy granted to the members of the church reflected the understanding that "we have three American-born generations, feel more American and are charged with greater responsibilities."[10] Taking a different approach, the traditionalists clung to the Ecumenical Patriarchate's statements that it was still overseeing Orthodoxy in America. *New Yorki* magazine noted that the new charter's main feature was that it increased the archdiocese's dependence on the patriarchate and showed that the patriarchate "has the last word on everything," which ought to please Greek Americans who "wanted Orthodoxy cloaked in the mantle of Hellenism the way we received it from our forefathers."[11]

Spreading Orthodoxy and Surveying the Orthodox

The Clergy-Laity Congress in Atlanta in 1980 highlighted the ways Greek Orthodoxy was confronting the task of adapting to the American environment. The archdiocese had commissioned a survey of the attitudes of its members from the Gallup organization. This unusual move was a sign that the church was adopting modern methods to document the views of its members. The survey was proposed by Father Alex Karloutsos, a young American-born priest who joined the public affairs department in 1977 and was destined to play an important role in the ways the archdiocese adopted a range of modern techniques and practices.

Iakovos's keynote speech in Atlanta focused on a spiritual theme, the need to revitalize the Greek Orthodox inheritance, which he presented as a strategy with which to confront the 1980s. His message reiterated the dual ethnic and religious dimensions of Greek Orthodoxy. The threshold of the new decade, Iakovos said, was "a most opportune time for commitment and action. . . . Our Greek legacy compels us to pursue education and excellence while our Christian legacy commissions us to go teach, baptize and commission others to the task of preserving and practicing all things, whatsoever Christ has commanded to his disciples. . . . Facing the eighties therefore, means arming ourselves with the panoply of the Greek Orthodox Faith and rearming our Christian conscience with purity and our mind with the determined will to live our faith in its fullness." The archbishop added that he saw the need for spiritual renewal as a way of transcending ethnic insularity: "Facing the eighties requires a new approach, study and understanding of our own status as well as of the course we should chart in our effort to consolidate the ground upon which we stand. . . . The time has come for us to disengage from everything that pushes us back into parochialism." He spoke about a path leading away from "parochialism" and toward creating an inclusive community of Orthodox Christians, and he spoke about the need to "close ranks with our Orthodox brethren to promote the ideal and the idea of Christian unity."[12]

Iakovos was outlining a new assertiveness on the part of Greek Orthodoxy in America, one in which it could open up to America without fear of
losing itself. The issue of the distinct character of the religion and the ethnic
group had been resolved: "There is no longer any fear of drowning in the
multi-ethnic and multi-ecclesiastical sea of this land. We no longer suffer
from an inferiority complex, which inhibited us in the past. We have self-
awareness and we are slowly acquiring our own physiognomy. We are not
yet fully organized as a serious power to be reckoned with, but gradually we
progress as a Church and as an ethnic group." With that process completed,
the next step after achieving distinctiveness and ensuring an existence was to
deepen the quality of religious life and strive for a more authentic religious
practice, because "our ecclesiastical perpetuity in this land will be ensured
the moment we cease vain and purposeless discussions and begin living our
faith through conscientious and fruitful actions."[13]

After Iakovos, the survey got top billing, and Dr. George Gallup Jr., president of Gallup Poll Inc., addressed the congress on its first day of business at
the Atlanta Hilton Hotel. He outlined the main points of the survey, which
were included in a 170-page booklet. The Gallup survey explored Greek
American attitudes in a broad range of fourteen areas, from religious beliefs
and practices to rating the functions of the church and the role of priests, and
interviewed 455 Greek Americans, of whom 60 percent were members of
the Greek Orthodox Church. The responses were divided among those given
by "Greek Americans" and members of the church. There were supplemen-
tary surveys of teenage and of adult members of the church. Significantly,
Gallup conducted its work not only in New York City but further afield, in
Chicago, Dayton (Ohio), Los Angeles, and Houston. Gallup also conducted
a series of seventy-five intensive interviews in Worcester, Massachusetts, and
Charleston, South Carolina. This geographical dispersion broke the near-
monopoly that the New York City area had enjoyed in terms of public responses to the archdiocese's affairs with the post-1965 immigrant influx. The
furor over the use of English in the Sunday liturgy that the Greek-language
press had roused in 1970 had relied almost entirely on protests emanating
from organizations of mostly Greek-born immigrants in and around New
York City. Now, a slice of the rest of Greek America, and from areas with
a high percentage of American born, was able to voice its opinions on how
the archdiocese conducted itself, including the ways the Sunday liturgy was
held in the church.

The language question appeared in the survey but was listed only after
a set of other findings that pointed to what Gallup described as "positive
elements" for Greek Orthodoxy in America. Levels of attested belief were

"extraordinarily high" among both the Greek Americans (i.e., non-church-member Greek Americans) and the church members. Eight out of ten Greek Americans were church members, and the church was "the focal point in their lives" and served them "in a great variety of ways, social as well as religious." Seven out of ten Greek Americans and eight out of ten church members had attended church in the last six months apart from baptisms, funerals, weddings, and special holidays, and eight of ten of both categories of those polled had prayed during the previous thirty days. A large majority thought it very important that their children received religious instruction and became religious persons. About half of Greek Americans and six in ten among church members said their church provided "enough leadership opportunities for them to use their own personal abilities and talents in performing volunteer work." Both surveyed groups gave a generally favorable rating to four key functions of the Greek Orthodox Church: its charitable efforts, its educational institutes, its communications and publications, and its leadership.[14]

After these positive elements, the survey went on to list the "warning signs," which included dissatisfaction with the ways the Sunday liturgy was conducted; a sense among younger respondents that the church did not offer them leadership opportunities and was not "warm or accepting of outsiders"; and a significant disjunction of the views of young respondents and the church on issues of personal morality. The survey also issued a warning about the church's finances, noting that the proportion of Greek Americans and church members who contributed 10 percent or more of their incomes to their church or other religious organizations was far below the national average. Of all those "warning signs," the most ominous were those regarding the church's relationship with the younger generation. "Pollster warns Greek Orthodox to provide more youth guidance," announced one of the Atlanta-area newspapers the next day.[15] Gallup told the congress not to assume that their children would remain in the church. Religious groups other than the Greek Orthodox Church were approaching young Greek Americans, Gallup reported, and in some cases the response they received was positive. In addition, according to the survey, both young Greek Americans and members of the church held views on moral and social issues that were much more liberal than the church's official positions. And, indeed, the congress confirmed the church's conservative outlook on social issues when it declined to endorse the proposed Equal Rights Amendment to the US Constitution that would guarantee equal rights for women and instead adopted a mild statement on the subject. The Congress also reaffirmed its stance against abortion.[16] Concerns about Greek Orthodoxy's ongoing ability to attract the younger generation also surfaced a few months later during a well-publicized discussion in its ruling body, the Archdiocesan Council. That discussion concerned how the church could no longer rely on incoming immigrants, how it should widen its appeal and even "edge away from its ethnic traits that make it seem foreign even to many of the young people raised within it," because "many young Greek-Americans do not understand Greek, for example, and therefore have difficulty following the church's liturgical rites."[17]

Next to youth policy, the language question was another major topic the survey addressed, indirectly, when it asked Greek American and church member interviewees about the Sunday liturgy. Generally the respondents most liked the hymns and music, followed by communion, tradition, comfort and peace, and beauty and meaning; what they liked least was the length of the service. Church members favored greater emphasis on singing of hymns, congregational recitation of prayer, reading the silent prayers aloud, and participation by the laity. The one thing they wanted less was the emphasis on the Greek language. The breakdown of the responses showed that after the liturgy's time-consuming length, the second least favorite thing about the liturgy was the Greek. Even those who reported the use of some Greek at home wished for less emphasis on the Greek during the service. The respondents in the Midwest (Chicago and Dayton) had the strongest reaction against the Greek. In response to the question "Do you feel that the worship services should have a greater emphasis on the Greek language, or less emphasis?" church members voted overwhelmingly for "less," though active members favored an emphasis on the Greek. The younger the age brackets, the less was the preference for Greek.[18] In the ten years that had elapsed since the archbishop's proposal to permit Sunday liturgies in English, the protests had prevented only the formal adoption of that measure. In practice, English was being used more and more in parishes across the country. The findings of the Gallup poll validated the archdiocese's policy of looking the other way when English predominated in the liturgy.

The Greek language press recoiled at the survey's findings about the Greek language and complained that "the Archbishop, the bishops and all the leadership of the Archdiocese have decided to follow to the letter the conclusions of the Gallup survey, of Mr. Gallup, which as is known give an overwhelming priority to the use of the English language." Reporters for *Proini*, a Greek language newspaper in New York, spoke to seventy parish priests and discovered that thirty-nine used only Greek in the liturgy, twenty-four used English and Greek, and only seven used only English. The article quoted priests from churches in New York, Florida, and Massachusetts who said they would only use Greek, but others said they would use both languages, and yet others only English. Nonetheless, the reporters concluded, their survey was an "anti-Gallup" that demonstrated that "the Archdiocese's Gallup" was unrealistic and disorienting.[19] The *Ethnikos Kyrix* wrote that the laity insisted on the use of Greek, "the authentic and traditional language of our faith," and English should be used only in an "explanatory way."[20] But by 1980 all the Greek-language press could do was manage to keep the language question alive among its readers in Astoria and the other scattered ethnic enclaves along the East Coast, in Chicago, and a few other places. For its part, the church continued to stress its commitment to Greek language education. It made no official pronouncement about English in the Sunday liturgy, thus avoiding unnecessary controversy while the steady spread of the use of English in parishes continued.

Despite the protestations of the Greek-language press, the Gallup survey met with overwhelming approval by the Clergy-Laity Congress. Bishop Anthony of San Francisco recommended that the report "include an expression of gratitude to Archbishop Iakovos for having the foresight to proceed with this study," and his amendment was accepted. There was one more amendment offered and accepted, that a summary of the report be translated into Greek for the benefit of parish council members "who do not read English"—a somewhat ironic footnote for a document that favored the use of English. It was a reminder that while some second- and third- generation parishes were drifting steadily toward more and more English, in some areas Greek was still predominant.[21]

Exploring New Frontiers: The 1982 Clergy-Laity Congress in San Francisco

Following the approval of the survey at the 1980 Clergy-Laity Congress, the church embarked on a course that was much more explicitly oriented toward addressing the challenges of Americanization. San Francisco was in many ways an ideal location to hold a congress that would build on the church's commitment to addressing the challenges of Americanization. Greek Orthodoxy had a long and distinguished presence in the city. More importantly, Greek Orthodox life on the West Coast was more accustomed to dealing with issues of assimilation and Americanization, and it was far away from the East Coast Greek enclaves such as Astoria and from the Greek language press that tended to regard both church and community as simply extensions of the Greek homeland. Of course, a clergy-laity congress reflected Greek Orthodox life on a national scale, but its particular locale served as a reminder of the geographical diversity and different conditions Greek Orthodoxy faced in the United States. And it had been thirty years since the last clergy-laity congress met on the West Coast, in 1952 in Los Angeles.

Bishop Anthony of San Francisco spoke about the need to rethink the standard procedures of the congress and "its familiar list of committees and its predictable pattern of reports and resolutions and financial statements," with a view to whether it "adequately expresses the nature and mission of the Church or fittingly responds to the challenges that confront us in these critical times." A major innovation introduced by the San Francisco diocese was a National Youth Rally scheduled in conjunction with the congress; its theme was "The Faith We Hold," and it was held at the Marriott Hotel in nearby Santa Clara, adjacent to the Marriott's Great America theme park. Another innovation was the inclusion of an ecumenical Christian service, which was held in St. Mary's Roman Catholic Cathedral, bringing together the leaders of all religious groups in the Bay Area, as well as the choirs of St. Mary's Cathedral and Grace Episcopal Cathedral, along with the Greek Orthodox choirs of the Western Choir Federation. One person who saw the 1982 Clergy-Laity Congress as an opportunity for even greater innovation and a new format was California state senator Nicholas Petris. In February 1982 he wrote to Archbishop Iakovos proposing two plenary sessions that would be addressed by a nationally recognized leader. The first would be on "World Peace and Nuclear War." Petris mentioned that several other denominations had passed strong resolutions condemning the nuclear arms race and calling for more intensive and continuing negotiations on arms control. Petris emphasized the point by saying, "The angels heralded the birth of Christ by singing 'glory to God in the highest and peace on earth.' In our own liturgy, the word *eirine* occurs more than thirty times. Our liturgy begins and ends with petitions to God for universal peace—*eirine tou cosmou*." The second issue that Petris suggested be the subject of a second plenary session was the role of women. He wrote: "It is time for us to open a frank and serious dialogue on the role of women in our church, with a view of elevating their status. The dualism which still painfully persists in our church is a relic of the past—reflecting a society of old which subordinated woman to man in all things." Another suggestion for change came from Dr. James Steve Counelis, a distinguished scholar of Orthodoxy who at the time was professor of education at the University of San Francisco. Counelis was especially interested in the way canon law construed the Orthodox Church as a legal body, and in the ways the church in America interacted with American constitutionalism and America's democratic ethos. He submitted an article titled "Historical Reflections on the Constitutions of the Greek Orthodox Archdiocese 1922–1982," which was included in the commemorative album produced for the congress. The album also included greetings from officials of the church and politicians, articles besides Counelis's, and the lists of committee members and the names of all those who worked to prepare the congress. Counelis's article, however, was not what most readers would have expected to find in a commemorative album. It went well beyond historical description and analysis and advocated for greater democracy in church affairs, based on the premise that American constitutional principles gave rise to the democratic expectations of American Orthodox Christians for an ecclesial structure that comported with the American experience. He concluded his article by noting, "There is no doubt that the American Archdiocese represents one of the adaptive forms of the Orthodox Church through her nineteen hundred years of history. And it should not come as a surprise that the American Orthodox ecclesial structure will take longer than sixty years fully to be indigenized. This writer believes that the development of an operative democratic church within the title of the Greek Orthodox Archdiocese of North and South America is inevitable, though he may not live to see it."

Ultimately, those bold recommendations for change did not get very far at the 1982 Clergy-Laity Congress—innovation of the format was one thing, but extending a greater role to women, or instituting more democracy, was beyond the church's ability to move quickly with the times. The issue of adopting a new format for future congresses was reported on by a special committee, which made several suggestions for greater inclusiveness and dialogue. The congress approved the report, and Archbishop Iakovos said the archdiocese would study it carefully. There was no special plenary session on peace and nuclear weapons such as Senator Petris had suggested, but a mildly supportive resolution on the need to halt the nuclear arms race was submitted and approved. The role of women was not discussed, even though the Ladies Philoptochos was holding its biennial congress at the same time, and in its report to the Clergy-Laity Congress it requested joint meetings in the future to discuss topics pertaining to its own future. The issues of governance that James Counelis raised were not accommodated in any item on the agenda, so they were not even discussed indirectly.

Yet because of the climate of change surrounding the congress, there was one item on the agenda that caused heated discussion—not surprisingly it had to do with the sensitive issue of Greek language education, which of course was connected to the bigger issue of the use of Greek in church life. As was the case very often, the discussion about the budget allocation for language education raised bigger issues. The Greek language education committee was requesting a substantial increase in its budget, and several delegates demurred, pointing out that the additional funds could be better used either for youth activities or for religious education, which was also directed toward the younger generation but was mostly in English rather than Greek. The debate between the supporters of increasing the funding for Greek education and the opponents of the measure was long and got heated at times. During the exchanges, one delegate suggested that since not all parishes ran Greek language schools, the other parishes should not receive less funds for youth work or religious education. At the heart of the exchanges were two different visions of the future of the archdiocese: one that sought to uphold the traditional emphasis on Greek language, and the other that sought to find other ways to attract the younger generations to the church. The difference was resolved only when Archbishop Iakovos made a forceful intervention underscoring the significance of Greek language education.

Iakovos wrote to Bishop Anthony to express his warm thanks for all he did to organize the congress, the ecumenical service in the Catholic cathedral, the youth event in Santa Clara, and the other events associated with the congress. Iakovos noted that clergy and laity demonstrated a satisfactory understanding of the problems facing the church and addressed them in a pragmatic way, "although," he added, "the ideal solutions of the problem situations were not found nor was their examination the most correct." Too many delegates, he said, succumbed to the temptation to appear as advocates of the devil in their speeches from the floor in order to earn easy applause. Nonetheless, he concluded, the twenty-sixth Clergy-Laity Congress was "a step forward, a very positive one if not a gigantic one, and it was gratifying and successful in terms of its organization, its appearance and its results." The archbishop did not offer any more information about his own assessment of the congress and which problems it left unresolved. But by the end of the decade, the new issues that had been raised as the congress approached were very much at the center of Greek Orthodox life. In 1986, a nuclear accident in Chernobyl in the Soviet Union reminded all of the seriousness of the problem of nuclear power. In 1987, the role of women in the Orthodox Church was brought to the fore by the publication of Eva Catafygiotou Topping's study *Holy Mothers of Orthodoxy*. That same year saw a group in Chicago establish a lay organization, Orthodox Christian Laity, which called for greater democracy and accountability in the structure of the church. One of its academic advisers was James Counelis. And finally, the issue of ministering to the needs of the younger generation became more and more important for Greek Orthodoxy. The success of the youth rally held in San Francisco in 1982 led Iakovos to establish what he called the Greek Orthodox Young Adult League (GOYAL, or YAL, which he preferred to call a "movement" rather than an organization), designed to foster Orthodox fellowship among church members whose ages ranged from about the late teens to the late twenties. The first national conference, involving workshops, discussions, and lectures, took place in Dallas in 1983, and conferences continued to be held annually.

Leadership 100

One issue raised in the Gallup survey could not be ignored, though it took the church several years to address. There does not seem to be any phase the church's history when it was not short of money and desperately trying to fund its manifold activities. This was the cost of the expansion of the parish's responsibilities that had begun in the Athenagoras era. With such a broad range of activities came a broad range of costs, and these inevitably affected a parish's abilities to pay its dues to the archdiocese, which itself was growing in size and in budgetary needs. The early 1980s appear to have been an especially difficult time for the archdiocese's finances, and the Gallup survey commented on this in terms of the relative percentage of donations made by the members of the church. There had been more reminders. At an Archdiocesan Council meeting in January 1981, lay member George Chimples, an Ohio-based businessman, presented the Finance Committee's response to the problem and said the committee was compiling a list of parishes that had not fulfilled their commitment to the archdiocese. He also appealed to those present to urge their parishes to pay up. This was imperative, he stressed, because "the Archdiocese does not have sufficient capital at the present time to continue for more than one year." In the discussion that followed, a number of ideas for reducing costs were aired, but nothing concrete was adopted. When the director of economic development Chris Demetriades, a real estate developer, told the council that although the expenses were greater than the anticipated receipts, the small budget shortfall was not an operating deficit, and that parishes just had to be urged to pay up. With that, the council concluded its discussion on finances.[22] But the problem was not going to go away. Three years later, at an Archdiocesan Council meeting in March 1984, Chimples announced there was a deficit of approximately $1 million that had accrued over the past three years and that it was obvious "the Archdiocese would have to either increase revenues or cut expenses." He suggested cuts in the budgets of Hellenic College and St. Basil Academy. The only thing that was decided was to form a committee to examine ways expenditures could be pruned—although everyone was in agreement after one member recommended that instead of "pruning" the council use the term "prioritizing."[23]

Luckily for the archdiocese, at a council meeting later that year in Denver, a group of lay members decided the only way the financial question could be resolved was to raise money to create an endowment fund. Among the founders was Michael Jaharis, the son of Greek immigrants from the island of Lesbos and owner of a successful pharmaceutical company in Florida. Jaharis had joined the council recently and had been taken aback by the lack of any serious businesslike management of its finances. Jaharis thought that creating an endowment through substantial contributions of its wealthiest members, a proposed $100,000 each over ten years, was the obvious solution. The archbishop was doubtful. Joining Jaharis were Chimples, Arthur C. Anton, Andrew Athens, Peter M. Dion, and George P. Kokalis. Years later Dion told a Greek American magazine, "Archbishop Iakovos did not believe we could get 10 Greeks to contribute $100,000 each. But we insisted and we won by one vote. . . . That evening in Denver my wife and my daughters became members. And of course, so did the rest of the founders. To make a long story short, when we left Denver we had 18 members! And they all paid the full amount of $100,000! And for some time we had to pay for operating expenses from our pockets."[24] Those six council members that took the initiative to form Leadership 100, as it was called, were representative of the type of either first- or second-generation Greek Americans who had done extremely well in the business world and were either already making donations to their parishes or to other causes and whom Iakovos had invited to join the Archdiocesan Council. Anton's father, Charles, had opened a dry cleaners in Lowell in 1913, and it had expanded into a chain that spread throughout Massachusetts and New Hampshire. Andrew Athens was born Andreas Athanasoulas to immigrant parents in Chicago in 1921, and he formed a steel manufacturing company with his brother Thomas in 1950 after being involved in postwar reconstruction in Europe with the US Army. Jaharis was also a second-generation Greek American, whose parents had emigrated to the United States from the island of Lesvos. He had gone to work in the pharmaceutical industry after receiving a law degree. Kokalis had arrived in the United States in 1920 at age eleven and went on to build a successful supermarket chain in the Chicago area. Peter Dion emigrated from Greece, became successful in the fur business, and then moved into real estate.

Initially, the creation of Leadership 100 was more important for what it said about the church's standing in the Greek American community than its financial impact. It was yet another sign of the archbishop's and the church's predominance in the world of Greek America in the 1980s. There was an obvious contrast to the Archons organization of lay members that Iakovos had created in 1966, which was associated with the Ecumenical Patriarchate and whose members made voluntary contributions of time or money to the church. Leadership 100 was explicitly associated with the archdiocese and had a required level of financial contribution. Very few of the wealthiest Greek Americans had not signed up by the end of the decade. In terms of the archdiocese's ailing finances, Leadership 100 was not an immediate panacea. The late 1980s saw the Holy Cross Theological School experience a serious shortfall of funds. But gradually, as Leadership 100's war chest grew, it was able to finance projects and lighten the load from the archdiocese's shoulders. And when a problem with an unwise real estate investment that the Archdiocese made grew much worse, Leadership 100 would come to the rescue.

Iakovos's Twenty-Fifth Anniversary

In 1984 Archbishop Iakovos, at the peak of his powers, marked the twenty-fifth anniversary of his enthronement. The year was taken up mostly by celebratory events, including the Clergy-Laity Congress that met in New York. In February, the archbishop received an honorary degree from Temple University in Philadelphia, his twenty-fifth honorary doctorate since taking office.[25] Plans for reform were mostly shelved, although in less public meetings, such as the gatherings of the Archdiocesan Council, issues such as the financial situation, the need to attract the younger generation, and of course the problems of schools surfaced frequently. But this was a year of pausing to mark all that had been achieved, rather than what needed to be done. The public relations agenda, which was the responsibility of Father Karloutsos, was very long. The encomiums had started a year earlier through one of Karloutsos's initiatives. He contacted two fellow Greek Americans at the *New York Times* and secured an interview with the archbishop by a young reporter, Maureen Dowd. Dowd, who later on would become a famously acerbic columnist, was evidently charmed by the archbishop and produced an article that lionized him and highlighted his controversial and militant support of civil rights, his leadership in building bridges between Greek Orthodoxy and other religions, his efforts to attract second- and third-generation Greek Americans by introducing more English language in the liturgy, and the attacks he faced from church conservatives. She also mentioned his (eventual) opposition to the Greek junta and his criticisms of Turkey's human rights record. She described Iakovos as unafraid of controversy and noted that he had told the National Council of Churches that the archdiocese would withdraw from that organization if it admitted a homosexual church, the Hollywood, California–based Metropolitan Community Church. Iakovos told Dowd he had received five death threats from Greeks and Turks, serious enough to require police protection. "To live dangerously is a kind of excitement," he said. "I expect criticism, even violent criticism. When it happens to be my belief I never feel any regret about what I say."[26]

In April 1984, the twenty-fifth anniversary of Iakovos's enthronement was marked with a glittering service held at the Greek Orthodox Cathedral in New York. Dignitaries of the Eastern Orthodox and Catholic and Protestant Churches were in attendance. Jimmy Carter, by then a former president, delivered a homily in which he called Iakovos "a distinguished servant of Christ and my personal friend."[27] Archbishop John J. O'Connor, the head of the Catholic Archdiocese of New York, prefaced his reading from an Epistle of St. Peter by pledging his loyalty, cooperative support, and deep abiding friendship toward Iakovos, whom he described as "a spiritual father." At the close of the service, Greece's ambassador to the United States awarded Iakovos the Greek Grand Cross of Honor on behalf of Prime Minister Karamanlis. There followed a luncheon at the Waldorf Astoria hotel attended by New York City mayor Ed Koch.[28] Later that year, again as part of his twenty-fifth anniversary, Iakovos was invited to offer invocations at the House of Representatives and the Senate in Washington.

In 1984 the archdiocese published a volume of essays on the history of the Greek Orthodox Church in America, two-thirds of which was devoted to what it described as the "Iakovian era" and in which most essays were encomiums to the archbishop's personality and his many achievements since his enthronement. It was the most substantive of a number of publications that appeared in Iakovos's honor that year. One of the editors, Rev. Milton B. Efthimiou, who had his own long record of service to the church, wrote in the prologue: "If there was one man that stood out in making Orthodoxy a major faith in this country and in the world it was Iakovos."[29] Theologian and historian of the Church Demetrios Constantelos, who often backed traditionalist views, struck one of the few carefully critical notes when he mentioned in his introductory essay that the emergence of criticism and internal dialogue was a healthy phenomenon in the church's life in recent years and offered examples, including "a great deal of reaction against the Archdiocese's pronouncements concerning the language problem, the development of the Church's institutions, such as Hellenic College, and the handling of the emergence of the Orthodox Church in America and of ecumenical relations."[30] If Constantelos's remarks were a reminder of the lingering feelings of past controversies, the essays on the "Iakovian era" in both their range and content attested to the archbishop's remarkable achievements in his quarter century as leader of the church. Much space was devoted to the

organizational work Iakovos had engaged in, the restructuring of the archdiocese with the creation of regional dioceses headed by a bishop, the creation
of a communications department for the archdiocese in 1980, the ongoing
efforts to develop and maintain the theological school and Hellenic College, the philanthropic work of the women's Philoptochos organization, the
schools and the other institutions, and the work to sustain a youth program.
Throughout there were nods toward the ways the church was adapting to
American reality and the emergence of an English-speaking Greek American
generation, but these were mostly implicit. Other essays, however, spelled
out that process. In his account of the ecumenical initiatives during Iakovos's tenure, Rev. Robert Stephanopoulos, the dean of the Greek Orthodox
Cathedral in New York City, described Iakovos's work in that particular area
as stemming from his ability to adapt to the American environment: "While
serving with distinction as Dean of the Boston Cathedral, the Archbishop
learned to love America and its unique way of life. He led in seeking ways
to apply Orthodoxy to the American reality and to transform the fabric of
society into conformity with the Kingdom of God." And further on, Stephanopoulos described the Greek Orthodox Church as existing in a definite and
special culture.[31] The volume's concluding essay, by John Charles, a member
of the Archdiocesan Council, also described Iakovos as leading the church
in an American environment. With regard to the language issue it took a
middle position between change and no change, noting that "the continuing
evolutionary development" of the church would determine how the language question would be settled, a position of course that indicated openness to reform.[32]

From Greek American to American Greek Orthodoxy

It was left to Iakovos himself to sum up the position of the Greek Orthodox
Church in the United States, and he did not shy away from outlining his
view that Greek American identity was transitioning from its ethnic character to an Orthodox identity rooted in American society. He was in Athens
in 1985 receiving a gold medal from the Academy of Athens, a hallowed
institution designed to promote the fine arts, humanities, and sciences in
Greece and which confers annual medals or prizes on worthy individuals. In
his speech at the award ceremony, he described, as he had back in 1968 at the
Clergy-Laity Congress, the nature of Greek America, only this time he had
to be brief. He therefore summarized by saying the Greek Americans were
becoming American Greeks (or Hellenes), "with all the basic and harmoni-
ously combined characteristics of Greek and American civilizations." And by

way of reassuring all those in attendance in Athens, Iakovos explained that concern for human rights was an element of this combination of Greek and American civilization, and that is why the "American Greeks" were vitally concerned with the rights of the Ecumenical Patriarchate, of Greece, and of Cyprus. The archbishop went on to assert that the previously ethnic community was changing into a religious or ecclesiastic community, more specifically "a Greek Orthodox community without losing a sense of its national, spiritual and cultural origins." At one point in his speech Iakovos conceded that the notion of American Greeks he was proposing was difficult to understand, but it was very true, he reassured everyone.[33] In retrospect, in an era when academics use notions of multiple identities and hybridity, Iakovos's vision is easier to grasp and appears to be a concept *avant la lettre*. He understood this American Greek entity as a part of America but retaining its own distinct characteristics, and that this made for a harmonious whole. He was essentially building on Moskos's view that the old diaspora had now become an American ethnic group, and he boldly defined that American ethnicity in religious terms. But, of course, in the case of the Greek Orthodox religion there was an implication of the old Greek ethnicity present.

Iakovos returned to the concept of "American Greek" the following year with his keynote speech at the 1986 Clergy-Laity Congress held in Dallas, Texas. He used the term in a hypothetical way, when he speculated about what the future held for the church. The archbishop asked the congress to consider and prepare for what the church's identity would be in the near future, specifically the year 2000. "Will we be identified as a Greek Orthodox Church and Archdiocese of America . . . or will we in fact be something else? If so, what will that 'something other' be—an American-Greek Church with greater emphasis on the Church's Greek-Christian origin and less on the American identity of our younger generations? Or will we become a phase or a part of what is called 'American Orthodoxy,' without discernment or identity as ethnic church jurisdictions, as is desired by some of our pious American born people?" Iakovos continued, laying out several questions about the possible future nature of the church, about what it would do, whether it would deal with spiritual concerns or also be involved in moral, social, and political problems. And then he dived into the language question, asking "Will it be a Church using only English as its official language, with hymns sung only in ancient Greek (perhaps because not all of them will have been translated into English), with petitions chanted in English and the choir usually responding in Greek?" and he continued, somewhat mischievously, to throw out his inquiries, saying "Will the sermons be heard in both languages, and rarely be inspiring in nature?" and "Will the Greek school conduct a weak and ineffectual program without concern for the teaching of linguistics?"[34] Iakovos was using a hypothetical format to get his audience used to and prepared for the changes the future held for Greek Orthodoxy. He was planting seeds that would eventually alert everyone that things were changing. But Iakovos was careful not to be explicit about his own views. Even the archbishop's severest public critic, Theodoros Kalmoukos, who was covering the congress for the *Ethnikos Kyrix*, found no cause for alarm for the traditionalists.[35]

The Dukakis Dilemma

Michael Dukakis, the son of Greek immigrants, had served two terms as governor of Massachusetts when he emerged as the strong favorite to the win his party's nomination for president in 1988. He would become the first candidate for president who was Greek American and also Greek Orthodox. His candidacy was met with widespread enthusiasm in the Greek American community, which rallied to his side in great numbers and through substantial money contributions. Yet that candidacy posed a dilemma for a church that had just consolidated its transition from an immigrant to an American church, for it behooved an American church to demonstrate a degree of impartiality in a presidential election.

Iakovos was no amateur when the need for political maneuvering came up. First of all he called the bluff of a group of conservatives who formed under the name "Orthodox Christians for Life" and launched public protests at Dukakis's self-identification as a member of the Greek Orthodox Church. They said Dukakis was not a "real" Greek Orthodox, for he was ineligible to receive communion because of his marriage outside the church to a non-baptized wife who was in fact Jewish. In response, Dukakis affirmed he was a member in good standing of the Annunciation Cathedral in Boston, and its pastor confirmed this. But protests continued, as the group also decried Dukakis's stance in favor of the right to abortion. Their campaign never amounted to much, although the media picked it up, including Rowland Evans and Robert Novak in their syndicated column.[36] Iakovos vigorously defended Dukakis. On arriving in Boston for the 1988 Clergy-Laity Congress in July, he said that Dukakis "is a member of the church, was baptized in it, and he has never left it," and described the attack as wrong and as coming from "small people." And, he added, "Why were none of us bothered by the years during which Dukakis was governor of the state [and] that he was married to a Jewish woman? . . . If the state of the Cabots and Adamses and Quincys and Lodges accepted to be governed by the son of a Greek immigrant, why should we be so resentful? . . . If Dukakis in the eyes of the American public is capable of governing the nation, it is their prerogative to choose him," he said. "I don't think that religious matters should be a criterion for the abilities or spiritual and moral power a man has."[37] In the fall, when the attacks resumed focusing on Dukakis's Jewish wife, Kitty, Iakovos continued to defend Dukakis in the same way, and he mentioned that mixed marriages were now the norm among Greek Americans, saying "Seventy percent of Greek Orthodox marriages are with those of other denominations, and an increasing number are with Jews."[38]

By decoupling Dukakis's ethnicity and religion from the church's attitude, Iakovos was signaling that the archdiocese was going to follow its customary bipartisan stance in the upcoming presidential election, which would likely pit the Democrat Dukakis against the Republican George H. W. Bush. Accordingly, both Bush and Dukakis were invited to speak at the Clergy-Laity Congress in Boston in July 1988, at a moment in which both men were all but certain of being nominated as their respective party's candidate. And despite the presence of both candidates, it was a measure of the ongoing issues the archdiocese was facing that the bishop of Boston, Methodios, told the *Boston Globe* that the three most prominent issues at the congress were going to be mixed marriages ("we have maybe 70 percent interchurch weddings, while 20 years ago 90 percent of all marriages were Greek Orthodox marrying Greek Orthodox"), the church's sponsorship of Greek language and cultural education ("the number of afternoon schools is shrinking, but we have a loud minority of newcomers who wish us to continue"), and raising money for the archdiocese's endowment fund. Another issue would be the ongoing difficulties of Hellenic College and Holy Cross Theological School, a complicated problem that Methodios summed up beautifully when he said, "Once we had a dream of building a Brandeis for Greeks, but the idea never caught and we were left with a $3 million debt."[39] Dukakis spoke at a specially organized "Tribute to Public Service" that enabled the governor's presence. He did not mention religion or Greek Orthodoxy in his address, although he did refer to both Greeks and ancient Greece and linked his quest for the presidency with classical Athens' democratic values, saying public service was in the Greek blood.[40] Bush spoke as the vice president, as he had done at previous clergy-laity congresses. Iakovos in fact had a close relationship to Bush through Michael Sotirhos, a leading lay member of the church and a member of the Archdiocesan Council. Sotirhos had been very active in the 1984 Reagan-Bush campaign, Reagan had appointed him ambassador to Jamaica in 1985, and in 1988 he played an important role in Bush's campaign. He was on hand to see Bush receive a warm welcome from the Greek Orthodox audience—many of whom would have been Republicans. Bush, who would launch a racially tinged series of attacks on Dukakis within a few weeks, prudently kept to a positive message, telling his audience, "Greek-Americans now can be found at every stage of our political life, and let me say this in all candor: I know how proud you are of Michael Dukakis. What a tribute it is to Greek-Americans, to our political system and to this great country of ours that we find it totally natural that the son of an immigrant is one of two men still contending to be president of the United States."[41]

In the end, Greek America did not produce a president from within its ranks, but by the time the 1988 presidential election took place, the Greek Orthodox Church had made substantial steps toward entering America's cultural mainstream. In a reflective article on religion in America in the 1980s, religion scholar Martin Marty spoke about how conservative religious movements were becoming prevalent and sealing the end of the liberal legacies of the 1960s. He spoke about the religious mainstream—the Protestant, Catholic, Reform and Conservative Jewish, and evangelical-moralist faith complexes—being joined by "Eastern [Asian] religions." He did not mention Eastern Orthodoxy anywhere in his article, but if he did he could have said about it what he did about those marginal religious movements, the "thriving cults," which he believed "had begun to fit quietly into the larger landscape."[42]

The way the archbishop balanced between Bush and Dukakis was no doubt driven by his own interest in maintaining his access to the White House whatever the election results, and was also enabled by the support the conservative, wealthy Greek Americans were offering to the Republican Party candidate. But by the same token it epitomized in many ways Greek Orthodoxy's repositioning as an American rather than ethnic religion, even though it preserved its place as the major Greek American institution. It was another sign of the church's ability to reconcile its Americanization while maintaining its ethnic identity, something that was not contradictory in multiethnic America.

CHAPTER 10

The Challenges for an American
Greek Orthodoxy

The peaceful, rolling hills of Ligonier, a small town in western Pennsylvania with a population of about fifteen hundred, was an unlikely site for where the future of Greek Orthodoxy in America would be decided. A five-hour westward drive from the archdiocese's headquarters in New York City, Ligonier is home to the Antiochian Village and Conference Center, which sits on a three-hundred-acre property and is administered by the Antiochian Orthodox Christian Archdiocese of America. The Antiochian Church, which had begun its existence in America under the auspices of the Russian Orthodox Church and had suffered internal divisions similar to those that Greek Orthodoxy faced in the 1920s, was by then unified and under the jurisdiction of the Greek Orthodox Church of Antioch based in Damascus, Syria. While most of its members continued to be Arab Orthodox immigrants or their children and grandchildren, the church had also admitted a number of converts from evangelical Protestantism in the 1980s, who formed a separate entity, the Antiochian Orthodox Evangelical Mission. The leader of that group of evangelicals, Peter Gillquist, has written about how his group was rebuffed by Archbishop Iakovos and the Ecumenical Patriarchate when they approached the Greek Orthodox archdiocese. Despite their different perspectives on the evangelicals, Iakovos and Metropolitan Philip (Saliba), the head of the Antiochian Archdiocese, had a close relationship. Iakovos had been present at Philip's consecration as archbishop in 1966.

Of all the hierarchs of the Eastern Orthodox Churches in North America, Philip was the greatest supporter of an American pan-Orthodox Church.[1]

It was at the Antiochian Village that the heads of twenty-nine Eastern Orthodox Churches met in late 1994, with Iakovos presiding. The meeting was the culmination of a long process of Orthodox contacts in North America that had been accelerated by the visit of Ecumenical Patriarch Dimitrios to the United States in the summer of 1990 in which he spoke in favor of greater cooperation between the Eastern Orthodox Churches in the New World. That same summer, at the Greek Orthodox Clergy-Laity Congress the patriarch attended, a church commission submitted its blueprint for the future in which it linked the Americanization within the Orthodox Churches with the need, indeed the inevitability, of the coming together of those churches. And at the Clergy-Laity Congress of 1994, the patriarch's representative, Metropolitan Spyridon of Italy, would speak effusively of the need to further the cause of pan-Orthodox cooperation in America.

The prospect of the emergence of an American pan-Orthodox entity of sorts conformed in many ways with the prevailing climate of globalization, in that Eastern Orthodoxy would be stepping out of its Old World ethnic enclaves and establishing itself as a religion with as much of a presence in the New World as in the Old. The Ecumenical Patriarchate's initial reaction to pan-Orthodox contacts was encouraging, though many details remained to be worked out, and indeed the role of the patriarchate remained unclear, perhaps on purpose on the part of Iakovos. As encouraging as the reaction was, it was also surprising, because on the whole, Eastern Orthodoxy, with the embrace of tradition as its ecclesiastical cornerstone, erred on the side of caution when confronted with new developments.[2]

The Ecumenical Patriarch's Pan-Orthodox Message

Dimitrios became the first ecumenical patriarch to visit the United States, and even though the Greek Orthodox Church was his host, and did all it could to ensure the patriarch was received as a head of state, Dimitrios made a point of reaching out to all Eastern Orthodox Churches during his stay. In the course of the twenty-seven-day visit, in which the patriarch traveled throughout the United States, he met with Greek as well as other Eastern Orthodox clergy and laity. On the eve of the patriarch's arrival, Leonid Kishkovsky, a Russian Orthodox priest and theologian who had become president of the National Council of Churches in America—a stronghold of major Protestant denominations—had expressed the wish that Dimitrios's visit would show there was a vital Orthodox community in the United States that was "multicultural, multiethnic, multilingual but also very American."[3] Dimitrios would not disappoint, and his experiences on the ground would convey how "American" the Orthodox had become, something that suggested to many that the next step should be forging Eastern Orthodox unity in America.

Dimitrios's outreach to the other Orthodox communities revived what had become a dormant process. The Standing Conference of Canonical Orthodox Bishops in the Americas (SCOBA) that Iakovos had established had made some headway in the 1960s but had little to show since then. The transformation of the Russian Orthodox "Metropolia" Church into the autonomous Orthodox Church in America in 1970 had put a damper on intra-Orthodox contacts. The best that Iakovos's twenty-fifth-anniversary volume, published in 1984, could come up with was a short one-page account that mentioned that SCOBA, "through much trial and tribulation, has been seeking ways and means of bringing its objectives to fruition."[4] The collapse of the Berlin Wall in November 1989 freed the Orthodox Churches in Eastern Europe from the control of the state and opened the possibility of closer interaction with the Patriarchate of Constantinople. There was no better way for the patriarchate to signal in interest in forging closer relations than by meeting with those Eastern Orthodox churches in North America.

Whatever the plans of spiritual communion with the Greek and other Eastern Orthodox Churches that Dimitrios had, the first order of business, wherever he visited, was to meet government dignitaries. Thanks to Iakovos's connections with the White House and Congress, as well as a good deal of planning, the visit became as high profile as possible, starting with the patriarch's landing in July 1990 at Andrews Air Force Base, where heads of state customarily arrived. The patriarch had a Secret Service escort during his entire stay in Washington, as he met with President Bush, visited Capitol Hill, where Vice President Dan Quayle and the Speaker of the House Tom Foley hosted a dinner in his honor in the Capitol Rotunda, and laid a wreath at the Tomb of the Unknown Soldier at Arlington Cemetery. In New York the patriarch met with the secretary-general of the United Nations Javier Pérez de Cuéllar. When the Archdiocesan Council had heard of all these plans at a meeting prior to the visit, it reacted "with an enthusiastic outburst of applause."[5]

The political aspects of the visit did not all go smoothly. Maybe someone could have predicted trouble at the grand occasion of the banquet in the Rotunda because it included senators and congressmen who were either Greek Americans or who supported Greek American lobbying efforts. When Senator Bob Dole made critical remarks about the Turks in his speech during the banquet, those traveling with Dimitrios were concerned that the criticism would be interpreted as being approved by the patriarch. The patriarchal delegation was also concerned because the archbishop awarded medals to the Greek American congressmen in appreciation of their support of the patriarchate's rights. They were right to worry: several daily newspapers in Turkey carried Dole's remarks on their front pages.[6] The patriarch himself studiously avoided any negative remarks about Turkey's policies during his trip, and as soon as he arrived in Washington he had made a courtesy visit to the Turkish embassy. The Turkish government had only recently given the patriarch permission to travel abroad, and true to the nonconfrontational style of his predecessor Athenagoras, Dimitrios had chosen not to refer to the travel ban publicly. The day after the Rotunda event, he hastily sent word to the Turkish embassy disassociating the patriarchate from the anti-Turkish remarks heard at the banquet.

Away from the politicized climate of Capitol Hill, Dimitrios's presence in Washington, where he was to be the honorary president of the archdiocese's Clergy-Laity Congress in early July, set the tone for the rest of the contacts with the Greek and other Eastern Orthodox communities. Upon his arrival Dimitrios had declared, "Today, Orthodoxy is not a strange and alien factor in America. It is flesh of its flesh and bone of its bones. . . . I greet warmly and without exception all the faithful children of the Orthodox in this country." He went on to underscore the need for the Orthodox Churches in America to come together, saying, "I convey to all the Orthodox of this country my love and . . . blessing, and assure them that the full unity of the Church, by canonical order has never ceased and will never cease to be my principal concern."[7] It was in Washington that Dimitrios made the most significant gesture when he went to the Cathedral of the Orthodox Church in America and prayed together with its head, the Metropolitan Theodosius. Theodosius had welcomed him by saying, "Your presence is a sign of renewed hope for unity, witness and mission of Orthodox Christianity in America. As 'the first among equals' within the brotherhood of Orthodox bishops throughout the world you have in your primacy a unique ministry of unity. We ask that through your prayers our ministry in America may bring even closer the full integration of our continued efforts, that the people and the society . . . may see that the Orthodox Church in North America is truly united in common mission, common witness, common purpose." Dimitrios responded by asserting that "it is truly a scandal for the unity of the Church to maintain more than one bishop in any given city, it clearly contravenes the sacred canons and Orthodox ecclesiology. . . . The Ecumenical Patriarchate, as a supra-national Church . . . will exert every effort in cooperation with the other Holy Orthodox Churches, and in accordance with canonical order, to resolve this thorny problem."[8]

The meeting with the Russian Orthodox in Washington was only the beginning. In New York, where Dimitrios spoke at a vespers service that brought together several Eastern Orthodox prelates at Holy Trinity Cathedral, he called on the fragmented Eastern Orthodox in America to unite.[9] Dimitrios's schedule also included a one-day visit to Allentown, Pennsylvania, a center of Ukrainian Orthodoxy, and meetings with Greek and other Eastern Orthodox clergy and laity in a total of eight US cities. In Chicago, his celebration of an open-air Mass in the city's Grant Park was attended by not only Greeks but all Eastern Orthodox faithful.

Dimitrios's visit to the United States was to be the last of the several pastoral missions he undertook in his life. A year later, in October 1991, he died of a heart attack in Istanbul. The Patriarchate's synod elected Metropolitan Bartholomew as his successor. The new patriarch, who at age fifty-one upon his election in November 1991 was much younger than his predecessor, would also advocate dynamically for pan-Orthodox unity but link it with upholding and enhancing the global stature of the Patriarchate of Constantinople. This would soon have a significant impact on Orthodoxy in America.

The 1990 Clergy-Laity Congress: Americanization and Religion

The thirtieth Clergy-Laity Congress echoed the patriarch's wish for pan-Orthodox unity, embedding it in the broader themes that had become the archdiocese's perennial concerns from the 1980s onward: facing the challenges of Americanization while deepening religious sentiment among the faithful. The community's demographic profile confirmed the urgency of that task. The 1990 US Census had recorded an increase from 1980 of 150,517, or 13.5 percent, in the total number of persons reporting they were of Greek ancestry, bringing the total to 1,110,373. But this still meant that the Greek Americans (or more accurately those who said they were of Greek ancestry) were 0.4 percent of the total population of the United States and were ranked thirty-first of all ethnic groups. The numbers also clearly showed that the foreign-born component of Greek America, of whom 80 percent had acquired US citizenship, was declining in numerical strength and aging.[10]

Aside from the patriarch's presence, the highlight of the congress was a report to the archbishop "Concerning the Future Theological Agenda of the Greek Orthodox Archdiocese," which amounted to a set of clear statements of how the Orthodox faithful were becoming more and more Americanized and the ways the church should adapt in order to ensure its survival and continued relevancy. It represented four year of deliberations of a commission headed by Metropolitan Silas, who had been bishop of New Jersey since 1979 and had also served as president of Hellenic College Holy Cross. Iakovos had appointed the commission after the 1986 Clergy-Laity Congress held in Dallas, where he had spoken of "a present crisis of identity in the Orthodox Church due to a weakening of ethnic, ecclesial and spiritual bonds in a secular, pluralistic society." This was yet another iteration of the perennial concern that the erosion of ethnicity and further acculturation into American society on the part of a growing number of Greek Americans would mean weakening ties to Greek Orthodoxy. The task Iakovos assigned the commission was "reflecting on the factors behind the identity crisis, formulating clear responses and offering recommendations pertaining to the Archdiocese."[11]

The commission included several senior faculty members of the Holy Cross Theological School and Greek American professors, but it was Charles Moskos's ideas that the report reflected. There was a theme running throughout—the evolving cultural and social characteristics of the Greek American community and how its relationship to its religion could be maintained—even though the commission divided the results of its deliberations into four parts: the faith crisis, the parish, leadership issues, and social realities. The findings, conclusions, and recommendations ranged from theological to practical, from grappling with the concept of faith to day-to-day administrative issues. In the first section, in discussing the contemporary crisis of faith, the commission noted that "we are an ethnic and religious minority in an open, secular society with powerful claims upon all especially the young," and therefore it recommended that "the Orthodox Church must take upon itself the prime responsibility for maintaining and strengthening the Orthodox identity among its members both as an intrinsic goal as well as a presupposition for effective mission in the world." Ethnic identity, which had played a major role and given cohesion to the Greek Orthodox Church, was on the wane. "With the weakening of ethnic ties due to various factors of sociological assimilation, most notably interfaith marriages, changes have occurred and problems have been created." The greatest problem was that "the offspring of interfaith marriages, of converts and of others already culturally assimilated, will continue to drift away unless they become linked to the Orthodox Church with clear ecclesial and spiritual bonds."

Significantly, while the report mentioned the children of converts drifting away, it did not comment on any influence converts might have had on diluting the church's ethnic character. A recently published ethnographic study of converts to Eastern Orthodoxy in the United States has concluded, surprisingly but very persuasively, that the converts themselves have a range of positive to negative reactions to the ethnic identity of the particular parish they joined, yet overall, they were not put off by any ethnic cliquishness. And the "cradle Orthodox" who were overtly "ethnic" in their understanding of their religion were in most cases very welcoming of the converts. Inevitably, in some cases the Greeks muttered in the background about the converts being *xenoi* (foreigners), though others greeted non-Greeks with the highest compliment: "You look Greek!"[12]

The commission then addressed a second problem in the new era. While attachment to tradition, to religious customs and forms, had contributed to perpetuating the church in the modern, open, and radically changing world in which novelty overshadowed tradition, the old, set way of doing things was no longer an obvious asset. The conclusion was the same: a new focus and spiritual investment were needed in the true goals and priorities of the church. And the way this could be achieved was by recognizing that "the faith commitment has more and more become a matter of personal choice than of social or cultural heritage." Thus the commission warned that Greek Orthodoxy could no longer rely on the weight of culture and tradition to sustain itself and instead should adapt to the modern era and help individuals embrace Orthodoxy on the basis of its content. The church had to clarify its doctrines, encourage prayer enlivened by a mystical sense of communion with the risen Christ, and provide a supportive environment that enabled the faithful to counterbalance their uncertain existence in a secular world by experiencing and living their Orthodox faith. It called for an internalization of the faith through a conscious personal conviction, because "we can no longer count on the spiritual investments of the past, that is to say, simply on the power of tradition and formal habits."[13] This was not a path to Orthodoxy that the first Greek immigrants to America would have recognized.

The second section of the report, on the parishes and why people either became members or left, included practical recommendations, from better planning and leadership to more inclusive engagement of parishioners, but it too referred directly to the sociocultural changes the Greek Orthodox were experiencing in the late twentieth century. The section opened with the observation that the problems facing the parishes, according to the commission, had to be understood through a sociological as well as a theological analysis. The parishes were not responding to the needs of the faithful because "as our people become more educated and more cosmopolitan, they are looking for more persuasive preaching and more prayerful liturgy than they once needed." The parishes were no longer as homogeneous as they used to be: "Our churches, with their strong ethnic and cultural heritage and values, well served this need of our people to belong and be involved in the past, but the increasing diversity of our faithful and the impact of the surrounding culture have begun to loosen the ties that formerly bound the parishioners together," and this meant the parish had to find new ways to bring its members together. As language and culture played less of a role in the consciousness of a parish, shared interests and values had to be emphasized more, because "as our people lose their cultural heritage, they will suffer more and more from American religious minimalism, and as a result they may not be able to recognize why they have to travel twenty or thirty minutes in order to go to an Orthodox church and not go to the Roman Catholic or Protestant church nearby since 'we all believe in the same God.'"[14] The third section, on leadership, addressed the inner workings of the church and the ways power was exercised throughout its hierarchy of organization, from the archbishop down to the parish, and included recommendations to improve those functions. At the very end of this section came a discussion about the importance of the Greek Orthodox reaching out to the other Orthodox churches. It spoke about how the Orthodox Church was "one, Holy, Catholic and Apostolic," and therefore its officials and its members were required to work toward achieving pan-Orthodox unity in America. This offered the commission yet another opportunity to frown upon past practices that reflected the church's ethnic character: "The cause of pan-Orthodox unity has been hindered because we have loved our own ecclesiastical customs and cultural traditions more than we have loved each other." It recommended that on a parish level, "more needs to be done to cultivate the awareness that members of all Orthodox jurisdictions, regardless of ethnic background, belong to the same Church."[15] The commission also called on bishops to do more to promote pan-Orthodox unity.

In the report's fourth section, on "social realities," the commission turned its focus away from issues of faith and the administration of the church and directly addressed the effects of the American environment on the faithful. It identified two major issues: the old, familiar topic of mixed marriages, and a new one for the clergy-laity congresses, the dichotomy in Greek American self-perceptions as either a Hellenic diaspora or as American ethnics—the very question Moskos, a key commission member, had raised a decade earlier in his book on the Greek Americans. It was this second issue the commission would concentrate on, though it did deal first with the issue of mixed marriages and recommended a more open treatment of this phenomenon, which the archdiocese had long considered a barometer of the erosion of Orthodox identity. The commission dispensed with the problem very simply by recommending a practical and realistic treatment of the growing phenomenon of intermarriage—namely, the church ought to be much more proactive in accepting non-Orthodox spouses and the children of mixed marriages, given the rising numbers of Orthodox marrying outside the faith.

As to the issue of whether the Greek Americans were a Greek diaspora or an ethnic American community, the report came down heavily in favor of the second and argued that in the current era, Greek American identity could survive only if it was expressed in terms of Greek Orthodoxy. The commission acknowledged that both the self-perception of being a diaspora and an American ethnic reflected Greek American reality, but it concluded, "Our own understanding of the Greek experience in America leans much more to the ethnic rather than the diaspora viewpoint" and went on to make a distinction between sacred and secular ethnicity. There was no doubt that secular ethnicity would erode over time, but that would not be the case for sacred ethnicity, which was defined by the Greek Orthodox faith. Sacred ethnicity, the commission believed, could strike roots in the New World because it could adapt to changing conditions "while not deviating from its holy traditions and transcendental truths." Conversely, if Greek Orthodoxy were to emphasize secular over sacred ethnicity, "its long-term future" in America would be in doubt. The report summed up this view with an easy-to-understand schema that described the relationship between Greek American ethnicity and religion as having gone through three different stages during the twentieth century: "For the immigrant generation, we might say that Orthodoxy was Hellenism—the two were virtually synonymous." The next stage was the second generation of Greek Americans, where "orthodoxy was found in Hellenism. To be Greek in America meant to be Greek Orthodox." And then, for the third and later generations, the initial relationship was stood on its head, because "Hellenism is to be found in Orthodoxy." In other words, the report explained, "rather than viewing the increasing Americanization of the Church as antithetical to Greek identity," it would only be with an indigenous—that is, American-rooted—Greek Orthodox Church "that we can expect any kind of Greek identity to carry on in the generations to come." And finally, this church, the commission concluded, had to accept non-Greeks, because, paradoxically, that is how it would guarantee some form of Greek American ethnic survival into the future.[16]

At the congress's closing banquet, the patriarch was treated to a spectacular example of the Americanization of the Greek Orthodox Church. With television news anchor and personality Ted Koppel serving as master of ceremonies, Dimitrios shared the dais with President George H. W. Bush. In a typical example of the public bonhomie and humorous exchanges that are common on such occasions, Koppel introduced a person whom the audience held in great reverence, then "apologized" to the president, saying he did not mean him. The president met the quip by replying that he thought Koppel was referring to his wife, Barbara. And when Koppel introduced Bush, he said he would not remind all present that he was the man who had prevented a Greek American from becoming president two years earlier. But the banquet attendees, happy and proud the president was honoring their church, gave Bush a rousing welcome.[17]

The Orthodox Christian Laity

Proof that many members of the Greek Orthodox Church supported the creation a pan-Orthodox, American Church came with the formation of a group that considered the church's moves too slow and insufficient. In April 1988, a press release announced that a group calling itself Orthodox Christian Laity (OCL) had just been chartered as a nonprofit corporation in Illinois. The purpose of the OCL was "to restore and strengthen the role of the laity in the Orthodox Church for the continuous regeneration of the Church in its Apostolic mission." All those listed as board members or participants in the group, which had been formed in Chicago the previous year, were members of the Greek Orthodox Church, some of them longtime activists, although the two-page press release did not mention the word "Greek" and spoke of the Orthodox Church, an early indication that the OCL would soon also be taking on the cause of Orthodox unity in America. There had always been critics within the church, and many had chafed at the archbishop's leadership style, his penchant for seeking constant validation from civil authorities, and the laity's inability to have its voice heard, but this was the first time such an organized group had appeared. Somewhat paradoxically, the OCL hoped it could enter into a dialogue with the archbishop whose very leadership style it opposed. In fact, most members of the group were long-serving, upstanding lay members of the church, and many had been involved in the archdiocese's youth organization GOYA when it was established in the 1950s. They knew Iakovos and had a close, respectful relationship with the archbishop. One of them who had an especially close relationship with Iakovos, Andrew Kopan, wrote to him in November 1988, saying he was eager to apprise him of the Orthodox Christian Laity movement, adding reassuringly it was composed of lay leaders who had been involved in GOYA, several members of the Archdiocesan Council, and several clergymen, "all of whom have nothing but the utmost respect for Your Eminence and your leadership of the Church." But, Kopan explained, "they are, however, concerned over some of the directions of the Archdiocese and seek to be heard," and he added, "I would advise Your

Eminence, with due respect that you accept this movement as the concerned movement as the 'voice' of the laity, indeed the 'conscience' of the Church and that you welcome their constructive criticism." Kopan concluded by requesting a meeting with the archbishop and signed with his first name only, in Greek: Andreas.[18]

The OCL believed the archdiocese had reached the point at which it was in dire need of changes. There was not one single event that triggered the formation of OCL; rather it was a culmination of complaints that grew as Iakovos strengthened his grip on the reins of the archdiocese and bolstered his personal authority. It is not a coincidence that the group formed in the wake of the lavish celebrations of Iakovos's twenty-fifth anniversary as archbishop in 1984. The accolades for Iakovos were not limited to the anniversary service and the events surrounding it in April of that year but were echoed at the Clergy-Laity Congress in July. The presence of the ABC network's news anchor Peter Jennings at a special banquet at the Waldorf Astoria hotel and a screening of a short video in which a picture of Jesus Christ morphed into an infant Iakovos were examples of what irked many members of the church and were catalysts for the creation of the OCL. The OCL hoped that if it could express the conscience of the church, as Kopan put it, it could gently redirect the archdiocese's practices away from the trappings of secular pomp and circumstance toward a more religiously oriented and inclusive way of church life. It was in no way a radical movement; rather it expressed the reformist wishes of a group that was in every other way part of the mainstream establishment of the Greek Orthodox Church in the United States.

The core of the archdiocese's establishment reacted in different ways to the appearance of the OCL. The Archdiocesan Council's minutes show great concern, but Iakovos evidently thought he could contain the movement, and it took a while for him to criticize it openly. When he was asked about "a certain lay movement in the Chicago area" at an Archdiocesan Council meeting in February 1989, he answered that to the best of his knowledge the group was not anti-ecclesiastical because its members were members of the church who had questions about the archdiocese's priorities. The issue did not go away. John Plumides, a council lay member and a former two-term AHEPA president, expressed alarm and suggested the archbishop call the leaders in for a special meeting. Iakovos responded that he was aware of their activities, that they were entitled to their opinions, and that he intended to meet them in the near future.[19] Iakovos in fact engaged in informal conversations with some of the leaders, including Kopan, and tried to persuade them to stop; he even offered to appoint a number of them to the Archdiocesan Council, but to no avail. At a council meeting in November 1991, the archbishop opened the proceedings by talking about the existence of "divisive forces" within and outside the church that took on three basic forms. He was alluding to a an array of critics that included the few "Genuine Orthodox" (the so-called Old Calendar) parishes, and the OCL, whom he described as "those would be reformers who choose to ignore the constant progress of renewal within the Church, as evidenced in the agenda for the Third Millennium"—a reference to the commission that had produced the blueprint for the twenty-first century at the 1990 Clergy-Laity Congress. Iakovos called here for "a continuation of the work of renewal by reexamining the nature of the church, comprehending it as a living spiritual organism, rather than an organization." He echoed that view when he wrote a stern letter to Kopan in which he told him the church was the body of Christ and thus could not accommodate separate organizations. After the archbishop, at a council meeting, expressed disapproval with the OCL, adding that the conversations he had with them only resulted in broken promises, a dam burst, and both clerics and lay members denounced the OCL. This put Dr. William Tenet, the one council member who had joined the OCL, in a difficult spot, and he apologized for a recent OCL publication that had criticized the archbishop sharply and called for more dialogue; but the council demanded a letter of apology. Kourides, the archbishop's legal adviser and right-hand man, suggested that the apology come with the assurance there would be no further OCL publications or public meetings. To the extent that no other, more moderate, views had been expressed at the meeting, these amounted to recommendations that the OCL disband and "return" to the church.[20]

The reason why the archbishop turned openly against the OCL at the November 1991 Archdiocesan Council meeting was that the OCL had taken a major step in October when it produced its own plan for Orthodox renewal, a response to the archdiocese's vision its commission had made public the previous year. The OCL's October 1991 gathering, which took place in Baltimore, was its fourth annual meeting. Its first had been in Chicago in early 1989; its second was later that year when the leaders met with Iakovos at a hotel near his residence in Rye, New York. The third meeting, in Chicago in 1990, featured lectures by both a Greek Orthodox theologian, Demetrios Constantelos, and Leonid Kishkovsky, the Russian Orthodox theologian. At that meeting it also commissioned a series of seven studies of key issues facing Orthodox Christianity in America. The topics the studies would cover were (1) faith, language, and culture; (2) spiritual renewal; (3) Orthodox women and the church; (4) mission and outreach; (5) selection of hierarchy; (6) administration and accountability; and (7) Orthodox unity. The authors of these reports submitted preliminary versions to the meeting in October 1991 for discussion. Clearly, by that time the OCL had crystallized into a potent force with a distinct vision for the future of Orthodoxy in America.

The OCL's vision, as it appeared in final form in 1993, had considerable overlap with that of the archdiocese, at least in terms of principles, but it differed in its treatment of the church's administrative structure and the role of the laity, its approach to Orthodox unity, and the role of women in the church. Where there were similarities, the OCL's vision represented an accelerated version of the direction in which Iakovos was leading Greek Orthodoxy and called for an immediate implementation of measures, in contrast to the slower process the archbishop preferred. Thus, in the preamble of the OCL's volume there were sixteen pages of enumerated recommendations corresponding to each of the seven essays. One area where the views of the archdiocese and the OCL were virtually identical was the relationship of faith, language, and culture. The reason was very simple: Charles Moskos, who had shaped that fourth section in the archdiocese's Third Millennium document, was the author of that particular study for the OCL, and there are entire sections in which both texts are identical. But the OCL's recommendations either called for changes beyond what the archdiocese would contemplate, or, where there was agreement, the OCL recommendations were very specific, something rarely found in the archdiocese's documents and its overall approach.

Two main themes ran through OCL's recommendations. The first one centered on the need for greater inclusiveness, namely the need for more lay participation in all aspects of church life, more democratic processes in the selection of church officials, a greater role for women, and an end to the differences in the way boys and girls were treated by the church. The other theme consisted of a cluster of measures that would make the Orthodox Church more indigenous and less ethnic. The OCL recommended that "Orthodoxy in America must evolve into an indigenous and American faith drawing on the best aspects of the American tradition while recognizing and respecting its ethnic roots" and also recommended that the use of English in the Sunday liturgy should be the standard practice. This call was repeated several times. The OCL stated that the preservation of ethnic identity should be the proper function of Greek ethnic associations and listed several suggestions to that effect. It acknowledged that governments also had a legitimate right to preserve ethnic identity, but added that the Greek Orthodox Archdiocese should separate itself from any influence of any government agency of any nation. The OCL acknowledged that accommodations over language and customs had to be made in the case of parishes with significant numbers of newly arrived immigrants, but steps had to be taken to ease their transition into American life as well. Finally, the OCL outlined two different models for achieving pan-Orthodox unity in the Americas, either through establishing an independent, autocephalous church that would rupture its ties with the Ecumenical Patriarchate, or a church that would be semi-autonomous from Constantinople.[21]

A measure of OCL's growing influence came when the organization sent its representatives to Istanbul, where they were granted an audience with Patriarch Bartholomew, even though at the time the archdiocese was keeping its distance and showed few signs of taking the organization's demands seriously. The OCL's meeting with the patriarchate was substantive, certainly not a mere photo opportunity, and it was followed by a private meeting between the patriarch and delegation member Peter Marudas, an OCL leader and aide to Senator Paul Sarbanes of Maryland, himself the son of Greek emigrants. George Matsoukas, an OCL leader who was on the trip, reported that Bartholomew conveyed that the institution of the patriarchate was above ethnicities and was itself a victim of nationalist policies and told the OCL members that Orthodox unity in the New World was his priority. When Matsoukas published his article on the subject in a volume that appeared long after the 1994 Ligonier conference, he added a postscript noting that ultimately the hopes that the patriarch would support Orthodox unity were dashed because Bartholomew "found comfort in his Ottoman roots" and chose instead to be the leader only of the Greeks in America.[22]

Meanwhile the archdiocese continued to discount the significance of the OCL demands, including those about giving women a greater role in church life. At the time, the World Council of Churches (WCC) had taken up the same issue of women in the church. When WCC representatives met with representatives of the archdiocese to inquire about the status of women in the church, they were told that "if something did not exist in the Early Church it could not be valid for church life today," and therefore the Greek Orthodox Church would not ordain women or even make them deaconesses (assistants to priests).[23] The WCC representatives came away doubly disappointed because they were unable to meet and talk to women, although they understood that the majority of Greek Orthodox women probably agreed with the archdiocese's position. But the encounter showed how the archdiocese was not prepared to even discuss the reforms the OCL recommended.

The Crisis over Finances

The clergy-laity congresses of 1992 and 1994 could have been remembered as occasions in which the church grappled with the evolution of a faith-based

American Greek Orthodoxy, but instead that spiritual and sociological issue was overshadowed by urgent concerns over the church's financial state. In retrospect it is easy to see that the cause of the financial woes was the ongoing pressure to fund the wide range of the church's activities, combined with the lack of expertise in dealing with major investments. A decade earlier the archdiocese had unwisely become involved in a real estate venture, which had subsequently gone sour and led to serious financial losses. Questionable bookkeeping practices were involved, along with an appearance of a conflict of interest for the director of economic development. In 1992 this all became public knowledge, and inevitably it became a major topic at the Clergy-Laity Congress in July. The Archdiocesan Council, no longer able to keep the issue under wraps, had to present a report, which was designed to minimize the damage and to smooth things over. And by way of demonstrating its new-found focus on money issues, the archdiocese presented a thorough overview of its membership's donations broken down by region, a springboard for reflection and planning ahead. But the real estate affair proved too toxic, and it ultimately overshadowed everything else. All this came at a particularly bad time, because it confirmed the OCL's critique of the church's hierarchical governance and was grist to the mill of the traditionalists, who were still harping on the issue of preserving the Greek language. And, needless to say, it damaged the archbishop's standing.

At the opening of the Clergy-Laity Congress in New Orleans in 1992, Iakovos's speech, titled "It's Time to Do the Lord's Work!" sought to focus the congress on helping and not criticizing the church. Opening in a confident mood, Iakovos proclaimed that Orthodoxy would survive as a faith, not as an ethnic culture, echoing the view of the 1990 commission. The legacy of those who first brought Orthodoxy to America, he said, "will depend on the degree and the extent to which our faith is able to shape and order our everyday life" and "would not depend on language" (a jab at the traditionalists) or "any reformations or adaptations" (no doubt a rebuke directed at the OCL). The archbishop had introduced some reforms so as to blunt the criticisms leveled by the OCL, but the real estate issue was destined to overshadow the proceedings.

The trouble had begun in the early 1980s when the archdiocese bought a fifty-one-acre tract in Purchase, New York, that it began to develop with a view to selling it for a profit. Chris Demetriades, a builder of luxury homes and a member of the Archdiocesan Council, was the archdiocese's director of economic development at the time and had proposed the venture. His own company bought an adjacent parcel and began developing it. In 1983 the archdiocese began building houses on its property, but in 1987, after having spent over $14 million to buy the land and develop it, it decided to sell the property, to avoid a new tax burden and to limit its risk. After finding other bids unsatisfactory, the archdiocese sold the property to Demetriades for a price of over $14 million, plus deferred interest that would be paid as houses were sold, and further payments based on the sales of homes to be built, which the New York Times reported would have brought the total to between $20 million and $22 million. According to the newspaper, Demetriades had sold thirty homes and repaid the church $6 million, but then he pleaded that he faced bankruptcy because of a drop in the real estate market. Over the next two years, the archdiocese released him from paying more than $10 million that he still owed for the purchase, and in exchange he made a lump-sum payment of a $1.3 million.[24] In January 1992 the archdiocese reduced his obligations by $5.5 million by deducting $2.3 million from the original price and writing off at least $3.2 million more in deferred payments and interest. But the Times reported that different figures were found in papers submitted to the church in 1987 to the New York Supreme Court in Westchester County, a requirement when not-for-profit religious organizations make major sales of their property. The papers indicated the church was to earn $19.9 million, including deferred interest payments of $7.5 million. From the floor of the 1992 New Orleans congress, delegates, some of them affiliated with the OCL, urged the archdiocese to authorize an independent counsel and accounting firm to explore the transaction and report on it.[25] They were not satisfied with the picture the Archdiocesan Council was offering, along with a Price Waterhouse audit of the financial tractions related to the real estate affair. A month earlier, when the Archdiocesan Council had considered the report that was to be submitted to the congress, one member had proposed that an "unbiased committee" handle the issue. The council members who were "in the legal profession" had withdrawn from the meeting for a while to discuss legal technicalities in the phraseology. Another member protested rumors concerning the personal liability of the members of the Finance Committee and the council. It was obviously a very difficult and uncomfortable meeting for all present. The council went forward and approved the report, though not unanimously.[26] Likewise, at the congress, delegates chose to close ranks around the church's leadership. An extraordinarily big congress finance report committee reviewed the budget. Demetriades apologized for the losses and was then warmly praised for his services. When George Karcazes, an OCL leader, stood up at the plenary session when the budget was being presented and proposed an independent investigation, he was ruled out of order. Theodore Prounis, the lawyer who represented the archdiocese in the real estate deal, told the New York Times that the critics "should stop all this nonsense when the governing bodies of the church have spoken."[27]

The real estate investment affair's repercussions continued for at least another two years. Immediately after the Clergy-Laity Congress at New Orleans, Simos C. Dimas, a New York–based lawyer active in church and community affairs, began a lawsuit against the archdiocese, claiming that it had not obtained proper court approval for either the original sale or the later change in its terms. The lawsuit, which Dimas had initiated without real hope of winning but in order to expose the deal, sent ripples throughout the Greek American community. Meanwhile, the OCL was finalizing the publishable version of its studies on issues facing Orthodox Christians in America, in which it listed recommendations calling for greater accountability for the church's financial position. It referenced the real estate affair directly: "Given the persistent questions relating to specific land deals involving the Church properties in New York state, one of which resulted in a write-off of $5 million of funds owed to the Archdiocese by a former employee, the Archdiocese should retain independent counsel and auditing firms to investigate the circumstances of these transactions and render a report to the Archdiocesan Council."[28] There was a general sense that the trouble the church ran into with its real estate investment was yet another indication of how difficult it was for a religious institution to maintain a range of activities that were not only ecclesiastical but also educational while also satisfying the growing administrative demands all its services created. In 1991, the church's $8 million expenses were distributed as follows: 30.9 percent to education; 25.9 percent to its dioceses; 12 percent to communications; 10.9 percent to the Patriarchate of Constantinople and for missionary work abroad; 8.2 percent to its administrative offices; 7.7 percent to operational expenditures; and 4.4 percent to community services. In 1992, the budget had reached $9.4 million.

A report submitted at the 1992 Clergy-Laity Congress listing the largest monetary contributions the archdiocese received from the wealthiest parishes served as an illustration of the enormous funds that were being handed over every year. The top two parishes, which contributed $96,000 each to the archdiocese, were Holy Trinity Cathedral in New York City and St. Paul Cathedral of Long Island (St. Paul's, located in Hempstead, had been formed after World War II and grew thanks to the move to the suburbs of thousands of Greek Americans beginning in the 1950s). The third parish on the list, with a contribution of $90,000, was St. Demetrios in Astoria, a reminder that the Greek-born were still an important factor in church life—a reality confirmed by the presence of St. Nicholas Church of Flushing, New York, in seventh place. Seven of the top twenty parishes were either in Chicago

(St. Demetrios, Assumption of the Virgin, and St. Andrew) or in its suburbs (Palos Hills, Des Plaines, Glenview, and Westchester, Illinois), attesting to the continuing size and significance of the Greek Americans in the Chicago area. The highest contributor of those parishes, Sts. Constantine and Helen in Palos Hills, was tied in fourth place with the Annunciation Cathedral of Houston, with $82,000. The rest of the report was devoted to outlining the archdiocesan departments that the parish contributions funded, and also made the case that almost all of them required the greater allocation of resources to be approved by the Clergy-Laity Congress.

The 1994 Congress Seeks a New Beginning

After two years of embarrassing and painful public exposure over the real estate deal, and with the issue finally resolved, the archdiocese held the 1994 Clergy-Laity Congress in Chicago with great hopes of forging a new beginning and returning to the challenges outlined in the 1990 commission's report—and responding to the questions the OCL was raising. Speaking at the Archdiocesan Council's meeting on the eve of the congress, Iakovos reiterated the view that the community had to be one of faith, not of people coming from the same race, heritage, and culture, and emphasized "we are moving fast towards a community of people having the same religious belief, the same worship. . . . It is imperative, therefore, that we see our Church in the Americas as a communion and a community . . . and foster this new concept as the one that will guarantee the survival of our religion." He touched briefly on the effects of the real estate deal, saying, "During the years 1992–94 we have been taught that trusting blindingly or delegating responsibilities which are ours to others is not the best way of success." It was the closest the archbishop had come to admitting his responsibility for the debacle.

Yet the new beginning Iakovos sought was being undermined by rumors that his relations with the Ecumenical Patriarchate had worsened to the point that the mother church was considering who would replace him in the near future. Bartholomew and Iakovos knew each other well—they were both from the island of Imvros—but Bartholomew was almost thirty years younger. The election for Dimitrios's successor had taken place three weeks after his death, and the fifteen-member synod had chosen Bartholomew in a unanimous vote. It was widely assumed that the Greek government and a prominent Greek businessman, Panayotis Angelopoulos, who had made considerable donations to the Ecumenical Patriarchate, had worked behind the scenes to secure at the minimum Iakovos's inclusion on the ballot, but the Turkish government had refused.[29] The new patriarch's dynamism and the opportunities opened to Eastern Orthodoxy following the collapse of communism in Eastern Europe made several observers assume that the patriarchate would be entering a new era of greater assertiveness and presence internationally.[30] The relationship between the archdiocese and the Ecumenical Patriarchate was about to change, with Constantinople claiming more and more rights of supervision over the affairs of Greek Orthodoxy in America.

At the Clergy-Laity Congress in Chicago, the patriarchate's representative, Archbishop Spyridon Papageorge of Italy, did not restrict himself to the status of the patriarch's messenger and observer, which was the norm with whoever was representing Constantinople at the congress. Instead he delivered a substantive speech to the congress and also addressed the Ladies Philoptochos and the archdiocese's youth organization, which were also holding their conferences in Chicago at the same time. Spyridon's strong presence in Chicago served to fuel talk of the patriarch's displeasure with the archbishop. The *Ethnikos Kyrix* gleefully reported that all the talk in the corridors outside the hall where the congress was taking place was about who would be the next archbishop.

Pan-Orthodoxy at Ligonier

Contacts among the Eastern Orthodox Churches in America had always been haunted by fears of how each of the respective mother churches would react. Their rivalries were a matter of public record and negatively affected the prospects of pan-Orthodox unity in North America. Beyond the homeland's assumption that its immigrants were a diaspora, the resources their respective churches in America offered was another important reason for the Old World Orthodox patriarchates to guard them jealously and look down on any moves that might lead to the creation of an autocephalous, semi-independent Orthodox Church in America. No wonder SCOBA, the Standing Conference of Canonical Orthodox Bishops in the Americas that Iakovos had created in 1961, was still in existence three decades later, though it was making little headway. The Old World patriarchates remained concerned about moves toward autocephaly and the introduction of the English language in church services. According to Thomas FitzGerald, in the United States those issues "had a chilling effect upon Pan-Orthodox cooperation," and from the 1970s to the early 1990s "the underlying tensions manifested themselves in the relationship among the clergy of the various jurisdictions, in the relationships among the theological schools, and, to some degree, in the work of the grassroots inter-Orthodox organizations," and the bad feelings "were fueled by the extreme views coming from partisans on all sides of the discussions." If anything, the thrust toward greater Orthodox unity only affirmed a sense of jurisdictional distinctiveness.[31]

The snail-pace contacts among Orthodox jurisdictions picked up in the 1980s when preparatory meetings, cumbersomely named "Pre-Conciliar Conferences," were held to clear an agenda for a future pan-Orthodox conference. The status of the Orthodox diaspora was eventually discussed in such gatherings in 1990 and again in 1993. The fist of those meetings took place at the Orthodox Center of the Ecumenical Patriarchate in Chambésy in Switzerland in November 1990. There, an Inter-Orthodox Preparatory Commission, after discussing the issue of the "Orthodox Diaspora," decided to submit a proposal to the forthcoming Fourth Preconciliar Pan-Orthodox Conference. All the Orthodox Churches were unanimous in their desire "that the problem of the Orthodox diaspora be resolved as quickly as possible and that it [the solution] be organized in a way that is in accordance with Orthodox ecclesiological tradition and with the canonical praxis of the Orthodox Church." The meeting also decided to initiate a transitional phase that would lead to the consideration of a canonical solution. This would entail the creation of "Episcopal Assemblies" in all the regions where a diaspora church existed. Their responsibility would be "to bear witness to the unity of Orthodoxy and to develop a common activity of all Orthodox living in the region; to represent all the Orthodox in contact with other confessions, as well as in the society at large in the region; to cultivate theological and ecclesiastical education."[32] In 1993, another meeting in Chambésy defined the regions in which the assemblies would be created and discussed the regulations by which they would function. It also confirmed the consensus of the participating Orthodox Churches on the prospect of autocephaly and how it would be proclaimed. The mother churches pledged their support to the work of the assemblies and their commitment to restore canonical normality in the diaspora. At long last, the issue of the autocephaly of the Orthodox Churches in the diaspora was moving forward. As FitzGerald notes, things were moving in the direction that many American Orthodox theologians had recommended, namely that there be greater administrative unity among the jurisdictions in the United States.[33] Yet it soon became evident that there was no consensus about how fast the process should unfold.

Iakovos wished to push forward. His plan to call a meeting of all the Orthodox hierarchs in America in 1988 had been shelved because of the celebrations that year of the millennium anniversary of the arrival of Christianity to Russia. This time there were no obstacles, and he proposed a meeting in late 1994. The Orthodox leaders whose churches were affiliated with SCOBA agreed to meet. The gathering would take place in Ligonier, Pennsylvania, at the facilities of the Antiochian Orthodox Church, whose leader, Metropolitan Philip Saliba, was a strong advocate of Orthodox unity. When the Ecumenical Patriarchate heard of this plan it made urgent inquiries, which Iakovos dismissed, explaining that this was an internal matter among the Orthodox Churches in America that need not concern Constantinople.

What happened at Ligonier and what happened in its aftermath epitomized the differences in perception and understanding of the position of the Orthodox Church in the America of the 1990s. The proceedings were videotaped, and a forty-minute documentary film was made, a sign of the openness with which the leaders of the Orthodox jurisdictions approached their gathering. At Ligonier, Iakovos, as the presiding bishop, opened the proceedings by saying that all those present were at a place were they could be transfigured from parochial to truly Orthodox Christian people, from separate jurisdictions to one jurisdiction, and from many ethnic groups to one, headed and dominated by Christ. Thus, he set the tone for three days of conversation and reflection, without an agenda, as Metropolitan Theodosius of the Orthodox Church of America said, to see how they could achieve administrative unity. Twenty-nine prelates from the eight separate North American–based Orthodox jurisdictions that belonged to SCOBA—the American Carpatho-Russian Diocese, the Antiochian Orthodox Christian Archdiocese, the Bulgarian Eastern Orthodox Diocese, the Greek Orthodox Archdiocese, the Orthodox Church in America, the Romanian Orthodox Archdiocese, the Serbian Orthodox Church, and the Ukrainian Orthodox Church—spent three days of prayer and formal and informal conversations and getting to know each other at the Antiochian facilities at Ligonier. It was the first time that they had all gathered under the same roof. As Metropolitan Saliba said in the conference's videotape, the time for Orthodox unity had come. It did not mean severing ties with the churches in the Old World—instead it meant helping them, because they could benefit more from a united rather than a fragmented Orthodox Church in America.

The meeting issued two statements at the end of its proceedings, one on the church in North America and the other on challenges of Orthodox missionary work. The statement on the church was the one that would cause controversy. It spoke of the forthcoming pan-Orthodox conference and its inclusion of the issue of the "diaspora" on the agenda, and humbly requested that the church in North America be part of the conversation. The statement went on to dispute the applicability of the term "diaspora" in the case of

the Orthodox churches in North America and pointed out that the churches
were growing closer together:

> We have agreed that we cannot accept the term "diaspora" as used to
> describe the Church in North America. In fact the term is ecclesiasti-
> cally problematic. It diminishes the fullness of the faith that we have
> lived and experienced here for the past two hundred years. Moreover,
> as we reflect on the ways in which the Church in North America has
> matured, it is important to recognize that much has been done as the
> natural and organic response of Orthodox Christians who share the
> same faith while living together in one place. We celebrate and build
> on already existing structures.

Those structures were SCOBA and other bodies, including representatives of
the Eastern Orthodox Churches in North America, the International Orthodox Christian Charities (IOCC), the Orthodox Christian Education Commission (OCEC), the Orthodox Theological Society in America (OTSA), and the
Orthodox Christian Missions Center. All those organizations, the statement
went on to say, gave witness to the strong foundation that the project for
greater unity had already acquired. The aim was "to organically become an
administratively united Church," and the statement concluded by emphasizing "this is presented as a broad outline or framework in which the whole
Church in North America can grow to manifest the deep unity of faith that
we share."[34]

If anything, the statement on the church in North America that came
out of Ligonier was scrupulously crafted so as not to give offense to the Old
World churches or create the impression that it was somehow a manifesto
of an upcoming break with the homeland and the creation of a united autocephalous or autonomous American Orthodox Church. But for all its care,
the statement had the opposite effect, and the Ecumenical Patriarchate and
other Old World patriarchates quickly issued condemnations. Even though
the patriarchate asked and received assurances from Iakovos that this did
not entail the creation of an autocephalous American Orthodox Church, it
stated that "it repudiates all the initiatives taken at the meeting in Ligonier,
Pennsylvania, for having overstepped its authority and states that it in no
way recognizes any of its decisions which are opposed to the pan-Orthodox
proposals and directions on the issue of Diaspora and the corresponding
procedure followed for its regulation."[35] Evidently, operating in the new era
of globalization, the patriarchate wished to retain the right to oversee any
major step toward the unification of the Orthodox ecclesiastical structure in
America.[36]

To understand why the patriarchate's reaction was so sharp, however, one has to search for any systematic analysis from within the Orthodox Churches in America. The 1994 Ligonier meeting is somewhat of a taboo subject, and official documentation is hard to access. One articulate and systematic criticism came from the OCL. In 1997 the organization held a meeting in Boston commemorating its tenth anniversary. The theme was "The American Church and the Ecumenical Patriarchate," and the program included a keynote speech by James Counelis and three response speeches, by Rev. Theodore Stylianopoulos, a Harvard Divinity School–educated theologian, Aristeides Papadakis, a scholar of Byzantine and religious history, and Valerie A. Karas, a scholar of church history with a particular interest in the role of women in the Orthodox Church, past and present. Counelis launched a comprehensive criticism of the Ecumenical Patriarchate's involvement in the affairs of Eastern Orthodoxy in America, describing the patriarchate as an institution beholden to a foreign government and exercising an authoritarian form of governance. He contrasted what he called the "Holy American Church" (it is unclear if he meant the Greek Orthodox Church or all Eastern Orthodox Churches in America) with the Ecumenical Patriarchate, stating that "the Holy American Church is a state-separated church. In contrast, the Ecumenical Patriarchate reflects a state-church. The Holy American church reflects a culture of direct lay involvement in church governance; the Ecumenical Patriarchate reflects a guild of priests with total control over church governance and its resources."[37] Of the three responses, it was Stylianopoulos's that took issue with Counelis's critique, though his rebuttal was scholarly in tone and content. He stated that "the Orthodox tradition plainly teaches that regional churches have a right to grow towards autonomy and autocephaly . . . however the proper way to arrive at the ultimate goal is through orderly canonical process on the basis of mutual Christian love and by means of prayerful dialogue and cooperation in order that God Himself may fill us with His energy and guide us to that glorious goal in His chosen time."[38]

Over the next few years, the OCL maintained its critique of the patriarch's intervention and returned again and again to the position that the Greek Orthodox in America were not a "diaspora" beholden to Constantinople. It was a position invoked by Papadakis at the OCL meeting in his response to Counelis's remarks, and it was repeated in 2003 by Leonid Kishkovsky. Speaking in 2003 at a conference in Moscow, Kishkovsky argued that Orthodoxy in America should not be considered as a diaspora by the Old World patriarchates, and in referring to Ligonier he noted with understatement that the Ligonier conference, "though intended to be respectful and meant to make a contribution to progress towards Orthodox unity under the guidance of the patriarchates, caused much controversy and harshly negative reactions. They failed to secure the support of the patriarchates for a coherent movement towards Orthodox canonical and administrative unity in America."[39]

There are of course interpretations of the patriarchate's reaction that center on the issues of personalities and power politics. A commonly held view is encapsulated in the words of one study, that "unfortunately the Ligonier statement was viewed by some of the patriarchates as a 'power grab' by Iakovos who heretofore had been accused sotto voce of cultivating a cult of personality," and moreover that "many feared he was on the verge of having himself elected Patriarch of America. . . . Some of the Old World Patriarchates were scared of losing their American diocese simply for economic reasons." And the specific reasons why Patriarch Bartholomew reacted negatively are assumed to be because one of the participants, Bishop Vsevolod of the Ukrainian Archdiocese, assured the patriarch that Iakovos was getting ready to have himself declared "Patriarch of America."[40]

In retrospect, and considering Bartholomew's next moves, there appeared to be a larger strategy at play, one that reflected a much greater assertiveness of the Patriarchate of Constantinople over the Greek Orthodox Archdiocese. The patriarch's reaction to Ligonier, whether justified or due to a misunderstanding or misinformation, or perhaps even a pretext for executing an already decided-upon plan, brought such a fundamental restructuring of Greek Orthodoxy in North and South America that it has to be recognized as a historic turning point that represents a reassertion of Constantinople's authority in America.

The fate of the Ligonier gathering can be interpreted as a reflection of the caution with which Eastern Orthodoxy, or at least its leadership, confronts innovation, especially in a globalized age. Or it can be understood as a difference over turf and possibly a personality clash. In terms of our narrative so far, Ligonier represents a moment at which the Greek Orthodox Church was unable to respond to the Americanization trend among its faithful. The church's ethnic character, and specifically its doctrinal dependency on the Ecumenical Patriarchate of Constantinople, brought an end to a decades-long journey during which the church had balanced between adapting to Americanization and retaining its ethnic character. Because that character was ethno-religious, and its religious dimension entailed a connection with Constantinople, Iakovos's strategy was ultimately answerable to a higher authority. And that authority, the ecumenical patriarch, evidently believed that the movement toward a pan-Orthodox American Church threatened his own authority and jurisdiction over Greek Orthodoxy in America. At a more abstract level, since the structures that shape a particular historical process exist because human agents observe and conform to their existence, Constantinople represents an external structure that had been present in the history of Greek Orthodoxy but had come into play only occasionally, as for example in the appointment of an archbishop of North and South America. And because "structures comprise rules and resources that human agents draw on and reproduce when they act,"[41] it is on this level at least easy to understand why both the archbishop and the clerical and lay leadership in America conformed to the wishes of the patriarch. As they saw it, it was not an outside intervention into the affairs of Greek Orthodoxy in America; it was merely a corrective move by the head of the Orthodox Church.

CHAPTER 11

Church and Patriarchate and the Limits of Americanization

The Ecumenical Patriarchate's sharp reaction to Ligonier demonstrated that there were limits to the Greek Orthodox Church in America's ability to choose its own path and shape Greek Orthodox identity in America, and it was the Ecumenical Patriarchate that defined those limits. The rights that the patriarch enjoyed over Greek Orthodox life in the United States put an end to the evolution of Greek Orthodoxy into some form of American Orthodoxy through its fusion with the other Eastern Orthodox Churches. Beginning in 1991, with Bartholomew as patriarch, the Great Church had begun to reassert its authority and invoke its transnational character. In 1995 the patriarchate opened a liaison office at the European Union headquarters in Brussels. Following Bartholomew's accession to the throne, the patriarchate experienced "a renaissance of sorts" with the rebuilding of churches and the refurbishment of its headquarters in Istanbul, thanks to the generous funding provided by businessman Theodoros Angelopoulos. With the help of former president Carter, Bartholomew had skillfully managed to improve the patriarchate's relations with the Turkish government. In both cases it is notable that Bartholomew apparently required little help from Iakovos, and there were rumors the archbishop was displeased. But clearly the patriarchate was less beholden than it had been earlier to the support provided by the Greek Orthodox Church in America, though the American connection was still important. A strengthened patriarchate had no qualms about blocking the process that had begun at Ligonier. In the United States, the church had remained relevant and powerful because it had managed to reflect the gradual Americanization of the Greek Americans and to a large extent shape their identity through running the Greek educational system and capitalizing on the importance of religion in American life—and it had relied on the personality and charisma of Archbishop Iakovos. Although the church remained Americanized, from the mid-1990s onward its course would rely as much on the goodwill and sanction of the mother church as it would on what went on in the New World.

A Relationship Redefined

The church's relations with the patriarchate, or more accurately the archbishop's relationship with the patriarch, entered a stormy period in the aftermath of Ligonier. Speaking at the Archdiocesan Council's meeting in New York in March 1995, the first since the controversial gathering had taken place, Iakovos gave an account of what had happened. He had sent both statements issued at Ligonier to the patriarchate, along with a report and a pledge of "full undying support to the Mother Church." But he then received a letter, dated December 23, 1994, "indicating that the statements were misunderstood," and he received a second and third letter "warning him to abide by the Ecumenical Patriarch's restrictions" or else the patriarchate would send a committee over to the United States. A fourth letter indicated that the issue had officially been closed, and there was no further correspondence.[1] Despite the archbishop's reassuring tone, it was clear that the repercussions were continuing. The patriarch had ordered the Ligonier plan to be scrapped, and rumors were rife about his displeasure with Iakovos. Bartholomew rejected a request by Archdiocesan Council member Andrew Athens for a meeting, though that may have also been prompted by Athens's involvement in a Greek government initiative to form a Greek diaspora organization, which Bartholomew saw as undermining the patriarchate's role.

Alarmed at this state of affairs, the council at its March meeting unanimously passed a motion commending Iakovos and the Greek Orthodox bishops for their participation at Ligonier and affirming its support for the two statements that meeting had issued. The motion was meant to reinforce a message the council had sent to Constantinople expressing its support of Iakovos. But the council balked at demanding a meeting with the patriarch, agreeing that instead some of its members travel to Istanbul along with Iakovos and some of the church's bishops. The council designated the members of the delegation headed by Iakovos that would travel to the Ecumenical

Patriarchate. They were Metropolitan Silas, Bishop Iakovos of Chicago, Father Chris Metropulos, Dimitri Moschos, who was the council's chair, Elenie Huszagh, John Plumides, Evan Chris, Peter Pappas, Chris Philip, representing the Archons, Mimi Skandalakis, the president of the Philoptochos, and Tom Kanelos of the church's Young Adult League. None of the clerics who had participated in the Ligonier meeting were chosen. The council unanimously expressed its concern and dismay at the news that Andrew Athens had been denied an audience with the Ecumenical Patriarchate. There could have been very few of those in attendance who left that meeting optimistic about future developments.

A cover of tight secrecy blanketed the communications between the archdiocese and the patriarchate over the months that followed. The more the spokespersons of each side stonewalled, the more they fueled the rumors of Iakovos's impending forced resignation. In August, Iakovos was visiting Greece. The Athens News Agency issued a short notice stating that the archbishop would visit the northern town of Alexandroupolis, and from there he would make the short trip to his birthplace, the island of Imvros (Gökçeada). The news bulletin also went on to tersely state that "Ecumenical Patriarch Bartholomew, also hailing from Imvros, will also be on the island the same day. Commenting on reports that Archbishop Iakovos might resign, Church circles did not rule out the possibility of important developments on Imvros on Aug. 15."[2] The agency's next report from the island described a joint church service that the patriarch and the archbishop held on the island as part of the festivities surrounding the August 15 feast day of the Virgin Mary. There were no reports of important developments, simply because both prelates chose not to disclose that on August 15 Iakovos had indeed handed Bartholomew his resignation. Iakovos had hoped to make that known after he arrived back in the United States within a few weeks, but Bartholomew waited only a few days and made an official announcement while Iakovos was still in Greece. The patriarchate's announcement had an addendum to the effect that "the retirement letter was submitted willingly and for reasons of health," which only confirmed the widespread suspicions that the archbishop had been pressured and was stepping down against his will. This triggered anger and shock in the Greek American community and among political leaders in Athens. Faced with an overwhelming outcry and pleas on both sides of the Atlantic that he remain in office, Iakovos wrote to the patriarchate in October rescinding his resignation.[3]

The rapidly unraveling situation led Bartholomew to send a delegation (a patriarchal exarchy) made up of three hierarchs to calm the roiling waters of Greek Orthodoxy in America. It was headed by Archbishop Stylianos of

Australia, Metropolitan Demetrios of Vresthena (a former professor at the Holy Cross seminary in Brookline who had been reassigned to a position in Greece), and Metropolitan Demetrios of Sevasteia, who was the director of Bartholomew's "personal office." Stylianos had a reputation of being blunt and outspoken and had gone through a long period of tension with the secular Greek community organizations in Australia. It did not look like the delegation had been charged with offering any olive branches. The archdiocese extended a very cautious welcome. Participants in the meetings between Greek Americans and the delegation informed the *New York Times* that often the discussions were tense, and the newspaper commented about the annual dinner held in October to honor Iakovos on his patron saint's day by noting that "praise for him was as thick as the slices of filet mignon. . . . Joining the chorus was Archbishop Stylianos. No one mentioned that Archbishop Iakovos had initially refused to receive Stylianos and his delegation . . . and banqueters interrupted a videotaped tribute from Patriarch Bartholomew with cries of 'No!' when the Patriarch referred to Iakovos's retirement. The Archbishop himself stepped to the lectern and asked the diners to remain respectful."[4]

Two days later, on Friday, October 20, the patriarchate's delegation attended the meeting of the Archdiocesan Council in New York—the formal setting for the official exchange of views between Bartholomew's representatives and the archdiocese's leadership. On the agenda was a discussion of the future of the Greek Orthodox Church in America and the patriarch's initiatives to put an end to the Ligonier initiative, Iakovos's resignation, and a more recent development, the censure of Bishop Methodios of Boston and his resignation as president of the Holy Cross Theological School in Brookline. Methodios, who had a close relationship with Iakovos, had been one of the signatories at Ligonier. Present also were twelve priests and seventy-three lay members of the church whose list of names read like a who's who of leading Greek Americans. But the two key persons in the room were Stylianos, who was the delegation's spokesperson, and Iakovos, who would be chairing the meeting that could determine whether or not he would remain archbishop beyond the date on which Bartholomew was insisting on his resignation. This was the largest and most important gathering of the clerical and lay leaders, other than a clergy-laity congress, to take place under Iakovos. It began in the morning in one of the ballrooms of the New York Hilton, as all Archdiocesan Council meetings did, with a prayer and a short reading from the scriptures. With the formalities over, Iakovos acknowledged the significance of the gathering and the potential for conflict. Two days earlier, at the banquet when there were cries of "No!" from the floor when his retirement was mentioned, he had gone to the podium and called for civility and order. Now he tried to avoid similar outbursts by taking the high ground, welcoming the patriarchal exarchy and adding that "the meeting will proceed in a very sound and Christian way, because this is an historic day in which we will arrive at decisions that will make sense and service the mission of this Church in this land." He told those assembled, "We must present ourselves as Christophers—bearers of Christ" and welcomed everyone as his "coworkers." Evidently Iakovos wished to avoid confrontation, at least at the outset of the meeting, in which two hours were put aside for questions to be posed to the patriarchal delegation. Stylianos followed in the same vein and told the meeting, "We are not here to search, judge[;] we came to assure you that we will try and do our best in whatever and whenever to assist you, so that unity in America becomes more evident and apparent." He thanked Iakovos "for the cordial way he cooperated with us from the very first moment we arrived," then said he would be happy to respond to "thoughts and anxieties that will be directed to us."[5]

There followed an apparently open discussion in which the members of the Archdiocesan Council spoke truth to the power of the patriarchate. Andrew Athens was the first to take the floor. He had been asked to present "the major concerns of the flock," which he cataloged in a list of eight items. These were the patriarchate's announcement of Iakovos's resignation; concern with the censure and forced resignation from his position at Holy Cross of Bishop Methodios; dismay at the patriarchate's lack of understanding of the legal status of the seminary; sadness with the patriarchate's misunderstanding of the unity among the Orthodox in the Americas; sadness with its misunderstanding of "who we are as Americans"; the need to assess the needs of the archdiocese in the twenty-first century; the need to ensure that Orthodoxy remained strong; and the belief among the Greek Orthodox that Iakovos should postpone his departure, or otherwise the stability of the church would be jeopardized. Next came short contributions from almost forty of those present, which echoed three main themes: an overwhelming sentiment of love and support for Iakovos along with a clearly expressed wish that he remained archbishop; criticisms of the Ecumenical Patriarchate's behavior toward Iakovos; and a sense that the patriarchate was oblivious to the environment that Greek Orthodoxy faced in North America. The praise for Iakovos expressed by Mimi Skandalakis, a daughter of Greek immigrants from Marietta, Georgia, who was in her third year as president of the Ladies Philoptochos, captured the love and loyalty to the archbishop that many others would echo. "Most of the people in this room," she said, "have worked with the Archbishop since we were young. We have brought up the next generation of leaders, our children. The Archbishop always taught us love for the Patriarchate. We would like to state that we want our Archbishop to stay and to retire when he feels appropriate. We respectfully request to be allowed to voice our opinion." Another one of the few women present, Yorka Linakis, also a second-generation Greek American and a former judge of the New York State Supreme Court, spoke eloquently of how Iakovos had promoted Orthodoxy in America and how he had inspired the women of the church. Many of those offering praise for Iakovos, such as Basil Foussianes, a member of the Archdiocesan Council since 1974, admitted that the Greeks in America did not know about the Patriarchate of Constantinople and had learned about it from their leaders, especially Iakovos.

Soon, speakers became more emboldened and turned their attention toward the patriarchate and its actions, venturing some criticisms. John Anggelis, a lawyer from Lexington, Kentucky, was the first of several speakers to openly criticize the patriarchate when he asked, "Will we have a voice in the future of our Church? Or will we be dictated to by the Patriarchate?" and added, "The Turks have a say on who will become Patriarch. If the Turks have that much voice, should we not have a voice in the elections of our leaders?" John Plumides, a senior member of the Archdiocesan Council, was a little more restrained, but he did say, "We do not want anyone from the outside to tell us how to run our church." If the support for the archbishop and the critiques of the way the patriarchate had behaved were spontaneous reactions to the events that had unfolded since the Ligonier meeting, the tirade also addressed a bigger and longer-term problem: the extent to which the patriarchate really understood the dynamics of Greek Orthodoxy in America. Bill Cokorinis, a Salt Lake City real estate agent, Greek language instructor at the University of Utah, and long-standing member of the Archdiocesan Council, was one of the first to raise that issue, asking, "Do they know the problems of the youth in America? We never see anything from the Ecumenical Patriarchate, or the Greek Government." Speaking right after him, one of the younger persons at the meeting, George Tsandikos, declared, "We are Americans, Greek Orthodox Americans. We are the next generation. Our voice must be heard in Constantinople. If we are not heard by Constantinople, we will be the lost generation." Father Thomas Paris of the Greek Orthodox Cathedral of the Ascension in Oakland, California, asked for a timetable for an autonomous church in the United States that would serve "the totality of the Orthodox in the United States," adding, "the Patriarchate must realize that we have grown . . . and we do not want to be patronized." Father Paris's tone and words were unprecedented in high-level meetings of the archdiocese and showed how wide the rift had grown between many leading members of the Greek Orthodox Church in America and the Patriarchate of Constantinople. And clearly, the Greek Orthodox in America were not going to watch passively as the patriarchate engineered changes. Elenie Huszagh went as far as proposing a resolution calling on the patriarchate to allow the Greek Orthodox in America to exercise their advisory rights in the selection of the new archbishop. It was passed.[6]

It is hard to imagine what Iakovos was thinking as the discussion on the future of the archdiocese—effectively a discussion on what had happened since Ligonier—became heated at times and combined unrestrained praise for himself and restrained but evident criticisms of the patriarchate. He must have certainly been moved by the succession of tributes of love and admiration and respect that speaker after speaker expressed. And there is no doubt that these were genuine manifestations of the archbishop's standing in the eyes of many of his clergy and laity. But he was also put in an awkward position, because the praise heaped on him was coupled with increasingly sharp critiques of the patriarchate. And even though these justified his decision to withdraw the resignation that he evidently had been pressured into submitting back in August, they also represented a rejection of the natural order of Greek Orthodox things, namely loyalty and obedience to the Patriarchate of Constantinople. The discussion had gone on for well over the two allotted hours, and almost four hours had passed before Iakovos decided to put a stop to the rising discontent. As the minutes put it, he "chastised those who spoke in a manner unbecoming to such a gathering" and reminded everyone that "we need to express our views in a Christian manner."[7] This was consistent with Iakovos's moves after Ligonier. In planning that gathering, he had excluded the patriarchate and must have known there would be some sort of sharp reaction, but he probably underestimated Bartholomew's retaliation. In the face of that response, Iakovos stepped back from confrontation. It was almost as if he wished for a united and more autonomous Eastern Orthodoxy in America beyond what the patriarch would tolerate but also did not want to go against the patriarchate's standing. At least some of those present must have wondered whether his roots in Imvros and his ties to the patriarchate simply proved too strong for him to make the necessary break and lead the archdiocese into the American Eastern Orthodox Church that his, and their, experiences in the United States had shown was necessary.

At last it was time for Stylianos to respond to all that had been said, and his speech was both conciliatory in a general sense but uncompromising on certain of the specific demands—after all, he was there to lay down the law and report to Bartholomew, and was not accountable to anyone in the room. He was also no stranger to confrontations between the clergy and the laity and had earned his reputation of blunt speaking. Yet maybe because he was representing the Patriarchate of Constantinople, it may have also crossed his mind that he himself could replace Iakovos in the near future. In any case, Stylianos was gracious and restrained in his asserting the authority of the mother church. He opened by trying to defuse the tension, reassuring all present that he had heard them and saying they were entitled to state their views but also obliged to love their archbishop and to express their dedication and love of the mother church "who has sent you this Archbishop." He explained that the exarchy was there to listen and would convey to the patriarchate the content and sentiment of what was said "not only in substance but also the emotions." He went on to explain that Iakovos's resignation "was done freely," while Methodios's case was different, and in any case "the Archbishop has changed his mind seeing the expression of your feelings." Having calmed the waters somewhat, Stylianos could not resist gently chiding the council. He asked, "Why is there such panic, why such a lack of confidence in the Mother Church? Were you consulted before any other Archbishop came? They were successful through the Holy Spirit. You had nothing to say then." Then he asked rhetorically, "If Archbishop Iakovos had been elected Patriarch, would you have done the same? I do not think so." Then he reassured them again, saying their fears were baseless. He asked them again not to panic, adding that the Holy Spirit was driving the Church.[8]

Stylianos was explicit about why the patriarchate disapproved of Ligonier, affirming what had been made clear over the previous months, namely that Bartholomew wanted the patriarchate to be directly in charge of any intra-Orthodox initiatives. Few of those in the meeting had mentioned Ligonier explicitly. One of the clerics did so, saying that Bishop Methodios should not be made its scapegoat, that Ligonier "opened new doors for Orthodoxy in the Americas." He also noted that Spyridon, speaking at the 1994 Clergy-Laity Congress as the patriarch's representative, had delivered a message against ethnocentricity. Stylianos responded by affirming the patriarchate's role in initiating any and all ecumenical openings, saying "the decision of Ligonier is sacred but the way it was attempted to obtain administrative unity was uncanonical" and suggesting that the process would be done sometime in the future "canonically" and by ensuring the patriarchate would remain the mother church. Nearly a year after that meeting in western Pennsylvania, it was obvious that the patriarchate's fears that Ligonier threatened its standing had not abated. It was also obvious that Orthodox unity in North America would have to wait and would proceed on Constantinople's terms. Ligonier was already "history."

The tension-ridden atmosphere of the meeting between the council and the patriarchal delegation was a new development in the history of Greek Orthodoxy in America. The presence of the delegation affirmed the Ecumenical Patriarchate's very direct involvement in the archdiocese's affairs, and it also reflected the patriarch's understanding that the clerical and also the lay leadership were owed an explanation for his decisions. But by the same token it was the first time that a delegation from the patriarchate had invited the lay members to express their views in a formal, "official" setting. And the members had openly expressed criticisms of the way the mother church was supervising the affairs of their archdiocese. All this would have been inconceivable in earlier times, certainly before the cooling of the relations between the archbishop and the patriarch. The distance that opened between the two of them allowed the Archdiocesan Council greater voice. The council had grown in stature under Iakovos, and this trend had only increased the more the archbishop relied on members such as Jaharis and others who were able and prepared to play a more activist role rather than perform the functions of mere yes-men. Post-Ligonier, the archbishop's standing was weakened, but not the council's. It remained to be seen whether the council would maintain its newfound assertiveness and whether the October 1995 meeting would be setting a precedent.

The Community Reacts

Like the Archdiocesan Council, the rest of the Greek Orthodox community were dazed by the developments and torn between their admiration and love of Iakovos and their respect toward the patriarchate. The Greek language media, including the *Ethnikos Kyrix*, were not speaking up in favor of the archbishop, though that was not surprising. One publication, which in its decade-long history had not adopted a particular stance toward Iakovos and the archdiocese's affairs, did stand out in its criticism of the patriarchate: the *GreekAmerican* was a weekly English-language newspaper produced by the Greek-language daily *Proini*, but it had its own editorial policy and addressed itself to an educated audience, carrying articles and opinion pieces by journalists and academics. An editorial that appeared in September 1995 described the ongoing post-Ligonier events as "a real power struggle" and stated that Patriarch Bartholomew was "seeking to impose his will on the Church of North and South America." The editorial acknowledged his right to impose his authority but advised great caution, adding that "Patriarch Bartholomew needs to understand that the Greek Orthodox in the United States, although they are in need of the Patriarch's spiritual leadership, are too independent-minded and self-sufficient to begin taking orders from someone who has never ministered or lived here, and whom they hardly know. They need to be treated with the respect and sensitivity they deserve. Embarrassing their religious leader whose achievements are too numerous to mention here, and whom they revere simply won't do." And the editorial included a parting shot, warning that "the Patriarch may be able to exact a resignation here and there by pulling rank, but if he continues this way he won't be able to exact what he really needs to succeed—the support and trust of the Greek American faithful."[9] The following month another critique of the patriarch's actions appeared. Lambros Sideridis, a Connecticut-based physician and member of the Archdiocesan Council, publicized his views in a Greek American English-language magazine. He described the patriarchate's attempts to gain administrative control over the archdiocese and dictate its policies as "very ill-advised" and harmful to the interests of Orthodoxy in the United States. The children of the Greek immigrants, he pointed out, who accounted for 75 percent of the community, had been deeply nurtured with the ideals of democracy and freedom, and it was "unconscionable, unacceptable and destructive to the Greek American community and its institutions to have their affairs and destiny" dictated by an institution that was unfortunately subject to the control and censorship of the Turkish government.[10]

The OCL, which had been so consistently against Iakovos, faced a dilemma: the archbishop was on his way out, but the Patriarchate of Constantinople's increased involvement went against its belief that the church in the Americas should be autonomous. In April 1995 the OCL issued a sharply worded statement supporting the outcome at Ligonier but saying it had come thirty-five years too late and that "the diaspora mindset has contributed to the loss of many Orthodox Christians and the non-acceptance of those who intermarry." Nonetheless, the OCL considered the statement issued at Ligonier as making good sense and leading to ecclesiastical order and potentially a historic turning point. But it criticized Iakovos, claiming the archbishop acted on his realization that the church in America was not a diaspora church only after he understood he would never become patriarch of Constantinople. The statement listed the ills of the archdiocese under Iakovos: it employed secular models and relied on lawyers to resolve its problems; it elevated lay members based on their monetary contributions, not their faith; it meddled in the foreign affairs of the United States; it perpetuated ethnicity and showed excessive deference to the ethnic press. And the OCL also believed Iakovos was responsible for the "unfortunate cacophony that is part of the aftermath of Ligonier" and for miscommunicating with the patriarchate—and that the ethnic press also contributed to creating a misunderstanding.[11] Focusing on poor communications between New York and Istanbul may have been a diplomatic way of saying Iakovos did not make it clear that the long-term goal was for the church in America to have autonomy rather than to become autocephalous, which was Bartholomew's fear. At that juncture, the OCL still hoped that somehow the patriarch would go along with the Ligonier statement and indeed take steps to enable its implementation. To allay any misunderstanding of the OCL's attitude at that sensitive moment, Andrew Kopan, one of the organization's leaders, sent a letter to the *GreekAmerican* pointing out that the OCL wished for a united Orthodox Church in America, which would "remain a province of the Ecumenical Patriarchate under its spiritual jurisdiction." There may have been individuals within the OCL who foresaw an eventual independent American Orthodox Church, but that was not the organization's official position.[12] Left unsaid but certainly implied was the OCL's disinclination toward offering Iakovos any direct support.

The Greek government, heeding appeals from community members but also concerned about how Greek foreign policy goals would be affected, tried but was unsuccessful in preventing Iakovos's departure from his post, but it managed to slow down its timetable. After both government and opposition politicians in Athens had expressed their shock at the confirmation of Iakovos's resignation, the Ministry of Foreign Affairs apparently extracted a promise from the patriarch to delay the process. Several news reports indicated that a major reason for this concession by the patriarchate was the concerns the Greek government had expressed at the prospect of not having Iakovos at the head of the Greek Americans in what was an election year in the United States. Ultimately, a decision was made that Iakovos would be stepping down on July 29, 1996, his eighty-fifth birthday. In a final indignity, rather than allowing the archbishop to announce the date himself, it was leaked to the public via the *Ethnikos Kyrix*. Even then there were reactions from Athens, with Iakovos's old foe Andreas Papandreou, in his final stint as prime minister, exchanging sharp words with the Ecumenical Patriarchate over the wisdom of the information being made public so prematurely.[13]

Years later, following Iakovos's death in 2004, Methodios of Boston offered a beautiful eulogy at the internment of the archbishop on the grounds of Hellenic College in Brookline. He spoke fondly of the archbishop's competitive spirit and vast erudition and recounted that anyone who ever played Scrabble with him on Martha's Vineyard, where he liked taking vacations, "learned words that weren't yet included in Webster's Dictionary of the English language. . . . He always played to win . . . and when the score was close and you thought you finally had a chance to win . . . Archbishop Iakovos would come up with a word that you knew didn't exist."[14] In the wake of Ligonier, the archbishop appeared to have run out of those words.

Iakovos Marches On

While the Ligonier aftermath was slowly eroding his standing, Iakovos was still carrying on his duties undeterred, including his role as an intermediary between Greece and Cyprus and the American political world. Iakovos had kept up a steady stream of correspondence with US presidents and Greek prime ministers throughout his career, and the 1990s were no exception. During the breakup of Yugoslavia into separate states, one of its constituent republics, the Socialist Republic of Macedonia, adopted the name "Republic of Macedonia" when it declared independence in 1991. Citing the history of ethnic enmity and territorial disputes in the Balkans and alarmed by the appropriation of ancient Greek names and symbols by the Slavic inhabitants of the neighboring republic that had become a sovereign state on Greece's northern border, Greece launched a diplomatic campaign to force the republic to adopt a compound name—in other words, not use the term "Macedonia" on its own. Greek immigrants who had emigrated from (Greek) Macedonia by the thousands to Canada and the United States zealously joined the effort and sought to put pressure on governments to take Greece's side with a campaign that began with big public rallies in Ottawa and Washington in 1992. The rally in Washington, jointly organized by the church and the Pan-Macedonian Federation of America, was huge, and the Greek American community and the archbishop were reliving the heyday of the Greek American mobilization following Turkey's invasion and occupation of the northern part of Cyprus. And here again, Iakovos was the titular head of the movement, even though the Pan-Macedonian Federation was the engine propelling the movement forward. But in terms of foreign policy, the Macedonia name issue not as clear-cut as the Cyprus crisis. But Iakovos soldiered on, advocating strongly for Greece's demands, and pledged his services in the cause of finding a solution, with messages to President George H. W. Bush and Greek prime minister Konstantinos Mitsotakis in 1992. The archbishop continued to raise the Macedonia issue with their successors, Bill Clinton, who became president in 1993, and Papandreou, who had won the Greek elections that same year. As it turned out, this was yet another Greek foreign policy goal that would defy an easy resolution and instead would drag on for years.[15]

While focusing on this new Greek "national issue," Iakovos never forgot about Cyprus, and just a few days after the turbulent 1994 Clergy-Laity

Congress, he was writing to Clinton about the theft of a valuable Greek Orthodox icon from a church in the northern part of Cyprus that was under Turkish occupation. His last message to Clinton as archbishop came only days before the 1996 Clergy-Laity Congress—it was a set of reflections on the rise of Islamic fundamentalism in Turkey.[16]

Meanwhile, Iakovos was planning a big exit, with a series of special events surrounding his last Clergy-Laity Congress in 1996. Most notably he decided that the opening of the congress would be marked by a huge open-air Mass (divine liturgy) held in Central Park on Sunday, June 30. And at the congress, he would show a brave face, hide any bitterness he felt toward the Patriarchate of Constantinople, and shepherd in the new era gracefully. Toward that purpose, he did all he could to prepare the faithful and all his collaborators, encouraging them to work toward overcoming their disagreements with the patriarchate and ensuring a smooth transition under the new archbishop. As early as November 1995, he wrote to the clergy, the parish councils, and the Philoptochos organizations, telling them of his wish that he had conveyed to the planning committee, namely that the upcoming congress, his last, be the best ever and should not focus on his resignation or the possible presence of the patriarch but should focus instead on producing a strong program. The encyclical ended by stating, "With your active participation, this Clergy-Laity Congress should prove to be a most successful and meaningful gathering, one which will enable us to reflect on the accomplishments of the past, to plan for the future." And then the archbishop added a twist designed to deflect the attention onto himself, saying it would also "permit me the opportunity to thank each and every one of you for your support and assistance during the 37 years of my Ministry to you as your Archbishop."[17]

Preparations for the 1996 Congress and Iakovos's Farewell

The Archdiocesan Council met in March 1996. At an earlier meeting of the council, held in September 1995, the archbishop had said that now that he had submitted his resignation, it was important the upcoming Congress would be "the best ever. . . . The focus of the Congress should not be on the resignation or the possible presence of the Patriarch, rather on a strong program."[18] With Iakovos unwilling to criticize the patriarchate, there was not much opportunity for anyone to express disgruntlement with how Constantinople had handled things. Therefore the council meeting was designed to plan a triumphant farewell at the upcoming congress in the summer and to make sure that any outstanding business, such as the final resolution of the real estate saga, would be taken care of before the new archbishop arrived. But even though there were no church political problems in the months before Iakovos's final clergy-laity congress, suddenly economic problems surfaced. Evidently, some of the wealthy lay members who usually supported the congress through sponsorship were dragging their feet and had not committed funds, which created a problem, because the additional events planned to mark Iakovos's farewell meant the budget this time was especially big. Some of the donors may have been uncertain whether it was wise to underwrite an event that was essentially focused on an outgoing archbishop who had displeased the patriarch.

The organizers began to get alarmed. At the end of May, Peter J. Pappas, the chairman of the upcoming congress, wrote to George Kokalis, one of the more prominent lay members, expressing his dismay at the situation. He wrote, "Surprisingly, many of our church leadership both Clergy and Laity seem to have taken a conspicuous back seat to this year's event," and then added, "I refrain from speculation but it seems we have begun marching to another drum beat." He explained that assumptions about last-minute increases were not true, and continued ominously, "The virus that has entered our Greek Orthodox Community is very dangerous. It is people, such as yourself and our commander of the Archons along with the President of the Executive Board of the Archdiocesan Council that have not reached out to their selective members to encourage them to partake in one of the many sponsorship programs." And Pappas ended forcefully, asking, "What happened to all the supposed loyalty that the above mentioned groups have had for His Eminence all these years?" and answered his own question, declaring "What a statement you are making. It seems we want him to go away quietly while preparing to greet our new leader. Something is wrong here[;] we should be able to do both."[19] Iakovos received a copy of the letter. Always a realist, he must have understood that he was now a lame duck and that some of his former followers were about to realign their allegiance with the patriarchate, if they had not done so already.

While publicly offering praise to Iakovos and speaking about the significance of the upcoming congress, many among the leaders of the clergy and laity remained more focused on the search for the new archbishop. The Greek American press reported rumors that the patriarch was considering two of the prelates who were on the delegation he had sent to the United States. The feeling was that Stylianos would be too controversial a choice because of his reputation for abrasiveness and his role as the spokesperson of the delegation. In contrast, Metropolitan Demetrios, a soft-spoken former Harvard Divinity School professor, appeared as a potentially popular choice.

Hidden away from the prying eyes of the Greek American media, Father Alex Karloutsos, the patriarch's representative in the United States, was hard at work trying to secure the best possible successor to Iakovos. Back in October at the Archdiocesan Council meeting, several members had complained about Bartholomew's decision to appoint Father Alex as his representative in the United States. Karloutsos, once considered Iakovos's right-hand man, had headed the Archdiocese's Communications Department, and after his dismissal following a falling out with the archbishop, he had become the executive director of the Leadership 100 organization. Karloutsos was widely considered as having been instrumental in the patriarch's decision to force Iakovos to resign, and those close to the archbishop considered Karloutsos a "traitor" to the cause. He was certainly directly involved in Bartholomew's search for a successor. That search, as it turned out, was becoming increasingly focused on Metropolitan Spyridon of Italy, who had represented Bartholomew at the 1994 Clergy-Laity Congress. Karloutsos arranged for trips to Italy of several leading lay members of the church, including Michael Jaharis, in order to pave the way for Spyridon's appointment. Jaharis and Karloutsos had developed a close relationship. They shared a sense of pragmatism and wanting to get things done—indeed, some consider them the architects of the succession.

Meanwhile, in New York City, preparations went on to honor the archbishop's wish that the 1996 Clergy-Laity Congress be the best ever. Nothing would be left to chance. A month before the congress opened, Timothy J. Maniatis, the head of the organizing committee, sent a sixteen-page set of instructions to the New York Hilton outlining the special requirements of the archbishop's party. Maniatis began by providing a profile of those participating in the congress who would be guests at the hotel: "The individuals attending the Congress," he wrote, "are serious, with over 35% of the members of the clergy." And in order to avoid any misunderstanding, Maniatis explained, "the Greek Orthodox Clergy are allowed to marry, many therefore will come with their families." And as far as the non-clergy were concerned, the typical profile was of a "successful, upper middle class businessman who also works diligently for his Church on both the local and national levels." There were several specific demands associated with the arrival of the archbishop: "The General Manager (or his representative) of the New York Hilton and Towers and/or other VIPs must meet His Eminence and escort him to His suite." The hotel was also expected to "provide ample amenities to His Eminence," while "the General Manager (or his representative) should visit for 5–10 minutes" and "after a reasonable time, everyone should leave the Archbishop's suite to allow Him to rest." The suggested amenities to be available at the suite included "Coffee, Tea, Soda, Evian Water; finger sandwiches; fresh fruit (sliced); feta cheese; hard cheese (not too salty) and crackers." There were special instructions concerning the archbishop's suite, where he would be holding numerous meetings, breakfasts, and working luncheons. All this required special catering needs: besides the above-mentioned beverages, the menu available during his meetings was to include "small Greek pastries, cheese, fresh fruit," and there should be a silver coffee service and crystal glassware and "china" porcelain plates.[20] For an archbishop who was legendary for insisting on the best quality in everything associated with the archdiocese's public events, it was a fitting set of requirements.

The End

The Thirty-Third Biennial Clergy-Laity Congress that opened on June 30, 1996, in New York City was more of a sending off party for the archbishop, with guest speakers and delegates delivering emotional tributes to Iakovos. And by Iakovos's standards, his keynote address was relatively short, running at fourteen pages double-spaced, probably because he wished to avoid controversy in what was his last formal speech as archbishop. Even the committee reports alluded to his tenure and his achievements. The Finance Committee, for example, noted, "When His Eminence Archbishop Iakovos was enthroned in 1959 the annual budget of our Archdiocese was approximately $600,000. There was no Clergy Pension Fund and no major endowment programs in the Archdiocese. Today we have reached annual operating revenues of $7.8 million . . . have a Clergy Pension Fund of $31.6 million . . . and the Archbishop Iakovos Leadership 100 Endowment Fund $25 million." Only then it would go on to say that despite that growth, the finances were still falling short of fulfilling even the basic needs of the church.[21]

The day the congress opened, the archdiocese held the huge open-air Mass in Central Park, officiated by Iakovos. All churches in the New York, New Jersey, and Connecticut metropolitan area were ordered not to hold services but instead bus the faithful into Manhattan to participate in the service. Couples who had scheduled weddings in Greek Orthodox churches in the tri-state area had to ask their parish priest to get special permission to remain and officiate the wedding service rather than attend the event at Central Park. Despite the rain, which started early in the morning and became heavy by midmorning, thousands braved the weather. Estimates of the crowd size varied; Iakovos reported to the patriarch a week later that twelve to thirteen thousand were there, the *Ethnikos Kyrix* estimated ten thousand in attendance, the *New York Post* reported six thousand, and the *New York Times* noted the rain kept away many of the ten thousand who were expected to attend, but "the steady drizzle seemed for the several thousand present, almost to become part of the religious experience." The Greek American television anchor who was presiding told the crowd that the apostle endured torture "and we can endure a little rain," as he stood before a large reproduction of an icon, hanging in Central Park's band shell, depicting Jesus giving communion to his apostle. In his sermon, Iakovos called on the congregants to brave every adversity facing their church and their national heritage the way they were braving the rain.[22] The participation of the Byzantine Choir of the Church of Athens added to the pomp of the occasion. It was the first time the Greek Orthodox Church had attempted to hold an open-air Mass on this scale, and its symbolism suggested this was Iakovos's way of publicly declaring what he had said many times, that the Greek Orthodox were an integral part of America and could attempt to do what that the Catholic and Protestant Churches did on their big occasions. The Greek language newspapers in New York were certainly impressed and declared that the event had been a triumph.

The congress itself opened its formal proceedings the next Monday morning, July 1, and continued through Friday, primarily focused on honoring the outgoing archbishop. In between the lines and the emotional words offered in praise of Iakovos were glimpses of the lingering tension over the church's relationship to the patriarchate and the issue that caused the rift, the push toward uniting all Eastern Orthodox Churches in America. On the Saturday before the open-air Mass, the *Washington Post* carried an article about Iakovos, focusing on Ligonier and its aftermath and mentioning that a few days earlier the outgoing archbishop had met with his Eastern Orthodox counterparts on the Standing Conference of Canonical Orthodox Bishops in the Americas, the group that had met at Ligonier, and he thanked them for their cooperation in settling differences in jurisdictions and asked them to continue meeting and not let time undermine their efforts. Asked by the *Post* reporter whether the unity plan resulted in his resignation, Iakovos dutifully replied in the negative, but added he was "indeed very disappointed" in not achieving a formal unification of the Orthodox Churches in America before retiring. "I will be happy before I die to see this dream of mine come to a successful end."[23]

Patriarch Bartholomew used his message to the Clergy-Laity Congress not only to praise Iakovos but also to remind the faithful of how the mother church regarded Greek Orthodoxy in America. He spoke about Greek Orthodox going forward and spreading the world over, creating the Greek Orthodox diaspora, adding, "The beloved eparchy of our Ecumenical Throne, the Greek Orthodox Archdiocese of North and South America constitutes the greatest part of this diaspora." There followed rich praise for Iakovos, a reflection on the passage of Saint Paul about walking by the same rule and being of the same mind, and then a reminder of the presence of the patriarchate in the lives of the Greek Orthodox in America: "In a vigilant way and with brotherly love, our Most Holy Apostolic and Patriarchal Throne follows the course of our Holy Archdiocese in the Americas. Like a loving mother, the Patriarchal Throne in all ways shared and continues to share in the common joy for its success and general progress, while supporting the vigilant and courageous implementation of the work and the accomplishments of the high mission entrusted to your Archbishop by the sacred center of Orthodoxy."[24] In other words, the patriarchate is here to stay in your lives.

One of Iakovos's last acts as archbishop was to send a brief two-page report to Patriarch Bartholomew on the 1996 congress, in which he deflected attention from himself and spoke of the state of the church in America, stressing the role of the laity. This was, he reported, the largest ever clergy-laity congress in terms of numbers of clerical and lay delegates, because all considered it their duty to be present for several reasons, one of them being to uphold the stature of the archdiocese, which, he added somewhat mischievously, some regarded as having been questioned. The outdoor liturgy was a huge success, with twelve to thirteen hundred attending in the rain, and three-quarters of them received Holy Communion. In general, Iakovos went on to say, the congress demonstrated that the Greek Orthodox were proud of their church and that they no longer had an inferiority complex about its being an immigrant church, for it was widely recognized and respected by the American people. The congress also confirmed that the Greek Orthodox Church in America played an important role in the ecumenical movement. The congress, Iakovos continued, witnessed a coalescing between the clergy and the laity, but the laity had several special characteristics that had to be observed. The laity quieted their voices only because the church was going through a transitional phase until the election and enthronement of the new archbishop. It is not known how the patriarch reacted to Iakovos's succinct report.

The months that followed the patriarchate's rejection of the Ligonier decisions were a time in which both clergy and laity began to absorb the change that had come over Greek Orthodoxy in America. Archbishop Iakovos played a crucial role in enabling all those around him to come to terms with the new status quo. That was all the more remarkable because not only had his pan-Orthodox vision been stymied, but he was also being forced to resign.

And yet he carried himself with great dignity; he concealed what must have been a profound bitterness and obediently went along with the Ecumenical Patriarchate's decisions. And he also ensured that the immense support he commanded from within the Greek American community did not translate into defiance of the patriarchate. Iakovos, of all people, knew the rules and the authority and rights of the Ecumenical Patriarchate over Greek Orthodoxy in America, and his public comportment, through to the moment he stepped down, was a lesson to all Orthodox about how the church's hierarchy should be respected, and also how the needs of the "mother church" must always come first.

On a more abstract level, we can say that Iakovos demonstrated a form of what Anthony Giddens calls "practical consciousness," in that his response to the patriarch's actions was conditioned by the fact he was socially constituted as a church leader himself. He was a person who had lived his life according to the church's hierarchical structures and regulations, and the new circumstances caused him to reflect on his social existence and play along with the rules. And significantly, the hierarchs of the other Orthodox Churches who were present at Ligonier appeared, at least publicly, to accept and go along with the patriarchate's decisions. The sense of Orthodox Church hierarchy and the doctrinal authority of Constantinople served to overpower the pressures of Americanization that had brought Iakovos and the other church leaders to Ligonier.

CHAPTER 12

Greek Orthodoxy in America Enters the Twenty-First Century

The end of the Iakovos era signaled the beginning of a new era in which the Patriarchate of Constantinople became a permanent force in the affairs of Greek Orthodoxy in America. The patriarchate not only appointed a new archbishop, Spyridon, but also radically restructured the church by "breaking up" the archdiocese of North and South America into the Archdiocese of America, with jurisdiction in the United States; the Metropolinate of Canada; and the Metropolinate sees of Central America and South America. The reorganization "was intended to serve the faithful more effectively and bring it under more direct supervision of the Ecumenical Patriarchate which historically has been given the responsibility to govern the Orthodox faithful of the diaspora."[1] By the same token it deprived Greek Orthodoxy in the Americas of a single, influential leader, although in practice Iakovos had derived his power and influence from the support of the Greeks of the United States. Nonetheless, the office's geographical limitation to the United States represented a symbolic diminution of the archbishop's status. An even greater blow to the archbishop's standing was the planned elevation of the regional bishops in the United States to the rank of metropolitan, a move that would grant them greater autonomy and correspondingly limit the powers of the archbishop. Finally, the archbishop was named as the "exarch" or representative of the Patriarchate of Constantinople in the United States, and in this way he would recoup some of his authority but only by virtue of representing the patriarch. Finally, the Patriarchate of Constantinople enhanced its standing in the United States even further by coming to an agreement with the few Genuine Orthodox churches (the so-called Old Calendar Orthodox), which abandoned their independent status in exchange for recognition as entities that enjoyed direct jurisdiction from Constantinople. The patriarchate became much more present in Greek Orthodoxy's daily life. And the "Archons"—the "Order of St. Andrew of the Ecumenical Patriarchate," the organization of prominent church lay members that Iakovos had founded in 1966—found a new raison d'être and became much more active over issues of religious liberty, with a focus on the rights of the patriarchate in Turkey. In ecclesiastical terms, the United States had become a province of Constantinople.

The new era also brought greater influence, at least within the archdiocese, to another lay element in the United States. During Iakovos's last years, the loyalty that the Archdiocesan Council had displayed in the face of the patriarchate's criticisms built upon its earlier demands for greater accountability over the real estate issue. Yet another sign of the laity's greater significance was the continued presence of the Orthodox Christian Laity organization. Although it had stayed relatively quiet in the aftermath of the patriarch's sharp reaction to Ligonier, the OCL remained an important element in the life of Greek Orthodoxy in the United States. The patriarchate's intercession satisfied the OCL's demands that Archbishop Iakovos's powers be curbed, but at the same time a greater role by the patriarchate in the affairs of the church in America was less positive, unless it was going to lead in the longer term to a more democratic functioning of the archdiocese and greater autonomy. The OCL was poised to make the most of the new era.

But what became the overwhelming, immediate concern for Greek Orthodoxy in the wake of Iakovos's departure was that his successor, Archbishop Spyridon, the patriarchate's choice, was not able to establish his authority. This was because of a combination of factors, ranging from his personality and what was considered an authoritarian leadership style, to his traditionalist outlook. On paper, Spyridon appeared able and qualified for the job. He was the first American-born head of the Greek Orthodox Church. Born George Papageorgiou in Warren, a town in eastern Ohio, he had graduated from high school in Tarpon Springs, Florida, home of a large Greek community. In 1962, at the age of eighteen, he entered the Patriarchal Seminary on Halki, and when he was ordained a deacon in 1968, he took the name Spyridon. He then served in several posts in Europe. Spyridon had attended the 1994 Clergy-Laity Congress in the United States as the patriarch's representative. During his ten-day visit he had a range of meetings

with clergy from all Eastern Orthodox denominations, and he gave interviews to several Greek American newspapers. In his report to the patriarch
about his visit, it is clear that Spyridon shared Bartholomew's unease about
the patriarchate's standing in the eyes of many Greek Orthodox, and in the
report he mentioned that during his visit he had tried to bolster Constantinople's image.[2] An American-born prelate, and one who was on record as
having spoken in favor of Orthodox unity in America and was also closely
identified with the patriarchate, did indeed seem an ideal choice to succeed
Iakovos at a time when both the leading laity in the United States were becoming more demanding and Constantinople was becoming more assertive.
As Elizabeth Prodromou notes about the changes Orthodoxy was experiencing in the post–Cold War era, "The growing sense of agency among Orthodox populations in the diaspora is now changing their relationships with the
'old countries' in general, and the 'mother churches' of those countries in
particular. Thus Orthodoxy is not only coming to grips with pluralism in
the outside world, but is also feeling pressure for greater internal pluralism
from influential quarters within its own ranks."[3] Spyridon was a beneficiary
of the new era, but also vulnerable to its democratic dynamic. Ultimately,
his tenure would turn out to be especially turbulent, and when protests grew
and influential members such as Michael Jaharis withdrew their support, the
patriarch asked Spyridon to step down in 1999. Ten days before the official
announcement in August of that year, Spyridon granted an interview to a
right-wing nationalistic newspaper in Greece and said that his opponents
were intent on "Americanizing" the church, which he believed had an important ethnarchic role to play.[4] In the end, he and everyone else would see
that the Ecumenical Patriarchate was not opposed to the church adapting
further to its American environment, although it was against moves toward
a pan-Orthodox American church that it might have difficulty controlling.

Spyridon did bequeath a few positive legacies to Greek Orthodoxy in America, including the publication of a report on the state of Greek language in the
United States, compiled by a commission he had appointed. The commission
was headed by the eminent Greek American language professor John Rassias, who was known for his creative and innovative teaching at Dartmouth
College. The outcome was a thorough, ninety-four-page, in-depth analysis
of both the state and the potential future of Greek language education in the
United States. It bore Rassias's imprimatur and evoked his enthusiasm and
optimism, and even expressed the hope that the Greek American community could create "a distinguished institution of higher learning that would
stand proudly beside a Catholic Georgetown, a Jewish Brandeis and a Quaker
Haverford!"[5] The Rassias report, as the study has come to be known, serves as

a reminder of what could have been during Spyridon's era. And Spyridon consistently spoke out on the church's role in Greek language education. In January 1999, in a speech on Greek Letters Day, the annual celebration of Greek Orthodoxy's contribution to Greek language and education, he spoke about his will "to promote, preserve and perpetuate the Greek language."[6] But language education, as it turned out, was one the few bright spots of his tenure.

Spyridon's treatment of an incident at Hellenic College Holy Cross had proved disastrous. The problems had begun in February 1997 at a traditional Greek celebration on campus of Tsiknopempti, literally "Smoky Thursday," which marks the penultimate Thursday before Lent, when large quantities of grilled meats are consumed. That particular celebration went awry, and rumors that a priest had made sexual advances to one of the students rippled through campus the next day. A disciplinary committee investigated the incident and found the priest was guilty of sexual harassment and should be censured. But Spyridon disagreed with the decision and moved to dismiss the three persons who were on the committee, which included the college's president and a tenured professor. The president, Alkiviadis Calivas, had joined the school as a faculty member in 1978 and had served in many capacities before becoming president. He was fired after he made public his objections to the archbishop's involvement. The Greek American media alluded to the incident and its repercussions, but the archdiocese and the college had managed to more or less keep a lid on the controversy. Greek Orthodox faithful throughout the country realized that things were not right on the Brookline campus but did not know the details, and in any case Hellenic College Holy Cross frequently seemed to be experiencing trouble. Then, the *Chronicle of Higher Education* reported on the story in its July 18, 1997, issue. The *Chronicle*'s comprehensive and detailed public exposé caused considerable embarrassment to the archdiocese and weakened Spyridon's efforts to establish his authority. Speaking in Boston in early March 1997, Spyridon had said the archdiocese would not tolerate "splitters" or dissidents; but dealing with a reputable publication's claims proved to be more difficult. The *Chronicle* picked up the story because events had spiraled precipitously within a few months. Soon after the firings, two deans resigned, and an administrator, Dr. Valerie Karas, was offered a deal to leave with full pay before her contract expired. She filed a complaint with the attorney general of Massachusetts alleging that the dismissals and demotions violated the institution's bylaws and threatened its accreditation. Some at the college, the *Chronicle* reported, continued to support the archbishop. They included Rev. George Dragas, who had resigned as dean in June and was quoted as saying, "The archbishop is the head of the house . . . it is right that he does what he needs to. . . . You cannot use academic traditions against ecclesiastical ones. This is an ecclesiastical institution. You know your parameters." But not everyone conveyed a similar sense of blind obedience. Others said the recent changes were more extreme than usual. "They saw the dismissals as a crackdown on academic priests who might seem too independent," the *Chronicle* noted, quoting one faculty member, who insisted on anonymity, saying, "He gives orders. We must blindly follow them without dialogue." Faculty members also said the dismissals and reassignments were ordered with little explanation or recourse for appeal. Father Alex Karloutsos, who was contacted by the *Chronicle* for the archdiocese's perspective, diplomatically tried to minimize what happened, although in doing so he acknowledged that there had long been problems. He stated that "the president of the school and the dean of the seminary and the dean of the college were all in conflict. . . . When Archbishop Spyridon arrived, he found turbulence. It was hard to determine who was at fault. It was like coming in and finding Adam and Eve fighting. Adam said, 'It's not me.' Eve said, 'It's not me. It's the snake.' So everyone was looking for the snake." A year later the dust had not settled. As a follow-up to complaints that were made to the state authorities about the college's personnel changes, two accrediting agencies gave the college six months to change its governance procedures and strengthen its faculty's role in hiring, promotion, and firing.[7]

In the wake of the ongoing crisis at the college, Greek Americans began wondering how the patriarchate would react. A growing number of them, resenting Spyridon's authoritarian style, openly wished that he would be replaced. An organization calling itself Greek Orthodox American Leaders (GOAL) kept publishing criticisms on a website it started precisely for that purpose. GOAL accused Spyridon of a range of failures in office, including authoritarianism, mismanaging church funds, repressive policies, failure to implement policies, and disrespect of priests. Others still supported Spyridon, and many looked to the patriarchate for a solution to the weakening of the archbishop's stature. An article in the *New York Times* that had appeared on the day of Spyridon's enthronement as archbishop in 1996 accurately identified the new, enhanced role the Ecumenical Patriarchate would play in Greek Orthodox affairs in the United States. "Unity with the Ecumenical Patriarchate," the newspaper reported, "was the dominant theme of Patriarch Bartholomew's charge to his new appointee." Paraphrasing Saint Paul's famous hymn to love, Bartholomew said in an announcement following Spyridon's appointment that if a bishop "does not have unlimited devotion and blind loyalty and lifelong gratitude" to the Ecumenical Patriarchate, then "he is but a noisy gong or a clanging cymbal." Bartholomew told the *Times* that "blind loyalty does not sound right to American ears," but he warned about making too much of such phrases.[8] Bartholomew had also said that the new archbishop would face many problems, differing views on how the church should face the future, and ideological currents in his new position.[9] The prediction turned out to be very true.

Bartholomew Makes His Mark in the United States

Patriarch Bartholomew did not leave the church's fate in the United States up to Spyridon, especially as he saw that the new archbishop was unpopular, so he made a monthlong, sixteen-city tour of the US that began in mid-October 1997 and which was nicely timed to calm the growing discontent in the church and raise his own profile. This was part of the new, more assertive presence the ancient institution adopted under Bartholomew. And his visit was a statement that despite his stopping the movement toward an American Orthodoxy at Ligonier in its tracks, he regarded Orthodoxy as not only a transnational force but also one compatible with universal humanistic values and, by extension, American values. Speaking at Tufts University, where he was awarded an honorary doctorate, he said that each of Orthodoxy's foundational concepts, of personhood, way of life, and integration, "suggests common points of solidarity between the Orthodox world and the increasingly transnational world of peacemakers. Specifically the principles of freedom and relationality with respect to human rights make Orthodoxy's conception of personhood fully compatible with democratic norms. Moreover, the heterogeneity and dynamism of personhood reinforce secular principles encouraging toleration of differences within society rather than defensive reaction against otherness," and he added with his American audience in mind, "Debates over multiculturalism within the context of the United States . . . would be enriched by attention to Orthodoxy's vision of the person."[10]

Bartholomew's first engagement was to attend a banquet marking AHEPA's seventy-fifth anniversary, and he used the opportunity to underline the organization's close support of Greek Orthodoxy and its ties to the Ecumenical Patriarchate. For those who remembered the visit in the United States of his predecessor Ecumenical Patriarchate Dimitrios, in which Bartholomew had participated, Bartholomew's visit as patriarch was clearly more dynamic. He used his public appearances to underline the patriarchate's close ties with the Greek Americans. In his speech he praised AHEPA's support of the patriarchate and Hellenism, which he described as a gift of God. Bartholomew used the terms "Hellenism" and "Greek Orthodox" interchangeably, saying "today to be a Hellene in America is to be admired . . . to be Orthodox in America is no longer to be a member of a small and little known religion."

And in highlighting the connections between AHEPA and the church, he listed several examples of their close cooperation. "Here in America, AHEPA has long supported the Church institutions. . . . Many church mortgages have been paid by AHEPA. . . . St. Basil's has been fostered and sustained by AHEPA and its sisters in the Daughters of Penelope. . . . Hellenic College / Holy Cross and its students have been the beneficiaries of AHEPA's love and support. . . . AHEPA also honors and obeys the message of our Church to welcome and shelter one's neighbors through its incomparable AHEPA Housing initiative."[11] Bartholomew was not exaggerating the patriarchate's ties with AHEPA, an organization that for many years had sent delegations to Constantinople and had fashioned its own close ties to the patriarchate, regardless of the status of the relationship of the Greek Orthodox Church in America and the patriarchate, especially in the Iakovos era, in which there had been some ups and downs.

The patriarch's visit included meetings with President Clinton and other officials, receiving the Congressional Award medal at the US Capitol, a speech to the United Nations, and participation in a symposium on the environment in Santa Barbara, California. In New York, Bartholomew held a service of divine liturgy on October 25 in Madison Square Garden, and Mayor Rudolph Giuliani named part of East Seventy-Ninth Street, the site of the archdiocese's headquarters, in the patriarch's honor. At Georgetown University in Washington, Bartholomew would speak at a first-ever gathering of Muslim and Orthodox representatives. Meetings with other Eastern Orthodox leaders were designed to reassure them that despite his censure of Ligonier, the patriarchate supported close contacts among Orthodox churches. Significantly, in receiving the congressional medal, he paid homage to America's religious liberty and tolerance and remarked that it was no wonder that Orthodox Christians the world over had found a haven in the United States. There was no mention of the existence of an Orthodox "diaspora."[12] In between all this, Bartholomew was expected to raise issues related with the patriarchate's status in Turkey and address the difficulties confronting Spyridon. George Matsoukas, speaking as president of Orthodox Christian Laity, told the New York Times "It's my hope and prayer that the Patriarch's visit will bring harmony back to the Orthodox church."[13]

Bartholomew, publicly at least, focused on the outreach goals of his visit rather than on the archdiocese's internal affairs. Religion media critic Andrew Walsh wrote,

Bartholomew needed to make an impressive showing in his first pastoral visit to these shores. And, by most measures, he scored a coup. His people flocked to see him and he snagged unprecedented notice from the non-Orthodox world. Previous pastoral visits by Orthodox prelates from Russia, Syria, Greece, and Eastern Europe had attracted scant public attention. The 1990 visit of Bartholomew's predecessor, Patriarch Dimitrios II—the first ever by a sitting Ecumenical Patriarch—was a particularly spectacular public relations flop. Given Bartholomew's dramatic descent on Washington, it's not surprising that extensive media coverage followed—although the visit never received significant national television coverage. And, despite their relative unfamiliarity with Orthodox Christianity in the United States, the complexity of the issues that Bartholomew invoked, and the challenges of dealing with Orthodox sources unaccustomed to aggressive press coverage, American journalists did a solid job covering the trip.[14]

Bartholomew even earned praise from the Washington correspondent of Turkey's mainstream newspaper *Hürriyet*, who noted that "when his visit is evaluated from the point of Turkey, it was not publicly used as an anti-Turkish platform, as in the case of past experiences. I tend to give credit to the patriarch and his new administration for restraining the machinery because anti-Turkish Greek elements are still very fervent in strategic positions in the Greek Orthodox Archdiocese of America's administration." And, he added, "If this visit is evaluated from the Orthodox religious establishment's point of view, without a doubt the Patriarch raised the visibility of the Orthodox Christian Church in the United States. He emphasized the point that Orthodoxy is not a museum religion, but a still living one."[15]

Bartholomew was unwilling to address the church's internal affairs in public. In Walsh's words, "In a month of travel heavily punctuated by sermons and speeches, he made only veiled references to the church's internal disputes. His silence was observed and reported almost immediately. 'Greek Orthodox clergymen and lay people who hoped to get some sense of his attitudes towards the controversial issues swirling within their church had to do some pretty creative exegesis of his remarks,' the *Chicago Tribune*'s Steve Kloehn remarked. . . . the patriarch isn't talking in-house politics."[16] Bartholomew granted interviews only at the end of his visit, and despite prompting from the *Ethnikos Kyrix*, he continued to avoid the issue of Spyridon's standing, conceding only that he was concerned about the Greek American community's unity. He attributed the discontent to difficulties that all new archbishops faced in the early stages of their tenure. The patriarch evidently believed that as long as he stood by his choice of archbishop, the storm would blow over. But it only got worse.

A New Beginning

There was one instance during Bartholomew's visit that appeared designed to offer Spyridon some coverage and legitimacy, and that was when the patriarch visited a monastery that a Greek Orthodox monk, Ephraim (Ioannis Moraitis), had established in the desert in Arizona in 1995. Fearing rejection from the Greek Orthodox archdiocese, Ephraim had initially turned to the Russian Orthodox Church for protection and legitimacy, but then sought and gained the approval of Archbishop Spyridon. The monastery, St. Anthony's, was closely modeled on the monastic life of Mount Athos, an important center of Eastern Orthodox monasticism in Greece, where Ephraim had served as a monk. Ephraim and his Arizona monastery had begun to gain considerable respect and popularity, even something of an aura, among the Greek Orthodox faithful across the country, with his supporters believing he had brought authentic Orthodox life to the United States. He also had his detractors, who considered his movement nothing more than a fundamentalist cult. Bartholomew evidently believed that the best way to deal with Ephraim was to acknowledge his services to Orthodoxy and try and co-opt him. He had done the same with the few "Genuine Orthodox" Greek churches in the United States that were very traditionalist and even followed the Julian Calendar. He offered them protection and the right to remain outside the jurisdiction of the archdiocese, as along as they recognized his authority as their patriarch. Bartholomew visited St. Anthony's monastery in much the same spirit, and in doing so also validated Spyridon's treatment of Ephraim.

Yet over the next months, many Greek Orthodox clerics and laypersons considered that Spyridon was treating Ephraim too kindly and tolerating his particular brand of tradition-oriented worship. GOAL and other critics used the Clergy-Laity Congress of 1998 as a venue in which they aired their many criticisms of the archbishop. Spyridon's chancellor—his right-hand man— Father George Passias, already a controversial figure thanks to his reputation as the archbishop's enforcer, added to his notoriety when it became known he was an ardent follower of Ephraim. In November 1998, Spyridon traveled to a monastery the Ephraim movement had established in Kendalia, Texas, where he took part in a conference on the Athonite monastic movement. Spyridon officiated at the Thyranoixia (the ritual opening of the doors) of the monastic church, and he also enthroned the newly elected abbot, Father Dositheos, which served to anger his critics even more.[17]

The archbishop decided to take a firm stance against his opponents in the wake of the battering he received at the Clergy-Laity Congress of 1998, but his actions would be ultimately dismissed by the Patriarchate of

Constantinople. The first step Spyridon took was to remove certain prominent Greek Americans from the Archdiocesan Council and its Executive
Committee, including its president Alex Spanos and Michael Jaharis, who
had helped broker the transition from Iakovos to Spyridon. The archbishop
continued an ongoing feud with the Philoptochos, and an influential member of the national Philoptochos board, Froso Beys, did not have her term
renewed. Spyridon was throwing down the gauntlet at his opponents. Unfortunately for him, it was Patriarch Bartholomew who picked it up. The
patriarch evidently thought that Spyridon had overstepped his mark and was
now threatening to alienate an indispensable group of lay leaders of the
church. He reacted by demanding that the archbishop immediately reverse
his decisions and declined his request for a private meeting after Spyridon
suggested only a compromise solution. According to Spyridon's biographer,
this was the beginning of the end, and he realized "he had been abandoned in
the pursuit of his mission in America."[18] This may have been true, although
Spyridon did appear to have several opportunities in the months to come to
regain the patriarch's trust and had several meetings with him.

Spyridon met with the patriarch in September 1998 and then again in
January 1999. In the time in between, the movement against him had grown
and, most crucially, had been joined by five senior bishops—their titles were
now "metropolitan"—who had made their criticisms of the archbishop public. The five metropolitans had accompanied Spyridon at his meeting with
the patriarch in September and had voiced a number of criticisms of the state
of the archdiocese, ranging from Spyridon's abolishing the synodic system
of governance, to an overindulgence of Ephraim's monastic movement, to
causing Orthodoxy to lose ground in the United States because of his autocratic style of governance. The archbishop was facing what amounted to
an open revolt both from within the church and from without, including
the Greek American press and prominent Greek Americans such as Simos
Dimas. Dimas had filed a lawsuit charging financial misdoings and seeking
access to the archdiocese's books. The judge denied part of the suit, declared
another part moot, but also granted Dimas access to some documents. And
Dimas succeeded in placing the archdiocese in the awkward position of not
wishing to disclose its finances, which embarrassed it, at least in the eyes of
its critics.[19] And several parishes were beginning to talk seriously about withholding their annual contributions to the archdiocese. Not since the church's
civil war in the 1920s had there been such a degree of dissent and division in
Greek Orthodoxy in America. In December, nearly a quarter of all the parish priests in the United States joined the bishops in publicly criticizing the
archbishop.

In January 1999 a paralyzing stalemate between the archbishop and his opponents descended on church life. The archbishop remained in a combative mood. It was a measure of the expectations of both sides when Spyridon returned to New York that month relieved to still be archbishop, without having had to submit his resignation as his opponents had hoped. Emboldened by what turned out to be a temporary reprieve, Spyridon continued to turn against his critics and dismissed Father Robert Stephanopoulos, the long-serving priest of Holy Trinity Cathedral in New York City. Stephanopoulos was widely popular, and the move not only shocked the parish faithful but surprised the entire Greek Orthodox community for the same reason and also because at the time, Stephanopoulos's son George was President Clinton's communications director and himself an immensely popular figure in the community. This was yet another example of Spyridon's tendency to make divisive moves and display remarkable tone deafness to their implications. What made Stephanopoulos's dismissal even worse was that Spyridon had simultaneously rejected the patriarch's instruction to get rid of his very unpopular chancellor, Father Passias. According to his biographer Justine Frangouli-Argyris, Spyridon "had some time ago come to the realization that he had to be left to his own devices. He knew that by removing the most reliable and capable of his advisors, he would be entirely at the mercy of his persecutors."[20]

While Spyridon dug his heels in, the national media seized on Father Stephanopoulos's dismissal from the cathedral because it was exactly the type of dramatic incident that illustrated the ongoing Greek Orthodox battles. In March, *New York Magazine* ran a story on the controversy with a telling title: "Crisis in the Cathedral." The writer, Christopher Bonanos, had attended a noisy and contentious meeting of the lay members of the church that had convened right after the news became known—they had invited the archbishop to attend, but he was apparently "out of town." Father Stephanopoulos had tried to placate the anger in the room, but to no avail—no one was siding with the archbishop. "Apparently installed to reel in the American parishes thought to be straying from the church leadership in Constantinople," Bonanos wrote, "Spyridon, the first American-born archbishop, has made a series of unpopular theological rulings and even less popular personnel changes. Statements of protest—one signed by the five top American bishops calling for Spyridon's resignation, another signed by nearly a quarter of the Greek Orthodox priests in America (including Stephanopoulos)—have been delivered to the church leaders in the old world, only to be rejected." Even when the author made an effort to present both sides of the argument, his conclusion was damning for the standing of the archbishop,

albeit punctuated by the inevitable cliché: "Whether Spyridon is a man pe-
culiarly, even astonishingly, ill-suited to his job or simply a misunderstood
figure clumsily growing into a difficult role, his tenure as archbishop has
triggered a battle, religious and secular, that can be described—in the most
literal sense—as Byzantine."[21] On his part, Spyridon sincerely believed right
through the end that he had fought the good fight against the engrained influence of Protestantism in America's Greek Orthodoxy and its worst effect,
the involvement of the laity in running the church's affairs.[22]

Spyridon's era ended as it had begun, with the patriarchate asserting itself
over the affairs of Greek Orthodoxy in America and again appointing as archbishop the candidate of Bartholomew's choice, a wise, scholarly theologian
who had taught at Harvard, Demetrios (Trakatellis), the metropolitan of
Vresthena. The transition from Archbishops Spyridon to Demetrios in 1999
appeared to go much more smoothly than had the previous appointment of a
new leader of the Greek Orthodox Church in the United States. And indeed,
Demetrios proved to be a wonderfully calming influence on the affairs of the
church. But over a decade later, Michael Jaharis, who had been instrumental
in Spyridon's appointment and in his replacement, spoke publicly about the
serious difficulties Demetrios had faced back in 1999. He described it as "an
incredibly unwelcoming state of affairs and political infighting" made worse
by the existence of "an inherited debt of approximately $7 million or more
resulting from accumulated annual operational deficits and legal costs." He
went on to explain that leading lay members of the church had to apply their
business savvy to rectify the serious financial problems the church faced.[23]

When the dust settled following Spyridon's departure and Demetrios's
enthronement, the new status quo, in which the Ecumenical Patriarchate's
presence in America was evident, quickly became even more apparent. The
patriarchate's powers over the affairs of Greek Orthodoxy were made official
by a new charter that the patriarchate, the new archbishop, and the regionally based metropolitans agreed on at a meeting in Istanbul and which was
introduced at the Clergy-Laity Congress in Los Angeles in 2002. Demands by
the OCL and others that the charter be put to a vote were rejected, causing
tensions on the eve of the congress. As the *Los Angeles Times* put it, "Some
church activists are warning that the new charter not only erodes rank-and-
file power, but further delays the 1.5 million-member American church's
eventual independence from its mother church." The controversy, the report went on to say, was "a classic example of a church built by immigrants,
who have come of age in America, intent on remaining loyal to the church's
ancient traditions and faith even as that church is reshaped by a new culture."[24] And any hopes that pan-Orthodox unity might still be on the agenda

were dashed in Los Angeles. Just before the congress convened, the (Russian) Orthodox Church of America announced that its head, the Metropolitan Theodosius, was to retire, and the Patriarchate of Antioch granted fully autonomy to the Antiochian Archdiocese in America. There was speculation that both bodies had timed their announcements so as to create the conditions for some form of close cooperation with the Greek Orthodox Church. But it soon became apparent that "unity was put on the back-burner and autonomy was out of the question."[25]

Spyridon and His Successors in Perspective

Archbishop Spyridon's tenure should not be dismissed as a parenthesis in the history of Greek Orthodoxy in America. Nor should its shortness be interpreted as some form of personal failing or ascribed to an idiosyncratic personality. Beyond whatever personal traits irked those around him, Spyridon appears to have embodied a very traditional form of leadership, one that would have been acceptable in a metropolis in Greece or in Europe but was unsuited to the circumstances that obtained in the United States. He himself can be forgiven for assuming that the patriarchate's takeover of Greek Orthodoxy's affairs in the United States signaled a rolling back of the Americanization that had taken hold. His treatment of leading lay members and his authoritarian-like handling of administrative issues, his attempts to introduce a more traditional way of doing things, and his tolerance of Ephraim's quasi-fundamentalism suggest as much. The growth of Ephraim's monastic movement reflected the challenges of maintaining a balance between adaptation to America and preserving Orthodox traditions. Many of those who believed that assimilation into American life also meant the secularization of Greek Orthodoxy or at least slipping into Protestant congregational practices turned viscerally toward traditional practices, and this laid them open to accusations of being too fundamentalist, as in Ephraim's case, or too traditional, in Spyridon's case.

The reactions to Spyridon's personality and his policies amply demonstrated that what he probably considered excessive forms of Americanization could not be rolled back. Greek Orthodoxy had adapted to its environment and had settled in its own way of doing things. And the patriarchate's intervention was designed solely to assert its control over Greek Orthodoxy in America rather than interfere with the process of integration into American society—with the exception, that is, of blocking any moves toward the emergence of an autonomous or autocephalous pan-Orthodoxy, which would diminish Constantinople's transatlantic reach. It is hard to understand why the patriarch chose Spyridon as Iakovos's replacement. It could have been an error in judgment, a lack of anticipation of how the new archbishop would comport himself, or an underestimation of the church's Americanized culture. What is certain is that as a historical agent, Spyridon was unable either to adapt or to manipulate the complex structural characteristics of Greek Orthodoxy in America.

There seem to be two main reasons why Spyridon fell short. One was that he misread the ecumenical patriarch's intentions, or at least he did not quickly readjust his policies when the patriarch adjusted his own in light of the reality that Greek Americans were, on the whole, Americanized Greek Orthodox. Bartholomew's speech at the banquet that AHEPA held in his honor should have demonstrated to all that while the patriarchate may have considered Greek Orthodoxy in America as a diaspora in an ecclesiastical sense, it was quite comfortable with the Greek Orthodox feeling at home in America, at least the America Bartholomew described, multiethnic and tolerant of others, which he regarded as perfectly aligned with the ecumenical values of Greek Orthodoxy. The other reason was that the Greek Orthodox Church in America had clearly become a victim of its own success. By co-opting the other Greek American institutions and assuming a wide range of responsibilities, including education—ranging from Greek language afternoon schools all the way to a Greek Orthodox seminary—the church had burdened itself with increasingly complex and difficult tasks. Indeed, Spyridon's successor, Archbishop Demetrios, would end his twenty-year-long tenure amid complaints that too many Greek language schools were closing and that the seminary was facing problems so severe that they were jeopardizing its very future.

Demetrios, nonetheless, possessed a personality very different from that of Spyridon and was credited with restoring calm and order to the affairs of the church, though he was ultimately brought down by questions concerning the way he managed the church's finances. An erudite and wise prelate, Demetrios quickly made his peace with most of the wealthy and influential lay members of the church, and in 2004 he persuaded a group of wealthy Greek Americans who were already contributing to the church through the increasingly influential Leadership 100 organization to underwrite another organization, named "FAITH: An Endowment for Orthodoxy and Hellenism," to support programs for young people that promoted an understanding of Orthodoxy and Hellenism. Spyridon's abrasiveness in the face of challenges from the lay element was absent in Demetrios's case. Demetrios was open to all and maintained a busy schedule of private meetings and public engagements, in which his speeches always included quotes from the Scriptures. Yet

Demetrios proved to be too accessible, too accommodating, and too agree-able for some, at least those in the church who pined for a dynamic leader in Iakovos's mold. As a leader and an administrator, Demetrios was cautious; he constantly invoked the authority of the Ecumenical Patriarchate over the Orthodox Church in America as a way of explaining why he was unwilling to consider changes to address the effects of the Americanization of the Greek Orthodox. And any steps along the path of Iakovos's vision of pan-Orthodox unity in America were left to the patriarchate, which was more concerned with establishing a pan-Orthodox community on a global (rather than an American) scale, a goal that would obviously enhance its own standing and protect it from any unwelcome developments in its host country, Turkey. In this respect the church's Order of Saint Andrew the Apostle—the Archons—whose national commander Anthony J. Limberakis took office almost at the same time that Demetrios was installed as archbishop, appeared more en-ergized than ever as it mobilized in support of religious freedom and the advancement of the Ecumenical Patriarchate. Overall, Demetrios's presence stabilized the church, and Demetrios himself was widely liked both for his comforting and dignified leadership and for his openness and close relation-ship with all major Greek American institutions.[26] Although he did so much to restore stability in the early part of his tenure, Demetrios had to suffer in-dignities in his last years as archbishop, as several prominent Greek Orthodox publicly sought his resignation because of concerns over the management of the church's finances and especially the stalled St. Nicholas project in Lower Manhattan. Nevertheless, when Demetrios eventually resigned, there were some who did not forget all the good that he had done. AHEPA issued a statement that eulogized his many qualities and expressed its appreciation that the archbishop had "walked side-by-side, hand-in-hand, with AHEPA family leaders at significant, even historical occasions for the community."[27]

Where Demetrios was deemed to be less successful was in controlling the church's budget and managing the very ambitious and costly project of rebuilding St. Nicholas, the small Greek Orthodox church that had been destroyed when the south tower of the World Trade Center collapsed on September 11, 2001. True to its confident place in American society, the Greek Orthodox Church envisioned a Byzantine-style structure designed by a modern architect, Santiago Calatrava, who had designed the nearby World Trade Center Transportation Hub as well as the roof of the stadium in Ath-ens for the 2004 Olympic Games. The planned St. Nicholas Church, which was described as a national shrine, would be open to all persons, believ-ers and nonbelievers, and also include a nondenominational bereavement center. The project was challenging on its own terms, but it soon ran into a series of problems related to concerns about the erection of a religious building near the September 11 memorial site, and more generally about the uses of the area where the World Trade Center had stood. The costs soared, while funds earmarked for St. Nicholas were apparently redirected to address other pressing financial needs of the archdiocese, and construction stalled in 2017. Yet again, it seemed, the Greek Orthodox Church had tried to do too much.

Bartholomew's choice for Demetrios's successor, one of the clerics of the patriarchate, Archimandrite Dr. Elpidophoros Lambriniadis, who was serving as chief secretary of the patriarchate's synod, confirmed the process of greater involvement of the patriarchate in the affairs of Greek Orthodoxy in America. The prospect of another home-grown leader of Greek Orthodoxy in America would have to wait. A few years before his appointment as archbishop in 2019, during a visit to the Holy Cross seminary in Brookline, Elpidophoros delivered a thoughtful analysis of the state of Eastern Orthodoxy in the United States, demonstrating that the leading clergy in Constantinople had a good grasp of the conditions affecting Orthodoxy in the United States. Nonetheless, Elpidophoros made sure to end his lecture by affirming the Ecumenical Patriarchate's hegemony over Orthodoxy in America, stating that "with regards to the United States, the submission to the First Throne of the Church, that is, to the Ecumenical Patriarchate is not only fitting with the American society and mentality but also it opens up the horizons of possibilities for this much-promising region, which is capable of becoming an example of Pan-Orthodox unity and witness. . . . The Mother Church of Constantinople safeguards for the Orthodox Church in America those provisions that are needed for further progress and maturity in Christ."[28]

The Ecumenical Patriarchate's rejection of the decisions of the pan-Orthodox gathering at Ligonier, Pennsylvania, and Archbishop Iakovos's forced resignation in 1996 were a turning point in the history of the Greek Orthodox Church in America. The patriarchate had held jurisdiction over the affairs of Greek Orthodoxy in America since 1922, but in practice the archbishops had been given greater and greater leeway in finding ways to navigate amid the conflicting demands of preserving an ethno-religious entity in an American environment. The arrival of Patriarchal Exarch Damaskinos in 1930 along with the subsequent appointment of Athenagoras as archbishop was a reminder of how the patriarchate could choose to intervene and shape the affairs of Greek Orthodoxy in America. The elevation of Archbishop Athenagoras to ecumenical patriarch in 1948 and his decision that his successor in the United States would be a prelate who had not served there were additional reminders of the presence and reach of the patriarchate. During the nearly four-decades-long tenure of Archbishop Iakovos, relations were close initially because Athenagoras was Iakovos's mentor, but ties between the archdiocese and the patriarchate became increasingly strained, especially after Athenagoras's death in 1972.

Meanwhile, however, the church had found ways to accommodate the steady assimilation of the Greek Americans and the emergence of the second- and third-generation American born. The church managed not only to adapt but also to thrive in those circumstances and retain its centrality in Greek American community life, despite the existence of a range of national and local institutions that lay claim to the allegiance and support of Americans of Greek descent. The responsibility the church had assumed as both the spiritual and the ethnic repository of Greek America allowed it not only to change with the times but also maintain its ethno-religious character and retain its hegemonic role. Hegemonic not only in an institutional sense but also in a discursive sense. It was able to define Greek Americanness, or rather determine the parameters of the conversations around Greek American identity and how to preserve it. Those parameters included the religious content of the ethnic identity. The ethno-religious church created an ethno-religious identity.

Led by Iakovos, the church, in its trend toward becoming more and more Americanized, eventually reached the crucial threshold of contemplating and imagining the establishment of a pan-Orthodox American Orthodox Church along with the other Eastern Orthodox Churches. This vision acquired its most articulate blueprint at the gathering in Ligonier. Evidently, Patriarch Bartholomew, who had been installed in 1991, decided that the process of Americanization endangered the patriarchate's ability to oversee Greek Orthodox life in America, and he forcefully intervened, reversing that process and inaugurating a new era in Greek Orthodoxy's life in America.

The new era brought several changes, including a restructuring of the church's organization, an increased presence of the patriarchate in Greek Orthodox life in the United States, and an increasingly religious inflection in the Greek American identity fostered by the church. Surveys taken at the turn of the twentieth century show that for many second- and third- generation Greek Americans, their Greekness is defined in large part by their Greek Orthodox faith. Greek American lobbying in Washington has registered an increasing concern with the status of the Ecumenical Patriarchate in Turkey and the continuing closure of the patriarchate's Halki Seminary by order of the Turkish government. Meanwhile, the church's continued centrality in Greek American social life and Greek language education indirectly enhances the standing of the Ecumenical Patriarchate in the minds and hearts of Greek Americans.

For most of the twentieth century, especially from the moment Athenagoras arrived in the United States in 1931 to assume his duties as archbishop, through the conclusion of Iakovos's tenure in 1996, the archbishops navigated as they saw fit to preserve Greek Orthodoxy in a steadily changing milieu and with a rapidly Americanized church membership. That membership was not a passive bystander but instead, judging by the ongoing influence of Greek Orthodoxy, responded positively for the most part to the changing navigational course. In other words, the church changed, and so did its members, in a dialectical interchange that kept Orthodoxy relevant over the decades. The ethno-religious character of Greek Orthodoxy no doubt gave it deep moorings in the understanding of Greek American identity and was crucial in its survival in a multiethnic and multi-religious American society. And American society's tolerance of ethnicity, albeit in its more symbolic manifestations in the later part of the twentieth century, was beneficial for the ethno-religious Greek Orthodox Church. The religion's transnational character, its attachment to the homeland and to its mother church in Constantinople, reinforced its ethnic identity and by extension strengthened religious attachments. The transnational dimension, in other words, complemented and strengthened Greek Orthodoxy's ethno-religious quality. The era of globalization, with its compression of geographical space and transcendence of borders and geography, brought a strengthening of the transnational dynamic, which was conducive to the increased presence and role of the Ecumenical Patriarchate of Constantinople. And this meant, in turn, a significant change in the overall conditions that shaped Greek Orthodoxy in America. Even as post–Cold War globalization was becoming a reality, the church was embarking on a course that would have weakened its ethno-religious character and made it part of an American supra-ethnic Orthodox entity. This course was either slowed or halted, depending on the true nature of the patriarchate's intentions. It may be that while Greek Orthodoxy in America is becoming mature enough to make the next step toward joining an American Orthodox community, the Patriarchate of Constantinople is asking it to slow down in the interests of helping it consolidate its ecumenical character. Throughout the twentieth century, Greek Orthodoxy in America had to adjust to its changing surroundings. Now, in the twenty-first century, it faces the challenge of adapting to a global environment.

NOTES

Introduction

1. National Geographic, "Best Food Festival in Each U.S. State."
2. Skopetea, *To Protypo Vasileio kai e Megale Idea*.
3. Hammond and Warner, "Religion and Ethnicity," 55–66.
4. Mavratsas, "Greek-American Economic Culture." See also Anagnostou, "Ceasar V. Mavratsas."
5. Handlin, *Uprooted*, 104.
6. Gordon, *Assimilation in American Life*; Herberg, *Protestant-Catholic-Jew*.
7. Williams, "Religion and the Making of Community."
8. Smith, "Religion and Ethnicity in America."
9. See Bodnar, *Transplanted*.
10. For example, in an otherwise excellent study on the new trends of immigration history, Virginia Yans-McLaughlin, in *Immigration Reconsidered: History, Sociology, and Politics*, mentions the Greeks only in passing, along with other southeastern European immigrants.
11. Morrow, "Transnational Religion."
12. Kim, "Religion and Ethnicity."
13. Vertovec, *Transnationalism*, 2–3, 145–46.
14. One study that does not ignore the Eastern Orthodox is Ahlstrom, *Religious History of the American People*.
15. Saloutos, *Greeks in the United States*.
16. Saloutos, "Greek Orthodox Church."
17. Saloutos, "Greeks of Milwaukee."
18. Moskos, *Greek Americans* (1st and 2nd eds.); Moskos and Moskos, *Greek Americans* (3rd ed.).
19. Scourby, *Greek Americans*.
20. Constantelos, *Understanding the Greek Orthodox Church*; Erickson, *Orthodox Christians in America*; Ferencz, *American Orthodoxy*; Fitzgerald, *Orthodox Church*; McGuckin, *Orthodox Church*; Michalopoulos and Ham, *American Orthodox Church*.
21. Karpathakis, "Whose Church Is It Anyway?"; Karpathakis, "Greek Orthodox Church and Identity Politics"; Kourvetaris, "Greek Orthodox Church in the United States"; Kopan, *Education and Greek Immigrants in Chicago*; "Greek Survival in Chicago"; Papadopoulos, "Role of Nationalism."
22. Prodromou, "Ambivalent Orthodox"; Prodromou, "Religious Pluralism."
23. Clapsis, "Challenge of a Global World"; Roudometof, "Transnationalism and Globalization"; Roudometof, Agadjanian, and Pankhurst, *Eastern Orthodoxy*; Roudometof,

"Greek Orthodoxy, Territoriality, and Globality"; Roudometof, *Globalization and Orthodox Christianity*.

24. Condos, "Greek Language School"; Diamandi-Karanou, "Relationship between Homeland and Diaspora"; Kunkelman, "Religion of Ethnicity"; Morrow, "Transnational Religion"; Soumakis, "Sacred Paideia"; Varlamos, "Quest for Human Rights"; Wisnosky, "Contemporary Orthodox Christian Theological Education."

25. Grammenos, *Orthodoxos Amerikanos O Archiepiskopos Voreiou kai Notiou Amerikes Iakovos*; Petrou, *O Ethnikos Dichasmos*; Theodosopoulos, "E Hellenike Orthodoxe Ekklesia."

26. Alex, "Twenty-First Century Participation"; Balodimas-Bartolomei, "Greek American Identities"; Kourvetaris, "Greek Orthodox and Greek American Ethnic Identity."

27. Moskos, "Greek Community in the United States."

28. See for example Hollinger, "'Secularization' Question."

29. Moskos and Moskos, *Greek Americans*, 105.

30. Gerber, "Forming a Transnational Narrative."

31. Anagnostou, "Where Does Diaspora Belong?"; Jusdanis, "Greek Americans and the Diaspora."

32. Giddens, *Central Problems in Social Theory*, 1–95; Giddens, *Constitution of Society*, 1–45.

33. Yates, "Using Giddens' Structuration Theory."

1. Greek Orthodoxy Arrives in America

1. Makrides, "Why Are Orthodox Churches Particularly Prone to Nationalization?"
2. FitzGerald, *Orthodox Church*, 41–43, 50–51; see also Alfonsky, *History of the Orthodox Church in America*.
3. Doumouras, "Greek Orthodox Communities."
4. Efthymiou, *Skiagrafia*, 81.
5. Gabriel, "Retrospective," 246–47.
6. *Chicago Tribune*, "Kiss Away Their Past Sins."
7. Kourelis and Marinis, "Immigrant Liturgy"; see also Ousterhout, "Holy Space."
8. Burgess, *Greeks in America*, 143–44.
9. Burgess, *Greeks in America*, 160.
10. Abbot, "Study of the Greeks in Chicago."
11. Contopoulos, *Greek Community of New York City*, 117.
12. Anagnostou, *Contours of White Ethnicity*, 41.
13. Hart, *Time, Religion and Social Experience*, 7–8, 121–23.
14. Stewart, *Demons and the Devil*, 34–35.
15. Kopan, "Greek Survival in Chicago," 278–79.
16. Constantelos, *Christian Faith and Cultural Heritage*, 3–5.
17. Saloutos, *Greeks in the United States*, 73.
18. Efthymiou, *Skiagrafia*, 84–87.
19. Perkins, "New Immigrants and Education."
20. Schmemann, "Clergy and Laity."
21. Xenides, *Greeks in America*, 118.

22. *Greek Star*, "Fall of the Greek Race."

23. Foreign Relations of the United States, "Greece: Illegal Immigration," 131–32.

24. Canoutas, *Hellenism in America*, 200.

25. Greek Embassy, Washington, DC, to GMFA, 25/8 July 1920, Historical Archive, GMFA.

26. Greek Historical Society of the San Francisco Bay Area, *Greeks in San Francisco*, 7, 32, 47, 88; *San Francisco Call*, "Peace Reigns Again in the Greek Church"; *San Francisco Examiner*, "Bishop and Church End 8 Years War"; *San Francisco Examiner*, "Pastor Wins Suit for Salary"; *Los Angeles Times*, "King Cupid Throws Londos."

27. Ambatielos, Freshman, and Loomos, *Celebrating the 100th Anniversary*, 24.

28. Contopoulos, *Greek Community of New York City*, 22.

29. Annunciation Greek Orthodox Church, "Our Parish History."

30. Saloutos, *Greeks in the United States*, 133–34.

31. Frazee, *Orthodox Church*, 124.

32. Zacharopoulos, "Beginning of the Organization."

33. *New York Times*, "Greeks Celebrate Independence."

34. *Chicago Tribune*, "Writ Welcomes King's Prelate"; *Chicago Tribune*, "Pastor Quits to Thwart Greek King's Bishop."

35. Encyclical of the Metropolitan of Athens, New York, 29/11 August 1921, LOIRP0001, box L1, Archives, GOARCH.

36. "General Convention of the Clergy (First Session)," 1921 LOIUM0001, box L1, Archives, GOARCH.

37. Efthymiou, *Skiagraphia*, 93.

38. McGuckin, *Orthodox Church*, 381.

2. Americanization and the Immigrant Church in the 1920s

1. Alexandris, *Greek Minority of Istanbul*, 69–76.

2. Agenda of New York District Meeting, November 11–12, 1924, E&D GOARCH, 35–36.

3. Higham, *Strangers in the Land*, 273.

4. Higham, *Strangers in the Land*, 318.

5. See Commons, *Immigrants in America*.

6. *Neighbors: Studies in Immigration*, 50.

7. *Neighbors: Studies in Immigration*, 56–57.

8. Heinze, "Critical Period," 158.

9. Leber, *History of the Order of AHEPA*, 148–66, 207–8.

10. *Saloniki-Greek Press*, "Greek American Progressive Association."

11. *New York Times*, "Many Banks to Aid Buyers of Bonds"; *New York Times*, "Sees Greek Glory Return."

12. "E Eklesia tes Amerikes apo tes elefseos tes Aftou Theiotates Agiotetos Meletiou" [The church of America from the arrival of His All Holiness Meletios], LO1KY0001, 1922, box L1, Archive, GOARCH.

13. Holy Synod Encyclical, July 18, 1923, in Manolis, *History*, 48.

14. Holy Synod Encyclical, July 18, 1923, in Manolis, *History*, 48.

15. Joachim, *Oi Kindynoi*.

16. Joachim, *Oi Kindynoi*, 6–14.

17. Joachim, *Oi Kindynoi*, 27.

18. Bukowczyk, *History of the Polish Americans*, 73.

19. Joachim, *Oi Kindynoi*, 54–58.

20. Ypomnima tes Ieras Synodou tes Ellinorthodoxis Archiepiskopes Amerikes pros ten Ellinikin Kyvernisin [Memorandum Holy Synod of the Greek Orthodox Archdiocese of America to the Greek government], March 20, 1928, L01G00132 1–2, box L1, Archive, GOARCH.

21. Namee, "Pews."

22. Minutes, Holy Synod Meeting, February 26, 1924, in Manolis, *History*, 55.

23. Minutes, Holy Synod Meeting, March 11, 1930, in Manolis, *History*, 173.

24. Greek Embassy in Washington, DC, to GMFA, June 30, 1923, Historical Archive, GMFA.

25. Greek Embassy in Washington, DC, to GMFA, June 30, 1923, Archive, GMFA.

26. Saloutos, *Greeks in the United States*, 290.

27. *Washington Post*, "Greek Envoy and His Wife."

28. Greek Embassy in Washington, DC, to GMFA, December 7, 1925, Historical Archive, GMFA.

29. Minutes, Holy Synod Meeting, March 10, 1925, in Manolis, *History*, 74.

30. Minutes, Holy Synod Meeting, March 1, 1927, in Manolis, *History*, 102.

31. Minutes, Holy Synod Meeting, March 1, 1927, in Manolis, *History*, 104.

32. Greek Embassy in Washington, DC, to GMFA, November 23, 1926, Historical Archive, GMFA.

33. Minutes Holy Synod Meeting, March 12, 1930, in Manolis, *History*, 179–80.

34. Damaskinos, Metropolitan of Corinth, to Archbishop of Athens Chrysostomos, Memorandum, January 14, 1930, Historical Archive, GMFA.

35. Papaioannou, *Odyssey of Hellenism*, 202–6.

36. Petrou, *O ethnikos dichasmos*, 279–320.

37. Ambatielos, Freshman, and Loomos, *Celebrating the 100th Anniversary*, 27.

3. Greek Orthodoxy versus Protestant Congregationalism

1. Chrissochoidis, *Spyros P. Skouras Memoirs*, 109.

2. Athenagoras to Patriarch Photios, May 24, 1931, Historical Archive, GMFA.

3. Archbishop Athenagoras, Keynote Speech at the 4th Church Congress of the Archdiocese, New York, November 16, 1931, LO2KY0001, box L2, Archive, GOARCH.

4. Athenagoras, Keynote.

5. Fahey, "Eastern Synodal Traditions," 254.

6. Vryonis, *Brief History*, 2.

7. Athenagoras, Keynote.

8. Saloutos, *Greeks in the United States*, 305.

9. Speech of Kallistos, bishop of San Francisco, on the Duties of the Archdiocese, 1931, LO2R00017, box L2, Archive, GOARCH.

10. George J. Chryssikos, "Observations of the Regulations of the Mixed Council," November 14, 1931, LO2CA0150, box L2, Archive, GOARCH.

11. Ambassador Simopoulos to GMFA, November 27, 1931, Historical Archive, GMFA.

12. Ferencz, *American Orthodoxy*, 178–86.

13. Papaioannou, *From Mars Hill*, 148–49.

14. Papaioannou, *From Mars Hill*, 142–43.

15. Papaioannou, *From Mars Hill*, 149.

16. Soumakis, "Sacred Paideia," 75.

17. Kitroeff, *Greeks in Egypt*, 172–76.

18. Zoustis, *O en Ameriki Hellenismos*, 239–40.

19. Memorandum from Athenagoras to Schoolteachers, June 10, 1935, E&D GO-ARCH, 330–32.

20. Memorandum from Athenagoras to Priests and Boards of Greek Orthodox Communities, August 26, 1938, E&D GOARCH, 351.

21. Consulate of Greece in Boston to GMFA, June 27, 1937, Historical Archive, GMFA.

22. Mackridge, *Language and National Identity*, 301–2.

23. Triantafyllidis, *Hellenes tes Amedrikes*.

24. "Semeioma M. Triandafyllidi."

25. Papaioannou, *From Mars Hill*, 150.

26. Papaioannou, *From Mars Hill*, 152. It was not a coincidence that the Russian Orthodox also felt the need to establish a seminary on American soil, and they established St. Vladimir's Seminary in New York City and St. Tikhon's Orthodox Theological Seminary in Canaan, Pennsylvania, both in 1938.

27. Poulos, *Pomfret*, 157–58.

28. Poulos, *Pomfret*, 132–56.

29. Guglielmo and Lewis, "Changing Racial Meanings," 177.

30. Kitroeff, "Greek-American Ethnicity."

31. Leber, *History of the Order of AHEPA*, 423.

32. Hart, *Time, Religion and Social Experience*, 15–17.

33. US Department of Commerce, Bureau of the Census, *Religious Bodies*.

4. The Greek Orthodox Church in between Greece and America

1. *New York Times*, editorial, October 29, 1940.

2. Sittser, *Cautious Patriotism*, 30–48.

3. Hennessey, *American Catholics*, 277–80.

4. Leber, *History of the Order of AHEPA*, 330–31.

5. Vlanton, "Documents," 96–97.

6. Encyclical, Athenagoras to Priests and Boards of Greek Orthodox Communities, July 27, 1940, E&D GOARCH, 155–56.

7. Encyclical, Athenagoras to Boards of Philoptochos Fraternities, November 26, 1940, E&D GOARCH, 282–83.

8. Encyclicals, Athenagoras to Boards of Philoptochos Fraternities, January 14, 1941; March 7, 1941; March 14, 1941; April 9, 1941, E&D GOARCH, 286–93.

9. Lackman, "Foreign Groups Join Federation."

10. Papaioannou, *From Mars Hill*, 171.

11. Nikolidakis, "E Symvole tes Akademias Agiou Vasileiou."

12. *Ethnikos Kyrix*, "To en Philadelphia Clerico-Laikon Synedrion."

13. *Athenai*, "To Clerico-Laikon."

14. *Ellinikos Astir,* "To Clerico-Laikon Syndedrio."

15. Veniopoulos, "Simeioseis apo to en Philadelphia Clerico-Laikon Synedrion."

16. *Ethnikos Kyrix,* "To en Philadelphia Episimon Deipnon tou Clericolaicou Synedriou."

17. Praktika 9es Clericolaikis Synelefseos [Minutes of the 9th Clergy-Laity Congress], November 4, 1946, box L7, Archive, GOARCH.

18. Praktika 9es Clericolaikis Synelefseos [Minutes of the 9th Clergy-Laity Congress], November 4, 1946, box L7, Archive, GOARCH.

19. Praktika 9es Clericolaikis Synelefseos [Minutes of the 9th Clergy-Laity Congress], November 4, 1946, box L7, Archive, GOARCH.

20. Bossard and Letts, "Mixed Marriages," 309.

21. Encyclical, Athenagoras to Priests, Board Members and Parish Members, April 9, 1948, E&D GOARCH, 236–38.

22. Encyclical, Athenagoras to Parish Priests, September 27, 1948, E&D, GO-ARCH 241–43.

23. Kourides, *Evolution of the Greek Orthodox Church,* 18.

24. Marty, *Modern American Religion,* 348.

25. *New York Times,* "'God Sent Roosevelt.'"

26. *New York Times,* "Rock from Athens"; *New York Times,* "Manning Receives Icon of St. John."

27. *New York Times,* "Greeks Honor 1,000 Dead."

28. Encyclical, Athenagoras to Board and Members of the Philoptochos, March 4, 1943, E&D GOARCH, 209–10.

29. Papaioannou, *From Mars Hill,* 179–80.

30. Sermon of his Eminence Archbishop Athenagoras at the Symphony Hall, Boston, November 3, 1946, box L7, Archive, GOARCH.

31. Alexandris, *Greek Minority of Istanbul,* 244–45.

32. *New York Times,* "Prelate Will Fly to Enthronement."

33. *New York Times,* "Athenagoras Goes to Istanbul Post."

34. Papaioannou, *From Mars Hill,* 274–77.

5. Assimilation and Respectability in the 1950s

1. Corrigan and Hudson, *Religion in America,* 385.

2. Corrigan and Hudson, *Religion in America,* 385.

3. Constantelos, *Understanding the Greek Orthodox Church,* 265.

4. *Ethnikos Kyrix,* "Sinenteuxi Athinagora Vostonis."

5. Daskalakis, "An Fygei o Athinagoras."

6. Constantelos, *Understanding the Greek Orthodox Church,* 264–65.

7. *New York Times,* "Greek Archbishop of Americas Is Here."

8. "The 11th Clergy-Laity Congress: The full key-note speech of the Archbishop Los Angeles 1952," LO9KY0001, box L9, Archive, GOARCH.

9. Prodromou, "Religious Pluralism," 746.

10. Inboden, *Religion and American Foreign Policy,* 301.

11. "Constitution Governing the Churches and Communities of the Greek Archdiocese of North and South America—As voted by its General Conventions of Clergy and Laity, amended by the 10th Convention of Clergy and laity (November 26th—December 1, 1950)," LO8DS0015, box L8, Archive, GOARCH.

12. St. Sophia Cathedral, "13th Biennial Congress"; Executive Committee Ladies Philoptochos, Encyclical, February 7, 1951; Archbishop Michael, letter to all Executive Committees of Ladies Philoptochos organizations, September 15, 1954, Basil J. Vlavianos Papers, Series 7, Associations, Subseries 9, Philoptochos Society.

13. *History and Consecration of St. John the Baptist Greek Orthodox Church*, 6.

14. St. Basil Academy, "History of St. Basil's Academy"; Leber, *History of the Order of AHEPA*, 385, 387, 389, 394, 430.

15. Encyclical, Michael to Priests, Parish Boards, Philoptochos Fraternities, Youth Organizations, Teachers and other organizations, March 12, 1954, E&D GOARCH, 512–14.

16. "Mr. Spyros Skouras' Speech St. Louis," 1950, L08SP006, box L8, Archive, GOARCH.

17. "Sermon by His Eminence Michael, Archbishop of the Greek Orthodox Church, CBS Church of the Air, Dec. 31, 1950," box L8, Archive, GOARCH.

18. Cornell, "One-Man Crusader."

19. "Sermon," in Constantelos, *Encyclicals and Documents*, 516.

20. Prevas, *History of the Greek Orthodox Cathedral*, 135–43.

21. Manis, "Outside Agitator Times Two."

22. Sotirhos, "Remembering Michael."

23. "First National Conference, Greek Orthodox Youth of America, August 1952," Vlavianos Archive, 1945–52.

24. Encyclical, Michael to Clergy, November 17, 1955, E&D GOARCH, 647–48.

25. Stephanopoulos, *Breath of Spiritual Fragrance*, 6.

26. Message of Archbishop Michael to the 5th Annual 4th Diocese District Conference of GOYA in Seattle, Washington, June 14–16, Vlavianos Archive, 1950–1958.

27. Theotokas, *Dokimio gia ten Amerike*, 226–32.

28. Alivizatos, *E Hellenike Orthodoxos Eklesia*, 5–6.

29. Michael, *Ofelomene Apanteses*.

30. Matsakis, *Growing Up Greek*, 48.

31. "The Archbishop's entire speech 14th Clergy-Laity Congress," LO9KY0001, box L12, Archive, GOARCH.

32. Stephanopoulos, *Breath of Spiritual Fragrance*, 6–7.

33. Iakovos, "Fifty Years of Life and Development."

6. The Challenges of the 1960s

1. Wuthnow, *Restructuring of American Religion*, 59.

2. Volaitis, "Orthodox Church as Church and Ethnic Community," 79.

3. Volaitis, "Orthodox Church as Church and Ethnic Community," 79–80.

4. Wuthnow, *Restructuring of American Religion*, 150–52.

5. Ambassador Pericles Skeferis, Ankara, to Greek Ministry of Foreign Affairs, January 21, 1950, KY 1950/161/5, Historical Archive, GMFA.

6. UN Permanent Representative Alexis Kyrou, New York, to Greek Ministry of Foreign Affairs, September 16, 1950, KY 1950/195/2, Historical Archive, GMFA.

7. Svolopoulos, *Constantinos Karamanlis*, 204–5.

8. Grammenos, *Orthodoxos Amerikanos O Archiepiskopos*.

9. Kourides, *Evolution of the Greek Orthodox Church*, 23.

10. Wiest, "Centenary of the Greek Orthodox Archdiocese," 3.

11. *New York Times,* "Greek Bishop Enthroned Here."

12. *New York Times,* "Service Is Held by New Primate."

13. Christopoulos, "Impact through Public Relations."

14. Bishop Athenagoras of Elaia to Callimachos, August 23, 1958, ff 64, box 11, Callimachos Papers.

15. *Greek Orthodox Archdiocese Yearbook 1986,* 103.

16. Constantelos, *Understanding the Greek Orthodox Church,* 270.

17. *Greek Orthodox Archdiocese Yearbook 1964,* 199–343.

18. "An Open Letter" and "Bulletin," both undated, Annunciation Church Philadelphia Papers.

19. Wuthnow, *Restructuring of American Religion,* 230–34.

20. Kourides, *Evolution of the Greek Orthodox Church,* 26–27.

21. Morris, *American Catholic,* 280–81; Carlin, *Decline and Fall,* 37–51.

22. "Report to the 17th Biennial Clergy-Laity Conference of the Greek Orthodox Archdiocese of North and South America by His Eminence Archbishop Iakovos," L15 KY0001, folder KY, box L15, Archive, GOARCH.

23. "Report to the 17th Biennial Clergy-Laity Conference."

24. "Keynote Speech to the Members of the 18th Clergy Laity Congress, Montreal 1966," L16500001, box L16, Archive, GOARCH.

25. March on Selma, "Statement Issued at 17th Biennial Ecclesiastical Congress."

26. Lambert, *Religion in American Politics,* 179–80.

27. March on Selma, "Statement by Archbishop Iakovos March 16, 1965."

28. Malouhos, *Ego o Iakovos,* 223.

29. March on Selma, "Archbishop's Letter to the Clergy, March 17, 1965."

30. "A Résumé of the Decisions and Statements 18th Biennial Clergy-Laity Congress of the Greek Orthodox Archdiocese of North and South America Montreal, June 25–July 2 1966," L16DR0018, box L16, Archive, GOARCH.

31. Dugan, "Greek Orthodox Church Backs U.S."

32. "Résumé of the Decisions and Statements."

33. Dugan, "Greek Orthodox Church Backs U.S."

34. "Report of his Eminence Archbishop Iakovos before the 15th Clergy Laity Congress, Buffalo New York, Sept. 19, 1960," box L13, L13KY0001, Archive, GOARCH.

35. "Report of his Eminence Archbishop Iakovos."

36. G. D. Vranopoulos to Greek Embassy, Washington, DC, July 7, 1962, KY 1962/14, Historical Archive, GMFA.

37. General Consulate in New York to GMFA, "Greek Schools and High Schools," May 28, 1963, KY 1963/11, Historical Archive, GMFA.

38. Montgomery, "Orthodox Church Can Use English."

39. "Résumé of the Decisions and Statements."

40. "Report of his Eminence Archbishop Iakovos."

41. "Report of his Eminence Archbishop before the 16th Clergy Laity Congress, Boston 1962," L14KY0001, box L14, Archive, GOARCH.

42. "Report of the Education Department 1960–62 Nov. 1962," box L14, Archive, GOARCH.

43. "Committee Report on 'The Church and the Educational Issue,'" L16RG0014, box L16, Archive, GOARCH.

44. E&D GOARCH, 1118–26.

45. "Report of his Eminence Archbishop Iakovos."

46. Vryonis, *Brief History*, 47–51.

47. Vryonis, *Brief History*, 21.

48. Vryonis, *Brief History*, 21–22.

49. "Archbishop Iakovos Message to the 19th Clergy-Laity Congress of the Greek Orthodox Archdiocese of North and South America Athens July 22, 1968," L17KY0001, box 17, Archive, GOARCH.

7. Greek Orthodoxy and the Ethnic Revival

1. Meagher, "Racial and Ethnic Relations," 212.

2. Moskos, *Greek Americans*, 59–61.

3. Patrinacos, "Role of the Church," 132.

4. Moskos, *Greek Americans*, 59.

5. Counelis and Kopan, "Orthodox Church and Its Language Problem."

6. Papaioannou, *Odyssey of Hellenism*, 452.

7. Patrinacos, "Change or Succumb."

8. Patrinacos, *Individual*, vii.

9. Patrinacos, *Individual*, 117–18.

10. Patrinacos, *Individual*, 131–32.

11. Papaioannou, *Odyssey of Hellenism*, 454.

12. Papaioannou, *Odyssey of Hellenism*, 455.

13. Archbishop Iakovos, "Keynote Address to the Delegates of the 20th Clergy-Laity Congress of the Greek Archdiocese of North & South America, June 29th," box L20, Archive, GOARCH.

14. Iakovos, "Keynote Address to the Delegates."

15. Papaioannou, *Odyssey of Hellenism*, 461.

16. *New York Times*, "100 Demonstrators Protest Greek Orthodox Plans."

17. Papaioannou, *Odyssey of Hellenism*, 462–63.

18. *New York Times*, "Iakovos, in Greece, Defends Reforms."

19. Germanos, *What We See and Hear*, 58.

20. Jameson, "Showdown in Orthodoxy."

21. *Ethnikos Kyrix*, "To 21° Clericolaikon Synedrion."

22. *Atlantis*, "Foni voontos en ti erimo."

23. Iakovos, "50 Years of Life and Development."

24. "Decisions of the 21st Clergy-Laity Congress of the Greek Orthodox Archdiocese," box L23, Archive, GOARCH.

25. "Decisions of the 21st Clergy-Laity Congress."

26. "Decisions of the 21st Clergy-Laity Congress."

27. "Decisions of the 21st Clergy-Laity Congress."

28. Greek Orthodox Archdiocese of America, "Emmanuel Hatziemmanuel Passes Away."

29. Ernest A. Villas, "The 21st Biennial Clergy Laity Congress," L23AC0004, box L24, Archive, GOARCH; see also *New York Times*, "1,000 at Banquet Weep at Patriarch's Death."

30. *Washington Post*, "Archbishop Banned at Athenagoras Rite."

31. *New York Times*, "Eastern Orthodox Church Chooses a New Patriarch."

32. Deno J. Geankoplos, "Enrichment through Diversity: The Greek Immigrant and the American Ideal," 23rd Biennial Clergy-Laity Congress of the Greek Orthodox Archdiocese, Sheraton Hotel, Philadelphia, July 2 to July 9, 1976, box L26, Archive, GOARCH.

33. Emmanuel Hatziemmanuel, "Greek Education Progress Report and Future Development," Report to the Clergy-Laity Congress of 1976, L27RE0003, box L26, Archive, GOARCH.

34. Hatziemmanuel, *O Amerikes Iakovos Hellenike Ekpaideuse*, 34.

35. Vaporis, "Church's Role."

36. Soumakis, "Sacred Paideia," 205–6, 114.

37. GOARCH, Office of Education, "The Greek Archdiocese System of Education," submitted by Emmanuel Hatziemmanuel, June 25, 1975, box V13, Archive, GOARCH.

38. Soumakis, "Sacred Paideia," 112.

39. *Nea Yorki*, "Liberation of Education."

40. Vaporis, "Church's Role."

41. Peter Kourides to Archbishop Iakovos, February 2, 1970, H12AL0002, folder RO box L20, Archive, GOARCH.

42. Arthur D. Little Inc, "A Report to the Greek Orthodox Archdiocese of North and South America," H12AL0031, folder RO box L20, Archive, GOARCH.

43. Peter Kourides to Archbishop Iakovos, February 2, 1970, H12AL0002, folder RO box L20, Archive, GOARCH.

44. Bukowczyk, *History of the Polish Americans*, 118–21.

8. Church and Homeland

1. Harakas, "Stand of the Orthodox Church." See also Harakas, *Contemporary Moral Issues*.

2. Anagnostopoulou, "Makarios III," 246–49.

3. Hadjipolycarpou, "Nation of Saints."

4. *New York Times*, "Patriarchate a Hostage."

5. Encyclical, Iakovos to Reverend Clergy and Esteemed Members of the Board of Trustees of the Communities of the Greek Orthodox Archdiocese of North and South America, August 13, 1964, E&D, GOARCH, 1167–68.

6. Greek General Consulate in New York to GMFA, January 18, 1965, Historical Archive, GMFA.

7. Wuthnow, *Restructuring of American Religion*, 164–65.

8. Fiske, "Orthodox Diocese of Americas."

9. "Archbishop Iakovos' Message to the 19th Clergy-Laity Congress of the Greek Orthodox Archdiocese of North and South America Athens July 22, 1968," box L17, Archive, GOARCH.

10. "Archbishop Iakovos' Message to the 19th Clergy-Laity Congress."

11. "Archbishop Iakovos' Message to the 19th Clergy-Laity Congress."

12. "Archbishop Iakovos' Message to the 19th Clergy-Laity Congress."

13. "Archbishop Iakovos' Message to the 19th Clergy-Laity Congress."

14. Vidalis, *Confronting the Greek Dictatorship*, 360–65.
15. Gage, "Iakovos Criticizes Greek Government."
16. Miller, *United States and the Making of Modern Greece*, 172.
17. Paul, "Study in Ethnic Group Political Behavior," 184–87.
18. Greek Orthodox Archdiocese, "Meeting on Cyprus Crisis"; *Chicago Tribune*, "Greeks Here Unify."
19. Watanabe, *Ethnic Groups*, 112, 141.
20. Kitroeff, "Diaspora-Homeland Relations," 33.
21. National Security Council Memorandum for Secretary Kissinger from A. Denis Clift, "Request from Archbishop Iakovos to See the President," ND18/CO40 Wars/Cyprus, President Gerald R. Ford Papers.
22. White House Memorandum of Conversation, September 25, 1974, President Gerald R. Ford Papers, http://www.fordlibrarymuseum.gov/library/document/0314/1552804.pdf.
23. White House Memorandum of Conversation, October 7, President Gerald R. Ford Papers, http://www.fordlibrarymuseum.gov/library/document/0314/1552819.pdf.
24. "President's Meeting with Archbishop Iakovos," October 7, 1974, Statement for White House Press Secretary, box 16, CO Cyprus 1974–75, President Gerald R. Ford Papers.
25. Evans and Novak, "Mr. Ford and the Greek Archbishop."
26. "Archbishop Iakovos Visits Athens and Pledges Assistance from Greek-Americans," August 21, 1974, from Athens, Greece T: State Department WikiLeaks, https://wikileaks.org/plusd/cables/1974ATHENS05956_b.html.
27. US Amb. Kubisch in Athens to Department of State, January 31, 1975, https://wikileaks.org/plusd/cables/1975ATHENS00877_b.html.
28. US State Department to US Embassies in Ankara and Athens and Consulate in Istanbul, January 1978, WikiLeaks.
29. US Embassy in Athens to State Department, February 10, 1978, WikiLeaks.
30. C. Ioannides, *Realpolitik*, 151.
31. C. Ioannides, *Realpolitik*, 157–75, 214–18.
32. *Washington Post*, "Fifteen Thousand Protesters," April 17, 1978; *St. Petersburg Times*, "Archbishop Meets with Mondale."
33. Malouhos, *Ego o Iakovos*, 353.
34. *Chicago Tribune*, "Mondale to Speak at Greek Fete."
35. American Presidency Project, "Jimmy Carter Remarks."
36. *New York Daily News*, "One Religious Leader."
37. Howe, "Primate Is Acting."
38. Grammenos, "O Archiepiskopos Voreiou kai Notiou Amerikes Iakovos."
39. Kalmoukos, "Davos kai Kerde."

9. Toward an American Greek Orthodoxy

1. Moskos, *Greek Americans*, 144–46.
2. *Greek Orthodox Archdiocese Yearbook 1986*, 103.
3. Anagnostou, "White Ethnicity," 103, 107.
4. Waters, *Ethnic Options*, 88–89, 121–24, 150–55.

5. Seraphim, *Quest for Orthodox Church Unity*, 78–91.

6. Moskos, *Greek Americans*, 74–75.

7. *Charter of the Greek Orthodox Archdiocese of North and South America 1978*, articles 1–3.

8. Basil Foussianes, "Administration of the Archdiocese," 229–30, 271.

9. "Archbishop Iakovos, Keynote Address 24th Clergy-Laity Congress July 3, 1978, Detroit, Michigan," box L29, Archives, GOARCH.

10. *New York Times*, "Greek Orthodox Church Approves Greater Role for Clergy and Laity."

11. Makrias, "E 24e Klirikolaiki," 5.

12. "Facing the Eighties," Keynote Address by Archbishop Iakovos, 25th Clergy-Laity Congress, June 30, 1980, Atlanta, box L31, Archives, GOARCH.

13. "Facing the Eighties."

14. Gallup Organization, "Study of the Greek Orthodox Population," 11–16.

15. *Rome (GA) News-Tribune*, "Pollster Warns Greek Orthodox."

16. *New York Times*, "Around the Nation."

17. *New York Times*, "Greek Orthodox Leaders Encouraged."

18. Gallup Organization, "Study of the Greek Orthodox Population," 100–101.

19. Vitalis and Nikitaides, "Oi iereis yper tes Hellenikes glossas."

20. Maraslis, "E Clericolaiki kai emeis."

21. "Minutes of the 25th Clergy Laity Congress of the Greek Orthodox Archdiocese June 30–July 4, 1980, Atlanta," box L32, Archives, GOARCH.

22. Meeting of the Archdiocesan Council Minutes, January 16, 1981, New York 3–7 A22550001, box L32, Archives, GOARCH.

23. Meeting of the Archdiocesan Council Minutes, March 23–24, 1984, Toronto 5, box L35, Archives, GOARCH.

24. Rhobotis, "Founding Father Peter M. Dion."

25. Lounsberry, "Greek Orthodox Archbishop Is Honored."

26. Dowd, "Vibrant Iakovos."

27. Efthimiou and Christopoulos, *History*, "President Carter's Homily," 205.

28. Briggs, "Archbishop Iakovos Marks 25 Years."

29. Efthimiou and Christopoulos, *History*, iii.

30. Efthimiou and Christopoulos, *History*, 38.

31. R. Stephanopoulos, "Archbishop Iakovos as an Ecumenist," 358, 363.

32. Charles, "Future of the Archdiocese," 384.

33. Iakovos, "Diagrafomenai prooptikai dia ton Hellenismon tes Amerikes," 454–58.

34. Archbishop Iakovos, "Rekindling an Orthodox Awareness," Keynote Address, 28th Clergy-Laity Congress Dallas, Texas, June 29, 1986, box L37, Archive, GOARCH.

35. Kalmoukos, "O archiepiskopos kyrixe tis ergasies tes clericolaikis."

36. Evans and Novak, "Question of Orthodoxy."

37. Franklin, "Orthodox Prelate Raps Criticism of Dukakis."

38. Goldman, "Dukakis's Ties to Orthodox Church."

39. Franklin, "Greek Orthodox Congress Opens."

40. Michael Dukakis, "Tribute to Public Service," July 6, 1988, L40TR0010, box L40, Archive, GOARCH.

41. Blake, "At Church Congress in Boston."

42. Marty, "Transpositions," 17.

10. The Challenges for an American Greek Orthodoxy

1. Gabriel, "Retrospective," 275; Gillquist, *Metropolitan Philip*, 275–87; Gillquist, *Becoming Orthodox*, chap. 10.

2. Agadjanian and Roudometof, "Introduction."

3. Steinfels, "Patriarch Begins 8-City Tour."

4. Efthimiou, "Establishment of SCOBA," 352.

5. Archdiocesan Council Meeting Minutes, March 30–31, 1990 6, box L41, Archive, GOARCH.

6. Kass, "Orthodox Await Visit by Patriarch."

7. FitzGerald, *Orthodox Church*, 118.

8. FitzGerald, *Orthodox Church*, 118–19; Pink, "Orthodox Patriarch Continues Busy United States Tour."

9. Steinfels, "Patriarch Reaches Out."

10. Berry and Henderson, *Geographical Identities of Ethnic America*.

11. "Report to His Eminence Archbishop Iakovos concerning the Future Theological Agenda of the Greek Orthodox Archdiocese 30th Clergy Laity Congress 1990," 2, box L42, Archive, GOARCH.

12. Slagle, *Eastern Church*, chap. 6.

13. "Report to His Eminence," 4–7.

14. "Report to His Eminence," 11.

15. "Report to His Eminence," 17–18.

16. "Report to His Eminence," 22–23.

17. Roberts, "Bush's Grecian Turn."

18. Kopan to Archbishop Iakovos, November 8, 1988, Andrew Kopan Papers, DePaul University Archives.

19. "Minutes, Archdiocesan Council Meeting Feb. 24–25 1989," box L41, Archive, GOARCH.

20. "Minutes, Archdiocesan Council Meeting Nov. 15–16, 1991," box L44, Archive, GOARCH.

21. Sfekas and Matsoukas, *Project for Orthodox Renewal*, 1–16.

22. Matsoukas, *Church in Captivity*, 5–7.

23. Liveris, *Ancient Taboos and Gender Prejudice*, 188.

24. Steinfels, "Real Estate Deal."

25. Steinfels, Church's Land Deal."

26. "Minutes, Archdiocesan Council Meeting May 15, 1992," Archive, GOARCH.

27. Steinfels, "Church's Land Deal."

28. Sfekas and Matsoukas, *Project for Orthodox Renewal*, 13.

29. Grammenos, *Orthodoxos Amerikanos O Archiepiskopos*, 115.

30. Steinfels, "Eastern Orthodox Prelates."

31. FitzGerald, *Orthodox Church*, 5, 109–10.

32. Bedrin and Tamoush, *New Era Begins*, 109–10.

33. FitzGerald, *Orthodox Church*, 115.

34. Antiochian Orthodox Christian Diocese of North America, "Statement on the Church in North America."

35. *American Church and the Ecumenical Patriarchate*, 11–12.

36. Roudometof, "Transnationalism and Globalization," 385.

37. *American Church and the Ecumenical Patriarchate*, 13.
38. *American Church and the Ecumenical Patriarchate*, 31.
39. Kishkovsky, "Orthodoxy in America."
40. Michalopoulos and Ham, *American Orthodox Church*, 182.
41. Yates, "Using Giddens' Structuration Theory," 161.

11. Church and Patriarchate and the Limits of Americanization

1. "Archdiocese Council Meeting Minutes March 10–11 1995," A225L0001, box L48, Archive, GOARCH.
2. Athens News Agency Bulletin #660, August 9, 1995.
3. Steinfels, "As a Leader Prepares to Leave."
4. Steinfels, "As a Leader Prepares to Leave."
5. "Archdiocesan Council Meeting Minutes Oct. 20, 1995," A225L0002, box L48, Archive, GOARCH.
6. "Archdiocesan Council Meeting Minutes Oct. 20, 1995."
7. "Archdiocesan Council Meeting Minutes Oct. 20, 1995."
8. "Archdiocesan Council Meeting Minutes Oct. 20, 1995."
9. *GreekAmerican*, "Ecclesiastical Turmoil."
10. Sideridis, "Archbishop's Retirement," 5–7.
11. Matsoukas, *Church in Captivity*, 9–11.
12. Andrew Kopan to the *GreekAmerican*, December 14, 1995, Andrew Kopan Papers.
13. Papandreou to Bartholomew, August 24, copy of letter, folder gg, box 15a, Archive, GOARCH; Grammenos, *Orthodoxos Amerikanos O Archiepiskopos*, 118–19.
14. Dragas, *Legacy of Achievement*, 182–84.
15. Grammenos, *Orthodoxos Amerikanos O Archiepiskopos*, 218–38.
16. Angelopoulos, *Ta apanta epi panauropinon dikaiomaton kai ethnikon thematon*, 457–548.
17. Constantelos, *Complete Works of His Eminence Archbishop Iakovos*, 250–51.
18. "Greek Orthodox Archdiocese 33rd Clergy Laity Congress, Planning Meeting Sept. 22, 1995," L48SC0002, box L48, Archive, GOARCH.
19. "Pappas to Kokalis May 30, 1996," L4BIS0004, box 48, Archive, GOARCH.
20. "33rd Biennial Clergy Laity Congress, Congress Specifications, June 30–July 4, 1996," LY8CS 0001, box L48, Archive, GOARCH.
21. "33rd Biennial Clergy Laity Congress Finance Committee Report July 3, 1996," box L49, Archive, GOARCH.
22. Steinfels, "Greek Orthodox Bid Goodbye"; Mornell, "Archbishop Iakovos Gives Final Mass."
23. Broadway, "For Greek Orthodoxy, It's the End of an Era."
24. "Ecumenical Patriarch Bartholomew, Message to the 33rd Clergy-Laity Congress," L49WP0003, box L48, Archive, GOARCH.

12. Greek Orthodoxy in America Enters the Twenty-First Century

1. Constantelos, *Understanding the Greek Orthodox Church*, 275–76.
2. Spyridon, Report to the Ecumenical Patriarchate.
3. Prodromou, "Ambivalent Orthodox," 67.

4. Archbishop Spyridon, "Theloun tin Amerikanopoiisi tes omogeneias."

5. *Future of the Greek Language and Culture in the United States*, iii.

6. Spyridon, "Value of Greek Letters."

7. Lively, "Faculty Firings"; Wilson, "Accreditors Tell Hellenic College to Change Policies"; Lively, "Accreditor Says Hellenic College Has Responded to Complaints."

8. Steinfels, "Greek Orthodox Prelate Enthroned Today."

9. "A Statement of the Ecumenical Patriarch July 31, 1996," box L49, Archive, GOARCH.

10. Chrysavgis, *In the World*, 27.

11. Bartholomew, "Address of His All Holiness Ecumenical Patriarch Bartholomew."

12. Chrysavgis, *In the World*, 40.

13. Niebuhr, "Patriarch's Visit Bolsters Orthodox Church."

14. Walsh, "Patriarch's Visit."

15. Kazaz, "Reflecting on the US Visit."

16. Walsh, "Patriarch's Visit."

17. *Orthodox Observer*, "Archbishop Spyridon Convenes Monastic Leaders."

18. Frangouli-Argyris, *Lonely Path of Integrity*, 194–97.

19. *Hellenic Chronicle*, "Dimas vs. Archdiocese Decision Issued."

20. Frangouli-Argyris, *Lonely Path of Integrity*, 233.

21. Bonanos, "Crisis in the Cathedral."

22. Stammer, "Easing Tensions of a Church in Transition."

23. Jaharis, "Full Text of Speech."

24. Stammer, "Clash between Autonomy, Tradition."

25. Michalopoulos and Ham, *American Orthodox Church*, 194.

26. It is too early to offer an informed scholarly assessment of Demetrios's tenure, and in any case the focus of this book is on the twentieth-century history of the church.

27. AHEPA, "Statement: Resignation of Archbishop Demetrios."

28. Elpidophoros, "Challenges of Orthodoxy in America."

BIBLIOGRAPHY

Primary Sources

Archival Collections

Andrew T. Kopan Papers, DePaul University Library
Basil J. Vlavianos Papers, California State University at Sacramento, Special Collections
Demetrios P. Callimachos Papers, University of Minnesota Archives
Greek Orthodox Archdiocese of America, Archives Department
Historical Archive, Greek Ministry for Foreign Affairs
Orthodox Christian Laity Records, DePaul University Library
Presidential Papers of Gerald Ford, Gerald Ford Library
WikiLeaks, Public Library of US Diplomacy

Published Collections of Documents

Constantelos, Demetrios J., ed. *The Complete Works of His Eminence Archbishop Iakovos.* Vol. 3, *The Torchbearer*, pt. 2. Brookline, MA: Holy Cross Orthodox Press, 2001.
——. *Encyclicals and Documents of the Greek Orthodox Archdiocese of North and South America, 1922–1972.* New York: Greek Orthodox Archdiocese, 1972.
Dragas, George D., ed. *Legacy of Achievement: Metropolitan Methodios of Boston, Festal Volume on the 25th Anniversary of His Consecration to the Episcopate.* Boston: Greek Orthodox Metropolis of Boston, 2008.
Manolis, Paul. *The History of the Greek Church of America: In Acts and Documents.* Vols. 1–3. Berkeley, CA: Ambelos, 2003.
Vlanton, Elias, ed. "Documents: The O.S.S. and the Greek-Americans." *Journal of the Hellenic Diaspora* 9, nos. 1–2 (1983).

Secondary Sources

Abbot, Grace. "A Study of the Greeks in Chicago." *American Journal of Sociology* 15, no. 3 (1909): 379–93.
Agadjanian, Alexander, and Victor Roudometof. "Introduction: Eastern Orthodoxy in a Global Age—Preliminary Considerations." In Roudometof, Agadjanian, and Pankhurst, *Eastern Orthodoxy in a Global Age*, 1–25.
AHEPA (American Hellenic Progressive Association). "Statement: Resignation of Archbishop Demetrios." News release, May 4, 2019. https://ahepa.org/statement-resignation-of-archbishop-demetrios/.

Ahlstrom, Sydney E. *A Religious History of the American People*. 2nd ed. New Haven, CT: Yale University Press, 2004.

Alex, Christine. "Twenty-First Century Participation in Two U.S. Greek Orthodox Churches." PhD diss., University of Pittsburgh, 2007.

Alexandris, Alexis. *The Greek Minority of Istanbul and Greek-Turkish Relations, 1918–1974*. Athens: Center for Asia Minor Studies, 1992.

Alfonsky, Bishop Gregory. *A History of the Orthodox Church in America, 1917–1934*. Kodiak, AK: St. Herman's Theological Seminary Press, 1994.

Alivizatos, Amilkas. *E Hellenike Orthodoxos Eklesia* [The Greek Orthodox Church]. Athens: n.p., 1955.

Ambatielos, Vicky Zafeiris, Timi Loomos Freshman, and Dean Loomos, eds. *Celebrating the 100th Anniversary of the Greek Orthodox Community Los Angeles and Southern California*. Los Angeles, n.p., 2008.

The American Church and the Ecumenical Patriarchate: Governance, Diaspora, Role of Women. Chicago: Orthodox Christian Laity, 1998.

American Presidency Project. "Jimmy Carter Remarks at a White House Reception Honoring Archbishop Iakovos." September 18, 1979. http://www.presidency.ucsb.edu/ws/?pid=31371.

Anagnostopoulou, Sia. "Makarios III 1950–1977: Creating the Ethnarchic State." In *The Archbishops of Cyprus in the Modern Age: The Changing Role of the Archbishop-Ethnarch, Their Identities and Politics*, edited by Andrekos Varnava and Michalis N. Michael, 253–309. Newcastle: Cambridge Scholars, 2013.

Anagnostou, Yiorgos. "Caesar V. Mavratsas: Contributions to Greek American Sociology." Ergon Greek American Arts and Letters, posted March 24, 2019. https://ergon.scienzine.com/article/essays/contributions-to-greek-american-sociology.

——. *Contours of White Ethnicity: Popular Ethnography and the Making of Usable Pasts in Greek America*. Athens: Ohio University Press, 2009.

——. "Where Does Diaspora Belong? The View from Greek American Studies." *Journal of Modern Hellenism* 28, no. 1 (May 2010): 73–119.

——. "White Ethnicity—a Reappraisal." *Italian American Review* 3, no. 2 (Summer 2013): 99–128.

Angelopoulos, Athanasios. *Ta apanta epi panauropinon dikaiomaton kai ethnikon thematon* [Complete works on human rights and national issues]. Thessaloniki: University Studio Press, 2007.

Annunciation Greek Orthodox Church. "Our Parish History." http://www.annunciationnyc.Org/our-parish/history.

Antiochian Orthodox Christian Diocese of North America. "Statement on the Church in North America." Standing Conference of Canonical Orthodox Bishops in America, Antiochian Village, November 30–December 2, 1994. http://www.antiochian.org/1040.

Athenai. "To clerico-laikon" [The clergy laity]. June 18, 1942.

Athens News Agency Bulletin, no. 660. August 9, 1995.

Atlantis. "Foni voontos en ti erimo" [A voice crying in the wilderness]. June 28, 1972.

Balodimas-Bartolomei, Angelyn. "Greek American Identities in the C21st: A Generational Approach." *Journal of the Hellenic Diaspora* 38, nos. 1 and 2 (2012): 71–97.

Bartholomew, Patriarch. "Address of His All Holiness Ecumenical Patriarch Bartholomew at the 75th Anniversary Banquet of AHEPA in His Honor at Union Station, Washington DC, October 21, 1997." https://www.patriarchate.org/-/

address-of-his-all-holiness-ecumenical-patriarch-b-a-r-t-h-o-l-o-m-e-w-at-the-75th-anniversary-banquet-of-ahepa-in-his-honor-at-union-station-washingt.

Bedrin, George, and Philip Tamoush, eds. *A New Era Begins: Proceedings of the 1994 Conference of Orthodox Bishops in Ligonier, Pennsylvania*. Torrance, CA: OTP, 1996.

Berry, Kate, and Martha Henderson. *Geographical Identities of Ethnic America: Race, Place, and Space*. Reno: University of Nevada Press, 2001.

Blake, Andrew. "At Church Congress in Boston, Bush Courts Greek Americans." *Boston Globe*, July 8, 1988.

Bodnar, John. *The Transplanted: A History of Immigrants in Urban America*. Indianapolis: Indiana University Press, 1987.

Bonanos, Christopher. "Crisis in the Cathedral." *New York Magazine*, March 8, 1999. http://nymag.com/nymetro/news/religion/features/973/.

Bossard, James H., and Harold C. Letts. "Mixed Marriages Involving Lutherans—a Research Report." *Marriage and Family Living* 18, no. 4 (November 1956): 308–10.

Briggs, Kenneth A. "Archbishop Iakovos Marks 25 Years." *New York Times*, April 2, 1984.

Broadway, Bill. "For Greek Orthodoxy, It's the End of an Era; Retiring Archbishop Says Effort to United Faithful Must Continue." *Washington Post*, June 29, 1996.

Bukowczyk, John J. *A History of the Polish Americans*. New Brunswick, NJ: Transaction, 2008.

Burgess, Thomas. *The Greeks in America*. New York: Arno, 1970; originally published in Boston, 1913.

Canoutas, Seraphim. *Hellenism in America*. New York: Cosmos, 1918.

Carlin, David. *The Decline and Fall of the Catholic Church in America*. Manchester, NH: Sophia Institute, 2003.

Charles, George J. "Future of the Archdiocese." In Efthimiou and Christopoulos, *History of the Greek Orthodox Church in America*, 183–203.

Charter of the Greek Orthodox Archdiocese of North and South America 1978. New York: Greek Orthodox Archdiocese, 1978.

Chicago Tribune. "Greeks Here Unify under a New Voice." February 13, 1975.

——. "Kiss Away Their Past Sins." April 15, 1901.

——. "Mondale to Speak at Greek Fete." June 9, 1979.

——. "Pastor Quits to Thwart Greek King's Bishop." August 15, 1921.

——. "Writ Welcomes King's Prelate." August 12, 1921.

Chrissochoidis, Ilias, ed. *Spyros P. Skouras Memoirs (1893–1953)*. Stanford, CA: Brave World, 2013.

Christopoulos, George. "Impact through Public Relations." In Efthimiou and Christopoulos, *History of the Greek Orthodox Church in America*, 233–46.

Chrysavgis, John, ed. *In the World, Yet Not of the World: Social and Global Initiatives of Ecumenical Patriarch Bartholomew*. New York: Fordham University Press, 2010.

Clapsis, Emmanuel. "The Challenge of a Global World." In *The Orthodox Churches in a Pluralistic World: An Ecumenical Conversation*, edited by Emmanuel Clapsis, 47–66. Geneva: World Council of Churches, 2004.

Commons, John Rogers. *Immigrants in America*. New York: Macmillan, 1920.

Condos, Athena Sophia. "The Greek Language School as a Transmitter of Ethnicity: A Study of Linguistic, Cultural and Religious Maintenance." PhD diss., Southern Connecticut State University, 1997.

Constantelos, Demetrios J. *Christian Faith and Cultural Heritage: Essays from a Greek Orthodox Perspective*. Boston: Somerset Hall, 2005.

———. *Understanding the Greek Orthodox Church*. 4th ed. Brookline, MA: Holy Cross Orthodox Press, 1998.

Contopoulos, Michael. *The Greek Community of New York City: Early Years to 1910*. New Rochelle, NY: Caratzas, 1972.

Cornell, George. "One-Man Crusader Battles for Eastern Church's Role." *The Day* (New London, CT), September 7, 1985.

Corrigan, John, and Winthorp S. Hudson. *Religion in America*. 7th ed. Upper Saddle River, NJ: Prentice Hall, 2004.

Counelis, James S. "Greek Orthodox Statistics of the United States, 1949–1989: Some Ecclesial and Social Patterns." *Journal of the Hellenic Diaspora* 16, no. 4 (1989): 129–60.

Counelis, James S., and Andrew T. Kopan. "The Orthodox Church and Its Language Problem." *Logos* 1, no. 8 (September 1968).

Daskalakis, Apostolos. "An fygei o Athinagoras" [If Athenagoras leaves]. *Empros*, February 2, 1948.

Diamandi-Karanou, Panagoula. "The Relationship between Homeland and Diaspora: The Case of Greece and the Greek American Community." PhD diss., Northeastern University, 2015.

Doumouras, Alexander. "Greek Orthodox Communities in America: Before World War I." *St. Vladimir's Seminary Quarterly* 7, no. 4 (1967): 172–92.

Dowd, Maureen. "A Vibrant Iakovos Marks 24 Busy Years as Archbishop." *New York Times*, October 29, 1983.

Dugan, George. "Greek Orthodox Church Backs U.S. on Vietnam." *New York Times*, July 2, 1966.

Efthimiou, Miltiades. "Establishment of SCOBA." In Efthimiou and Christopoulos, *History of the Greek Orthodox Church in America*, 352.

Efthimiou, Miltiades B., and George Christopoulos, eds. *History of the Greek Orthodox Church in America*. New York: Greek Orthodox Archdiocese, 1984.

Efthymiou, Vasilios. *Skiagrafia ton apodemon Ellenon tes Amerikes kai istoria tou kathedrikou Neas Yorkes* [A sketch of the Greeks in America and a history of the cathedral of New York]. New York: n.p., 1949.

Eggebroten, Anne. "Americanizing Greek Orthodoxy." *Christianity Today*, July 31, 1970.

Ellinikos Astir. "To Clerico-Laikon Syndedrio" [The Clergy-Laity Congress], June 26, 1942.

Elpidophoros, Archimandrite. "Challenges of Orthodoxy in America and the Role of the Ecumenical Patriarchate." March 16, 2009. https://ocl.org/challenges-of-orthodoxy-in-america-and-the-role-of-the-ecumenical-patriarchate/.

Erickson, John H. *Orthodox Christians in America*. New York: Oxford University Press, 2007.

Ethnikos Kyrix, "Sinenteuxi Athinagora Vostonis" [Athenagoras of Boston Interview], June 13, 1949.

———. "To en Philadelphia Clerico-Laikon Synedrion" [The Clergy Laity Congress in Philadelphia], June 25 and 29, 1942.

———. "To en Philadelphia episimon deipnon tou Clericolaicou Synedriou" [The Official Dinner of the Clergy Laity Congress in Philadelphia], June 30, 1942.

———. "To 21° Clericolaikon Synedrion" [The 21st Clergy-Laity Congress], June 25, 1972.

Evans, Rowland, and Robert Novak. "Mr. Ford and the Greek Archbishop." *Washington Post*, November 11, 1974.

———. "A Question of Orthodoxy." *Washington Post*, May 18, 1988.

Fahey, Michael A. "Eastern Synodal Traditions: Pertinence for Western Collegial Institutions," in *Episcopal Conferences: Historical, Canonical and Theological Studies*, edited by Thomas J. Reese, 253–65. Washington, DC: Georgetown University Press, 1989.

Ferencz, Nicholas. *American Orthodoxy and Parish Congregationalism*. Brookline, MA: Holy Cross Orthodox Press, 2015.

Fiske, Edward B. "Orthodox Diocese of Americas Opens 19th Congress in Athens." *New York Times*, July 22, 1968.

FitzGerald, Thomas. *The Orthodox Church*. Westport, CT: Greenwood, 1995.

Foreign Relations of the United States. "Greece: Illegal Immigration of Greeks into the United States." #16408 401–03 *FRUS* 1908. http://digital.library.wisc.edu/1711.dl/FRUS.FRUS1908.

Foussianes, Basil. "The Administration of the Archdiocese." In Efthimiou and Christopoulos, *History of the Greek Orthodox Church in America*, 221–32.

Frangouli-Argyris, Justine. *The Lonely Path of Integrity*. Athens: Exandas, 2002.

Franklin, James L. "Greek Orthodox Congress Opens on Words of Worship." *Boston Globe*, July 4, 1988.

———. "Orthodox Prelate Raps Criticism of Dukakis Based on His Faith." *Boston Globe*, July 3, 1988.

Frazee, Charles. *The Orthodox Church and Independent Greece, 1821–1852*. London: Cambridge University Press, 1969.

The Future of the Greek Language and Culture in the United States. New York: Greek Orthodox Archdiocese, 1999.

Gabriel, Antony. "A Retrospective: One Hundred Years of Antiochian Orthodoxy in North America." In *The First One Hundred Years: A Centennial Anthology Celebrating Antiochian Orthodoxy in North America*, edited by George S. Corey, Peter E. Gillquist, Anne Glynn Mackoul, Jean Sam, and Paul Schneirla, 244–49. Englewood, NJ: Antakya, 1995.

Gage, Nicholas. "Iakovos Criticizes Greek Government." *New York Times*, July 27, 1973.

Gallup Organization. "Study of the Greek Orthodox Population in the U.S." January 1980.

Gerber, David A. "Forming a Transnational Narrative: New Perspectives on European Migrations to the United States." *History Teacher* 35, no. 1 (November 2001): 61–78.

Germanos (Polyzoides), Metropolitan. *What We See and Hear in a Greek Eastern Orthodox Church*. New York: Divry, 1961.

Giddens, Anthony. *Central Problems in Social Theory: Action, Structure and Contradiction in Social Analysis*. London: Palgrave Macmillan, 1979.

———. *The Constitution of Society: An Outline of the Theory of Structuration*. Malden, MA: Polity, 1984.

Gillquist, Peter E. *Becoming Orthodox: A Journey to the Ancient Christian Faith*. 3rd ed. Chesterton, IN: Conciliar, 2010.

———. *Metropolitan Philip: His Life and His Dreams*. Nashville, TN: Thomas Nelson, 1991.

Goldman, Ari L. "Dukakis's Ties to Orthodox Church Stay Warm Despite Abortion Stance." *New York Times*, September 7, 1988.

Gordon, Milton. *Assimilation in American Life: The Role of Race, Religion and National Origins.* New York: Oxford University Press, 1964.

Grammenos, Athanasios. "O Archiepiskopos Voreiou kai Notiou Amerikes Iakovos stis Helleni-Tourkikes scheseis" [Archbishop of North and South America Iakovos and Greco-Turkish Relations]. *Valkanika Simikta* 17 (2015): 171–86.

——. *Orthodoxos Amerikanos O Archiepiskopos Voreiou kai Notiou Amerikes Iakovos stis Ellinoamerikanikes scheseis (1959–1996)* [Orthodox American Archbishop of North and South America Iakovos and Greek-American relations (1959–1996)]. Thessaloniki: Epikentro, 2018.

GreekAmerican. "Ecclesiastical Turmoil." September 1995.

Greek Historical Society of the San Francisco Bay Area. *Greeks in San Francisco.* Charleston, SC: Arcadia, 2016.

Greek Orthodox Archdiocese. "Meeting on Cyprus Crisis Held in Chicago on September 12, 1974." News release.

Greek Orthodox Archdiocese of America. "Emmanuel Hatziemmanuel Passes Away in the Lord." September 22, 2015. https://www.goarch.org/-/emmanuel-hatzi emmanuel-94-passes-away-in-the-lord.

Greek Orthodox Archdiocese Yearbook 1964. New York: Greek Orthodox Archdiocese, 1964.

Greek Orthodox Archdiocese Yearbook 1986. New York: Greek Orthodox Archdiocese, 1986.

Greek Star. "The Fall of the Greek Race and the Byzantine Empire. . . ." June 3, 1904. https://flps.newberry.org/article/5422062_5_1189.

Guglielmo, Thomas A., and Earl Lewis. "Changing Racial Meanings: Race and Ethnicity in the United States, 1930–1964." In *Race and Ethnicity in America*, edited by Ronald H. Bayor, 167–92. New York: Columbia University Press, 2003.

Hadjipolycarpou, Maria. "A Nation of Saints: The National Theological Rhetoric of Archbishop Makarios III (1913–1977)." *Journal of Modern Greek Studies* 33, no. 1 (May 2015): 127–53.

Hammond, Phillip E., and Kee Warner. "Religion and Ethnicity in Late-Twentieth-Century America." *Annals of the American Academy of Political and Social Science* 527, Religion in the Nineties (May 1993): 55–66.

Handlin, Oscar. *The Uprooted: The Epic Story of the Great Migrations That Made the American People.* 2nd ed. Philadelphia: University of Pennsylvania Press, 2002.

Harakas, Stanley S. *Contemporary Moral Issues Facing the Orthodox Christian.* Minneapolis: Light and Life, 1982.

——. "The Stand of the Orthodox Church on Controversial Issues." https://www. goarch.org/-/the-stand-of-the-orthodox-church-on-controversial-issues.

Hart, Laurie Kain. *Time, Religion and Social Experience in Rural Greece.* Lanham, MD: Rowman & Littlefield, 1992.

Hatziemmanuel, Emmanuel. *O Amerikes Iakovos Hellenike ekpaideuse, philosophia kai epiteugmata 1959–1996* [Iakovos of America, Greek education philosophy and achievements, 1959–1996]. New York: Greek Orthodox Archdiocese, 1996.

Heinze, Andrew R. "The Critical Period: Ethnic Emergence and Reaction, 1901–1929." In *Race and Ethnicity in America: A Concise History*, edited by Ronald H. Bayor, 131–66. New York: Columbia University Press, 2003.

Hellenic Chronicle. "Dimas vs. Archdiocese Decision Issued." June 23, 1999.

Hennessey, James. *American Catholics: A History of the Roman Catholic Community in the United States.* New York: Oxford University Press, 1981.

Herberg, Will. *Protestant-Catholic-Jew: An Essay in American Religious Sociology.* Chicago: University of Chicago Press, 1983. First published in 1955.

Higham, John. *Strangers in the Land: Patterns of American Nativism, 1860–1925.* New Brunswick, NJ: Rutgers University Press, 2002.

The History and Consecration of St. John the Baptist Greek Orthodox Church, Las Vegas, Nevada, June 4–5, 2005. N.p, n.d.

Hollinger, David A. "The 'Secularization' Question and the United States in the Twentieth Century." *Church History* 70, no. 1 (March 2001): 132–43.

Howe, Marvin. "Primate Is Acting to Ease Greek-Turkish Hostility." *New York Times,* December 11, 1987.

Iakovos, Archbishop. "Diagrafomenai prooptikai dia ton Hellenismon tes Amerikes" [The unfolding prospects for the Greeks in America]. *Academy of Athens Minutes* 60 (1985), Special Session of November 7, 1985: 454–58.

——. "The Fifty Years of Life and Development of the Greek Orthodox Archdiocese of the Americas—1922–1972—an Appraisal." New York: Greek Orthodox Archdiocese, 1972.

Inboden, William. *Religion and American Foreign Policy, 1945–1960.* New York: Cambridge University Press, 2008.

Ioannides, Chris P. *Realpolitik in the Mediterranean: From Kissinger and the Cyprus Crisis to Carter and the Lifting of the Turkish Arms Embargo.* New York: Pella, 2001.

Ioannides, Lakis A. *Archiepiskopos Iakovos O egetes tou Hellenismou tes Amerikes* [Archbishop Iakovos, the Leader of Hellenism in America]. Thessaloniki: n.p., 1989.

Jaharis, Michael. "Full Text of Speech Given by Archdiocesan Council VP Michael Jaharis." *National Herald,* December 20, 2012.

Jameson, Harris P. "A Showdown in Orthodoxy." *Hellenic Chronicle,* March 2, 1972.

Joachim, Bishop of Boston. *Oi kindynoi tou en Amerike Ellinismou kai ta mesa diasoseos autou* [The dangers for Hellenism in American and the means of salvation]. Boston: n.p., 1926.

Jusdanis, Gregory. "Greek Americans and the Diaspora." *Diaspora* 1, no. 2 (Fall 1991): 209–23.

Kalmoukos, Theodoros. "Church Life in America Is Being Trivialized." *National Herald,* November 11, 1998.

——. "Davos kai kerde—Oi vathyteres epidioxeis tou Archiepiskopou k. Iakovou" [Davos and gains—the deeper aims of the Archbishop of America Iakovos]. *Ethnikos Kyrix,* February 29, 1988.

——. "He Is Suffering from the Tragic Loss of His Son to a Monastery Where He Became Ill." *National Herald,* October 27, 1998.

——. "O Archiepiskopos Iakovos, e diadoche kai kapoioi epidoxoi diadchoi tou" [Archbishop Iakovos, his successions and certain hopeful successors]. *Ethnikos Kyrix,* January 19, 1995. http://www.archbishopspyridon.gr/spyridon_1995/ek_diadoxi-iakovou_20jan95.html.

——. "O archiepiskopos kyrixe tes ergasies tes clericolaikis" [The archbishop signaled the opening of the work of the clergy-laity]. *Ethnikos Kyrix,* July 1, 1986.

Kaloudis, George. *Modern Greece and the Diaspora Greeks in the United States.* Lanham, MD: Lexington Books, 2018.

Karpathakis, Anna. "The Greek Orthodox Church and Identity Politics." In *New York Glory: Religions in the City,* edited by Tony Carnes and Anna Karpathakis, 374–87. New York: NYU Press, 2001.

———. "Whose Church Is It Anyway? Greek Immigrants of Astoria, New York, and Their Church." *Journal of the Hellenic Diaspora* 20, no. 1 (1994): 97–122.

Karpozilos, Kostis. *Kokkine Amerike: Hellenes metanastes kai to orama enos Neou Kosmou* [Red America: Greek immigrants and the vision of a New World]. Heraklio: University of Crete, 2017.

Kass, John. "Orthodox Await Visit by Patriarch." *Chicago Tribune*, July 20, 1990.

Kazaz, Harun. "Reflecting on the US Visit of Patriarch Bartholomew." *Hürriyet Daily News*, November 29, 1997.

Kim, Rebecca Y. "Religion and Ethnicity: Theoretical Connections." *Religions* 2 (2011): 312–29.

Kishkovsky, Leonid. "Orthodoxy in America: Diaspora or Church?" Paper delivered at the International Theological Conference of the Russian Orthodox Church, Moscow, 2003. https://oca.org/holy-synod/statements/fr-kishkovsky/orthodoxy-in-america-diaspora-orchurch.

Kitroeff, Alexander. "Diaspora-Homeland Relations and Greek-American Lobbying: The Panhellenic Emergency Committee, 1974–78." *Journal of Modern Hellenism* 11 (1994): 19–40.

———. "Greek-American Ethnicity, 1919–1939." In *To Hellenikon: Studies in Honor of Speros Vryonis, Jr.*, vol. 2, edited by Jelisaveta Stanojevich Allen et al., 353–71. New York: Caratzas, 1993.

———. "Greek American Identity in the 1980s." In *Arméniens et Grecs en diaspora: Approches comparatives*, edited by Eric Bruneau, Ioanis Hassiotis, Martine Hovanessian, and Claire Mouradian, 299–306. Athens: L'École Française d'Athènes, 2007.

———. "Greek America's Liturgical Language Crisis of 1970." Ergon Greek American Arts and Letters, February 26, 2019. https://ergon.scienzine.com/article/articles/liturgical-language-crisis-of-1970.

———. *The Greeks in Egypt, 1919–1937: Ethnicity and Class*. London: Ithaca Press for the Middle East Centre, 1989.

———. "The Limits of Political Transnationalism: The Greek-American Lobby, 1970s–1990s." In *Greek Diaspora and Migration since 1700: Society, Politics and Culture*, edited by Dimitris Tziovas, 141–53. Burlington, VT: Ashgate, 2009.

Kollias, Sifis. *Archiepiskopos Amerikes Michael o apo Korinthias* [Archbishop Michael of America from Corinth]. Athens: n.p., 1964.

Konstantellou, Eva. "Greek American Day Schools in the Context of U.S. Educational Multiculturalism: History, Present State, and Future Prospects." In *Studies in Honor of His Eminence Archbishop Iakovos*, edited by Nomikos Michael Vaporis, 379–88. Brookline, MA: Holy Cross Orthodox Press, 1995.

Kopan, Andrew T. *Education and Greek Immigrants in Chicago, 1892–1973*. Chicago: n.p., 1990.

———. "Greek Survival in Chicago." In *Ethnic Chicago: A Multicultural Portrait*, edited by Melvin G. Holli and Peter d'A. Jones, 260–302. Grand Rapids, MI: Eerdmans, 1995.

Koularmanis, Anastasios. "Greek Orthodox Education and the Saint Demetrios School of Astoria, 1956–2015." PhD diss., St. John's University, New York, 2015.

Kourelis, Kostis, and Vasileios Marinis. "The Immigrant Liturgy: Greek Orthodox Worship and Architecture in America." In *Liturgy in Migration: Cultural*

Contexts from the Upper Room to Cyberspace, edited by Teresa Berger, 155–75. Collegeville, MN: Liturgical Press, 2012.

Kourides, Peter T. *The Evolution of the Greek Orthodox Church in America and Its Present Problems*. New York: Cosmos Greek-American Printing, 1959.

Kourvetaris, George. "Greek Orthodox and Greek American Ethnic Identity." In *Studies on Greek Americans*, 51–70. Boulder, CO: East European Monographs, 1997.

———. "The Greek Orthodox Church in the United States: (Private) Crisis or Transition?" In Roudometof, Agadjanian, and Pankhurst, *Eastern Orthodoxy in a Global Age*, 245–74.

Krindatch, Alexei, ed. *Atlas of American Orthodox Christian Churches*. Brookline, MA: Holy Cross Orthodox Press, 2010.

Kunkelman, Garry A. "The Religion of Ethnicity: Belief and Belonging in a Greek-American Community." PhD diss., University of Pennsylvania, 1986.

Lackman, Libby. "Foreign Groups Join Federation." *New York Times*, February 9, 1941.

Laliotou, Ioanna. *Transatlantic Subjects: Acts of Migration and Cultures of Transnationalism between Greece and America*. Chicago: University of Chicago Press, 2004.

Lambert, Frank. *Religion in American Politics: A Short History*. Princeton, NJ: Princeton University Press, 2008.

Leber, George J. *The History of the Order of AHEPA, 1922–1972*. Washington, DC: AHEPA, 1972.

Lively, Kit. "Accreditor Says Hellenic College Has Responded to Complaints on Governance." *Chronicle of Higher Education*, May 14, 1999.

———. "Faculty Firings Throw a Greek Orthodox College in Turmoil." *Chronicle of Higher Education*, July 18, 1997.

Liveris, Leonie. *Ancient Taboos and Gender Prejudice: Challenges for Orthodox Women and the Church*. Burlington, VT: Ashgate, 2005.

Los Angeles Times. "King Cupid Throws Londos; Jimmy Plans World Tour." August 17, 1939.

Lounsberry, Emilie. "Greek Orthodox Archbishop Is Honored." *Philadelphia Inquirer*, February 6, 1984.

Mackridge, Peter. *Language and National Identity in Greece, 1766–1976*. New York: Oxford University Press, 2009.

Makrias, Panayotis. "E 24e Klirikolaiki" [The 24th Clergy-Laity]. *Nea Yorki* 31 (August 1978): 5.

Makrides, Vasilios N. "Why Are Orthodox Churches Particularly Prone to Nationalization and Even to Nationalism?" *St. Vladimir's Theological Quarterly* 57, nos. 3–4 (2013): 325–52.

Malouhos, Georgios. *Ego o Iakovos* [I, Iakovos]. Athens: SKAI & Livanis, 2002.

Manis, Andrew. "Outside Agitator Times Two: Father Sam Gouvelis and Birmingham's Greek Community Face the Civil Rights Movement." https://www.researchgate.net/publication/267536421_Outside_Agitator_Times_Two_Father_Soterios_Gouvellis_Yankee_Greek_Orthodox_Priest_in_Birmingham_and_Selma.

Maraslis, Fontas. "E Clericolaiki kai emeis" [The Clergy-Laity Congress and us]. *Ethnikos Kyrix*, July 3, 1980.

March on Selma. "Archbishop's Letter to the Clergy, March 17, 1965." GOARCH Archive, folder CD, box E24 1965.

——. "Statement by Archbishop Iakovos, March 16, 1965." GOARCH Archive, folder CD, box E24 1965.

——. "Statement Issued at 17th Biennial Ecclesiastical Congress on the Occasion of the Signing of the Civil Rights Bill." http://civilrights.goarch.org/ecumenical.

Marty, Martin E. *Modern American Religion.* Vol. 2, *The Noise of Conflict, 1919–1941.* Chicago: University of Chicago Press, 1997.

——. "Transpositions: American Religion in the 1980s." *Annals of the American Academy of Political and Social Science* 480, Religion in America Today (July 1985): 11–23.

Matsakis, Aphrodite. *Growing up Greek in St. Louis.* Chicago: Acadia, 2002.

Matsoukas, George Edmund. *A Church in Captivity: The Greek Orthodox Church of America.* New York: iUniverse, 2008.

Mavratsas, Caesar V. "Greek-American Economic Culture: The Intensification of Economic Life and a Parallel Process of Puritanization." In *New Migrants in the Market Place: Boston's Ethnic Entrepreneurs,* edited by Marilyn Halter, 97–119. Amherst: University of Massachusetts Press, 1995.

McGuckin, John Anthony. *The Orthodox Church.* Malden, MA: Wiley-Blackwell, 2011.

Meagher, Timothy. "Racial and Ethnic Relations in America." In *Race and Ethnicity in America: A Concise History,* edited by Ronald H. Bayor, 193–240. New York: Columbia University Press, 2003.

Michael, Archbishop. *Ofelomene apantesis* [An answer that is owed]. New York: Greek Orthodox Archdiocese, 1955.

Michalopoulos, George C., and Herb Ham. *The American Orthodox Church: A History of Its Beginnings.* Salisbury, MA: Regina Orthodox Press, 2003.

Miller, James Edward. *The United States and the Making of Modern Greece: History and Power, 1950–1974.* Chapel Hill: University of North Carolina Press, 2009.

Montgomery, Paul L. "Orthodox Church Can Use English; Iakovos Announces Decision at Congress in Denver." *New York Times,* July 4, 1964.

Mornell, Mara. "Archbishop Iakovos Gives Final Mass before 6,000 in Central Park." *New York Post,* July 1, 1996.

Morris, Charles R. *American Catholic: The Saints and Sinners Who Built America's Most Powerful Church.* New York: Vintage, 1997.

Morrow, Eric V. "Transnational Religion in Greek American Political Advocacy." PhD diss., Baylor University, 2012.

Moskos, Charles C. *Greek Americans: Struggle and Success.* New Brunswick, NJ: Transaction, 1st ed., 1980, and 2nd ed., 1989.

——. "The Greek Community in the United States." In *The Greek Diaspora in the Twentieth Century,* edited by Richard Clogg, 197–224. New York: St. Martin's, 1999.

Moskos, Peter C., and Charles C. Moskos. *Greek Americans: Struggle and Success.* New Brunswick, NJ: Transaction, 2014.

Namee, Matthew. "Pews (or Lack Thereof) in Early Orthodox Churches." Orthodox History Blog, December 9, 2009. http://orthodoxhistory.org/2009/12/09/pews-or-lack-thereof-in-early-orthodox-churches/.

National Geographic. "The Best Food Festival in Each U.S. State." https://www.nationalgeographic.com/travel/travel-interests/food-and-drink/top-food-festival-every-US-state/.

Nea Yorki. "Liberation of Education." June 1980 (vol. 33), 13.

Neighbors: Studies in Immigration from the Standpoint of the Episcopal Church. New York: Domestic and Foreign Missionary Society, 1920.

New York Daily News. "One Religious Leader for Both Democratic and Republican Conventions." August 23, 2008.

New York Times. "Around the Nation." July 6, 1980.

——. "Athenagoras Goes to Istanbul Post." January 24, 1949.

——. "Eastern Orthodox Church Chooses a New Patriarch." July 17, 1972.

——. " 'God Sent Roosevelt,' Greek Archbishop Says." January 20, 1934.

——. "Greek Archbishop of Americas Is Here." December 16, 1949.

——. "Greek Bishop Enthroned Here." April 2, 1959.

——. "Greek Orthodox Church Approves Greater Role for Clergy and Laity." July 6, 1978.

——. "Greek Orthodox Leaders Encouraged to Try to Widen Church's Appeal." January 18, 1981.

——. "Greeks Celebrate Independence." April 11, 1921.

——. "Greeks Honor 1,000 Dead." May 31, 1933.

——. "The Hour of Greece." Editorial. October 29, 1940.

——. "Iakovos, in Greece, Defends Reforms." July 12, 1970.

——. "Manning Receives Icon of St. John." October 22, 1936.

——. "Many Banks to Aid Buyers of Bonds." October 6, 1918.

——. "100 Demonstrators Protest Greek Orthodox Plans." July 13, 1970.

——. "1,000 at Banquet Weep at Patriarch's Death." July 8, 1972.

——. "The Patriarchate a Hostage." Editorial, April 21, 1965.

——. "Prelate Will Fly to Enthronement: 'Sacred Cow' Will Bear Party of Greek Patriarch-Elect to Istanbul Ceremony." January 9, 1949.

——. "Rock from Athens Given to St. John's." June 16, 1933.

——. "Sees Greek Glory Return." October 30, 1918.

——. "Service Is Held by New Primate; Iakovos Celebrates His First Divine Liturgy at Greek Cathedral." April 6, 1959.

Niebuhr, Gustav. "Patriarch's Visit Bolsters Orthodox Church." *New York Times,* October 19, 1997.

Nikolidakis, Nikolaos. "E symvole tes Akademias Agiou Vasileiou sten Ellinoglosse ekpaideuse ton EPA" [The contribution of St. Basil's Academy to Greek language education in the United States]. In *Istoria tes Neoellinikes diasporas erevna kai didaskalia* [History of the Modern Greek diaspora research and teaching], vol. 2, edited by Michales Damanakis, Vasiles Kardases, Theodosia Michelaki, and Antonis Chourdakis, 142–55. Rethymno: EDIAMME, 2004.

Orfanos, Spyros, Harry J. Psomiades, and John Spyridakis, eds. *Education and Greek Americans: Process and Prospects.* New York: Pella, 1987.

Orthodox Observer. "Archbishop Spyridon Convenes Monastic Leaders in Texas." November 20, 1998.

Ousterhout, Robert. "The Holy Space: Architecture and the Liturgy." In *Heaven on Earth: Art and the Church in Byzantium,* edited by Linda Safran, 81–120. University Park: Pennsylvania State University Press, 1988.

Papadopoulos, Yannis G. S. "The Role of Nationalism, Ethnicity, and Class in Shaping Greek American Identity, 1890–1927." In *Identity and Participation in*

Culturally Diverse Societies: A Multidisciplinary Perspective, edited by Assaad Elia Azzi, Bernd Simon, Bert Klandermans, and Xenia Chryssochoou, 9–31. Hoboken, NJ: Wiley-Blackwell, 2010.

Papaioannou, George. *From Mars Hill to Manhattan: The Greek Orthodox in America under Athenagoras I*. Minneapolis: Life & Light, 1976.

——. *The Odyssey of Hellenism in America*. Thessaloniki: Patriarchal Institute for Patristic Studies, 1985.

Patrinacos, Nicon. "Change or Succumb to the Inevitable." *Orthodox Observer* 35, no. 603 (June 1970).

——. *The Individual and His Orthodox Church*. New York: Orthodox Observer, 1970.

——. "The Role of the Church in the Evolving Greek American Community." In *The Greek American Community in Transition*, edited by Harry J. Psomiades and Alice Scourby, 123–36. New York: Pella, 1982.

Paul, John Peter. "A Study in Ethnic Group Political Behavior: The Greek Americans and Cyprus." PhD diss., University of Denver, 1979.

Perkins, Linda M. "The New Immigrants and Education: Challenges and Issues." *Educational Horizons* 78, no. 2 (2000): 67–71.

Petrou, Themistoklis. *O ethnikos dichasmos sten omogeneia tes Amerikes kai e archiepiskopia tou Athenagora* [The national schism among the Greeks in America and Athenagoras's tenure as archbishop]. Athens: Periplous, 2008.

Philippou, A. J., ed. *The Orthodox Ethos*. Oxford: Holywell, 1964.

Pink, Daniel H. "Orthodox Patriarch Continues Busy United States Tour." *Washington Post*, July 14, 1990.

Poulos, George. *Pomfret: The Golden Decade*. Brookline, MA: Holy Cross Orthodox Press, 1988.

Prevas, Nicholas M. *History of the Greek Orthodox Cathedral of the Annunciation, Baltimore, Maryland*. Baltimore: John Lucas Printing, 1982.

——. *House of God . . . Gateway to Heaven: A Centennial History of the Greek Orthodox Cathedral of the Annunciation*. Baltimore: Greek Orthodox Cathedral of the Annunciation, 2007.

Prodromou, Elizabeth. "The Ambivalent Orthodox." *Journal of Democracy* 15, no. 2 (April 2004): 62–75.

——. "Religious Pluralism in America: Problematizing the Implications for Orthodox Christianity." *Journal of the Academy of American Religion* 72, no. 33 (September 2004): 746.

Rhobotis, Demetrios. "Founding Father Peter M. Dion." *Neo Magazine*, 2014. http://www.neomagazine.com/2014/04/founding-father-peter-m-dion/.

Roberts, Roxanne. "Bush's Grecian Turn." *Washington Post*, July 13, 1990.

Rome (GA) News-Tribune. "Pollster Warns Greek Orthodox to Provide More Youth Guidance." July 1, 1980.

Roudometof, Victor. *Globalization and Orthodox Christianity: The Transformations of a Global Tradition*. New York: Routledge, 2017.

——. "Greek Orthodoxy, Territoriality, and Globality: Religious Responses and Institutional Disputes." *Sociology of Religion* 69, no. 1 (2008): 67–91.

——. "Transnationalism and Globalization: The Greek Orthodox Diaspora between Orthodox Universalism and Transnational Nationalism." *Diaspora* 9, no. 3 (2000): 361–97.

Roudometof, Victor, Alexander Agadjanian, and Jerry Pankhurst. *Eastern Orthodoxy in a Global Age: Tradition Faces the 21st Century.* Lanham, MD: Alta Mira, 2005.

Saint Basil Academy. "The History of St. Basil's Academy." http://www.stbasil.goarch.org/about_us/.

Saloniki-Greek Press. "Greek American Progressive Association," September 28, 1933.

Saloutos, Theodore. "The Greek Orthodox Church in the United States and Assimilation." *International Migration Review* 7, no. 4 (Winter 1973): 395–407.

——. *The Greeks in the United States.* Cambridge, MA: Harvard University Press, 1964.

——. "The Greeks of Milwaukee." *Wisconsin Magazine of History* 53, no. 3 (Spring 1970): 193.

San Francisco Call. "Peace Reigns Again in the Greek Church." October 7, 1910.

San Francisco Examiner. "Bishop and Church End 8 Years War." December 16, 1929.

——. "Pastor Wins Suit for Salary, Court Tells Trustees of Greek Church to Pay Arrears." October 10, 1937.

Schmemann, Alexander. "Clergy and Laity in the Orthodox Church." *Orthodox Life,* no. 1, 1959.

Scourby, Alice. *The Greek Americans.* Boston: Twayne, 1984.

"Semeioma M. Triandafyllidi pros ten Archiepiskope Voreiou and Notiou Amerikes Schetika me to Ekpaideutiko Programma tou Hellenismou tes Amerikes, 1939" [Memorandum from M. Triandafyllidis to the Archdiocese of North and South America about the Education of the Greeks in America, 1939]. University of Thessaloniki Digital Archive, http://invenio.lib.auth.gr/record/40931?ln=el.

Seraphim, Archimandrite. *The Quest for Orthodox Church Unity in America.* New York: Sts. Boris & Gleb, 1973.

Sfekas, Stephen J., and George Matsoukas, eds. *Project for Orthodox Renewal: Seven Studies of Key Issues Facing Orthodox Christians in America.* Chicago: Orthodox Christian Laity, 1993.

Sideridis, Lambros. "The Archbishop's Retirement and Its Effects on Our Community." *Greek-American Review,* October 1995, 5–7.

Simon, Andrea Judith. "The Sacred Sect and the Secular Church: Symbols of Ethnicity in Astoria's Greek Community." PhD diss., City University of New York, 1977.

Sittser, Gerald L. *A Cautious Patriotism: The American Churches and the Second World War.* Chapel Hill: University of North Carolina Press, 1997.

Skopetea, Elle. *To Protypo Vasileio kai e Megale Idea* [The Model Kingdom and the Great Idea]. Athens: Polytypo, 1988.

Slagle, Amy. *The Eastern Church in the Spiritual Marketplace: American Conversions to Orthodox Christianity.* DeKalb: Northern Illinois University Press, 2001.

Smith, Timothy L. "Religion and Ethnicity in America." *American Historical Review* 83, no. 5 (December 1978): 1155–85.

Sotirhos, Michael. "Remembering Michael." Greek Orthodox Archdiocese of America. https://www.goarch.org/-/remembering-michael.

Soumakis, Fevronia. "A Sacred Paideia: The Greek Orthodox Archdiocese, Immigration, and Education in New York City, 1959–1979." PhD diss., Columbia University, 2015.

Spyridon, Archbishop. Report to Ecumenical Patriarchate, July 19, 1994. http://www.archbishopspyridon.gr/spyridon_1994/asp_synedr-vlad_19jul94-p.html.

——. "Theloun tin Amerikanopoiisi tes omogeneias" [They want the Americanization of the Greeks in the United States]. Interview with Georgios Vasileiou,
Eleftheri Ora, August 9, 1999. http://www.archbishopspyridon.gr/spyridon_
1999/el-ora_synenteuxi_09aug99.html.

——. "The Value of Greek Letters to the Greek Community of America." January 31,
1999. http://www.archbishopspyridon.gr/spyridon_1999/parak_omil-grk-
letters_31jan99.html.

Stammer, Larry B. "A Clash between Autonomy, Tradition." *Los Angeles Times*,
June 29, 2002.

——. "Easing Tensions of a Church in Transition." *Los Angeles Times*, August 19, 2000.

Steinfels, Peter. "As a Leader Prepares to Leave, a Church Struggles to Keep Its Independence." *New York Times*, November 12, 1995.

——. "Church's Land Deal Stirs Call for Inquiry." *New York Times*, July 12, 1994.

——. "Eastern Orthodox Prelates Name Ecumenical Patriarch." *New York Times*,
October 24, 1991.

——. "Greek Orthodox Bid Goodbye to Their Leader." *New York Times*, July 1, 1996.

——. "Greek Orthodox Prelate Enthroned Today." *New York Times*, September 21,
1996.

——. "Patriarch Begins 8-City Tour of US." *New York Times*, July 3, 1990.

——. "Patriarch Reaches Out to Embrace Far-Flung Flocks in Orthodoxy." *New York
Times*, July 15, 1990.

——. "Real Estate Deal Puts Archdiocese in a Controversial Light." *New York Times*,
April 4, 1994.

Stephanopoulos, Nikki, ed. *A Breath of Spiritual Fragrance: The Treasure of Archbishop
Michael*. New York: Greek Orthodox Archdiocese, 2008.

Stephanopoulos, Robert. "Archbishop Iakovos as an Ecumenist." In Efthimiou and
Christopoulos, *History of the Greek Orthodox Church in America*, 353–64.

Stewart, Charles. *Demons and the Devil: Moral Imagination in Modern Greek Culture*.
Princeton, NJ: Princeton University Press, 1991.

St. Petersburg Times. "Archbishop Meets with Mondale." April 29, 1978.

St. Sophia Cathedral (Washington, DC). "13th Biennial Congress of the Greek Orthodox Archdiocese." Press release, September 30, 1956.

Svolopoulos, Constantinos. *Constantinos Karamanlis: Archeio, gegonota kai keimena*
[Constantinos Karamanlis: Archive, events and texts]. Vol. 4. Athens: Karamanlis Foundation, 1994.

Theodosopoulos, Georgios. "E Hellenike Orthodoxe Ekklesia stes Enomenes Polit-
eies Amerikes" [The Greek Orthodox Church in the United States of Amer-
ica]. PhD diss., University of Thessaloniki, 2012.

Theotokas, Georgios. *Dokimio gia ten Amerike* [An essay on America]. Athens: Estia,
2009.

Triantafyllidis, Manolis. *Hellenes tes Amedrikes: Mia omilia* [Greeks in America: A talk].
Athens: n.p., 1952.

US Department of Commerce, Bureau of the Census. *Religious Bodies: 1936*. Vol. 2,
pt. 1, *Denominations A to J*. Washington, DC: Government Printing Office, 1941.

Vaporis, Michael. "The Church's Role in Preserving the Greek Language." *H Nea
Yorki* 34 (June 1981): 26–27.

Varlamos, Michael. "A Quest for Human Rights and Civil Rights: Archbishop Iakovos
and the Greek Orthodox Church." PhD diss., Wayne State University, 2018.

Veniopoulos, Nestor. "Simeioseis apo to en Philadelphia Clerico-Laikon Synedrion" [Notes from the Clergy-Laity Congress in Philadelphia]. *Atlantis*, June 30, 1942.

Vertovec, Steven. *Transnationalism*. New York: Routledge, 2009.

Vidalis, Orestis E. *Confronting the Greek Dictatorship in the U.S. Years of Exile: A Personal Diary (1968–1975)*. New York: Pella, 2009.

Vitalis, Stavros, and Giorgos Nikitaides. "Oi iereis yper tes Hellenikes glossas" [Priests in favor of the Greek language]. *Proini*, July 3, 1980.

Volaitis, Constantine E. "Orthodox Church as Church and Ethnic Community in the United States." *St. Vladimir's Seminary Quarterly* 5 (1961).

Vryonis, Speros, Jr. *A Brief History of the Greek-American Community of St. George, Memphis, Tennessee, 1962–1982*. Malibu, CA: Undena, 1982.

Walsh, Andrew. "The Patriarch's Visit: Pouring Oil on Troubled Waters." *Religion in the News* 1, no. 1 (Summer 1998). http://www.archbishopspyridon.gr/spyridon_1998/rin_ptr_sum98.html.

Washington Post. "Archbishop Banned at Athenagoras Rite." July 10, 1972.

——. "Fifteen Thousand Protesters Back Retention of U.S. Arms Embargo on Turkey." April 17, 1978.

——. "Greek Envoy and His Wife Are Feted at Home." December 6, 1929.

Watanabe, Paul Y. *Ethnic Groups, Congress, and American Foreign Policy: The Politics of the Turkish Arms Embargo*. Westport, CT: Greenwood, 1984.

Waters, Mary C. *Ethnic Options*. Berkeley: University of California Press, 1990.

Wiest, Walter E. "The Centenary of the Greek Orthodox Archdiocese of North and South America: An Appreciation." In *The Orthodox Ethos*, edited by A. J. Philippou, 3–20. Oxford: Holywell, 1964.

Williams, Preston N. "Religion and the Making of Community." *Journal of the American Academy of Religion* 44, no. 4 (December 1976): 603–11.

Wilson, Robin. "Accreditors Tell Hellenic College to Change Policies on Hiring and Firing." *Chronicle of Higher Education*, June 25, 1998.

Wisnosky, Mark. "Contemporary Orthodox Christian Theological Education in the United States of America." PhD diss., University of Pittsburgh, 2015.

Wuthnow, Robert. *The Restructuring of American Religion*. Princeton, NJ: Princeton University Press, 1988.

Xenides, John P. *The Greeks in America*. New York: G. H. Doran, 1922.

Yans-McLaughlin, Virginia, ed. *Immigration Reconsidered: History, Sociology, and Politics*. New York: Oxford University Press, 1990.

Yates, JoAnne. "Using Giddens' Structuration Theory to Inform Business History." *Business and Economic History* 26, no. 1 (Fall 1997): 159–83.

Zacharopoulos, Nikos. "E Aparche tes Organoses tes Hellenikes Orthodoxes Eklesias ste Vorio kai Notio Amerike" [The Beginning of the Organization of the Greek Orthodox Church in North and South America], edited by Kostas Mpeis. In *Timetikos Tomos Archiepiskopou Demetriou* [Festschrift for Archbishop Demetrios] (electronic publication). http://www.kostasbeys.gr/articles.php?s=3&mid=1096&mnu=1&id=23150.

Zoustis, Vasilios. *O en Ameriki Hellenismos kai e drasis tou* [Hellenism in America and its activity]. New York: n.p., 1954.

INDEX

Abbot, Grace, 22
Aghia (Hagia) Sophia, Istanbul, Turkey, 21
Agnew, Spiro, 153
AHEPA. *See* American Hellenic Progressive
 Association
Albanian Autocephalous Church, 67
Alex, Christine, 9
Alexakis, George, 29
Alexakis, Louis, 29
Alexandros, Archbishop: appointment of,
 40; at Clergy-Laity Congress of 1921,
 35, 36; Damaskinos's visit and, 56;
 dismissal of, 55–56; Joachim's proposals
 on education and, 45, 47–48; personality
 of, 46, 52; as resident bishop in America,
 33–34; splintering of Greek Orthodox
 Church in America and, 50, 52–53
Alexiou, Alexandros, 36
Alivizatos, Amilkas, 33, 109, 110
American-born Greek Americans: in church
 leadership, 119; church outreach to, 3–4,
 9, 105–7; and language question, 72–73,
 143; Orthodoxy and Hellenism for, 211;
 Patrinacos's book and, 144–45
American Greeks, notion of, 199
American Hellenic Institute, 170
American Hellenic Progressive Association
 (AHEPA): Americanization promoted
 by, 43, 61, 87, 91, 138; Athenagoras and,
 61, 75, 81; Bartholomew and, 252–53,
 260; Cyprus crisis and, 170; Damaskinos
 and, 56; Demetrios and, 261; Great
 Depression and, 75–76; influx of new
 immigrants after 1965 and, 141; Michael
 and, 113; public acceptance of Greek
 Orthodoxy by, 61; support for St. Basil
 Academy, 102–3; support for war effort
 in World War II, 81; visits to White
 House, 91
Americanization: in 1920s, 39–40, 41,
 42–43, 48; in 1960s, 119–20, 134; in

1980s, 182–83; AHEPA and promotion
 of, 43, 61, 87, 91, 138; Athenagoras
 on, 58, 60–61, 87, 88, 94; balancing
 act in response to, 11, 12, 16, 77, 79,
 114, 118, 138–39, 141, 154, 155, 202;
 church response to pressures of, 3–4, 9,
 11, 15, 43–44, 45, 48–49; Clergy-Laity
 Congress of 1990 on, 207–8; concern
 about, 87–88, 101, 103, 115–16, 132;
 Ecumenical Patriarchate's position on,
 249, 260; and ethnic identity, retention
 of, 182, 183; Greek language schools
 as buffer for, 24; Iakovos's response to,
 16, 121–24, 138, 139, 143, 146, 149–50,
 182, 185, 198–99; impact on small
 religious denominations, 11; Joachim
 on, 45–46; limits of, 16, 226, 229, 259;
 vs. Orthodox Church hierarchy, 246;
 postwar rise in religiosity and, 95;
 religious affiliation of ethnic groups
 and, 4, 5, 6, 7
Anagnostou, Yiorgos, 183
Angelis, John, 233
Angelopoulos, Panayotis, 220
Angelopoulos, Theodoros, 228
Annunciation Cathedral, Boston, 116–17
Annunciation Cathedral, Houston, 150, 220
Annunciation Church, Chicago, 19, 21–22
Annunciation Church, New York City: early
 years of, 30; establishment of, 19, 25;
 school associated with, 25–26
Annunciation Church, Philadelphia:
 establishment of, 19; move to suburbs, 121
Anthony, Bishop of San Francisco, 190,
 191, 193
Antiochian Church, 19, 203–4, 223, 259
Antiochian Orthodox Evangelical
 Mission, 203
Anton, Arthur C., 195
Anton, Charles, 195
Arab Orthodox community, 11, 19, 203

Spyridon, 256, 257; restoration in 1970s, 185. *See also specific names*

boards of trustees, church, 30–31; community organizations transformed into, 63; relations with parish priests, 33

Bonanos, Christopher, 257–58

Boston, Massachusetts: Annunciation Cathedral in, 116–17; Athenagoras's visit to, 60

Botasis, Dimitrios, 30

Brademas, John, 119

Brookline, Massachusetts, theological school in, 73. *See also* Holy Cross Theological School

Burgess, Thomas, 21

Burt, Richard, 179

Bush, George H. W., 201–2, 205, 211–12, 239

Byron, Lord, 126–27

Caesaro-papism, 37

Calatrava, Santiago, 261

California. *See* San Francisco

Calivas, Alkiviadis, 250

Callimachos, Demetrios, 14, 36, 50, 55–56, 119

Calvocoressi, Mrs. L. J., 83

Calvocoressis, Leonidas, 36

Canada: concentration of Greek immigrants in, 132; Metropolinate of, 247

Canoutas, Seraphim, 28, 74

Capadalis, Nick, 136

Carter, Jimmy, 176–78, 197, 228

Catholicism: de-ethnicization of, 6, 122; phasing out of Latin in, 142–43; social and cultural upheaval of 1960s and, 116. *See also* Roman Catholic Church

CBS Radio, *Church of the Air* program, 104

charity. *See* philanthropy

Charles, John, 198

Chicago, Illinois: Annunciation Church in, 19, 21–22; Athenagoras's visits to, 60, 74; clergy-laity relations in early years in, 31; concentration of Greek immigrants in, 132, 141; Dimitrios's visit to, 207; first Greek immigrants in, 18, 22; first Greek Orthodox churches in, 19; Holy Trinity Church in, 20, 25, 35, 49; parishes in, financial contributions by, 219–20; Socrates school in, 25, 132; Sts. Constantine and Helen Church in, 25, 220

Chicago Tribune (newspaper), 20, 254

Chimples, George, 194, 195

Chris, Evan, 230

Christophoros (Kontogeorge), Father, 67

Chronicle of Higher Education, on sexual harassment incident at Hellenic College, 250–51

Chrysostomos, Archbishop: forced resignation of, 164; as head of Church of Greece, 40; recall of Bishop Germanos by, 49

Chryssikos, George J., 66

church: as bridge to homeland, 10, 22; as facilitator of assimilation, 4, 6, 7; as haven for newly arrived immigrants, 4, 5, 6. *See also* church(es), Greek Orthodox; immigrant church(es)

church(es), Greek Orthodox: Americanization of service at, 49; architectural model for, 20–22, 81; and community organizations, 26, 27; first in US, 17, 18–20; new, spread to suburbs in 1960s, 121; schools associated with, 24–26; as social spaces, 23. *See also* Greek Orthodox Church in America

Church of Greece: archdiocese's efforts to maintain independence from, 53; as autocephalous church, 32; under Chrysostomos, 40; and debate over Athenagoras's successor, 97–98; early parishes in US and, 30; and Ecumenical Patriarchate of Constantinople, 2, 32, 40; embassy as informal representative of, 28; and Greek government, subservience to, 32–33; jurisdiction over Greek Orthodox in America, 32, 40, 55; under Theokletos, 28, 33, 34

Church of the Air program, CBS Radio, 104

civil rights movement: and ethnic revival, 140; and Greek Orthodox priests, 105; and Iakovos, 15, 105, 124–26, 164

classical Greek civilization, and Greek Orthodoxy, 24–25, 69

Clergy-Laity Congress(es), 13; of 1921, 35–37; of 1931, 61–66; of 1933, 67; of 1939, 70, 76; of 1942, 81, 83, 84–87; of 1946, 87–88, 92; of 1950, 101, 103–4; of 1952, 111; of 1956, 102; of 1958, 112; of 1960, 121, 128–30, 133, 135–36; of 1962, 121, 130, 132–33; of 1964, 120, 121, 122–23, 146, 151; of 1966, 123–24, 127–28, 131, 134; of 1968, 164, 165–67; of 1970, 142, 143, 145–46, 151, 154; of 1972, 149, 150–52; of 1976, 155; of 1978, 185; of 1980, 186–87, 190; of 1982, 190–93; of 1984, 196, 213; of 1986, 199–200, 208; of 1988, 201; of 1990, 204, 207–12, 214; of 1992, 216, 217–18; of 1994, 204, 216, 220, 221, 242, 248; of 1996, 240–41, 242–45; of 1998, 255; of 2002, 258–59; reports of Supreme Educational Board at, 70

Greek Orthodox Young Adult League
(GOYAL/YAL), 193–94, 230
Greek Orthodox Youth of America (GOYA),
105–7, 112, 212
Greek War of Independence (1821), 2, 80;
parades celebrating, 9, 23, 60, 76; role of
religion in, 2
Greek War Relief Association (GWRA), 9,
78; Athenagoras and, 80, 82; Philoptochos
branches and, 82–83
Greeley, Andrew, 4
Gregory the Theologian, 134

Hadjis, Meliton, 117
Hagia (Aghia) Sophia, Istanbul, Turkey, 21
Halkias, Michael, 147
Ham, Herb, 7
Handlin, Oscar, 4, 11
Harakas, Stanley, 161
Hatziemmanuel, Emmanuel, 152, 155, 156,
157, 158
Haviland, John, 81
Hellenic Chronicle (newspaper), 149
Hellenic College: AHEPA's support for,
253; archbishop's control over, 13;
establishment of, 73–74; financial
problems of, 159, 160, 194, 201; mixed
record of, 160; Patrinacos as dean of, 144;
sexual harassment incident at, 250–51; St.
Basil Academy incorporated into, 84
Hellenikos Astir (newspaper): on church
and community, 27; on Greek language
schools, 24; support for Athenagoras, 86;
support for Vasilios, 51
Hellenism, and Orthodoxy, 24–25, 69,
103–4, 211
Helleno-Amerikanikon Ekpaideutirion, 25
Herberg, Will, 4, 95–96
Higham, John, 41
Holy Cross Theological School: AHEPA's
support for, 253; archbishop's control
over, 13; chapel dedicated to Archbishop
Michael at, 106; financial problems of, 196,
201; founding of, 72–73; issue of Greek
language at, 74; liberal arts institution
added to, 159; Maliotis Center at, 159–60;
Methodios as president of, resignation of,
231, 232; mixed record of, 160
Holy Trinity Cathedral, New York City:
Cyprus crisis and special service at, 169;
Dimitrios's visit to, 207; early years of,
30; financial contribution by, 219; first
Clergy-Laity Congress in (1921), 35–36;
Iakovos's 25th anniversary celebration in,

197; Iakovos's inauguration in, 118–19;
joint service of Eastern Orthodox
churches in, 91; rivalry with Annunciation
Church, 25–26; Russian Church's claim
of authority over, 19; Stephanopoulos as
dean of, 198, 257; women's charity group
associated with, 23
Holy Trinity Church, Chicago, 20;
appointment of Bishop Germanos and,
35; call for autonomous church by, 49;
language school associated with, 25
Holy Trinity Church, Lowell, Massachusetts:
architecture of, 21; farewell service by
Bishop Germanos at, 49; and Greek
language school, 25; splintering of
congregation of, 51
Holy Trinity Church, San Francisco, 29
homeland: church as bridge to, 10, 22;
closer interactions with, in postwar era,
113–14; and diaspora communities, 130;
Greek Americans' ties to, 5; Iakovos and
ties to, 156, 162, 164–68; Michael and ties
to, 111–12; resources from churches in
America, 221; Sunday liturgy as return to,
148. *See also* Greece
Hoover, Herbert, 56, 90
Houston, Texas, Annunciation Cathedral in,
150, 220
Hürriyet (newspaper), 254
Huszagh, Elenie, 230, 234

Iakovos, Archbishop, 9, 15; 20th anniversary
of, 178; 25th anniversary of, 196–98,
205, 213; achievements of, 197–98, 243;
Americanization of Greek Orthodox and,
16, 121–24, 138, 139, 143, 146, 149–50, 182,
185, 198–99; on American society, dangers
of, 166; Archdiocesan Council's loyalty
to, 229, 232–33, 234, 248; archdiocese's
50th anniversary and, 149–50; and
Archons (organization), 195–96, 248; and
Athenagoras, 116, 117, 119, 148, 149, 153,
175, 184, 263; and Athenagoras's funeral,
153–54; and autonomy issue, 183–84;
awards received by, 178, 197, 198; and
Bartholomew, 220, 230–31, 234; and Bush,
201, 202, 205; and Carter, 176–78, 197;
centralization plan of, 135–38; civil rights
movement and, 15, 105, 124–26, 164;
at Clergy-Laity Congress of 1960, 121,
128–30, 135–36; at Clergy-Laity Congress
of 1964, 122–23; at Clergy-Laity Congress
of 1968, 165–67; at Clergy-Laity Congress
of 1970, 142, 145–46; at Clergy-Laity

World War I: Greek immigration to US after, 22; Greek Orthodox Church in America during, 43; political polarization during, 29, 32–33
World War II: aid to Greece during, 9; Athenagoras's support for US during, 91–92; Greece in, 78–79; immigration after, 102, 141; and patriotism, 80; and religiosity, 78, 95
Wright, Frank Lloyd, 7

xenophobia, in early 20th century, 23–24, 35

Young Adult League (YAL), 193–94, 230
younger generation, church's relationship with: Clergy-Laity Congress of 1982 and, 191, 193; under Demetrios, 260; Episcopal Church's appeal and, 103; Gallup survey of 1980 on, 188–89; under Iakovos, 105, 193–94, 198; under Michael, 105–7, 112

Zambelis, Mike, 136
Zepatos, Speros, 136
Zoustis, Vasilios, 70